DOMINANCE AND SUBMISSION

THE BLUE ÖYSTER CULT CANON

MARTIN POPOFF

DOMINANCE
AND SUBMISSION

THE
BLUE ÖYSTER CULT
CANON

MARTIN POPOFF

WP
WYMER
PUBLISHING
Bedford, England

First published in 2023 by Wymer Publishing, Bedford, England
www.wymerpublishing.co.uk Tel: 01234 326691
Wymer Publishing is a trading name of Wymer (UK) Ltd.

Print edition (fully illustrated): **ISBN: 978-1-915246-32-5**

Edited by Agustin Garcia de Paredes.

Printed and bound in Great Britain by CMP, Dorset.

A catalogue record for this book is available from the British Library.

Typeset/Design by Andy Bishop / Tusseheia Creative.
Cover design by Tusseheia Creative.
Front cover photo © Greg Olma.

TABLE OF CONTENTS

Introduction

There are millions of Blue Öyster Cult fans out there, and for good reason: it is my opinion that the band and its storied assembled writing teams over the years have turned in some of the best lyrics in the business. On top of that, there's so much variety and complexity to the music, any deep rock 'n' roll fan can potentially go down the rabbit hole of this band and become obsessed but quick.

But I gotta tell ya, this book, surely has the potential to expand that fan base further, and further beyond any absorption of the three BÖC books I've written so far. Let's dwell on that for a minute. I really didn't imagine it was possible—or useful to the world—for me to write another Blue Öyster Cult book, but *Dominance and Submission: The Blue Öyster Cult Canon* erased that notion.

To be sure, my first BÖC book, *Agents of Fortune: The Blue Öyster Cult Story* is the typical ground zero narrative booky book on the band. Then we have *Blue Öyster Cult: A Visual Biography*, which offers a detailed timeline along with 400 pictures, in a coffee table format, hardcover, full colour throughout. Both are available through Wymer Publishing, who are also the publisher of the present volume. Then I did *Flaming Telepaths: Imaginos Expanded and Specified*, complete with 39 illustrations by me, which was a crazy, occult, conspiracy theory, deluxe blossoming of the *Imaginos* saga. That is also still available along with prints of the drawings, directly from my website, martinpopoff.com.

The point is, I suppose that's my version of BÖC's black-and-white trilogy, and *Dominance and Submission* is the *Agents of Fortune*, as it were (or maybe the *On Your Feet or on Your Knees*). In other words, I'm absolutely thrilled to report that a fourth Blue Öyster Cult book from me is entirely useful and even, regularly, blindingly illuminating. And I can say that without measuring modesty because this book is not about me. Fact is, I didn't think there was any way for me to write another Blue Öyster Cult book, until this concept came along. To be sure, I've done a bunch of books like this in the past, and even recently, with Wymer wanting to create a bit of a series. But with this band in particular, once I had done the trivia-stuffed, interview-intensive *Agents of Fortune* book and then the detailed timeline book with all those live shots and pictures of memorabilia completing the circuit, I didn't think another book on this band from me was possible.

Enter our esteemed panel, our dozen or so Knights Templar, our alchemical cabal of Rosicrucians with rosy-coloured glasses. Because fact is, these guys had tons and tons of stuff to say that I didn't say in any of my three books so far. Turns out I'm not so smart, and in fact nowhere near the sharpest tool in the workshop of telescopes when it comes to Buck and Eric and Albert and Joe and Allen. And so I let these guys talk, which is the process with all these books, but even more so here versus previous titles I've penned, where indeed, each chapter starts with some manner of intro material from myself. In this case, I've made the conscious decision not to overlap with the books I've done already, and left the space reserved for intro material as just the hard goods on each album. I had reservations about that, but as soon as I started talking to these guys, that hesitation melted away. Pleasantly, almost joyously, I found myself regularly and continually amazed at the proposed new ways to look at this band that these guys conjured. I found myself excited as they explained trends across songs that I had never noticed, and then dozens and dozens of times, hearing about details within songs that I had possibly never noticed or at least never written about in my other books, or maybe just plain hadn't thought about in years.

Therein lies the beauty of *Dominance and Submission*: even though my previous books on the band inevitably serve the purpose for which they are intended, that is turning any prospective reader into a Blue Öyster Cult fan, this book will do that too, and possibly more forcefully and purely. Because, again, the things these guys say about the songs will get you excited about checking them out for the first time or listening to them with fresh ears. They certainly had me scurrying back to the original texts and appreciating the immense talent for music and words inherent across this band's 14 studio albums.

So again, I do admit a certain amount of scepticism that this exercise would turn out to be of use, but I quickly had my mind opened and then efficiently and substantially filled up with all sorts of great new ways to think about Blue Öyster Cult. It's a process that got me really interested in the band all over again. Which surprised the hell out of me, frankly, because before I started, I really thought, pompously, that I was just going to hear a bunch of stuff I already knew, or opinions that I already shared and thus would be bored to tears hearing for the millionth time. Absolutely not the case. I found myself hanging on every word that these guys said, and all along, in the back of my mind, pleased with myself that I picked my panel right!

I guess there's one other point I'd like to make. There was still the reservation that there was not enough of "me" in this thing (after all, I stuck my name on the front!). So keeping in mind the fact that I adamantly did not want any overlap between this book and my other three books, what I did do is make sure that I was somewhat, substantively but not overbearingly, part of the conversation. In other words, there are opinions and theories and factoids regularly massaged into my questions, but hopefully not to the point of making those questions of the "leading" variety. Because really, that's the only place I am, right here in this introduction and in my part of these Q&As, my questioning, my interrogation. And hey, to put it in perspective, myself, all these guys, we are all super-fans, and I fully expect that the first book anyone needs from me on this band is *Agents of Fortune*, and then this one possibly in the #2 position, maybe tied with the coffee table book. And then if you claim to be as occulted and Ö'Culted as I am, last and most psyche-destroying is my *Imaginos* expansion and explosion, *Flaming Telepaths*.

But it must be said that of the four, I love the fact that *Dominance and Submission* can serve as a casual and easy-reading entry point, because it's just a bunch of dudes explaining the pleasures and virtues of Blue Öyster Cult, no heavy history or statistics, just straight to the lyrics and the music and the people making it. That's what's so cool about this book and that's what was so cool about talking to these guys, frankly, again, with myself realizing I didn't have all the answers, and realizing that listening to a bunch of other smart music fans talk about this band could greatly enhance my appreciation of the records they constructed.

So with that said, fans new and old, I present to you *Dominance and Submission*, the best pure appreciation of Blue Öyster Cult that ever came from a book with my name stuck on the cover.

Martin Popoff
martinp@inforamp.net; martinpopoff.com

C31063   BLUE OYSTER CULT

SIDE I   MATRIX #AL31063   PUBLISHER

1 TRANSMANIACON MC   3:40   B. O'Cult Songs, Inc.
2 I'M ON THE LAMB BUT I AIN'T NO SHEEP   3:17   (ASCAP) 1971
3 THEN CAME THE LAST DAYS OF MAY   4:00
4 STAIRWAY TO THE STARS   3:30
5 BEFORE THE KISS, A REDCAP   4:40

SIDE II   MATRIX #BL31063

1 SCREAMS   3:20   B. O'Cult Songs, Inc.
2 SHE'S AS BEAUTIFUL AS A FOOT   2:50   (ASCAP) 1971
3 CITIES ON FLAME WITH ROCK AND ROLL   4:00
4 WORKSHOP OF THE TELESCOPES   3:00
5 REDEEMED   4:45

WE'RE VERY EXCITED ABOUT THIS NEW GROUP ON COLUMBIA RECORDS AND KNOW
THAT YOU WILL BE ALSO.

JIM BROWN
NATIONAL ALBUM PROMOTION MGR.
COLUMBIA RECORDS

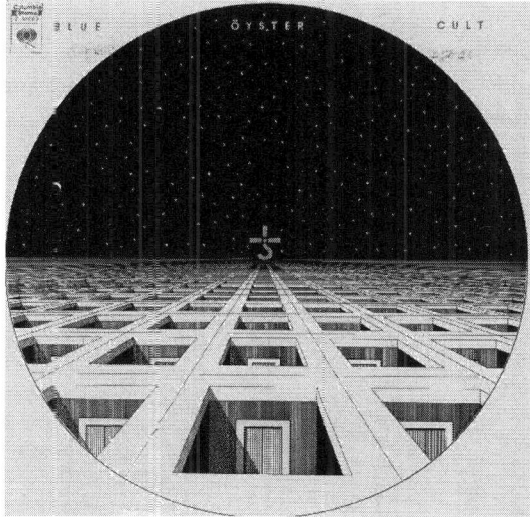

BLUE ÖYSTER CULT

Blue Öyster Cult
January 16, 1972
Columbia C 31063
Produced by Murray Krugman and Sandy Pearlman; Associate Producer, David Lucas
Engineered by David Lucas and Bill Robertson
Recorded at The Warehouse, New York, NY
Personnel: Eric Bloom – lead vocals, stun guitar, keyboards; Donald "Buck Dharma" Roeser – lead guitar, vocals; Joe Bouchard – bass, vocals; Allen Lanier – rhythm guitar, keyboards; Albert Bouchard – drums, vocals

Side 1
1. "Transmaniacon MC" (Sandy Pearlman, Albert Bouchard, Donald Roeser, Eric Bloom) 3:20
2. "I'm on the Lamb but I Ain't No Sheep" (Pearlman, A. Bouchard, Bloom) 3:09
3. "Then Came the Last Days of May" (Roeser) 3:29
4. "Stairway to the Stars" (Richard Meltzer, A. Bouchard, Roeser) 3:42
5. "Before the Kiss, a Redcap" (Pearlman, Murray Krugman, Allen Lanier, Roeser) 4:57

Side 2
1. "Screams" (Joe Bouchard) 3:09
2. "She's as Beautiful as a Foot" (Meltzer, A. Bouchard, Lanier) 2:56
3. " Cities on Flame with Rock and Roll" (Pearlman, Roeser, A. Bouchard) 4:04
4. "Workshop of the Telescopes" (Pearlman, Bloom, Roeser, J. Bouchard, Lanier, A. Bouchard) 3:50
5. "Redeemed" (Pearlman, Henry Farcas, A. Bouchard, Lanier) 4:01

Martin talks to John Alapick, Bill Schuster, Henry Tenny and Matt Thompson about *Blue Öyster Cult.*

Martin Popoff: So here we are with Blue Öyster Cult's very first album. What kind of band are they in 1972 and how did they get to this place?

Bill Schuster: My big impression was that they still had one foot entirely in their previous incarnations as Soft White Underbelly and Oaxaca and Stalk-Forrest Group, and then that tentative other foot going forward, trying to be what the record company wanted them to be, as they say, America's Black Sabbath. But essentially, I found this album to be Stalk-Forrest Group part two. Many of the songs could be interchangeable with what became known as *St. Cecilia: The Elektra Recordings*, which was their shelved material come to life in 2001, especially stuff like "Redeemed," obviously, and "I'm on the Lamb," the song that keeps on going and gets a new title on the next record (laughs). Honestly, that one's never been a favourite of mine in any form, though I know it's a fan favourite overall. But it's like the band doesn't quite know who they want to be at this point.

Personally, I'm a big fan of the Stalk-Forrest Group material. I love the *St. Cecilia* stuff for what it is. You can definitely get to the Blue Öyster Cult vibe there without, say, the over-the-top creepiness. And one thing I found on this particular album, lyrically, they have that creepy vibe but they don't have the cartoon horror aspect that will come later with stuff like "Godzilla." This is subtly scary as opposed to the later more like, say cartoony stuff.

John Alapick: They were coming out of a psychedelic period there in the late '60s, and they were recording seriously in studios before they became the Blue Öyster Cult. And when you listen to some of that work in retrospect you hear like a Steppenwolf sound with a lot of organ. We have the *St. Cecilia* thing, but as bonus tracks on the *Blue Öyster Cult* remaster, we got demo versions of "Donovan's Monkey," "What Is Quicksand," "A Fact About Sneakers" and "Betty Lou's Got a New Pair of Shoes." You've got the organ thing mixing in with the guitar and it was very loose. So especially on the first album, you really heard a lot of remnants of their sound before they became the Blue Öyster Cult.

Henry Tenney: I think part of what we get with the first album is due to the technology of the age. The production of the record, the dynamic range isn't quite what later became available and so everything feels a little darker and dustier. And I think a big part of it is that Eric Bloom's voice is more mysterious. He's got a rasp and it's sort of gravelly, without being crunchy, and it's got this vibe of like someone telling a mystery story. And then that combined with these lyrics that are so dense and evocative, it's really unclear as to what they're evoking a lot of the times. And not in an annoying way but more like a "Let's dive into this mythology" way.

I'm sort of retroactively putting this spin on it, because it took me a while to actually read H.P. Lovecraft, but for me, this feels like that. It feels like a lot of the songs have this honest undercurrent. Yeah, and I say honest in opposition to something that's really, you know, this is our mythology, this is all figured out, everything has a plan. It seems like this is just what they did with the Sandy Pearlman and the Richard Meltzer influences and stuff, but it feels like the music you would write if you were really aware of the deep, terrifying void of space around you, the timeless, endless void of space. They hearken to that a little bit more in some tunes that comes up later. Obviously "Astronomy" is a big one.

But there are all kinds of moments of madness in this album that I think relate to that. And I know that later on they had some specifically Lovecraft tunes—or more like *Imaginos* saga tunes heavily influenced by Lovecraft—beyond the ones we're going to talk about. But anyway, this first record just feels like it's soaked in the sort of gothic horror of stoner times, the things that people were reading in college in 1967 or whatever. I think that really informs a lot of the music and gives it its particular feel of creepy without being self-consciously creepy.

Matt Thompson: This is a band that has been a band for a while. They had the Soft White Underbelly, then they go through that middle period where they are Stalk-Forrest Group and a bunch of other names, playing bars and stuff, so they are rooted in the '60s. So this is a '60s band releasing an album in the early '70s, striving to be heavy metal, trying to be heavy metal, because now we have heavy metal, which didn't really exist when they were Soft White Underbelly. So they're intentionally trying to do that. But production-wise, it's very reverb-y, it sounds old and it does not sound like a Black Sabbath record of the time at all. It sounds like The Doors. You've got the organ- and keyboard-type stuff, so it's much more of an atmospheric kind of thing with noticeable remnants from the '60s. Songs like "Redeemed" or "Then Came the Last Days of May" are very much in the Stalk-Forrest Group sphere, and then you have some legit heavy metal. It's a 'tweener album. It's not really of its time period. It's about an older time period, and I think they clean that up a bit production-wise for the second album, *Tyranny and Mutation*.

Martin: Excellent, okay, into the first song we have "Transmaniacon MC," which is *Munsters* rock from the '60s if there ever was. It doesn't sound like Columbia were getting their American Black Sabbath.

Bill: No, they weren't (laughs). I'd say it's that whole not knowing who they are yet thing, and going with what they originally wanted to do mixed with what the record company wanted them to do. It's that war between who they were and who they're going to be and they're not quite there yet. I will say that right off the bat they establish themselves as a biker band, given that this is about a fictitious biker gang. They play all the Sturgis festivals and roadhouses and everything like that. And the very first song on the first album, here we are talking about Altamont and establishing their biker cred, so to speak.

As for the sound picture painted with this first track, it's murky and muffled but I think with this particular material, and really with the whole black-and-white period, this production works for it. If it was too clear and bright like some of the later stuff, I don't think it would have the mysterious vibe that it does. I'm glad al their albums don't sound like this, but songs like "Transmaniacon MC" sort of need that sense of mystery and fog.

John: As Bill says, this song references the Altamont free concert and the MC stands for motorcycle club. On this album, Eric Bloom was doing most of the singing. And right from the get-go, when you hear Eric sing, his voice isn't the greatest at this point. But he's got a lot of swagger; there's a lot of confidence about him. It's s milar to Bon Scott from AC/DC—he didn't have the greatest voice but he commanded a room with it. That's what I get from Eric Bloom. "Transmaniacon" is a great introduction to Eric and a really cool opener overall. The chorus features a nice call-and-response between Eric singing "MC" and then Buck Dharma coming in with that guitar line—that really makes the chorus there.

Henry: Yeah, I mean, is there a better opener for a record than "Transmaniacon MC?" I actually don't think so. It's like the mission statement for the band. It's got all the elements. It's got like a boogie beat going on, it's got Buck Dharma, who is obviously the most important piece of the Blue Öyster Cult puzzle. Possibly—I mean, it all comes together. Buck Dharma's guitar playing, you get your first taste of it here and you realize that he is above and beyond what hard rock guitarists were doing. He's got swing, he's really clean, he's really crisp, he's got this incredible feel that's beyond crunching guitar. It's got a fluidity and a lyric quality. He brings it up, he jumps in, does it and gets out. He jumps in again and he does a nice little lick and he gets out. That propels the song; it doesn't hold down the song.

A lot of guitar solos at this time, even for the great guitarists, they were just extended musical masturbation, really. And there's nothing wrong with that if you're really great at it, but he didn't do that. He fit himself into the songs. Other bands were more like, let's feature that guitarist and let the guitarist do his thing. Buck was featured by being part of the song instrumentally, not as an extension. There's not a moment where the song takes a break and he does this partitioned guitar thing. Plus he's got swing.

And "Transmaniacon," with all the, you know, mouthfuls of crazy lyrics, "beers and barracuda, reds and Monocaine"... I mean, that's always been one of my favourites, Monocaine being this substance in *The Invisible Man*'s potion that makes him go crazy—that's called Monocaine. And so the fact that they would name-check a fairly obscure, you know, horror movie reference or book reference, and that it's about motorcycles and it's dark and it's dusty, it's just a great way to start.

Matt: You get the chromatic hard rock riff, which is kind of early for that kind of stuff. You're getting a tremendous, high-quality Pearlman lyric. It's mystical and you've got the motorcycle club and Altamont. Here they actually are creating their own version of heavy metal. They don't get to do it that much. But where Sabbath's lyrical sensibilities are different and not nearly as weird—they're war and things like that—here it's like this alternative occult history. You're starting to get that right away with the first record; it's stuff you can really sink your teeth into.

Martin: Next comes "I'm on the Lamb but I Ain't No Sheep," which finds this sort of already small band getting smaller, like they're playing in a matchbox.

John: Yeah, it's interesting when you hear this version and then when you hear what it became on *Tyranny and Mutation* in the form of "The Red & the Black." Here, it's mid-tempo, very loose, and it sounds like a blueprint of what would come later. It's a cool track but it pales in comparison. Famously about the Royal Canadian Mounted Police.

Henry: You probably have a special affinity with this song being Canadian (laughs). It's basically about going up Hwy 87 and like, zipping across the border and avoiding the draft. But the fact that they later did an alternate version of this that's equally good and a completely different song with a completely different feel even though it's the same melody and song structure, that just shows you the versatility and the songwriting strength of that song, the strength of its imagery, the strength of, you know, "Frontenac Chateau, baby."

I love it. The other thing is, friends of mine who grew up on Long Island feel a real pride in Blue Öyster Cult and a real kinship with them. And I've lived in New York for 40 years now and so that creeps over to me. A lot of the songs have New York mentions and New York feels. That also brings in one thing that most other bands of the era don't have, which is a sense of humour and certainly a sense of absurdity.

But "I'm on the Lamb but I Ain't No Sheep" is like, it took me a long time to figure out what the hell the song was about, really. And then I realized, okay, Canadian Mounted Police wear red and black. Red and black is also possibly the coolest colour combination available and it says a lot. Red and black says a lot even if you're not thinking in terms of the Mounties. There's just this really strong imagery that's not so specific that you get sick of it. It's not so totally laid-out. It's not laid-out clearly at all!

A lot of songs where, for example, there's a hook or a riff that's too, too perfect, that gets boring after a while. It's like, wow, this is so great but it's too perfect. It's the ones that have something off about them that endure. And for me, the thing about BÖC is that their music has just enough "off" about it. I think Bowie is the same. A Bowie lyric, you puzzle over it, it's not cut-and-dried, you don't know what's being said, really. You have an idea and it gives you a feeling, but you can't nail it down and put it away. It stays there, because you're constantly working on it. I think "Walk on the Wild Side" is kind of the same thing. It's like the gender shifts so much that your brain can't fully grasp what's being said or who's who or who's what. But you feel compelled. And I think that's true with a lot of the BÖC lyrics.

And then the music is also rarely, if ever, cut-and-dried. I mean it gets a little cut-and-dried later but I think they're doing it honestly. Right now, in this record, as is common with a lot of first records, there's no chance to really see who you are and try to do who you are and try to recreate who you are. This is the creation moment where they are just being—they're just putting it out. They're just being who they are without thinking or knowing maybe even fully who they are or what they're saying.

Martin: Which is kind of an anachronism, right? There's a lot of The Doors in this band at this point, really across all of the first three albums.

Henry: Yeah, definitely. They have the same kind of rumble underneath them. I think Jim Morrison was such a strong influence on so many people that it's hard in their year, in 1972, as a lead singer at least, not to think about Jim Morrison. He was such a strong presence. It's in the DNA of the time. The Doors definitely had a lot of boogie and so there's tons of boogie. A lot of it to me, you know, the bass playing is great, but Buck Dharma just has this feel that's a little jazzy and a little boot-stompy. And he plays so cleanly but with such emotion, that I think it really helps propel a lot of this stuff along. But his jazziness is Doors-y and of course there's Allen Lanier's organ playing.

Bill: I will say that even though "I'm on the Lamb" is not a favourite, "Hornswoop me bungo pony on dogsled on ice" is a classic Sandy Pearlman line that to this day, I'm not 100% sure what it means and that's part of the coolness of it. I like that mystery of those early lyrics, especially from Pearlman and Meltzer. If they were clear, they wouldn't be as effective. Later on, they spell things out more obviously.

Martin: Next we have a ballad, maybe even a murder ballad in the traditional sense.

John: Yes, and "Then Came the Last Days of May," that's one that Buck Dharma wrote all by himself. The thing with Blue Öyster Cult was that on the majority of their songs, they had a lot of other writers doing the lyrics. You had their manager and sort of conceptualist Sandy Pearlman and you had Richard Meltzer, one of the first rock critics. Patti Smith came in a bit later, as did Helen Robbins or Helen Wheels. But this one Buck writes on his own, and it's a true story about a drug deal that went bad and two of the three kids were killed during it. And one of them I think was one of Buck's acquaintances from when they went to school at Stony Brook University in Long Island.

What's interesting about this song is that it's the first time you really hear some of those harmonies that they excelled at later on in their career, particularly on *Agents of Fortune* and *Spectres*. They do the song live to this day, but whereas on record it's just a laid-back, three-minute song about something that was tragic, now it's like a ten-minute tour de force because Richie Castellano and Buck Dharma will both play these long amazing solos during it. And it has a lot more energy live than it used to. It's become one of their more enduring tracks.

As for Buck, he's very melodic, but when he wants to shred he can. In his most memorable works, you can sing his solos—to this day. I mean, he's in his mid '70s now and still a fantastic guitar player and has lost nothing vocally as well. But from this first album, his sound was down. The other guys, not really; they weren't as good musically as they would be later. But Buck already had his sound down at this point. His solos were already pretty impressive on this first album. He's an unsung player; when the great guitar players are discussed, his name doesn't get mentioned enough.

Bill: Like many people, I prefer the live version from *On Your Feet or on Your Knees*; it gets to shine there. But I love the original too. It's actually a more straightforward story than most of their songs, which is kind of unusual. Probably because it's a Donald lyric and that's typically more his thing. But I think it works well. It gives an early indication of the beautiful sound that he can get from his guitar when he's just allowed to play.

Henry: This song's another example to me of like, what's going on? I mean, you know to a certain point. It's also about Dharma's singing, and his voice is totally different from Eric Bloom's. It's very clear and honest-sounding. It doesn't sound like it's sneaky or whatever; it's really playing in an emotional way. It's like, this is what's happening, almost Midwestern-y. Like I say— honest.

But you're hearing the tune and you're hearing the lyrics and you don't really know, what is the West in this case? Like, they go out and they do this thing and that's all pretty clear. It's just another reason why it sticks with you. Or sticks with me. "I'll be breathin' dry air." Where is that? And, "Spilled three boys' blood." Does that mean literally spill their blood? Are they all dead and he's about to die? You never know.

But then the other thing is like, this is the sweetest Buck Dharma playing. There are moments that are almost like country. You feel the landscape with the music very much in this. You feel people driving in the West, packed into this rented Ford, you know, all sitting on the bench seats of a hot car, driving through like West Texas or crossing the border into Mexico or whatever. And the music really gets you there without cliché.

Matt: I think the cool manoeuvre on this one—and it took me a little while to figure this out—is that chronologically the last verse is the first, right? That always kind of confused me. "I'll be breathin' dry air/I'm leaving soon/ The others are already there,/You wouldn't be interested in coming along, instead of staying here?/It's said the West is nice this time of year." It's that optimism before the trip that then ends in their deaths. It's a sophisticated lyrical approach, which we'll see in other BÖC crime-type songs like "Deadline."

Martin: We're back to thorny, anachronistic hard psych music with "Stairway to the Stars," aren't we? I mean, with a whole different mindset this could be modern heavy metal but these guys aren't thinking and arranging that way.
Henry: Yeah, it's a boogie and maybe even a glam tune, but I think it's fantastic. It's sort of talking about rock star access and being the rock star

which is the true essence of that early glam era in the UK. It's less about wearing super-high platforms and more about the content of the music and the feel of it. So yeah, it's got that boogie feel. It's like a boot-stomper, which is very Slade in a way—it feels like it could be a Slade tune.

And the imagery of a stairway to the stars reminds me of "I'll build a stairway to paradise" and all these other pieces of music in the past that were sweeter and from a musical or a movie or whatever. It's an image that's been used before. But this one, this stairway to the stars, he's not talking about him or his people or the people up on his level. He's talking about a stairway to the literal stars, it feels like. Even though he's also bragging about the stuff he has, like a rapper would. You know, "You can drive my motorcar/It's insured to 30 thou." That tells you when it was written (laughs).

John: A song about fandom. It's a great rocker with one of the first really good choruses and Eric sings this with a lot of passion. I'm surprised they don't play it live as much as they used to.

Bill: One thing I noticed about "Stairway to the Stars" that I don't think I've ever picked up on before is that there's a narrative going through that lyric. It's suddenly creepy where it begins with the "You can drive my motorcar/ It's insured to 30 thou/Kill them all if you wish." Then you go down a little, "Mow 'em down now!" Then, "Upon the cast, your broken arm," which I had never thought of before. Perhaps the arm was broken in the crash when this person was using the star's vehicle to mow people down. And then toward the end of the song we get, "I hope you heal up real quick."

Matt: You're getting a live rocker suitable for the time they're in—it fits really well with their desire to be heavy. Straightforward with a sturdy hard rock riff. And I love the little twist in the lyrics, with the broken arm and signing of the cast. It's a little bit of that humorous sensibility. They're not doing just a straightforward, "We're going to the stars" or "We're going to be superstars" song. You get this lyric that is both cynical and funny, which I appreciate.

Martin: Closing side one is "Before the Kiss, a Redcap," which is sort of two songs in one, something BÖC does well—"Golden Age of Leather" and "The Vigil" also do this.

Bill: Yes, this is musically, possibly, the most interesting song on the album. Donald really gets to shine here. It has multiple parts to it musically, which I really like. And the story behind the lyrics, another classic. The fact that it's based on a true story makes it even better. Essentially, it's about a bunch of druggies in a bar and we see the exchange of the redcap with the extended tongue and everything. That's really at the heart of the song for me; it's just such a vivid image, and so creepy.

Henry: Yeah, I've always really loved it. I don't know, it sounds kind of dirty to me. I don't know exactly what's being said but it feels vaguely pornographic. And musically, such a different feel. It's a real boogie song but in a different way from "Stairway," with really neither being a rote boogie or what we think of when we say boogie. It's quite dynamic and it's got that weird little break in the middle which is announced by this bass lick from Joe. Then it goes skiffle or something. I mean, it really goes all over the place but it holds together somehow.

John: They recently brought this back as live track. It's the longest song on the album but it's not so much because it's a progressive track; it's because it's more of a boogie. And then they go into this little jam and there's a great lyric over the jam that Buck sings. Like I say, they play this quite often these days. It's a tune about Conry's Bar, and the redcap is a pill they exchange while they kiss before they go on with their night. It's a memorable tune. An interesting thing about this album, Martin, is that the first half is like the rockin' side. And now we're gonna talk about the second half which is the psychedelic side surrounding their first great anthem.

Martin: Yes, over to side two and I'd say with "Screams" things get creepier—and even more Doors-like.

Bill: I'd agree with that. This is Joe's first song and I absolutely adore this song. I think it pairs up with "She's as Beautiful as a Foot"—I don't ever want to play those songs separately. They need to go back-to-back like this. Joe really came in with a bang here with his first writing credit. If you look at the lyrics, it's not nearly as horrific or supernatural as it might seem on the surface. And listening to it, you can just let the sounds wash over you, and granted, from a music standpoint, yes, it's a horror fest (laughs). But basically, it's just a ride through the city at night—a simple story. So I think that's a testament to the power of the recording and the music that it seems like so much more than what the lyrics actually say.

Matt: With "Screams," you've got Joe Bouchard trying to describe the Hell that is New York, right? And trying to write a lyric that would fit into a hard rock record. The thing that I enjoy the best is the drum transition to the next song. On the first three albums they spent time thinking about the transitions between songs. They do much more of it on the next two records but you also see it right here.

Martin: I'm still trying to grapple with the band's sound at this time, and what I think I hear more than anything is *Love It to Death*- and *Killer*-era Alice Cooper. What do you think of that idea?

Matt: Sure, that's a better comparison than Black Sabbath, and they love Alice Cooper, right? And they forge lifelong friendships with Dennis Dunaway and Neal Smith. So yeah, it sounds like that. And they're really inspired by that band to put on a professional rock show after opening up for them. They were a bar band, a psychedelic bar band before that, who didn't know how to do what they were trying to do. But yeah, you're right. Alice Cooper's got a little bit of a '60s sound to it as well, more than Black Sabbath does.

So neither one, neither BÖC or Alice Cooper, are really heavy metal. I mean, it's fake, right? And I don't mean that in a derogatory way. But they are intentionally trying to be something that they're really not. They're not heavy metal. It's not quite an honest representation. But they're such smart musicologists that they can at times execute. But that's not what they are. Still, these guys as Soft White Underbelly don't sound like the first BÖC record. There is this new sinister feel and atmosphere. But the psych is still there, and maybe even somewhat derived from The Grateful Dead. They loved the Dead. Buck loves Jerry Garcia, who is much more of an influence on his playing that any heavy metal guy or even any British blues boom guy like Jimmy Page.

Henry: "Screams" is super-psychedelic, with some insane piano, which sounds like a kid banging on the piano—it just takes it into madness. Super-slow and then it builds with the crazy piano. It's sort of a mad man's ramblings and rantings and ravings and it's a great way to start the second side, right? This is another thing about the whole record—and at least the first three records—is that there's never a break between songs, which I love. It's like a rock opera, in a way, although not thematically. But everything goes into the next song and into the next song. There's no blank space between tracks, which is hell for DJs, which maybe got in the way of why it didn't get played as much as it probably should have. But the fact that at the end of this, going into "She's as Beautiful as a Foot," it ramps down and then sort of falls apart in this drum frenzy. Then those low, sort of Indian music notes of "She's as Beautiful as a Foot" slide in after this big tumble of drums from Albert.

John: "Screams" is a really cool tune. Allen Lanier's bubbly, burbly organ brings a lot of that spooky feel to it. Initially it's slow and druggie and then it picks up. But it's the organ work and that slow intro that make it for me.

Martin: Before we move on, what does this album cover do to your brain?

John: The cover itself? Well, you've got the Chronos symbol, which is iconic now. It's a fairly altered version of the symbol for Saturn. Bill Gawlik came up with that and the band instantly loved it. It's a black-and-white cover of something that looks like a horizontal building, like a skyscraper on its side. And then it looks like night there in the background, along with some stars.

Bill: I could paint an entire wall with that album cover and just get lost in it. It's great. It seems to go on into infinity with these odd little... are those elevator doors? Yeah, that's almost what they look like, which gives me the impression that it's going down somewhere as well as forward and out into space. And of course, the Chronos symbol. I'm pretty sure Gawlik had no idea that he was coming up with something so iconic and I doubt the band did either.

Henry: Well, that's another thing—that album cover. When I first saw that, I was in, I guess, early high school, and it was what we were drawing, what boys were drawing. We had just learned about drawing to the vanishing point. And these are like super-rudimentary, two-dimensional perspective drawings. That's literally the vanishing point, those little blocks to the BÖC logo. It's a stoner thing; you could sit there and look at that album cover for hours. Because it was intricate, it was something relatable because it was what you had just learned how to do in art class in ninth grade or whatever.

It's incredible; I mean, how genius is that? To have a logo for your band. That icon for your band is like branding 101 now. But nobody did that. And the umlaut in Blue Öyster Cult really made the name stand out. I mean, I guess they didn't invent the heavy metal umlaut. Maybe Amon Düül was the first band to do the umlaut. But they're the first American band, probably. And that single graphic move helped create an entire iconography. It turned into a joke where you'd put umlauts over things just for no reason other than it looked cool. But that created this whole mythology and this whole way of talking about a certain kind of music and that album cover was the start of it.

It's also black-and-white, which speaks to the black-and-white quality of the music. It's not really highly dynamic, the music; it doesn't go all over the place. It's not bright at all. It's very dark, but dark without being dark. There are bands that want to be dark and they say, "Let's make dark music" and they make dark music. I don't think Blue Öyster Cult set out to make dark music. And it's not all dark. I mean, "Redeemed" is like the least dark song of all, you know, in the world. And that's later on in this record.

But as I said earlier, there's an honest exploration of who and what this music is, and that album cover is certainly part of it. It really does look like an H.P. Lovecraft world too. He always talks about Cyclopean architecture and it feels like this thing just rose from the sea. I mean, *Tyranny and Mutation* even more so, which is by the same artist, and a very similar feel, black-and-white, simple perspective. But there's this tower or some kind of structure. And that feels like Cthulhu's home that rises out of the South Seas, which sank, you know, untold millennia before humanity when the great Old Ones were ruling. The endlessness of time and the endlessness of space and the loneliness of humanity is really well illustrated, I think, in that album cover.

Martin: Okay back to the track sequence, next comes "She's as Beautiful as a Foot," and if BÖC were sort of in a proper commercial Alice Cooper zone with some of their other songs here—at least *Love It to Death* and *Killer*— now we're back to what those guys were like on *Pretties for You* and *Easy Action*.

John: Yeah, good point, and both these bands have a lot of Doors in them with similar pretty bleak production, right? Bob Ezrin isn't doing much better with sound over there, even though those guys are starting to sell some records. Anyway, yeah, "She's as Beautiful as a Foot" is more like a dirge. It just stays in that slow tempo the whole time. Again, eerie and spooky, very much like Alice Cooper, who they toured with and who made a big impression on them.

Bill: You might call this the first of their vampire songs, which, they have a long, long history of—vampire songs. But again, it's vague. It's not like say "Nosferatu" much later, which, I love "Nosferatu" but it's a much more straightforward and clear-cut story where this is very mysterious. Yeah, what does a fallen arch tastes like? I don't know. "The bloody tooth mark place"—where is that? How did it get there?

Henry: And the most absurd title. Yeah, I would definitely agree. "Don't put your tongue on the bloody tooth mark place" and "It tasted just like a fallen arch"… I mean, it's a little corny, but to say "She's as beautiful as a foot" puts it into a totally different realm. It's not like they're trying to fit into another idiom. They're making their own idioms. And it's not anything you would ever hear anyone say. I guess it depends on how you feel about feet. If you're a foot fetishist, being as beautiful as a foot is probably really great. But a lot of people aren't.

Martin: Next is "Cities on Flame with Rock and Roll," the band's famous almost made-to-order song, where, to be the label's Black Sabbath band, Albert and Donald take a listen to "The Wizard" and create a variant!

Bill: Yeah, famously stolen from Black Sabbath and to a degree King Crimson. I like how Albert will come out and admit, hey, you know what? We ripped this off, just like he did later for "You're Not the One I Was Looking for." He's not shy about saying, "Hold up guys; this is where we got this." I appreciate that about him. Yeah, this one's a perfect concert staple. Lyrically you've got, "Gardens of Nocturne, forbidden delight/Reins of steel and it's all right" and then "Marshall will buoy but Fender control," relating to the actual equipment. But if you don't think about it in terms of the equipment, it's just this cool mysterious lyric. At its heart, it's an early metal song. It just wants to be played live and to rock.

Henry: Incredible, and from this album it's the most obviously accessible rock 'n' roll jam that that they have. It's big, it's anthemic, it's got incredible guitar parts, it's got a great riff, it builds beautifully, it shreds. Buck is obviously in top form, although he never dips below top form for me. It's the closest thing they have to heavy metal at this point, although it's definitely not metal. I don't know, I don't like metal per se. I think metal's sort of a cheap version or cheap bastard child of *this*! This is original heavy metal to me, the honest stuff. It's really one of the great songs of the genre, but still not quite of the genre.

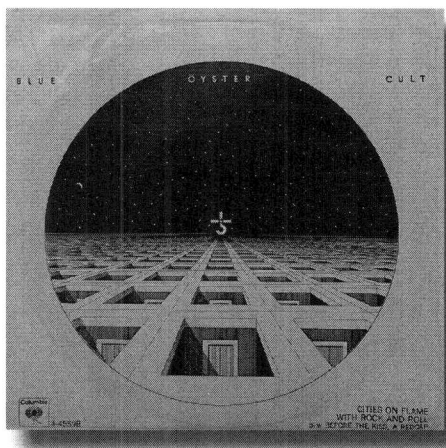

John: Interestingly, it's Albert Bouchard, the drummer, who sings this. With this band eventually all five of these guys would sing, even though you usually think of Eric Bloom and Buck Dharma. But Joe and Albert Bouchard, they're a wonderful rhythm section, but they sang some great tunes and classics. "Cities on Flame" is just a wonderful song with a very memorable riff and cool chorus. When you go see them live, they still play it as an encore. For encores there'll be "Cities on Flame with Rock and Roll" and whatever else they want to throw in there. Because they'll always end the main set with "(Don't Fear) The Reaper." But it's a fantastic track and I love the jam that happens after it goes through its main theme. Then the organ comes in playing these really fast runs and then it goes back into another little jam that's really killer. All of this is going on in like four minutes and three seconds but it always feels like a longer song because it takes you in. It's their first really great anthem and to this day it always sounds great live.

Martin: What can you tell me about Sandy's sort of philosophy about the potential political or societal power of rock 'n' roll?

Matt: Yeah it's a little hard to be brief about it but that's an obsession for him. Through this band he's sonically trying to create a sort of pure sound that has the ability to bring about a revolution, where '60s social activism is usually more about lyrics. He's fascinated with sort of pre-rock heavy music, classical Wagnerian type stuff, Anton Bruckner. So he's got this vision. He's kind of the svengali of the band at this point. But yeah, instead of '60s peace and love activism, this is Altamont and the dark power of rock that was felt there in what happened, revolution, totalitarianism. He's thinking history is going to be changed, and he believes that certain aspects associated with things like a distorted guitar that have these mind-altering sonic qualities can create change independent of what the lyrics are saying.

Martin: Excellent, and really, you can sort of see that in action in "Cities on Flame" in both the lyrics and the music. But then it's back underwater—or underground—for "Workshop of the Telescopes."

Bill: Yeah, but the lyrics are very cool here. I like the fact that Albert re-covered that song with his "Black Telescope" version recently, too, for his regeneration of the *Imaginos* story. It was never a favourite in the old days, but it's definitely grown on me over the years. I like the fact that you've got a full band credit along with Sandy here. I'm not sure if there was ever another song like that in the catalogue, come to think of it, where all five band members and Sandy get a credit like that.

John: Good tune, and you're right, more psychedelic like "Screams." Well, actually it's got a little more energy than "Screams" does.

Henry: "Workshop of the Telescopes" has always been my favourite on the album. It's so thorny and difficult to figure out—the lyrics are nuts. But the music is fantastic. There's this constant reverb-y, echoey guitar from Buck that sort of shimmers throughout the song. This is some of his finest work. Lyrically, it's just so strange. t hearkens back to this whole infinite terror of space. You know, "By silverfish imperatrix whose uncorrupted eye/Sees through the charms of doctors and their wives/By salamander drake and the power that was undine"... it's like speaking in tongues or something and not the Talking Heads album. It's like a chant without the rhythm, just crazy imagery. "By those who see with their eyes closed"—it's just mystery and fog and shrouding.

Matt: Musically quirky, with some dissonance at the intro and a great mystical lyric with a bunch of references involved with alchemy. I've done a lot of research on this song for another project that I'm doing, but you've got the salamander, which is an alchemical creature that has the fire that is needed for calcification and all this stuff. You have a reference to an "undine," which is this alchemical water spirit. And then there's the ability to see into the unknown, so, "Sees through the charms of doctors and their wives" and "When my vision was oh so cloudy" and "I saw things through two eyes." It's the alchemical search for answers to the world, to be able to see beyond what is there. It's right in line with the *Imaginos* sensibilities and lyrics and mysticism.

Martin: All right, well, with "Redeemed" we're in new territory, sort of The Grateful Dead circa *Workingman's Dead* and *American Beauty*.

Bill: Long ignored! (laughs). It's just this odd little song. I never really thought of it as a country song, but I've heard and read many times people saying that. It's really grown on me. t would've fit perfectly on the Stalk-Forrest Group *St. Cecilia* album. It almost seems like a holdover. That Grateful Dead influence is one of the things that I actually like about this song and the Stalk-Forrest Group. It's not the typical Blue Öyster Cult sound. I think if they would have followed that course further and not been steered towards being the American Sabbath, they could have come up with some pretty cool stuff. I wonder. I mean, I know you're a fan of the mid to late '70s Dead stuff—you're a big Donna Godchaux fan, right? I'd be kind of curious what these guys could have come up with in that vein, if they'd continued throughout the '70s.

But I think with the next album they find their new identity much more clearly. This one is still questing, and it's a little bit all over the place but in a fun way. Fortunately it's not one of those albums where a band comes out and boom!—here's our greatest material and we're never going to equal this. One of the cool things about Blue Öyster Cult for me is that they didn't start out with their best. They continued to grow, unlike so many artists who seem to just go "Pow!" and that's it—it's all downhill from here.

John: I was talking about the harmonies earlier on "Then Came the Last Days of May." Here, the harmonies really shine as well. This is a wonderful song. I've read reports that this is a song about someone's dog. I don't know how true that is, and also that they actually bought the lyrics from someone else. It's a cool closer to a pretty versatile album, although they would make more versatile albums in the future. And when it ends, it ends really quiet and then it gets loud again and then it just stops. They slowly reduce what they're doing and then go into the mini-frenzy and then choke it off. One thing about Blue Öyster Cult on these earlier albums, they would end these songs really abruptly. But lot of times the volume would really rise before it ends, making it feel like you saw an event.

Henry: In "Redeemed," because of the bear, Sir Rastus Bear, to me it always felt like the story of a teddy bear or some toy. It's so bright, it's country, it's cheerful, it's hopeful. There's nothing else on the album that has those feelings of positivity. And once again, I'm gonna say that the rest of the album is not self-consciously negative, because they're not doing anything self-consciously at this point to me at all. But nothing is this positive. It's an outlier. And if it wasn't so good, it would seem... I mean, I'm sure there are a lot of people who love this record and think "Redeemed" is the stupidest thing ever. I've never been like that. I think that it's the palate-cleanser before we get into *Tyranny and Mutation*. It's like, let's leave them with a song you can sing as you walk out of the theatre. And we'll pick it up next time with something that will drive them back down into our madness.

Matt: It's a previous song, right? Co-written with Harry Farkas, it's from the material that predates *Blue Öyster Cult*. It has some of that country, Grateful Dead sound to it. Sir Rastus Bear is mentioned in it, which is just the name of a dog. You just have to trip a little bit to make it sound weirder than it is. But it has that change at the end. It's this major key, Grateful Dead-style song up until the end. And then it suddenly changes. You get the chord change, much more minor-sounding, and then it outros in an unsettling way that overall nicely sums up the off-putting, sinister nature of the sound of the first record. Because it's not a '60s or a '70s record—it's somehow, intriguingly completely of neither era. It's got this undercurrent of sinister-ness because it's a heavy metal record that is not a heavy metal record, significantly—but not solely—because it doesn't have heavy metal production on it. But yeah, it has this off-putting, sinister weirdness that is unique and frankly kind of creepy.

Martin: Another thing that makes it not heavy metal is the fact that none of the singers in this band are singing particularly aggressively. There's more crooning and even some mumbling.

Matt: That's a great point, Martin. They don't have a heavy metal singer at all, right? Even Eric, on the most heavy metal of songs, is not gritty. Nor is he Ozzy by any stretch, who is not gritty but regularly has to exert himself. And especially early on, they're not pushing air; there's no power. You can barely hear the vocals. They're buried in the mix.

Martin: And with Joe and Albert, you've got something of a fragile style. Heck, most of Eric's style is also about fragility. Buck isn't fragile but it's still a small, modest sound.

Matt: He's a smooth, melodic, pop singer, and the other ones... fragile is a great way to put it. And that, to me, also adds to the off-putting aspect to it. But I do love your idea. It's really hard for these guys to execute heavy metal. In some ways, I don't know if it's on purpose or not, but *Imaginos* is an attempt to be heavy. But it doesn't do it in a Sabbath way at all. Maybe *Imaginos* would've been more successful if you had the Sabbath of that time period doing it. But again, BÖC are not heavy metal, so it's an outsider's opinion of what heavy metal should look like. You get its own version of the thing that is not that thing.

TYRANNY AND MUTATION

Tyranny and Mutation
February 11, 1973
Columbia KC 32017
Produced by Murray Krugman and Sandy Pearlman
Engineered by Tim Geelan
Recorded at Columbia Studios, New York, NY
Personnel: Eric Bloom – vocals, stun guitar, all synthesizers; Donald "Buck Dharma" Roeser – guitar, vocals; Joe Bouchard – bass, vocals, keyboards; Allen Lanier – keyboards, rhythm guitar; Albert Bouchard – drums, vocals

Side 1
1. "The Red & the Black" (A. Bouchard, Bloom, Pearlman) 4:20
2. "O.D.'d on Life Itself" (Bloom, A. Bouchard, J. Bouchard, Pearlman) 4:50
3. "Hot Rails to Hell" (J. Bouchard) 5:12
4. "7 Screaming Diz-Busters" (A. Bouchard, J. Bouchard, Roeser, Pearlman) 7:00

Side 2
1. "Baby Ice Dog" (A. Bouchard, Bloom, Patti Smith) 3:28
2. "Wings Wetted Down" (A. Bouchard, J. Bouchard) 4:12
3. "Teen Archer" (Roeser, Bloom, Meltzer) 3:57
4. "Mistress of the Salmon Salt (Quicklime Girl)" (A. Bouchard, Pearlman) 5:07

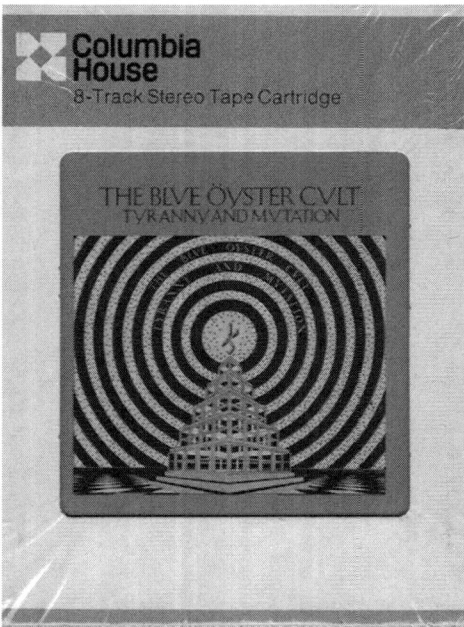

Martin talks to John Alapick, Jamie Laszlo, Steven Reid and Matt Thompson about *Tyranny and Mutation*.

Martin Popoff: The sophomore album, as they call it. This was the first Blue Öyster Cult album I got as a new release and my first BÖC album ever. And I didn't come on board as a huge fan at ten years old in 1973, I gotta say. It sounded creepy and old compared to Deep Purple and even Led Zeppelin, and of course I couldn't tell what the hell they were talking about. Frame this one up in context for us, Matt, to get us started.

Matt Thompson: Well, okay, I think the biggest change is it's informed by their life experiences of supporting the first record. So they have the two tours; they've got the tour with The Byrds, but more interestingly with Mahavishnu Orchestra, and of course, the Alice Cooper stuff. And they write *Tyranny and Mutation* on the road. The debut had a longer gestation period; it has some Stalk-Forest Group stuff still in it.

I think *Tyranny and Mutation* is really informed by what they want to deliver live. Production-wise, it's certainly punchy. They get rid of all the reverb, it's less Doors-y, a little less murky-sounding, the guitars definitely cut through more. And then from a songwriting standpoint, I think there too they have the live experience in mind. One example is the reworking of "I'm on the Lamb but I Ain't No Sheep" into "The Red & the Black." It opens the record and it opens a bunch of their shows going forward, right? So they're kind of designing an opener for the live set. It's great as an encore as well, so in later years they use it as a closer.

To me, that's sort of the most symbolical and literal way that they're leaving the psychedelic '60s origins of the bands, by leaving SFG/SWU stuff behind and kind of becoming what they're trying to be. So they're purposely trying to be a heavy metal group. And that's sort of the directive: they want to be America's answer to Black Sabbath from a commercial direction standpoint. They don't really do that on the first album much at all. And I think they've settled into how they're going to try to do it with *Tyranny and Mutation*. They're trying to describe Hell and kind of come up with their own version of heavy metal.

Martin: I wonder if you're over-stating the transformation, because they still do sound kind of old, right? And they still sound sort of 1969/1970 even on *Secret Treaties*, no?

Matt: Sure, well, so some of that is probably in their DNA. They're an old band. They're not a new band, right? They've been together from the Soft

White Underbelly days. To your point, as a quote unquote heavy metal record, something like "7 Screaming Diz-Busters" has some proto-speedy, maybe metal-ish elements to it, and it's a little bit proggy and it influences certainly thrashy bands, right? That's a song that Metallica would like. But the guitars are not very distorted. It's got a significant organ-type sound to it, not in a metal way but more atmospheric. Plus there's a boogie element.

But I think *Tyranny and Mutation*, to my ears, does have a unique sound to it among the first three records that is more appealing to the ears of people who like heavy stuff. And I would include punk in that. "The Red & the Black" becomes the first of their two punk songs, meaning songs that punk-ish and punk-influenced bands like, right? You get Mike Watt covering it in every band that he's in going forward. BÖC do that again on *Agents of Fortune* with "This Ain't the Summer of Love." So they write these two things that actually appeal to the punk set.

Jamie Laszlo: I like how the first three albums are all black-and-white, because they're almost like a different band. And you've got guys who like only the black-and-white albums. Well, they like them the most. I think if they would have made the first two or three albums and then broke up, we'd be talking about them the same way we talk about a lot of proto-metal bands, like Sir Lord Baltimore, you know, as part of this forgotten proto-metal thing.

But this is what they had going for them, I think, Martin. Proto-metal: how do you describe a sub-genre that isn't even a sub-genre? Is it just an age? An era? How do you describe the sound of proto-metal? And the best way I can describe it is not by how it sounds exactly. I just say it sounds like guys trying to figure it out. You know, throwing crap to the wall and seeing if it sticks. Some guys figured it out quicker than others—Black Sabbath, Deep Purple, Uriah Heep. But for those bands that were just trying to figure out, I think that's why we like listening to it—because it sounds very experimental. But the weird thing is, Blue Öyster Cult sound like they have figured it out, but what they've figured out is proto-metal and, importantly, not heavy metal. It's almost like they've figured out that proto-metal is what they were meant to do. They sound natural within this sub-genre that is not a sub-genre, but more like a brief period of time, or something necessarily linked to time by being deemed proto.

It's funny to see how they were framed back then. I have this copy with a reproduction of the hype sticker, with these period quotes from the magazines at the time on it. Very cool how, you know, everybody seemed down, when you read all the hype on this sticker. It seems like everyone thought that they were the next big thing.

Martin: What's it say?

Jamie: Okay, so Jon Tiven from the *Yale Daily News* writes, "Call it killer, call it heavy, but it is the best non-pretty American group in a long while, in the same (urban) league with The Doors and the Velvet Underground." Robert Christgau, writing for *Newsday* says, "The Blue Öyster Cult centres on Buck Dharma. He may very well be the best hard rock guitarist in America." Okay, well, Jimi's dead by this time. And I like how they say The Blue Öyster Cult. It's kind of like when Batman first came out, everyone said the Batman. Then we've got Mike Saunders writing for *Phonograph Records* magazine saying, "If any group has the potential to match the recorded work of Led Zeppelin and Black Sabbath—and much more importantly to possibly transcend the whole heavy metal field—Blue Öyster Cult should be it."

So yeah, I mean, they had the hype. These magazines probably don't even exist anymore. And at the bottom it says that a *Creem* readers poll called them the number one new group. Well, yeah, that readers poll probably came from the first album, from people listening to the first album. I don't know if this hype sticker was on the album when it was first released. Or maybe like a year after it was released, they put the hype on there because they were starting to get more notoriety. Plus there's Lester Bangs here who must've said in *Creem* that, "*Tyranny and Mutation* will blow you over like no record in recent memory. They have all the equipment necessary to become the best band in America." Wow.

John Alapick: Love it. What I'll add is that back in the '70s, the record companies would work with the artist. They would give them a few albums to help them find their sound. You heard it with Rush, you heard it with Queen, you heard it with Scorpions, you heard it with Judas Priest. Those early albums, they were still trying to find their way. Blue Öyster Cult had an idea of what they wanted to do on their self-titled debut, but on *Tyranny and Mutation* they found it. It was there. They're tighter, they're playing faster tempos, the musicianship is really increased. And now the whole band sounds confident, not just Eric Bloom. When you hear the first song, it just grabs you. And that first half is one of the more exciting halves of music I've ever heard in rock music.

Martin: Again though, there's still vestiges of psych in their sound, albeit of the bad acid trip variety.

John: I just think that was part of their foundation from when they were coming up as Soft White Underbelly. That was gonna be there. And as you listen to their catalogue, that part remained there, however faint. I mean, maybe not every album, but they always had that part of them.

Martin: Jamie, what's your take on the production?

Jamie: I think it's better than the first one and it's probably on par with the third one. Yeah, I don't want too slick of a production on this album, Martin. People always say they had proto-punk tendencies in their music and I think that stems from the first three albums. It's a little bit of that MC5 and Stooges thing going on, and that works well with these songs. Now I like the remake of "Astronomy" better than the original "Astronomy." We've never heard these particular songs produced in an '80s way either—I guess besides "O.D.'d on Life Itself" from *Cult Classic*, but that's '90s—so I have nothing to compare them to. But if someone gave me the choice, you know, take the gamble. You can have what's behind door number one or door number two, where we do them all with bigger production values but you haven't heard it yet, put this away I'll stick with door number one.

Martin: All right, so into the album, we have "The Red & the Black," which always struck me as a sort of MC5-meets-Amboy Dukes song, very Detroit rock. I can see Deadly Tedly—The Whackmaster, The Tedinator—coming up with this riff. Steven, I'll get you to chime in here.

Steven Reid: Thanks, yeah, I can hear that too (laughs). If you want a fast and frantic start to the album, this is it. This is almost garage rock or punk rock, topped with real attitude. The way the songs on this album are produced—this is Sandy Pearlman but Murray Krugman too—it almost sounds live, doesn't it? It's so raw. And I think it's rare to capture that amount of energy in a studio recording. If you're not on board by the time the song finishes, I don't know what's wrong with you. And the guitar work is so tight, so fiery, it absolutely takes your head clean off. Same again rhythmically: the whole thing is taped together so tight. It sounds so ramshackle and it's so *not* ramshackle. There's a skill in that.

Lyrically, "The Red & the Black" is a strange one. I mean being on the run from the Mounties is an unusual topic, isn't it? It's not what you would expect from a rock 'n' roll album. It's early on in their career and they're taking risks already. I like the lyric. It's a lot of fun. A lot of fun is not necessarily something I would always associate with a Blue Öyster Cult lyric and I mean that in the right way.

Jamie: I do like how they call side one the black and side two the red.

They're adding to that Blue Öyster Cult mystique right away on their second album. See, these guys knew what they were doing; they had it down before other bands. "The Red & the Black" opens with just this very jarring guitar sound. It's hard to pinpoint what you want to call it because some people would call it heavy. But then everyone has a different definition of what heavy is. Some people call heavy something like Black Sabbath, where you have that doomy sound. Some people call anything that's a little jarring and hard on the ears heavy. Early black metal is jarring and hard to listen to a little bit, but is it heavy? Depends on the person.

But this song is very, very fast, especially for 1973. You know, they call "Stone Cold Crazy" maybe the first speed metal song. This was a year before that. Is it proto-speed metal? When there's no such thing, I just make something up. It probably blew people away back in 1973, how fast they were playing and how jarring that guitar was. It was something your parents would definitely hate.

John: Fantastic track. They used "I'm on the Lamb but I Ain't No Sheep" as a blueprint and they made it faster. They make it this fantastic rock song that to this day they will occasionally bring out as an opener. It's a song that really gets you into the show and also gets you into their second album.

Matt: Yes, it's designed to be an opener but it also works well as a closer. Perhaps in the reworking of an old lyric, they're symbolizing that transition. This is their way of saying goodbye to the old stuff.

Martin: The guys take it way down for track two, which is "O.D.'ed on Life Itself," a kind of small-ish retro-rock thing.

Matt: Yeah, this one is lyrically much more interesting than it is musically interesting. You're getting a lot of the Sandy Pearlman purple prose, his very wordy lyrics, but it's consistently interesting. But the music is actually really straightforward, a bluesy boogie-type riff. To me it's the least successful song on the album. But what an awesome title—looks great on the album cover. But they right away rearrange it live. They punch it up , with the "O.D.'ed" stop "On life"—it's made more rhythmic. It's like it wasn't fully finished. It got written on the road very fast to record this album.

Steven: It almost makes the song before seem even more clever because it's this kind of relaxed blues shuffle that basically stumbles along. It provides juxtaposition though; it's not what you expect. You never get too comfortable or uncomfortable. It's a bit spaced-out but it's still got focus.

As I say, it's a million miles disconnected from "The Red & the Black" and yet it's still really connected! They feel like they join together. When it's spinning, I like this song, but if you were to ask me in a couple of days time, how does it go? Probably couldn't tell you, outside of the chorus. It's not quite got the hooks and memorability that so much of this album does.

Jamie: "O.D.'ed on Life Itself," man, this song comes off as a crowd-pleaser at a concert and they're still doing it. That hasn't gone away from the set list. I can see a lot of people in the crowd, you know, they're tired of the bullcrap that life sometimes hands them. And I could see them all singing together, "O.D.'ed on life, life itself." When you're in a crowd like that, doing that, getting out your frustration, it's a form of group therapy. There's all kinds of different forms of therapy, Martin, but you may as well try going to a BÖC concert first and see if that works.

John: To me it sounds like T Rex's "Bang a Gong (Get It On)." It's mid-tempo, the organs play a really cool part in the song and Eric sounds really confident. It's just a great party tune although it's not fast. And yes, they still play it live.

Martin: Next is "Hot Rails to Hell," which would be metal with different production and arranging, but here, heavy as it is, I still feel like we're in that proto-metal nether-zone.

Matt: Yes, and to complicate matters, you have the sort of legendary story on the recording of that one where the producer didn't like the way that the drums were recorded for whatever reason, whether it's performance or the quality of the recording. Albert's got to re-record the drums on it, and they don't have enough tracks to leave the original drum track there so he can't play along to himself. He has to play along to the guitar and bass and it works out okay. Albert always credits Buck's steadiness as a rhythm player for him to be able to pull that off. That's the only time they've really overdubbed a full drum track. Pretty interesting.

Lyrically, it's also interesting because you get the references to Phil King. He helps get "Cities on Flame" on the radio. He's an important person in their early history. But the lyric is kind of a combination of the references to Phil King and the story of Joe with Bill Gawlik taking the subway into New York City. That's a crazier time in New York City than it is today. And again, there's that missive of trying to write songs about Hell and the metaphor of the craziness of New York City at night equating to Hell. And there we have it—Joe has his signature song. For as long as he's in the band, that's his kind of showcase moment in concert.

Steven: Snarling guitars, superb layered vocals. All told, there's a bit of Steppenwolf in here. There's a power in the percussion that brings a threat and a potency that you wouldn't necessarily expect if you just heard the music on its own—really important and vital to what's going on here. But to me, the best thing about the song is the panning guitars at the song's end, the howling and then the screaming and the screeching. At the same time there's that descending surf guitar line going on. That doesn't belong here, but it dead belongs here! Why would you put that in there?! It's just so good. But I mean the volume… it's a tough listen at the end. It's really genuinely hard work.

Jamie: They sure did have the song titles early on. You know you're not buying a John Denver record. When you see the song title "Hot Rails to Hell," it sounds like it should be a Judas Priest song, something off of *Stained Class* or something. Here's the image I get: it's a beer-guzzling, doing 70 on the freeway in 1973 with your buddies kind of song. And why do I say 1973? Because today's kids are not going to do dumb things like that to an old song like this. And if you're a teenager in 1973, doing dumb things, you're way too old now to do dumb things like that. So it's perfect for doing 70 on the freeway while guzzling beers—but only in 1973.

John: What I like is that Joe's talking about the subway but the chorus, in particular, is about what you would feel if you were in Hell. "The heat from below can burn your eyes out." Wicked track, great anthem, and the band's second great anthem, after "Cities on Flame."

Martin: Well, they might have a third, with the next song on this album being "7 Screaming Diz-Busters," or a fourth if you count "The Red & the Black."

John: Yes, good point. This one is dramatic, but heavy at the same time. It starts out really psychedelic during the verses, with some great countering, octave-jumping bass lines in there from Joe. Over to the main theme, you've got a signature BÖC call-and-response—Eric sings a line and here comes Buck Dharma with a cool guitar run right after. And they're going back and forth before they go into the chorus of the song itself. A lot of songs on here are pretty tightly wound, tightly written. This song is seven minutes, but it doesn't feel like seven minutes because it's so exciting. There's a lot of drama. It gets really quiet and explodes. And each guy gets a brief showcase to add to the drama, with the bass and drums and then Allen Lanier's organ, which brings a spooky monster movie feel. It builds momentum until it goes into the chorus again. At the end, they're repeating "Lucifer the light" over a jam. It's pretty creepy—and culty!—if you think about it. And it's very loose musically, to the point of sounding chaotic. Each pass it's getting quieter and quieter and in the background you are hearing this counting. On the count of seven, that's when the song ends with that ringing guitar, and right before it's over, this strange screeching feedback. Wonderful track.

Matt: I want to compare this one to a later track, "Wings Wetted Down." Joe works a lot on the lyrics, and there's a difference in Joe's approach to lyrics whether he's writing them or Sandy's writing them. "Diz-Busters" is a Sandy Pearlman lyric, and Joe heavily edits the lyrics that he gets from Sandy. That's not the case, I don't think, with other band members. And Albert does the most work with Sandy. If you listen to the Albert/Sandy songs, you get those lots of mouthfuls of lyrics, like he's trying to cram them in there. And in some of them that really creates something cool, right? Like you'd never write a melody that way otherwise. If you're just humming a melody, you would never have come up with one like those necessitated by trying to cram all these Sandy Pearlman words in there and keep the order and things like that. Joe doesn't do that. Joe heavily edits Sandy's lyrics and makes the end result more musical.

In any event, "7 Screaming Diz-Busters" is pretty epic; there's a lot to it. You've got time changes both sort of real and imagined in terms of how it builds up and goes down at different times. But lyrically it all fits in. It's not the mouthful style. You actually get kind of a nice... even though the lyrics don't make sense as a chorus in a pop song, "On each and all those holy nights/When duster's dust becomes the sale," actually feels like a chorus. It's really weird even though lyrically it's not something you put in a pop song. But it's pretty hooky for such an epic-type song.

And there's the great organ stuff going on in it that becomes, again, a live highlight. The song leaves room for the jamming parts that they love to do in concerts. It's got plenty of room for that. It has room for the Eric

Bloom rants, or just kind of going off and telling a story, right? So there's *On Your Feet or on Your Knees* and *Live in the West*, the heavily-traded tape, where you get two totally different stories. It's Eric Bloom just going off, which is fun.

And overall the album is pretty abrasive-sounding to the ears, right? So trebly. And in "Hot Rails to Hell" you get the insect buzzing sounds at the end. You've got the one guitar really trebly throughout, and then there's the guitar that's the closest thing to this supposed "stun guitar" credit, although it's actually Buck playing it, not Eric. That provides the sort of deeper sound on there.

Steven: Even with everything we've said already, "7 Screaming Diz-Busters" goes on to outshine everything that's come before for me on this album—and possibly everything else on side two as well. Beautiful bass line, galloping riff, but when the reins come off, phenomenal. The urgency and the absolute 100% belief that the band have in the song, that's what makes it so impressive. They're not just playing this song or recording this song. They're attacking this song with everything they've got, right? It just happens to have been captured in the studio As for the production at this point in the band's career, is it perfect? No. It kind of *is* though, isn't it? Because it's perfect for what the intention appears to be. And the intention genuinely appears to be as ferocious as you possibly can without ever taking too many steps over the line. You don't want to play it safe. They are over the line at certain points in this album but it's never out of control. But it's mighty close.

Jamie: And another great title. That's the best thing about this song. And this can only come from talented people. I have no idea what seven screaming diz-busters are. I have no idea what they look like. But when I hear this song, I kind of get an idea of what they look like. You know, you've got the buzzing, swirling guitar over the charging guitar, which gives me an image that a few of these diz-busters, they travel by land—but a few are flying as well. I don't know if it's four and three or three and four. And these things are attacking and they're wreaking havoc, whatever they are. So after hearing the song, if you gave me a multiple choice of three pictures and said, "Pick out what the diz-buster is," I think I'd be able to pick it out. And

I might not even need the multiple choice. Just give me a pen and I think I could draw one at this point. That is very cool how they do that.

Martin: Nice. Before we venture over to side two of the original vinyl, what does this album cover do for you?

Steven: Everything. It does everything for me. It's such a good album cover. This is a message on high, isn't it? We are beaming to the world. We are about to take control. I mean, you've got the symbol in here and it's phenomenal. I absolutely love it. And yes, we're in the black-and-white era but I do like the touch of red, which alludes to the song and the titling of the sides; it's so clever.

Martin: I never noticed that! You're right—it looks like a radio tower!

Steven: Oh, yeah, to me that's always what it's been. This is the epicentre of what you're about to enter. From here we take over the world. And I absolutely adore how you've got the radio waves emanating out. And then these strange tiles. But the circular pattern continues all the way through, into the tile pattern, sort of like super- or mega-radio waves. The perspective of that is fantastic. So effective. I couldn't imagine going through the record racks and not picking that out. How could you not pick that out? I always think that a band should announce their name on the front of an album really boldly. This is one of the times where they got it absolutely right, just putting the name in there as part of the circle pattern, and no bigger than the album title. Phenomenal. Yeah, love it.

Matt: It's the second of the Bill Gawlik covers and they do correspond, or agree, don't they? I mean, maybe it oversells it, really, because now I'm thinking a little more about what you were saying. Those first two records have two great heavy metal album covers, but they aren't convincing heavy metal albums like *In Rock* or *Master of Reality* or whatever. But they're very mysterious. You stare at the album cover until you see God. That's in your black-lit room with incense burning, right? So it's of its time. It really fits into the imagery of what they're still trying to do at that time.

Matt: What do you know about Bill Gawlik?

Matt: Well, not a lot of people know much about Bill Gawlik. You even hear different stories about where he went to school, right? Did he go to RISD; did he go somewhere else? He's this sort of maniacal art student.

He allegedly contributes the title to the album because after listening to the first album while working on the art he says something to the effect of "Listening to this album is like tyranny and mutation." Sandy picked up on that and used it for the album. No one knows what became of him. He does these two legendary album covers and disappears. Which I think adds to the mysticism of them. It's perfect for the story.

Jamie: That cover hypnotizes. And if you spin it, it kind of reminds you of the legendary early Vertigo label. And of course Black Sabbath was signed to Vertigo.

Martin: All right, what do you guys think about "Baby Ice Dog?"

Matt: Yeah, so you get your Patti Smith lyric and my understanding is that Patti had given "Revenge of Vera Gemini" to Albert around the same time and he's really struggling to do anything with it. But he writes the music to "Baby Ice Dog" like really fast. So for whatever reason he's able to do something with it very quickly. It cops a Blues Project riff which probably helps expedite that music writing process, to borrow a little bit from one of their early heroes. So that was a big influence on the Soft White Underbelly, The Blues Project. The song is "I Can't Keep from Crying Sometimes." That's the song he kind of cops it from.

For a fairly short song, it's got a lot kind of going on in it. You get the little breakdown in the middle. You can even hear a little finger-snapping in the background. Then Eric does the "Lead me 'round like a broke-down hound now/Crossing me once too often," and then into this, you know, sort of single line music part. But they don't stay on anything too long. It's not like a jam band thing; it's got a lot of interesting parts. So it has a lot of things that great Blue Öyster Cult songs have, including weird, cool lyrics that you can just throw your own interpretation into—and they're written by a genuine, stamped and approved poet.

Steven: It's the shortest song on the album and it's pure '70s rock bliss, isn't it? Built on a great rhythmic bass riff that highlights the really quick and dexterous playing behind the kit from Albert. I'm not sure anyone does those quick-fire snare and tom rolls the way that he does them here. They're so clean, so sharp, so pronounced. I mean, they become hooks in their own right. His overall playing is just an absolute joy, full of swing, full of vigor. And yet he keeps such a tight hold on everything else that's going on. He's so good that you nearly forget to mention the guitarwork and Buck's tone and the great sort of classical piano runs in what, I guess, serves as the chorus. The way it all comes together is absolutely phenomenal. You know, you get to howl along with the song at the beginning and you get to howl along with the song at the end. You've got scorned lovers getting revenge. He really is ice-cold inside. Everything coming together, message and music.

Jamie: This one has that start/stop thing going on that I'm not really the biggest fan of. But it finds its groove often enough. Plus you gotta love the extra effort of putting the howling dogs in both at the beginning and at the end.

John: This is just at the time when, I believe, Patti Smith was seeing Allen Lanier and that's how she got involved with writing some of their lyrics before she became a singer on her own and had a very legendary career, even though it was more underground. But a wonderful lyricist. "Baby Ice Dog" is really cool. As a side-opener, it's up-tempo and frantic, although not as extreme as "The Red & the Black." Allen Lanier's piano plays a very key role in it. Another cool part about this song is how it just breaks down completely and Eric will sing a line and then the band will come in and then it goes back into its main theme. Again, call-and-response but between vocal and instrumentation, which is a blues trope.

Martin: Next is a heck of a creep show, with Joe delivering the lead vocal on "Wings Wetted Down," written by him and Albert.

Steven: Yes, and in a similar way to side one, the second track here suddenly pulls things back in. But this time it's more malevolent. Joe sings the verses and Eric joins him, harmonizing, on the chorus and that works a treat. There really is only a slight difference between the two, but it's just enough to add a different tone and a different feel; it puts you a bit off balance. I like that. Because it's a really gentle but unsettling musical soundscape that's going on below all of that.

It's an intriguing lyric. I mean, are you travelling with the four horsemen of the apocalypse? Or are you flying the skies during World War II? It seems like you're left to make up your own mind and I absolutely love that. There's so much similarity between the two ideas, and yet those topics couldn't be any more different. But same again, the music is doing an equal shift on the storytelling. It's such a strength of the band at this stage. That they present a lyric and create something else from it because the music is so connected to the whole ethos of the song. It's quite breathtaking in places.

Matt: Probably the best attempt at sounding like Sabbath, at least melodically—it's more like a Sabbath dirge than one of their rockers. Plus Iommi wouldn't play it that way. Joe takes some lyrics from Pablo Neruda, a Spanish poet, right? That's another aspect of Joe Bouchard's writing style. He takes it wholesale from "Ode with a Lament," although it's only a couple lines. And what's interesting is that it's written in Spanish; it's translated and there's different translations. So he's working off of a particular one. If you looked at other ones, you're not going to see the exact same lines.

He does the same thing in "Nosferatu" later on. Some of those lyrics are right from the silent movie. The words show up on the screen and they're right in the song. He does such a great job, but he quite literally takes those inspirations and then he works them and turns it into a song. So there's some really great imagery on that song taken from Neruda, but much of it is his own. I think the "echoes of empires" is his own. It fits the music beautifully. It's very moody and it's heavy in a way that's neither fast nor loud.

Jamie: I'm glad this one comes after "Baby Ice Dog" because if there's one thing "Baby Ice Dog" does is it makes this awesome song seem even more awesome because it's following my least favourite song on the album. The opening to this song is so inviting, so welcoming. Maybe you're being welcomed to Hell, but Martin, at least you're still being welcomed somewhere. In fact t kind of reminds me of the opening of "Heaven and Hell." You just want to step into the song if the song had a doorway.

But speaking of proto-metal bands at the time, these guys knew how to slow things down and still keep things heavy-sounding and a little bit evil. You had proto-metal bands like Dust and they're doing a slower song like "Thusly Spoken." There is nothing heavy about that song. If that was the only song you heard by Dust, you wouldn't even know they were a heavier band. Again, they're trying to figure out this new modern heavy music. BÖC already had it down. They had the doomy riffs over the melody, they had a spooky guitar solo that was also beautiful and they even fit in some lyrics about black horsemen soaring over churches and armies of birds in the rain. You know, there you go, done. There's your blueprint for heavy metal, even black metal.

Martin: But it's funny, and I don't want to keep coming back to it, but I have to stress that it's more proto-metal they have figured out, rather than heavy metal. I find that intriguing, even a little meta.

Jamie: Yes (laughs). They don't have heavy metal figured out but they have proto-metal and hard rock figured out. Yes, that's true. For real metal, there were the British bands and then I think Judas Priest came along, in '76 and '77, and figured out heavy metal for a whole new generation. But for the tools that they had to work with, Martin, I think BÖC were doing just fine.

Martin: And to drive the point home, "Wings Wetted Down" sounds like Black Sabbath if they had put out an album in 1969 when they were called Earth.

John: Sure, it's very spooky, very dark and mysterious, but the song's pretty slow. It doesn't really pick up steam. Plus Allen Lanier's sort of elegant piano playing serves a vital role. There's some great harmony guitar work on this song as well. I also like how it ends on this sort of soaring, bluesy note from Buck.

Martin: Okay, on the home stretch and we get another sort of deep track no one ever remembers, "Teen Archer."

Matt: Yes, and you get a Meltzer lyric for this one, but there's not a lot of lyric to it. It's a very short, strange lyric. You get a Buck Dharma vocal that's not on a Buck Dharma-written song in terms of the lyrics, with music by Buck and Eric. Time to talk about the drumming on the album. So the Mahavishnu experience... Albert feels like those guys blew them away musically on stage. He really wants to play stuff with a lot of chops on this record and he does. It's far and away the busiest drumming album for them. You get that in here. You get a little drum solo part in "Teen Archer." He's trying to do the Billy Cobham-type stuff on the record, which, to me, differentiates it from *Secret Treaties* and the first record. It's a much different drumming style. Although I don't want to exaggerate it—this is not Mahavishnu Orchestra by any stretch (laughs). And there's a very tasty Buck lead on that song as well.

Steven: "Teen Archer" doesn't quite step up as high as some of the other tracks on the album, but it's got some great guitar rolling through it. Don't get me wrong, Buck is always able to walk that fine line between perfectly played for the song and adding those flashes. It's got a keyboard solo, which is quite unusual. And then you get a quick, smart hammered bash around the kit. It's almost like someone decided to try and even-handedly hand out some spotlight. I mean, I used to play the drums and I'm never a fan of even a short drum solo in the middle of a song. It never feels like it needs to be there. It's fun, but at the end you're thinking what was the process that brought all of those aspects together?

It feels much more constructed than a lot of their songs, especially on this album. This album is energetic and raw. And this song has those sections where you think someone took a step back and planned, "I know what we'll do here." That's not what you get elsewhere. Lyrically, are we with a crazy drug addict or promiscuous young lady? I'm not so sure that the song itself knows. And certainly they're not going to tell us. No, it's left ambiguous. Is it about stepping too far in one direction or another, and neither direction is necessarily where you really want to go? Who knows?

Jamie: I will say that with side two of this album, there's a certain flow to the songs. Now it may not be exactly like another 1973 album, *Dark Side of the Moon*. It doesn't have the same flow as that. But it's not too far off. "Teen Archer" is an interesting song and I notice the drums here more than anything. You tell me if I'm full of it. You're the drummer. I only played for a couple years in high school to try to get chicks. But I feel like the beat doesn't come from the bass pedal hitting the bass drum. I sense that the beat comes from the snare, which is so energetically played that I hear his lift off the thing more than I hear the downstroke. It's got that light, nimble feel of upswing rather than downbeat or a big backbeat. Anyway, Albert is jazzy, I guess is what I'm trying to say.

John: Something I'd like to add, "Teen Archer" is the only song that Buck sings on the album, which is interesting because he'd become the voice on many of their more popular songs. I like how the second guitar doesn't kick in until after they sing the second line of the first verse. You hear the one guitar in this ear and then they sing the second line and you hear that heavy riff. I like when bands do subtle things like that.

Martin: Nice! Okay, last song on this fright-fest: "Mistress of the Salmon Salt (Quicklime Girl)." Successful close to the record?

Matt: Yes, to me, this is the masterpiece on it. You've got the best Sandy Pearlman lyric on here, one that really fits in with his Lovecraftian obsession. It is kind of a Lovecraftian story in a very wordy way. It keeps going at the end, right? There's some additional lyrics you don't expect and the music even changes—the song doesn't end the way it starts. Instead it kind of fades away with these really weird lyrics. "The necks like swans that seem to turn/As if inclined to gasp or pray;" like, what is that about? Because that's not part of the story. But it is story song-ish, in that there's some killing going on and this harvesting, the "A harvest of life/A harvest and death" thing. But it's very obtuse, and sort of rewarding to continue to go back to the lyrics to try figure out what it means.

And then musically I really enjoy it too. You've got that hard-hitting riff, really rhythmic, but then it goes into some other places. And then you get this beautiful harmony part from out of nowhere, with the "Where Coast Guard crews still take their leave/Quite listless in the sun." They're sounding like the Beach Boys there—just one little part and that's it! Everywhere else, there's no real backing vocals to it. So they throw in a lot of the stuff that is showing some of their musicology. Like, hey, let's just add this in there because we can, because we love the Beach Boys. Let's throw in something super-melodic on this otherwise sinister song.

Martin: And no *Imaginos* lyrics on this record.

Matt: No, we don't get that. But soon we will, right? It starts exploding on the next album, where you get some of the most important ones. So yeah, we take a break from *Imaginos*.

Steven: "Mistress of the Salmon Salt" is just marvellously ridiculous, isn't it? And I mean the song title in itself. You read that on the back of an album and you go, "I have absolutely no idea what we're talking about here." This band was never better than when they injected a little horror into their sound, and that's what this is. But it's not blatant in that it deals with death. Is it about getting out of dealing with death? Is that what's happening? This is so patient. We have a sense of waiting, knowing that that lack of release, which, same again, is kind of alluded to in the lyric and kind of not. It heightens the impact of the unsightly deeds that are happening in the lyric. You're waiting for that release. You're waiting to kind of let free of everything that's going on here. This is unsightly, unseemly.

It's not the most obvious way to end an album. It absolutely sits with you. It brews and it broils and it's just masterful songwriting. I really do like that. The lyric is very clever. And with that "Quicklime girl, quicklime girl," you've got that complete opposite of here's a catchy hook that you're going to sing. It sounds really smooth and really beautiful. And everyone's going to be happy and smiley and "Quicklime girl, quicklime girl." And yet listen to what's going on: that is not a happy, smiley lyric that you're singing along with. Really clever. I really like that they fool you so many times that you're thinking, we're in cheerful territory, and then you get below the skin of the song and you go, yeah, that's a different thing entirely.

Jamie: Ah yes, "Mistress of the Salmon Salt" and then the parenthetical extra. Now follow me on this one. This was my thought process. Quicklime is a calcium oxide. Calcium oxide is used in basic oxygen steelmaking. That is when carbon-rich pig iron is made into steel. And today we're going to call steel more or less a metal, for today. And the centre of the steel industry in the '70s and '80s was Pittsburgh. So I believe this song is about a metal chick from Pittsburgh. And being from Pittsburgh, I think I remember this chick. I think we hung out a few times in 1987. But on a serious note, it's got great drumming by Albert Bouchard, great guitar tone and a great solo at the end. Eric Bloom's vocals are awesome. All-around great song. And it's a little over five minutes. I like when great albums end with one of the longer songs; it provides an epic ending.

Martin: And isn't the pig iron of this explanation sort of proto-metal? Isn't this quicklime stuff helping the mill make proper heavy metal, steel, out of pig iron, which is the proto-metal?

Jamie: Sure, whatever you like, Martin. Whatever makes my conspiracy theory work (laughs).

Martin: The song is actually about using quicklime to help get rid of corpses. But that's actually a fallacy—even though it gets rid of the smell, it actually does the opposite and helps preserve them.

Jamie: How do you know all this?

Martin: John, over to you! (laughs). Any thoughts on "Mistress of the Salmon Salt?"

John: Worthy closer, very memorable, great harmonies and changes in mood. It's quite an upbeat song, but then when it goes into what would be the solo, they slow it down. Then this very Doors-y organ come in before Buck plays this wonderfully sparse solo. They go back into the verse and then the chorus and then they end it slow again. It's a wonderful way to end a great album—my favourite Blue Öyster Cult album.

Martin: Wow, okay. One other thing, the chorus makes me think, again, of this '60s girl group vibe we hear in BÖC from time to time. Agree? Disagree?

John: Yes, but I think that's more apparent later on, maybe most significantly on *Spectres*. What's really great about Blue Öyster Cult is that they stayed true to themselves for the most part, but they kept expanding their sound. I mean, maybe you weren't gonna like everything they did, but it was always interesting.

Martin: Jamie, you wanted to add something?

Jamie: Yeah, I just think that of the three, *Tyranny and Mutation* represents the sweet spot one. I think the first one is a bit more raw and the third one gets a little more experimental. So this is the sweet spot. If their career ended after these first three albums, this would be the band's *Ride the Lightning*, which is the sweet spot between *Kill 'em All* and *Master of Puppets*. There are a lot of pretty dedicated Metallica fans who love *Ride the Lighting* and I suspect there are more *Tyranny and Mutation* fans out there than we think.

SECRET TREATIES

Secret Treaties
April 5, 1974
Columbia KC 32858
Produced by Murray Krugman and Sandy Pearlman
Engineered by Tim Geelan; Second Engineer, Jerry Smith
Recorded at Columbia 30th Street Studio, New York, NY
Personnel: Eric Bloom – lead vocals, keyboards, stun guitar; Donald "Buck Dharma" Roeser – lead guitar, vocals; Joe Bouchard – bass, vocals; Allen Lanier – keyboards, rhythm guitar, all synthesizers; Albert Bouchard – drums, vocals

Side 1
1. "Career of Evil" (A. Bouchard, Smith) 3:54
2. "Subhuman" (Bloom, Pearlman) 4:37
3. "Dominance and Submission" (A. Bouchard, Bloom, Pearlman) 5:22
4. "ME 262" (Bloom, Roeser, Pearlman) 4:45

Side 2
1. "Cagey Cretins" (A. Bouchard, Meltzer) 3:15
2. "Harvester of Eyes" (Roeser, Bloom, Meltzer) 4:40
3. "Flaming Telepaths" (A. Bouchard, Bloom, Pearlman, Roeser) 5:18
4. "Astronomy" (J. Bouchard, A. Bouchard, Pearlman) 6:23

Produced by Murray Krugman
MAX EFFORT
BLUE ÖYSTER CULT
SECRET TREATIES
including:
Career Of Evil | Dominance And Submission
ME 262 | Flaming Telepaths | Astronomy
Aggression unchallenged
is aggression unleashed.
"Secret Treaties" of
the Blue Öyster Cult
On Columbia
Records and Tapes

Martin talks to Rick LaBonte, Reed Little, Steven Reid and Henry Tenney about *Secret Treaties*.

Martin Popoff: Here we are at the end of the so-called black-and-white trilogy. How is *Secret Treaties* an improvement over *Tyranny and Mutation*? Or is it?

Reed Little: Oh gosh, in every possible way. I figure every band has that album you listen to and go, "This is where it all came together." And for me *Secret Treaties* is the album where Blue Öyster Cult gets it all together. Maybe this is redundant when talking about Blue Öyster Cult, but it's another very strange album, especially lyrically. For 1974, there's still a lot of the '60s on this album. Some of it's like heavy Doors or Grateful Dead. Some of it's garage rock like the MC5 or the Stooges. There's even some straight-up psychedelia. But it's so '60s in places, it's weird. They don't sound anything like their peers at this time. Who would you consider their peers?

Martin: Well, in America, Montrose and Kiss both have an album out and Aerosmith has two. The Alice Cooper band is already done and Alice is onto his solo career. Man, Sabbath's got five albums. Mark I Purple is over with and *Burn* is already out. Uriah Heep have already accomplished their life's work (laughs). There's a lot of reason for them to not sound this old!

Reed: Man, you're right. So those are your hard rock peers, and it doesn't sound anything like that stuff, except maybe closest would be Alice Cooper, who also always seemed to have a foot in the '60s. Very true, yep. '69 or '70 like Haight Ashbury, still on a trip, just making more aggressive music.

Martin: Rick, how about a few adjectives to describe *Secret Treaties* in a general sense?

Rick LaBonte: Sure, it's uncanny, it's unpredictable, artistic, the result of thinking outside the box. And we've got to remember the time or the era. This is 1974, Columbia Records, they ended up getting a gold record for this—although not until 1992 (laughs)! But the point is that with every album they're doubling their sales from the first album to the third and then the fourth. They have momentum, they feel like they've got their bearings on things. But they're still under the direction of Sandy Pearlman, who brings his imagination, his science fiction mind or... forget fiction, his knowledge about secret sciences like alchemy, so I guess historical science.

That's what I get from *Secret Treaties* generally, that it's about secret and esoteric science, from the start to the very end of "Astronomy," just the idea of being dark and mysterious and not so forthcoming. These songs aren't obvious. You have to read between the lines. You really have to think about what they're talking about.

Martin: Before we move on, Rick, I mean, they're still not living up to that brief of being Columbia's answer to Black Sabbath, are they?

Rick: Yes and no. One thing Black Sabbath don't have is harmonies, and in BÖC, everybody sings in the band and there's multiple singers in many of the songs, even when it's not harmonies. I think it's just about them writing doomy riffs, or at least getting some doomy riffs in there fairly regularly. Also maybe because they seem to write about war like "War Pigs," and violence and creepy things, I'd say that's where the American Black Sabbath thing comes from, the themes that they write about, going down the dark path. I don't think it was the music itself, because as you've said, even for 1974 there's still a lot of The Doors and dark psychedelia to it.

Plus BÖC uses keyboards, which Black Sabbath do not have. It puts them in the neighbourhood of Deep Purple and Uriah Heep, which was happening around this time, but then again, more piano and '60s tones and textures, rather than majestic Hammond organ. So if they're following that idea, maybe it's more in just the writing, because the arrangements and the outcomes are not nearly as beefy and heavy as Black Sabbath.

Steven Reid: I agree, there's really something quite backwards-looking about the BÖC sound at this point. Their influences are certainly at play in a way that you wouldn't necessarily expect here, for a band that are a few albums down the line now. Yes, I do think that there is—and it may come back to bite them later on—a lack of willingness in certain ways to maybe play the current game. This is a sound we like, this is a sound we've come from and this is what we're going to do. It's definitely there; yes, there is that.

And I'm not a massive fan of The Doors, so thankfully it's only touched on with these albums, that Doors edge. There's enough of it here that I go, "Oh, sounds like The Doors!" But not enough for me to go, "Hmm, sounds like The Doors." And for me personally, who is not a Doors fan, that's quite important because I don't mind the odd touch but if they were to kind of go down that spiral, it'd be too far for me. But yeah, production-wise, you might call it naive in certain places. And I think that informed some of the production choices that they made later on too, interestingly. I mean, through '77, the productions are nice. There's a bad word. They're still solid, there's still a roundness to them, there's still some dynamic in there. Which is vital I think for this album because it is about dynamics and a difference in approach and showing different aspects, whilst not necessarily revealing all in one go, and that's a real strength.

Having said that, I think they've progressed massively. I think they're a different band from how they began. It's less frantic. I would suggest that it's not more crafted, but I think that there's more craft. Does that make sense? I think that, yeah, the earlier albums are still crafted and the arrangements are clever. What they do is clever, how they interact. The chemistry is really good. But on the first two albums they seem to be holding things. But now they're at a point where it's getting moved along. It's now more about the songcraft and less about just raw energy. Don't get me wrong; the raw energy that's there early on is fantastic. But what shows up here is a kind of amalgam of experience, alongside that kind of impetus for aggressive playing that they've never really lost.

But it does evolve as the catalogue moves on, massively. And *Secret Treaties* one of the first big steps. They've moved from one thing to another. They lose the punkiness, if that makes sense. What I've said about *Tyranny* is there's kind of an up-and-at-'em attitude. It feels a bit like a war that you're facing. Whereas now we've started to maybe back off a little bit and it's more impactful because of that. Interestingly. And that's one of the things that I really liked about this band. There's a lot of sleight-of-hand, I think, in the Blue Öyster Cult. Because they're viewed as a really heavy band, they're viewed as a really evil band, they're viewed as a band that have got all these jagged edges. No, not really. It's all there but it's subverted and delivered in a different, clever way. It's so smart, because you get to the end of some songs that are beautiful, melodic, really smooth and easy. But you feel unsettled by it. It's really clever. There aren't many bands that manage to knock you off-kilter in that sense, and *Secret Treaties* to me was the start of that. This was the start of them beginning to actually work out that they didn't have to necessarily go for the throat all the time, but they could still take your head off.

Martin: Okay, into the album and we get "Career of Evil," and it's like we're tossed back into 1968. Pretty crazy. But outside of the music, we get a pretty incredible and inscrutable lyric.

Reed: Yes, that was my first thought. I love "Career of Evil." I think it's a fantastic song. Lyrics by Patti Smith, based on a poem about Isidore Ducasse, which I won't attempt to pronounce. You Canadians do much better with the French than we southern Americans do. As for the music, I keep getting back to this theme. This is Blue Öyster Cult in a nutshell for me: the music is not as heavy as the lyrics. Even though Blue Öyster Cult was always thrown in with the heavy metal bands, they rarely did heavy metal songs, at least what I would consider heavy metal as somebody who got into metal in the '80s. But their imagery is heavy metal. And that's a very interesting space to occupy. This is exactly the type of lyric that Megadeth could have done in the mid to late '80s. And I love the drum breakdown when Eric goes, "I will not apologize;" that's very '60s. I don't know what you call that style of music, but it's not what anybody else in 1974 was doing.

Henry Tenney: I agree. "Career of Evil," incredible Patti Smith lyric, so good. You know, "I'd like your blue-eyed horseshoe/I'd like your emerald horny toad/I'd like to do it to your daughter on a dirt road/And then I'd spend your ransom money, but still I'd keep your sheep." It's like absurdism. There's a lot of great, funny absurdism, sort of word play, and some of it is nonsensical but all of it is evocative of something. It's not just like saying stuff. It's not just backing up the word truck and dumping words in randomly. They all have a certain beat poetry to them. They don't just go by as words, like sometimes the Jethro Tull stuff does. "Bungle in the Jungle" goes by as just like a boatload of words. These don't do that—these hit. They have a resonance when you hear them and that's one of the things that really appeals to me about the band.

Rick: Sandy Pearlman is writing, rock critic Richard Meltzer is writing, Patti Smith is writing. And they're having an input because the band believes in the vision that Sandy is creating, not to mention Patti is dating the keyboard player, Allen Lanier. So there's a think tank, where they get lyrics in front of the music. Which is an odd thing to do when you're doing singing, taking these lyrics, which are basically poems, and then putting music to them. Some of it is a mouthful of words and yet they manage to do it. This is one of the first bands that would really do something like that, although there's another big one, ironically—The Doors. But "Career of Evil," if you buy the single version, theychanged "do it to your daughter" to "do it like you oughta."

Steven: With "Career of Evil," here we go, it's a theme right across the whole catalogue. This, to me, is a perfect example of it being mean and dark and yes, it's evil, but it's also really sweet. The melodies here are well considered, well-constructed, and there's a good riff here but it doesn't snarl. You know, there's some cool rock 'n' roll rhythms, which is exactly what you alluded to. There are many looks to the past, because it is a real rock 'n' roll feel.

It's interesting. I think you can hear this influence right now. When I hear Ghost, I'm often brought right back to Blue Öyster Cult, because there's a band that have a great image, a great feel and evil look. People look at them, ooh heavy metal! There's no heavy metal in Ghost—zero, zilch, nil. There's a very, very small amount of heavy metal in Blue Öyster Cult. They like to bring it to you and take it away.

And right from the off here, that's what's going on. The effect is memorable, really catchy, with great guitar lines. It's full of melody, there's loads of feel. I mean, it's one of Buck's real go-tos; it's all about him—you feel him and his guitar solos The keyboards, as well, really dig deep into the mind. Slow, hypnotic, they work their way into you. And the vocals are subtly layered. By the time the song is over, you kind of go, wow, that was so much more than it felt at the time. You almost have to lift the needle and go, "Did that really just happen in there?"

They're being really clever, and I get the impression that this was the point where Blue Öyster Cult began to know it. But they knew how to use it. They're not clever, clever. They're not one of those bands where you go, yeah, it's pretentious. For want of a better phrase from the UK, it's not that. They never got to that stage of, hmm, I should look away now. They're always kind of welcoming you in; there's always more to discover. This is actually quite a cheerful little ditty, in those terms, about somebody going around and taking the lives of others. It sounds like lots of fun, doesn't it? It's really strange. You get to the end of it and you're thinking, hmm, I'll do that too! (laughs).

Martin: Next is "Subhuman," which is a critical song in the *Imaginos* saga, perhaps the most substantive in terms of plot. But man, again, the band is busy underscoring why they have a back-and-white period.

Reed: Yes, "Subhuman" could be off any of those albums and it sounds like heavy Doors to me. Clearly one of the two songs from the album taken from the *Imaginos* concept, although like everything involving *Imaginos*, you would never get that by reading the lyrics. Like you say, there's at least some kind of story in it. The guy is left on the shore by his buddies and he's waiting for these subhuman things to come and save him. But other than that, you would have no idea what anybody's talking about (laughs) if they weren't familiar with *Imaginos*. Which makes it kind of an unusual inclusion for an album that's not a concept album.

But Blue Öyster Cult had already established that they could do weird lyrics and there were enough people, I think, willing to listen to hippie-trippy psychedelic lyrics. It was still part of the rock landscape in 1974, I

guess I should say. And this one, it's clearly meant for long instrumental digressions. So when they get to *On Your Feet or On Your Knees*, it's three minutes longer than the album version. And I bet that this is one of those songs that if they needed to stretch out, they could just do 15, 20 minutes like The Grateful Dead with this song.

Rick: I love the dual harmony guitar work. This is one of many reasons why they should be recognized as important pioneers of heavy metal because that's something that got really popular with Judas Priest, Thin Lizzy and Iron Maiden. It's also an ear candy moment because they do it hard left and right, Eric in one side and Buck on the other side, and you can follow the whole song that way. And then the harmonies are doubled and they would trade places. It's fantastic writing.

Henry: "Subhuman" might be my favourite all-time BÖC song because it's a great example of their lyrical madness. Intentionally or not, tied-in with the *Imaginos* thing, it's very H.P. Lovecraft, because he's got these half-human, half-fish people and there's the sea. The vastness of space is mirrored in the vastness of the sea, and the unknowability. And so this whole thing, you know, "I am becalmed, lost to nothing/Warm weather and holocaust." Yeah, I've always really loved "Subhuman." In fact, I have a friend who in high school, I didn't know him until after, but he said that he painted the lyrics to "Subhuman" on his ceiling in glow-in-the-dark paint. So he'd have the lights on and then when he turned them off, he'd be lying there and he'd see "I am becalmed." So that's always been like our sign-off when we send each other emails and stuff.

Steven: Like yourself, I'm an album guy. Still these days, I put an album on and I'm there for the journey. I know that some of that may be rocky. But therefore, when songs kind of segue into one another, that I really like; it creates a real flow and you can't help but be swept up in it. You've gone from one mood to another. I love the snare drum work here, and that is a feature right across Albert's time in this band. It's so precise, so locked-in tight. He's leading the band. He's entitled to everything that goes on but he's not just staid. It's not just, you know, this is what I do. Because if I don't do this, everything else falls apart. He'll take some risks. But the band are locked-in tight. That makes the guitar sound really neat and the keyboards really tidy, but without it sounding safe. And it allows everything to hit in different directions.

And there's easy listening vocals here. The vocals from Eric Bloom here are quite peaceful. There's no real need to snarl and bite. And there's a lovely guitar solo—it dances. It's as though a country outfit stepped into the band's shoes for just a few little sections here. But you know that at the same time it's Blue Öyster Cult, and that is what has always struck me about this band, is that you can go okay, rock 'n' roll. Okay, country. Yep, heavy metal. But always you go, mmm, Blue Öyster Cult. That's a real skill. And even when they change a little down the line, that's a real skill. But I feel that already two songs into this album, you're already going, "Hmm, okay, what's next?"

Martin: Nice! All right, "Dominance and Submission," famous one of theirs—and great title (laughs).

Reed: What a wonderful song this one is, again, with those strange lyrics, possibly taken from an actual incident in Sandy Pearlman's life coming home from New York's Times Square on some New Year's Eve in the back of a car with a woman and somebody who he said was her brother, right? I think most of Sandy's lyrics are kind of nonsensical, and this one may or may not be talking about the effect of music on the human psyche. But it's also talking about this weird sexual encounter in the back of the car on the way home from New Year's Eve. And I'll admit it: I don't understand the lyric "radios appear" that they repeat over and over again. What does that mean? I don't know what that means. The riff, again, is very '60s and very Detroit, maybe The Stooges more than MC5. It's kinda garage rock too.

Henry: Incredible, and yes, a song about New Year's Eve in New York City. Yeah, love that whole back and forth, the two characters and the person who's getting crushed under the boot lyrically, starting to crack, like being interrogated to the point of breaking. It reminds me of the Mott the Hoople song "Violence," where he's going "Violence, violence" and you get a sense of the character sort of breaking down while he's singing. And that quality in "Dominance and Submission" is interesting to me, and really dynamic.

Rick: "Dominance and Submission" is a great rocker, a popular concert staple, one of the ones that has to be done. I love the way they did the vocal trade-off with one person going "Dominance!" and then the other, quieter, "Submission," like a call-and-response thing. It's like they all share the title and bring their different personalities to it. It kind of reminds me of The Who's version of "Summertime Blues" with John Entwistle going, "You're too young to vote" and they would trade places with the lyric line. They did that in a way that was pretty creative, to coordinate that. And it had to be wild to watch on stage as well as hearing it go from one vocal to another.

Steven: The arrangement here is just incredible. There's so much going on. And yet it's so tight, so compact. I mean, there's very nearly a kind of '50s, '60s rock 'n' roll jive going on underneath everything here. And it makes you smile, it gets you on board, it fits perfectly into the era that the song is set as well—1963—which is a nice touch; I like that. There's an awful lot of musical storytelling on this album. They don't just go, here's the song, here's the lyric, you work it out. They often come together. They are tonally linked, I think; the music is linked tonally with the lyrics and vice versa.

And there's a kind of twin guitar solo that works really well. It's a hint of days gone by but they drag it into the here and now. And the way that grinding beat at the end goes, it undoubtedly leads towards what can only be described as a sharp and welcome climax. That is what this song has always been building towards. There's quite a journey to get there and there are those peaks and valleys. But right at the end, yeah, yeah, yeah, we know where we're headed. And it doesn't let you down; it doesn't back off.

But that "Dominance, submission, radios appear" vocal section... you're left repeating that, like the automaton that this song has turned you into. It just refuses to let you go. I mean, "ME 262" has already started and I'm still going "Dominance, submission, radios appear." Because it's just so in there. As soon as you think of this song, you chant it the way that it's chanted in the song. In any case, you're all in. It's so good.

Martin: And speaking of MC5, ever since I was a kid, "ME 262" made me think of MC5, and not just because of the title, but the tough boogie and the support vocals.

Reed: Yeah, it's got the "ME" and the numbers, right? When I saw Blue Öyster Cult in concert in 2021 they did this song, so clearly it still has staying power in the catalogue and people liked it. Now I came to Blue Öyster Cult too late to know if this song was controversial. I know in the early '70s it felt a lot closer to the end of World War II. So I don't know how people felt about a song about a German fighter pilot shooting down English bombers. I don't know if that caused controversy or not.

In any event at this point of the album you're feeling like, oh, this is an unusually straightforward story, right? It's more like an Iron Maiden lyric; it's so straightforward. The ME 262 is a pretty rare aircraft to bring up and base a story on so that makes it interesting. Again, I find it very garage rocky. It's got an unusual amount of vocal reverb. They didn't really do a lot of vocal treatments on Eric, I feel like, but there is on some of this. And they've got that barrelhouse piano in it which instantly gives it a boogie feel, but away from how a heavier band might do it.

Henry: Love it. Very catchy. Very propulsive. I guess this is the song at least on the live record where they all played guitars—they did the big guitar circle. Lyrically insane and it's historically accurate from what I can tell about the type of planes and the type of ammo. Like you, Martin, I sent away my 50¢ back in 1977 or whatever and got back those dot matrix printed sheets, all caps, no punctuation, and just pored over those. And seeing the lyrics to "ME 262:" "Junkers Jumo 004/Blasts from clustered R4M quartets in my snout/And see these English planes go burn." I mean, they're all stuck in there. It was such a doorway into all sorts of things at the time when I got those sheets. I love that one. Yeah, "Bombers at 12 o'clock high." And the live version of that is fantastic.

Rick: Obviously a great fast-paced rocker with great drums right from the beginning. But I love the dynamic, where right in the middle you start hearing the jets and the warning sirens and all that and it makes you feel like there's a war happening. So it becomes a visual experience as well as an audio experience. You can't help thinking, what is going on?! If you didn't catch that the ME 262 was a jet or whatever, you did by the middle of the song. And making it into a boogie, it's uncanny. They're very strange in that way. Even when they write a song that sounds happy, it's a pretty depressive lyric or if it's a song that sounds dark, they make it like a fire dance. It's unbelievable. The lyric doesn't always go with the mood of the song. But it works for them.

Steven: With "ME 262" there's a real theatrical and excessive rock 'n' roll approach. It's like we're leading Jim Steinman down the path here, is what we're doing. You know, "Hi, Jim. We're Blue Öyster Cult. Would you like to be us later on? Do you think?" And he goes, "I think I probably will do." But the difference here is we're not doing girls and paradise by dashboard lights. We're doing bombs dropped from planes, which ties in with the cover—it's like the cover should have been the picture sleeve to the single version of "ME 262."

You've got air raid sirens, there's those huge chanting hordes of people on the ground that seem to be encouraging the whole thing to happen. Really heady stuff; it really takes you there. It has that swirl of so much going on and belief in what's happening. And then there's the benefit of having really a full band's worth of genuine singers—that really comes to the fore here. I mean, the main vocal from Eric is just fantastic. But the whole thing, everyone's involved, and the levels come and go and there's a real storytelling ability. It's all kind of sitting on top of tribal drums with the guitars weaving in and out. You're in this world. You can close your eyes and picture we're in the air, everything's happening, your senses will be heightened, there's so much threat, there's so much danger.

And again, when you walk away from this song, the impression it leaves is that of a kind of heavy metal monster. But the energy doesn't come from a mega-heavy riff or sledgehammer drums. It comes from the clever use of dynamics. You're in this journey. It feels intense, the arrangements are really clever, but they have that ability to let the song grow. They're happy to kind of start them off—and none of these starts particularly small—but we build; we always build.

And I love the fact that the lyric keeps you hanging at the end. I mean, we know what the fate is going to be. The fate is not going to end well; we're aware of that. But they don't feel the need to just lead you down that path all the way. You're left hanging in the sky. And so is he. So is the pilot. So is the plane. Yeah, it's really clever, just beautifully well-done and really well-observed.

And that is considering that you should not trust a band, in my opinion, that don't write their own lyrics. That's a genuine rule. If a band doesn't write their own lyrics, no no, don't trust them. They have nothing to say. You know, hmm. they need outside input. But when you pick the right people to do that, well, it's a different thing entirely. And they've been able to create music that is so well linked to those lyrics. That's really rare. It's really difficult to go through many bands' catalogues and pick out songs that were written by outside members and go, yeah. But musically it is so joined together, as if they were created simultaneously. And that, to me, is what is happening here.

Martin: Interesting you say that, but in this special case, it's never crossed my mind to think of Sandy Pearlman as not a band member! I mean, obviously he's not on stage with an instrument, but there's something about this relationship that is ever beyond Pye Dubois with Max Webster or John Barlow and Robert Hunter with The Grateful Dead. I'd put Richard Meltzer in that camp, but not Sandy. And then neither of them—or Patti or Helen or John Shirley—feel particularly outside of the creative cauldron.

Steven: Yes, fair enough. They go back to the same sources on a regular basis, and that allows the whole catalogue up to a point to feel linked. There are even characters who reappear. You get the same names, like Susie, coming backwards and forwards, and you get Michael Moorcock's sci-fi lyrics later down the line. You have those things to hang yourself on: "Ah, I'm in a Blue Öyster Cult album." But I agree; it's different from, "Here's a great song for you, guys. I think this will fit you perfectly." This has obviously been worked on together. There's a huge amount of synergy going on here. And relationships, too. That has to be said. So there are close bonds and real friendships and real relationships. And maybe that in itself explains why outside writers are able to come in and you don't notice.

Martin: Before we flip the vinyl, what does that album cover say to you?

Henry: It's sort of intimidating. It feels a little Nazi-ish, frankly, especially because the ME 262 is on it and you've got the logo and the German Shepherds and Eric is wearing a cape! It's a dark, record cover, for sure.

Rick: It reminds me of Led Zeppelin *II*—you know, blimp, plane, bomber jackets—where you also have members of the band in the picture but it wasn't colourful. And here it's less confusing because on the Zeppelin, there's like ten people. And then with the BÖC, on the inner sleeve you've got the colour illustration, so now the picture really popped.

Martin: All right, thoughts on "Cagey Cretins?" I mean, here's another one that is written heavy metal but then not presented that way.

Reed: I think this is probably the weakest song on the album. The most interesting thing about it is that you've got three vocalists. So you've got Eric and both Bouchard brothers singing on it. And beyond that, there's just not a lot to it. Except now this one we step out; we're beyond garage rock. We're beyond The Doors.

Martin: The drums are "trapsy" and there's no bottom end.

Reed: Right. With different production choices you can see it almost being heavy metal. But then they wouldn't be the same band. And you know, I think Albert was the most psych of the players. Buck is very much more the jam band player. He could have been a prog rock guy if he was English. And Albert is the psychedelic guy.

Rick: This is one that doesn't get played live. Good rocker, but verging on filler. It's short and sweet and it hits you where it hits you.

Steven: That is just such a good song title—let's just start with that. We've got both Bouchards and Eric here together and I like that. Remarkably similar voices across a lot of this catalogue. It took me a lot of years before I could pick them out. Back in the day, you really had to think about it. But I like the way they share the vocal load on this song. There are a few different angles that it offers. There's the bass line, which darts and it dances. And again, I'm gonna bore you to death about Albert's snare drum work. It's just so good. His snare's getting constant abuse in this song. The ghost notes add a real urgency. And that's picked up by the keyboards work; the way that the keyboard interjects and comes in and out, it's not by accident. That's been thought-out and put together. And this is one of those songs where I've often felt that at this stage of their career, there's so much energy happening with Blue Öyster Cult, it's almost like you're in a battlefield. You just see these figures appear and they're charging towards you. That is exactly what "Cagey Cretins" is; that's what's happening here. It's one of those songs where you almost want to take cover but it's so much fun at the same time.

Martin: I feel like the eccentric tone of the album is maintained as we roll into "Harvester of Eyes," kind of busy, oddball, heavy in BÖC's own special way.

Reed: "Harvester of Eyes" is the song that comes closest to being like an Alice Cooper song, especially with the lyric about this madman who collects eyes. You could see "Harvester of Eyes" on *Welcome to My Nightmare*. My favourite weird little factoid about "Harvester of Eyes" is that one of the lyrics references Supreme Court Justice Abe Fortas, where he apparently had said that he didn't serve in World War II because he had ocular TB, ocular tuberculosis. For anybody reading this now, tuberculosis was the number one killer of human beings up until the 1950s, when it was eventually replaced by cancer. So he claimed he had ocular TB. And they put a Richard Meltzer lyric about that in "Harvest of Eyes." So they're taking a stab at a Supreme Court Justice. That's not something that a lot of bands can say.

Rick: Yes, epic song, very creative. It's where BÖC deliver this serious metal overtone, but one where people would provide a whole album's worth of that. It's at least indirectly doomy like Black Sabbath, so here's your American Black Sabbath, but with a great arrangement and some proggy parts. As Reed says, the lyric is based on Abe Fortas, a former US supreme court judge who did some controversial things, although Meltzer just takes one line of something he said and twists it and runs away with it. So it's confusing, not clear.

Steven: Another great song title, isn't it? If you heard that now, in 2023, you would presume that we are in black metal territory, wouldn't you? This is the sort of song title that's going to howl and spew gargling guts at you. That is not what we're doing here. This is 1974 and it is equally hard-hitting. That's what I like about this. We don't need to be growling and screaming and shouting or have guitars that are as distorted as they could possibly be, to be that dangerous. This song is that dangerous.

It's the tale of a serial killer that's doing away with his victims and removing the eyes as visual trophies. I mean, this is really gory stuff. And I think the fact that the song allows that lyric to be laid out really quite clearly is much more threatening, because of the nuanced feel about the song. It's not a sweet melody, so you're not humming along to it. But it's not something that makes you go, yeah, I know what we're gonna get here.

And then you listen to the lyrics and you're pulled in and thinking, wow, they're really doing this?! Is that really what we're doing here? But the guitar work is off-kilter and there's these kind of wavering backing vocals that keep you on your toes. Again, we're lyrically and musically linked, but only so far. This is a spooky story that's being told in an eerie fashion musically, but it's not put on a tray for you; it's not heavy metal.

But yeah, it's quite graphic lyrically, quite sinister, and yet the lyrical matter-of-factness of removing the eyes to reveal the inside of your skull, I mean, it's delivered with a skip in its step, isn't it? It's almost like, mmm, this is what I do! Why would I not? Why do *you* not? So this is a killer enjoying his work. He's not out to scare you to death. I mean, that's gonna happen. But that's not the intention. Or it doesn't appear to be the intention. That will just happen along the way. He's almost doing you a favour. He's removing your sight. He'll look after it for you. I've got it here. It's all safe; it's all good.

Martin: I like that skip-in-your-step idea, because back to the music, you hear that in the bouncy bass line, and also in Albert's drumming, which is almost innocent or naive. And yet it's a heavy guitar riff. But even the guitars aren't way up in the mix or anything, right?

Steven: Absolutely; it's musical juxtaposition, which characterizes an awful lot of what's going on in this whole catalogue. Because we are building one thing and building something else and bringing them together in the middle and making it sound like it was always like that. There's a joyfulness. It seems to me that the more kind of demonic and possessed this band became, the happier they wanted to make you feel about it. And that is much scarier than the guy screaming in your face. Don't get me wrong, I like black metal and all that but it's about one note. You get it, you put it on, you listen to the whole thing, wow, okay, that was a journey. You put this on and you listen to it and you think, wow, *that* was a journey. You know, I didn't know where that was gonna go.

Martin: All right, *Secret Treaties* closes strong with a couple of significantly *Imaginos*-related songs. What do you make of "Flaming Telepaths?"

Reed: For years and years I didn't really know what to think of "Flaming Telepaths." It's over-the-top, quite camp, right? It feels like a show tune.

Martin: Like Meat Loaf?

Reed: They're kind of dancing around and Meat Loaf is a great example, yes. Maybe not quite as bombastic as Meat Loaf. But then if you accept the whole "And the joke's on you" part as being literal, it kind of makes sense. These days you would call that trolling, right? They're writing this over-the-top song with all of these over-the-top lyrics about, you know, "I know the secrets of the iron and mind" and "It's a flaming wonder telepath" and what does that mean? Anyway, it's a joke, and the joke's on you, audience member. But for all of that, you don't feel like you're the victim of anything because it's still a pretty good song.

Henry: I love the live version of "Flaming Telepaths" because the patter is so great. "Can't stand the light, baby, can't stand it now. Not talking about the light above. I'm talking about the hellfire down below. That's right. That's the Lucifer light."

Rick: Another great favourite of mine. The song is supported with brilliant keys and then that stark Moog synthesizer solo. Eric's vocal is just incredible and beyond that, this is a great early example of those signature harmonies that make records like *Spectres* and *Fire of Unknown Origin* so great. Yeah, you hear these wonderful harmonies that come in to support this weird song.

Steven: "Flaming Telepaths" is set up by this sort of haunted music box music at the end of "Harvester of Eyes." It demonstrates that the album has been crafted and thoughtfully created. Yeah, it's a song and we're gonna move on, but we're on a journey and we want you to take the whole journey with us. And it's interesting because the synthesizers at the start of "Flaming Telepaths," they feel really out of place on here—it's almost dayglo by comparison. It's like they're ten years ahead of their time, almost. Suddenly you think, where did that massive slab of '80s keyboards come from?

But it doesn't last. It's a really interesting kind of segue where you think, okay. But this is Blue Öyster Cult asking you to take stock. Hold on, hang on, let's have a breath. And whether you connect with that or not might have a strong effect toward whether you then love or loathe the song. But the keyboard/guitar trade-off that wafts through "Flaming Telepaths," oh, wow. It just holds it all together—really, really strong.

I mean, this is a song of mad scientists experimenting on themselves, a tale of drug use gone wrong. It seems like the music does the hard work for you. You're left to ponder the lyrics. You're not left with conclusions. But the music also leaves you to ponder. It doesn't necessarily leave you with conclusions. And that's what I mean by it's clever. That's why you come back to albums like this again. The best albums are not the ones that on first listen you go, oh, that's the best thing ever. It's the ones that when you listen to them for the tenth, 20th, 50th time, you still can go, "I wonder what they meant there. Do I get the same as what they get? Or not." And that matters and it doesn't. That's why bands shouldn't explain their lyrics.

And it is fascinating because Blue Öyster Cult have done a fantastic job I think of mis-explaining quite a lot of their lyrics over the years. I think they've been quite clever to drop off red herrings. They quite often take you down a path where some people ask direct questions about lyrics and we're fed a load of bull intentionally. Because they don't want you to know. They don't need you to know. If you can't make your own mind up, we're good with that.

Martin: Maybe so, but I think you also have to mix that with the fact that depending on who you ask, they might not know the true intention, given that there are outside lyric writers. Or maybe they don't remember! But I get your point. All right, the album closes with "Astronomy," the band's "Stairway to Heaven," famously.

Henry: An apt comparison. Because "Astronomy" is really one of the greatest songs of all time. It's so beautiful and haunting and feels like the subject matter, you know, musically and vocally. It feels like what's being discussed, it feels like someone's telling a sort of far-away campfire horror story or a story about the heavens. And maybe you're hearing it directly from some sort of 15th century astronomer. And it's really evocative vocally. I mean, that beautiful, "Astronomy, a star," the way that sort of spreads out and the way the harmonies kick in with that and the beautiful bass underneath it? It's really a masterpiece of songwriting and singing and performance, so evocative, so beautiful and strong—and haunting and haunted and scary and mysterious. I can't say enough about "Astronomy."

Reed: Ah, man, tied for my favourite BÖC song with "Veteran of the Psychic Wars." I love "Astronomy" so much. Now I will say I find it fascinating that if you're a very casual listener, it really looks like "Harvester of Eyes," "Flaming Telepaths" and "Astronomy" are going to form kind of a trilogy of songs, that they're thematically linked, right? And yet they're utterly different. They really don't have anything to do with each other. And I don't think you get that kind of scatterbrained mentality in modern music. But yeah, of any song on any BÖC album, if somebody had never heard of Blue Öyster Cult and they asked me, "What is Blue Öyster Cult?" I would play them "Astronomy." This is the song that defines the band like "Hallowed Be Thy Name" defines Iron Maiden.

I love the keyboard intro. I don't think Allen Lanier got a better keyboard part until "Joan Crawford," of all songs. It's an amazing keyboard part. And then after doing the piano melody—or sometimes even dovetailed *with* the piano melody—he's doing these big synth pads. Probably weren't synths at the time, but keyboard pads He was always providing the atmospheric base for the music. It's a very spare song. Once again—and I keep coming back to this theme—it's not super-heavy. But it feels like it could be; you know, Metallica covered it on *Garage Days Revisited*. You feel like, oh, this could have been a heavy metal song. And yet I'll take BÖC's version any day over Metallica's version of it. There's so much air; there's so much space. The guitars are very trebly. It's succinct playing and not giant, lingering power chords like you would get from Tony Iommi playing that riff—there'd be no air in it anymore, right?

Lyrically, again, we're dealing with the incredibly loose *Imaginos* concept. But once again, the lyrics, they are not linear, they don't tell a story. But they are evocative. The closest thing I can relate this to is actually David Bowie and his cut-up lyric technique, right? I know he didn't come up with it. William Burroughs came up with this idea, I think. But he would write out his lyrics and then he would literally take scissors and chop them up and he'd lay them out. It's supposed to dredge up subconscious images to make you think more about the themes than a linear narrative. And that's what I get out of "Astronomy." You're talking about this bar and there's the mirrors and the light that never warms. It seems like it could be a story, maybe, but it's not—there's nothing happening here. You know, the closest you get to a narrative is, "I know you'll soon be married/And you'll want to know where winds come from." What does that mean? It produces, if not a movie in your mind, a feeling. It produces a theme, a bit of unease, this kind of mystical aura. It's dreamlike, rather than narrative. And that is the perfect feeling for a song that you're going to call "Astronomy."

And then you have the percussion break. Albert was not Bonzo; he didn't get to do massive drum fills or anything. When he's playing by himself he's doing like these military bits. What do you call them? Maybe just snare rolls, right? And then it breaks down; it quiets down. So you've got dynamics, with songs going at one level even though there's a lot of space. And then it quiets down and builds back up.

And you've got the part at the end where they just repeat "Astronomy, a star" over and over again until the end of the song. That is one of my favourite musical moments of the entire 1970s. It fits. Again, it doesn't particularly say anything, but it feels like it should say something. And this is controversial, but I think this is where a lot of conspiracy theory comes from right? It looks like it should mean something and therefore it *has to* mean something. So people are going to assign it a meaning and that's what they do with BÖC.

Rick: I love the eerie piano and the whole idea of some sort of hidden, secret science behind the lyric. Of course they're rocking the BÖC formula and it's epic. As Reed says, it builds and builds, with all these well-reasoned parts. It's an incredible finale to the album.

Steven: This is the second notice on the album for "Susie, dear." The other one here is "Dominance and Submission" and then we see her on "The Marshall Plan." We're in the land of astronomical musings and the music fits that bill perfectly. It's deep and it's the considered groove that sets the scene for arguably the most considered song in terms of pace and delivery on this album.

But it's also got a guitar solo to die for. It really does. It's soaring, gently searing, expertly crafted, and it's the perfect vehicle to lift it to the star-laden skies that have been built earlier by the pianos and those calming vocals. They're leaving you not quite knowing what your fate will then become. Especially with that whispering wind that closes the track and album out. It's really mysterious.

Another strength is how the guitars and keyboards interlock. The spoken but still really forceful chants of "Hey!" add yet another layer. It's almost ritualistic but really smart stuff. The album's willingness to continually change its focus, move around… it alternates its attack and it makes it so much more impactful. And it could have been much more blunt; this album could have been much more forthright and it would have been much more immediate because of it. But I love the way that these kind of rounded tones will be employed to get the message across.

And yeah, we touched on the production earlier on. What I like here on the production is that nobody dominates. You can't say, you know what? This is Buck's album. No, it's about the song. It's about the essence of what the message is. It's about dynamics. And if anything, the main theme that comes through in the production is some phenomenal bass lines—really phenomenal bass lines. They often take the songs by the hand and gently lead them to where they need to go. There's nothing been dragged here. Yes, sometimes it's a bit more forceful, but these songs are allowed to grow and be different. And very often the bass drives it. Sometimes it's quite brutalist, but often it can be quite beautiful.

Martin: And to what extent do you think the *Imaginos* concept is represented here?

Steven: It's difficult to know. How far are we in? That narrative certainly adds to the mystique of this album. It's interesting that those songs are kind of dotted around other things that are really far removed. One of the things I really like about this era of the band is that it always feels like the temptation to go that whole hog and do the concept was respectfully avoided. And that decision was really key. Because it stopped any of these ideas from being too overt. We now look at them and go, are they linked? Where are they linked? How are they linked? Which part of the story are we dealing with at this point? We're not always linear; we're dotting around. Who is this? What's happening?

It didn't need to be revealed in one solid lump where we go yeah, okay, you want a story, we'll give you a story. Don't do that. Please don't do that. So at this point, what we're doing is we're dotting it with songs that are completely different lyrically and tonally. It makes you much more interested in that *Imaginos* idea. Because in my opinion it was always meant to remain mysterious, slightly distant. It was always meant to be that thing that kind of whispered its way through the albums, "Oh, what was that?" And it's gone again. That makes it much more intriguing, doesn't it? Because when the next one's coming out, you always want to go, "Is there more?" It's a seductive hook, isn't it? Against just giving us the full experience. It was a good decision.

Martin: Interesting. Okay, to sum up, would you agree with the overwhelming consensus out there that this is the pinnacle of the band's black-and-white period? I mean, many smart buddies of mine call *Secret Treaties* the greatest album BÖC would ever make.

Henry: I don't know, because there's a consistency with all of them. Those three records, it's almost like they're one song because they don't break in between. They seem to pick up where the last one left off. And they don't go astray. It's hard to do, to have a second record and a third record that are consistent like that, and have them still interesting. They haven't dropped off, they haven't tried to do something else and they haven't bought into their own hype and tried to recreate their own sound. Across all three, they feel really organic. It feels like they're honest and they're doing what they feel like doing.

And then when they get to *Agents of Fortune*, they still have that, but the outside influences are starting to come in, not just technologically but also musically. The change has started, and I think the result is still a really successful, really great album that's very much in the spirit of the first three.

Reed: Yes, I think the debut had some decent songs. *Tyranny and Mutation* I like better than the first album. I mean, from the first album, I'd say "Cities on Flame with Rock and Roll" is the only triumph, although "Last Days of May" matters as well. *Tyranny and Mutation* has better constructed songs, and by the time they get to *Secret Treaties*, they've got it nailed. They're able to do longer-form pieces and they're able to combine the parts to make better music.

Actually, let me talk a little bit about the bonus tracks. *Secret Treaties* on CD had four bonus tracks, including the indefensibly misogynist song, "Mommy." I just cannot help but absolutely love that song. It's a wonderful song. Just from the very opening where they come in with that barrelhouse piano and Eric Bloom goes, "This song's about your mutha—your mutha!" He's fantasizing about killing his mother and his wife and his daughter. And at the end he goes, "I hate them dames!" Which is... I don't know. That kind of thing would get you cancelled so fast these days. But yeah, I love that song. I'm sorry, mom.

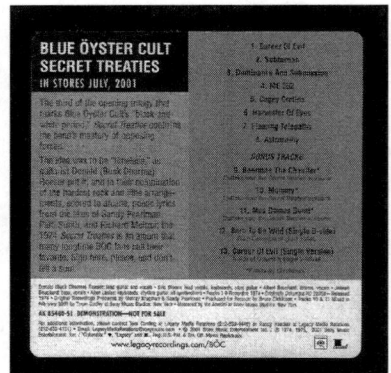

AGENTS OF FORTUNE

Agents of Fortune
May 21, 1976
Columbia KC 34164
Produced by Murray Krugman, Sandy Pearlman and David Lucas
Engineered by Andy Abrams and Shelly Yakus
Recorded at The Record Plant, New York, NY
Personnel: Eric Bloom – vocals, guitar, keyboards, percussion; Donald "Buck Dharma" Roeser – guitars, vocals, synthesizer, percussion; Joe Bouchard – bass, vocals, piano; Allen Lanier – keyboards, vocals, guitar, bass; Albert Bouchard – drums, vocals, acoustic guitar, percussion, harmonica
Guest performers: Michael Brecker, Randy Brecker, David Lucas, Patti Smith

Side 1
1. "This Ain't the Summer of Love" (Krugman, A. Bouchard, Don Waller)
2. "True Confessions" (Lanier) 2:55
3. "(Don't Fear) The Reaper" (Roeser) 5:05
4. "E.T.I. (Extra Terrestrial Intelligence)" (Roeser, Pearlman) 3:43
5. "The Revenge of Vera Gemini" (A. Bouchard, Smith) 3:48

Side 2
1. "Sinful Love" (A. Bouchard, Helen Robbins) 3:28
2. "Tattoo Vampire" (A. Bouchard, Robbins) 2:40
3. "Morning Final" (J. Bouchard) 4:14
4. "Tenderloin" (Lanier) 3:53
5. "Debbie Denise" (A. Bouchard) 4:12

Martin talks to Jim Bacchi, Rich Davenport, Henry Tenny and Matt Thompson about *Agents of Fortune*.

Martin Popoff: We've taken a pause for BÖC's first live album, *On Your Feet or On Your Knees*, issued in February of '75, but now the band is back renewed, changed somehow. What do you make of *Agents of Fortune*?

Henry Tenney: Yeah, agreed, it all changes with this record—but in a great way. It's still fantastic. They've had chances to work on things more at home and bring in demos and do all that, so things are less idiosyncratic but they're still really good. The technology of the day allows for more highs and lows. It's clearer music; it's brighter. It's not like the dusty, smoky, foggy stuff from the first record. It has this dynamic quality that they hadn't really had before. And the songs reflect that because maybe they have more time to work on them, or time to figure them out. They're tighter and poppier, they're less rambling and weird, but they're still successful and good. It's got obviously, their most successful thing: one of the best American rock songs in history is on this record, and it holds to many, many, many, many repeated hearings. Every day it's still a good song. I'm still not sick of "(Don't Fear) The Reaper" and I don't think I ever will be. Even songs I really like I can get sick of if I hear them too much. But that's a masterwork of songwriting.

Matt Thompson: Right, so everyone gets the TEAC four-track and everyone's coming to the band with more fully realized ideas. For good or bad, right? So you get less in-band collaboration, but there's probably a lot of pent-up creativity that each band member gets to realize. So there's a lot of material that gets presented for this album. And the leftovers that don't make it are terrific. You think of what gets left off, like "Hansel and Gretel," "Fire of Unknown Origin," "Dance the Night Away" and "Sally." So you get things that feed *Fire of Unknown Origin*, a Jim Carroll record and several Brain Surgeons records, right? There's a lot of high-quality material that the band is creating.

And to me, this album is their most New York-ish album. It's got a big city urban feel and I think some of this comes from the people they're hanging out with and collaborating with. You've got the Patti Smith and Helen Robbins/Helen Wheels collaboration going on with the band members, both musically and socially. And then the material itself is very different than the first three records, which are these sort of gothic, *Imaginos*-y, sinister songs that are trying to be heavy metal. Here they're trying to be sophisticated New Yorkers. It's coming from a different headspace. And what's cool is they've got the chops to pull it off. They can actually be that kind of band.

But one caveat to that is that everyone is coming with ideas except Eric, right? Eric had the most stuff for *Secret Treaties*. He writes the most for *Secret Treaties*, way more than he usually does, and he's not here for this one. Which I always kind of felt bad about. He just needed a break, probably. He did so much heavy lifting on *Secret Treaties*, and then on this record that sells the most, he doesn't get the writing credits, nearly as much as on other records. I just kinda felt bad about that.

Jim Bacchi: *Agents of Fortune* came out in 1976 and I was 13 years old and just starting to buy rock records as it were. My older sister was nine years older than me and she had The Monkees and all the Beatles 45s. And then my older brother is five-and-a-half years older than me; he was into Chicago and Steely Dan and Led Zeppelin, but not really heavy rock per se. So *Agents of Fortune* is me discovering heavy rock, as it were. That year, "(Don't Fear) The Reaper" was everywhere and it's still one of my favourite Blue Öyster Cult songs.

Which brings up a point: overall, they're supposed to be this heavy band but they're not really that heavy. And that's the weird thing that always tripped me up about Blue Öyster Cult. One of my best friends growing up was a huge Blue Öyster Cult fan. We'd always talk about the band and I'm like, you know, they're not as heavy as Kiss or Rush or Led Zeppelin. It's kind of weird, but I think of their heaviness in terms of their imagery and amazing song titles and their great album covers. Albert wasn't a hard hitter, not like the guy they have now. Albert was more of a modern rock-type drummer, which gave them a lightweight sound, and Eric didn't have a powerful voice—no one did. But then they would rock. They're very mysterious to me. Are they a heavy rock band? Are they just spooky and weird? That's the most intriguing thing to me. I didn't like them as much as a kid as I do now. They grew on me more as time went along.

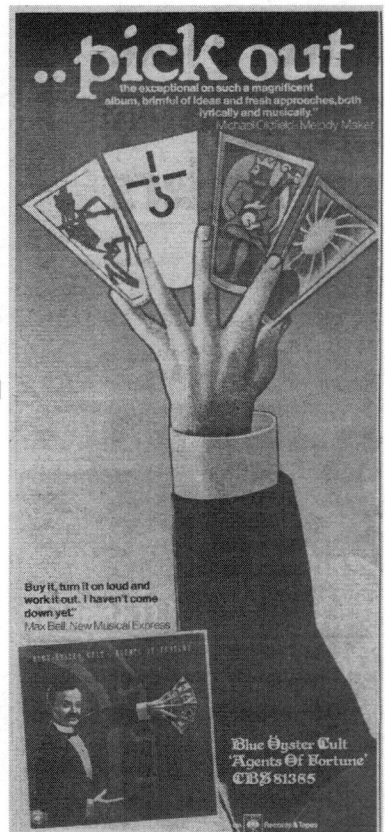

..**pick out**

the exceptional on such a magnificent album, brimful of ideas and fresh approaches, both lyrically and musically."
Michael Oldfield- Melody Maker

Buy it, turn it on loud and work it out. I haven't come down yet."
Max Bell, New Musical Express

Blue Öyster Cult
'Agents Of Fortune'
CBS 81385

Rich Davenport: This was my first BÖC album and I kind of digested it in a different order because the UK cassette version which I bought in 1987, they did the old trick they used to do with cassettes and eight-tracks as well, where they shuffled the track listing from the actual one that the band designated to make it fit the length of the cassette. So my version for years, I first knew it opening with "True Confessions," which I thought was an odd choice for an opening track. And they bumped "This Ain't the Summer of Love" to the start of side two.

But I love this album. There's so much variety and most of the tracks sit together really wel . And it doesn't strike me as the band doing anything odd to get airplay or watering anything down. It's a little less heavy than some of the earlier albums, but it sounds like a natural evolution of the band's sound. As they get to be better songwriters, they integrate the different elements. It's not quite as seamless as, say, *Fire of Unknown Origin*, where you might get all those elements within one song and also have the benefit of this tight, correct Martin Birch production job, but they all sit together fairly well despite all the different styles brought over from the different guys working on their own.

Martin: Okay, for everybody but Rich, the album opens with "This Ain't the Summer of Love," and for a magic moment there, it sounds like Blue Öyster Cult are heavier than they'c ever been.

Henry: Yeah, what a great way to start the record, with that great sinister chugging guitar and the slide down the neck and stuff. Next album they do "Golden Age of Leather" and this is like that, an anthem that has its position as an anthem in m nd. "R.U. Ready 2 Rock" is another one I'm thinking of which is like this, where they got to the point. And maybe it hearkens back to "Cities on Flame," where it's like, this is going to be our crisp, rock-solid mission statement in large caps. It's got great instrumentation, rock moments, the stur guitar of Eric Bloom, whatever a stun guitar is. It comes across very well; it's snappy, singable, it's got all the stuff you need, plus some great lyrical and vocal moments in it. A very strong opener.

Martin: It's a quas -cover, with this band The Imperial Dogs writing it and playing it in 1974.

Matt: Yes, that's exactly rig nt, hence the Don Waller co-credit. It adds to their punk credibil ty. They're like the classic rock band that a punk band can cover, which started with "The Red & the Black." It's pretty straightforward and works as both a punk song and a Blue Öyster Cult song. Eric doesn't sing it punky, but it works both ways.

Jim: "This Ain't the Summer of Love" I really like, especially because of that great opening riff. It's delivering that Blue Öyster Cult darkness, as does that whole cynical, "Things ain't what they use to be and this ain't the Summer of Love" line. I mean, he's basically saying, like, this is not a happy situation here, which goes great with the whole New York in the '70s situation. Just a great song with a great guitar solo.

Rich: Agreed; great guitar solo, and dark and menacing. As a drummer, Albert can play really regimented beats like he does here, set rhythm patterns that recur throughout the song, but then there are some pretty off-the-hook drum fills in this one as well. He can move between both worlds. Also that phrase, "This ain't the Summer of Love," that's something that people were saying about punk around this time, and Blue Öyster Cult was saying that here. I'm sure you know this, but *Sniffin' Glue*, the legendary UK fanzine, had Blue Öyster Cult in the first issue. So they were lumped in with punk quite mistakenly.

But I can see how they might resonate with someone who was into punk. There's that dark vibe, to the point where they're saying this is definitely not the Summer of Love in the opening song. At least in the UK, we were feeling that hangover from the '70s and what a lot of the prog bands were singing about. Conversely this a subversive thing for a band to be saying, when so many bands were still into a sort of post-'60s, new age hippie kind of vibe. That's a real sock to the jaw.

Martin: Next is "True Confessions," written by Allen, and where we find out that Allen is at least as good as singer as Joe or Albert and nudging up to Eric too.

Henry: Yeah, and it's a nice counterpoint to the first song. And the way it jumps in, like the black-and-white period albums, there's not really much in the way of blank space between the songs, which is such a cool thing to do. It's got some great parts. I love the "Naked, exposed like fine rock 'n' roll/ Perfect as strangers, imperfect as love/We're never sorry, we're never sad/ We're modern lovers, what fun we had." You could hear it being played on stage at Max's Kansas City or something. And that bendy guitar part that comes in is a little punky—singable, very catchy.

Martin: And then when the sax comes in, it's like the *Saturday Night Live* theme music. Which again is evocative of New York, not to mention the fact that there are stories about BÖC members and *SNL* people partying together.

Henry: Yes, sure. The saxophone has a David Sanborn-y kind of brightness to it.

Jim: With "True Confessions" they lose me for a second because it's like, this sounds like '70s E Street Band, with the piano and sax and stuff. That's the weird thing about Blue Öyster Cult: they're a heavy rock band and then they do something like this that's just like, "Huh? Okay." It's almost like a '60s Motown thing. Cool song but not one of my favourites. But yeah, I'm thinking, here comes Clarence Clemons. What's happening? And the rest of the record really isn't like this.

Rich: I get that too, but I was thinking more like Elton John or Randy Newman. I remember liking it but I just thought, "This isn't why I bought it. Is it all gonna be like this?" And the guitar has a country feel, although the lyric is quite sinister. They're offsetting a sweet melody and poppy feel with something that's, oh, hang on, listen to those lyrics. It's about what he's reading in these magazines. It's not typical lyrical fare. These two elements, they make them fit and it's not incongruous, but there's something subversive going on.

Martin: Okay, then the boys find themselves with a hit on their hands, and dare I say, something of a novelty hit. What do you like about "(Don't Fear) The Reaper?"

Henry: What don't I like about it? (laughs). It builds beautifully, the story that's being told... it's basically an upbeat song about suicide. Like, that would never, ever fly now. They would have been run out of town. But it builds so beautifully, the guitar line is fantastic, the solo is incredible, the vocals are so good and moody. It's scary but it's hopeful.

And it's romantic, but it's the romance of falling in love with death. That's just such a crazy way to position a song: as a love song to death. But it's a beautiful song with so many beautiful parts. And the breakdown sort of feels like a wake-up call to like, this is what we're talking about when we talk about death. And it works beautifully with the rest of the tune and the beautiful guitar work. But now it's jagged, with these shards of guitar all over the place—it gets gothic. It's like, oh, by the way, you're romanticizing death. You're falling in love with the thought of death. But this is what death

really is. And it's a little scarier than you think; it's scarier than your teenage dreams are. Like I say, it's the wake-up call.

But then it comes right back in with the beautiful guitar part and the cowbell (laughs), which we've all seen wonderfully parodied. I mean, hilarious—hilarious! That whole thing is so funny. And it just shows how important the song is to society, to the world, as a piece of art, that someone could parody it, that someone could bring that motion into it. And it doesn't diminish from the song. They're making fun of the song but it doesn't make the song a laughingstock at all. It makes the song *more* lovable. Which I think is the power of the song.

Matt: When you hear the "Reaper" demo, you realize how fully realized a song it was. You see the spark of genius that Buck tapped into there. He's not a prolific guy. He doesn't write because he thinks of himself as a writer. He just writes every once in a while, when he gets an inspiration. And here he's inspired and he gives the band its biggest hit.

Rich: There are certain rock classics that are on every compilation and you know them from the jukebox. Personally, I never get tired of hearing this one because the melodies are amazing. And it's a hit where again, the lyrical theme is very dark. It's not typical hit single fare. In fact, songs that have a dark theme like this, by the '80s the label would probably say you can't put this out as a single—it's too dark. Because I know The Replacements had a lot of grief with "The Ledge." MTV wouldn't play it. And that's a similar sort of dark lyric about death and suicide.

But I think the band deserved the hit because they wrote something that was typical of their own style. It's like the charts and the radio moved to come in line with Blue Öyster Cult rather than the other way around. I love the bombastic middle section as well, which I hadn't heard at first because I first heard it on a compilation that used the edited single version. But yeah, I love the solo and the big melodrama of the middle section.

Jim: "(Don't Fear) The Reaper" is when Blue Öyster Cult became what everybody knows as Blue Öyster Cult now in terms of mass popularity. Unfortunately it's been ruined by that *Saturday Night Live* skit, as funny as it was. Now as soon as you mention Blue Öyster Cult it's "More cowbell!" But such a unique-sounding song, right? The guitar solo is maybe the best guitar solo section in a rock song ever. The freakin' chorus ends and all of a sudden you're in the *Arabian Nights*.

But again, even more so now with this song, we're back to the mystery of this band and where they fit. Because they started out as this post-MC5 biker rock kind of thing, and then Buck started singing more, right? Buck has that smooth, beautifully velvet voice and those harmonies. And yeah, as a young kid hearing "(Don't Fear) The Reaper," you only realize later that it's about a teen suicide pact. Super cool. Yeah, seventh grade, that song was everywhere.

Martin: Also years later, now as a guitarist, when you look back at the song, what's your impression of hearing this odd, Byrds-y sort of guitar signature to it that they never ever revisit again?

Jim: Well, it's funny because it's Byrds-y in the vocals *and* the guitar, because I mean, you've got those amazing harmonies that have that super-lower part that just makes the whole song, if you really listen to the harmony. I'm really into vocal harmonies. It's like a lower third part. And I'm like, wow, that's a very interesting choice, to put what would be a third above the root note down below in the harmony. It's super-prominent, and I think it makes the whole harmony. And then obviously that guitar signature is incredible, with all that reverb. It was weird. They're in the mid '70s and they're really showing their '60s influence, right? Those old kind of Byrds and Hollies and Beatles things. But it's mystical; there's so much magic to it.

Martin: Next we have "E.T.I. (Extra Terrestrial Intelligence)," a men in black tale set to a sort of funky Aerosmith "Last Child" riff.

Rich: Yeah, great riff, very odd lyrics, talking about Balthazar, whoever he is. I'm not usually a fan of the voice box, which a lot of bands were using. Obviously Peter Frampton was well known for it. Most bands use it to make it sound like a wah-wah pedal, that kind of effect. And my theory is that when platform boots came in, in the '70s, no one could operate a wah-wah pedal safely without falling over backwards. So they started using the voice box instead. But then Buck, or whoever's playing the voice box, uses it in quite an original

way, as you would expect from Blue Öyster Cult. It's quite dark, almost belching. It's this dark cloudy sound that fits with it. A voice box can sound really dated, but it doesn't here. I like the feel of the song. And again we see the band's theme of juxtaposition, with the cheerful verse riff and cheerful chorus set against the UFO lyric.

Matt: For "E.T.I.," I think the interesting thing here is something that plays out on other songs, which is that Buck comes up with great music and they have to match a lyric to it. So, trying to find the lyric. Buck's original lyric was the one about traffic (laughs), a song about having too much traffic. It's a silly lyric. And instead they match it up with a great lyric that so fits into the Blue Öyster Cult mythology with UFOs and everything. In the end it totally succeeds as a band number.

Henry: I love how the first words we hear are, "Psst, come here!" (laughs). As a music track, it's almost proggy, with a great bass line, pumping but pretty spare, with the guitar doing that main circular run. It's got the banging piano thing—that's really cool. And you know, it's got the title in it: "Don't report this, agents of fortune!" plus "All prey, he's found the awful truth. Balthazar." It feels like a chant to a space god. So they're continuing that aspect of their mythology and their iconography. They're sticking with what they've done before which I think is great. They're not trying to divorce themselves from it.

Jim: That's one of those riffs where, like, I pick up a guitar and that's one of the riffs I like to play. One of my top five BÖC songs. The space imagery takes it out of just being a regular rock 'n' roll song. It's weird but it's got that great, smooth chorus and you still have that piano there but the song kind of rocks. Again, for a band that's as heavy as they supposedly were, they had three- and four-part harmonies. They all sang and contributed to these amazing vocal harmonies. So when you kick into that chorus, man, I'm so surprised it didn't become a radio song. Those harmonies are real ear candy on top of that chorus. The heavier bands kind of left the vocal harmonies out—Blue Öyster Cult left them in, and that's what I like about them. They all had good voices and they harmonize really well together in that song. When they leave that ascending riff and hit that chorus, it's so big because of those harmonies.

Martin: Definitely. Okay, side one of the original vinyl closes with "The Revenge of Vera Gemini," a sort of dreamscape-y shuffle. Highlight of the album, as far as I'm concerned. Or this tied with "Tattoo Vampire."

Rich: I agree; I absolutely love this song. It's just a stone-cold classic for me. And it was my favourite from the album at the time when I heard it, even ahead of "(Don't Fear) The Reaper." It's a real sort of goosebumps moment, quite chilling, very atmospheric. And the interplay between Albert and Patti Smith is amazing. I read somewhere, in some interview with the band, that we're to view it as a sort of *Wuthering Heights* Cathy and Heathcliff kind of thing. And I don't want this to sound pretentious, but if you're listening on headphones, it's mixed so that it sounds like Patti Smith's voice is floating around more ethereal and covered in reverb and Albert's is more front and centre. So in terms of the mix, she's floating around the guy almost like this ghost floating around the other half of the duet. It's like a dialogue between the two partners and one of them is all floaty and ethereal and the other one is solid.

Jim: "Vera Gemini" gets us back to the New York feel of the album, the sort of art punk thing, with Patti Smith writing lyrics and actually singing. So it gives this heavy rock band cachet, credibility, as part of the whole Lou Reed/Andy Warhol thing, almost. And they were just a band from Long Island, with a couple brothers from an upstate New York small town in the middle of nowhere. But it's weird, because that spoken intro comes right at the end of "E.T.I." What I mean is if you have your "E.T.I." on a CD, you play it and just at the tail end we start to hear Patti and then it cuts off.

Henry: Great song, and I love her voice, doing these little things in the background. And that intro, "You're boned like a saint with the consciousness of a snake;" so cool. And it's so obviously Patti's words. I mean, so much so that that she would have been better singing the lead. I think that she could have handled those lyrics better. But as it is, it's really moody and it adds a certain level of cool to them. Plus she's singing about horses here and the *Horses* album comes out right at the end of '75. So she's referring to her record when she says that. On *Secret Treaties* she wrote the lyrics to "Career of Evil," which has always been one of my favourites. I mean, like, really clever, crazy, warped, cool stuff. But I really love "The Revenge of Vera Gemini." Once again, you know Gemini, astrology, the stars, space. It's the first female vocal on a BÖC song and it really brings a new dimension. It's just cool that it's Patti Smith and Patti Smith being Patti Smith is just such an incredible addition to the album and the whole sort of mythos of BÖC.

Matt: Yeah, one of the strongest ones on that album. Now they're delivering the sophistication, the poetic goods. Patti gives the lyric to Albert a long time ago, for his birthday. The joke that Albert talks about, or the irony part to it, is that it mentions the 24th of May, which is Albert's birthday. He thinks that's in there because Patti is giving it to him as a birthday present, but the song is more about Bob Dylan and it's Bob Dylan's birthday (laugh). That's the O. Henry story there for you. And it's very much unlike "Baby Ice Dog," which doesn't feel like a Patti Smith lyric. This feels like a Patti Smith lyric. And they're doing it a little more like a Patti Smith song, with this cool groove to it. I love the call-and-response with the two singing, Albert singing and her doing her little parts. They play off of each other really well—love it.

Martin: To change the topic, I've always loved this album cover, based on an old photograph of a magician. How does it speak to you, if at all?

Henry: I mean, it's fun, with hidden meanings. You have the logo, which is great for consistency. I don't have any tattoos, but at some one point or another I said, you know what? I could probably get the Blue Öyster Cult symbol tattooed. But I wouldn't want people to mistake it for something else, because it's a little sinister. But the album cover is kind of a throwback. The illustration looks like it's from the early 1900s. It doesn't hit me deeply in the same way that the first few album covers do. Those covers feel like an invitation to a madness party or something, a little more like the records. This one's a little more front-facing.

Jim: Oh, one of the great spooky album covers of all time. It portrays them as The Addams Family of rock. It's mysterious. When I think of "(Don't Fear) The Reaper" and how ethereal that song is, that cover fits it so perfectly.

Martin: Over to side two and we have "Sinful Love," which I've always bookended with "Nosferatu" for some reason. In fact, now that I think about it, it's like you say, Jim, that they make me think heavy band but they aren't actually heavy.

Jim: Right, but it's still classic poppy Blue Öyster Cult with the plinking piano. But again it's not sugary pop; there was always a darkness to their pop. Blue Öyster Cult didn't sing about their dick, which is what most bands did in the '70s. Even their relationship lyrics were oddball, off the beaten path, dark. Like, what are they actually about? I asked a friend that as a kid and he said, "Oh yeah, they're basically vampires and outer space." I'm like, okay, I guess. I don't know if they were going for that, but that's kind of the vibe you get from them. Even their logo: three exclamation points and a question mark that all share a dot. What is that supposed to be? There's been so much mystery to this band as long as they've been around and still playing.

Henry: The piano gets pretty at some point and the vocal is almost chanting and it's a little dirty. But they have that nice break where it's got a groove, almost like a Steely Dan kind of groove with the piano. It's like clabbering piano for a lot of it and then it sort of gets sophisticated. Lyrically I like that, "The power that I give you, I'm so sick of your voice/My body, you don't give me no choice/But to boot you, honey, to give you the shove" and then also, "Dare-devil, she-devil, printer's-devil, evil/I love you like sin, but I won't be your pigeon."

Matt: To me, this is like a Brain Surgeons song before there's a Brain Surgeons. It has all the strong aspects of that band and of course Albert does it with them as well later on. It's very Albert. And it's also, I guess, very Helen Wheels. They collaborated a lot. With the "she-devil, printer's-devil" bit, you know, it's another Blue Öyster Cult song that's making you reach for the dictionary. What's a printer's-devil? And there are some interesting answers around that.

Rich: I love this one. Great keyboards, the band's really locked-in, the way they're all playing together. I like Albert's vocal, the stacked harmonies, the dark vibe. It's one of a couple of songs on this where there's a sense of drama and a punch to it, even though it's a slightly mellower track.

Martin: Then we're into "Tattoo Vampire," which I think is squarely the heaviest thing they'd ever come up to that point, once more, music by Albert, lyrics by Helen.

Rich: Yeah, classic Blue Öyster Cult rocker, with a dark, hammering riff. As you say about BÖC not thinking like a heavy metal band, it's a really concussive, attacking riff but it's not moronic or generic; it's not like Muppet metal. It's a really clobbering riff but there's some thought gone into it. It initially follows almost a blues pattern and then when it comes into that section about the grizzly smiles that don't flake off, it goes somewhere else. There's a strange vocal effect that's quite spooky. What the band is so good at is putting so much into an arrangement, so many different feels within one song, but it all fits. It's quite inviting in a melodic sense, but it's unsettling at the same time.

Henry: "I went down last night with a tattoo madam;" Eric singing with lyrics by Helen again. Yeah, that's Eric really doing his full rocker, rising to the opportunity on a really strong, super-rockin' jam. "Tattoo vampire, sucking the skin." There's that weird break that's got the laughing and the swirling and the funhouse/spook house thing—so cool. That's really taking it through all of its steps. They don't miss a trick on "Tattoo Vampire."

Matt: Lars Ulrich says that's his favourite Blue Öyster Cult song. It's a true heavy metal song. The production on *Agents of Fortune* is not heavy though, right? So it's a great heavy metal riff, but it never feels as heavy as it could've been. And you get a vampire song, which is kind of a staple of Blue Öyster Cult ethos.

Jim: When I hear "Tattoo Vampire," I'm transported back to old black-and-white era Blue Öyster Cult. That riff and the vocal and everything sounds like the old first couple albums.

Martin: "Morning Final" is yet another song on *Agents of Fortune* that represents quite a shock and a shift from what came before.

Rich: I must admit I absolutely love "Morning Final." Very atmospheric, and the way it builds up with the keyboards, that's a great intro from Allen. It's almost like a mini-movie in the form of a song, isn't it? There's an obscure '70s funk feel to it, which is kind of dated but not dated in the way an '80s drum sound is. It's kind of a welcome, easily identifiable '70s trope that fits well. And then the lyric is a crime story with the way the lyrics are describing the story there. The chorus is quite arresting and the harmonies are great. Joe wrote this one and also sings it and it's a highlight of the album for me.

Henry: I like the "Paper, mister? Read all about it!" And "Oh baby, don't it make you feel so bad"—great singalong. "Dark clouds are over the street." This one to me feels more like the old BÖC than some of these on the record, at least lyrically. I feel like it has a certain melancholy to it.

Martin: It's almost like a dream that you'd classify in between a dream and a nightmare.

Henry: Yeah, yeah, maybe that's what it is. And the subway is obviously something that they deal with too—"Hot Rails to Hell" is about the subway. It's very New York. And there's the guy selling papers on the street, although that's not the New York they grew up with; that's like the New York of 1905. He's a newsie!

But yeah, it's got some real nice parts to it. You know, if you get sick of one of the parts, you're gonna come to one that makes the other one makes sense. I think some of the best songs can have a part that's not necessarily all that pleasing, maybe? But then it becomes like an "aha!" moment when you get to the part following it, where it now all makes sense. Like there's some connection with the chords used or something's resolved that isn't resolved in isolation. I think one of the best examples of that is not in BÖC but in Led Zeppelin. "The Rover" is good and it's funky, but it's ugly. And then when it gets to the second half of the verse or whatever you call it, the chorus, you're just, oh! Like your whole head expands because you've just made sense of everything you've heard before. You retroactively go back and bring that into this position of making sense or being beautiful. It's such a cool songwriting technique and ability.

Matt: Very cool song, and a story song, with Joe continuing with the subway theme, but in a more straightforward manner than "Hot Rails to Hell" lyrically—and musically, come to think of it. It's about a death, a murder, but it's a good shtick he's got going, telling it through the lens of a newspaper headline. And of course it gives the Blue Öyster Cult fan club zine its name— *Morning Final* becomes the fan club zine. Plus it really contributes to the diversity of the record.

Martin: "Tenderloin" is about as dark as BÖC can get, and yet it's couched in some virulent form of pop. I'm hearing The Stranglers in this one circa *The Raven*, and The Stranglers haven't even been invented yet.

Matt: Well, so here's where Allen really is getting to influence the band. "True Confessions" and "Tenderloin" are not like other Blue Öyster Cult songs chord-wise. They're much more sophisticated than your typical Blue Öyster Cult songs. "True Confessions" he even sings; it's the one and only song he actually sings on and he does fine. It's a vision of what could have been. Because he really gives the band that urban sophistication that sometimes is missing. "Tenderloin" is brilliant. It's lyrically brilliant, evocative lyrics, cool chord progression and like I say, lends the band a specific type of sophistication that you don't normally get.

Martin: I've always grouped "Tenderloin" less with "True Confessions" and more with "Morning Final" and "Vera Gemini," and I suppose it's because they are written rock but lack heavy guitar, so all three are left sort of murky.

Matt: And I would say that those songs are cool, right? This is a band whose coolness has ebbed and flowed throughout their career. They started out cool, and now they're kind of entering their not cool period, where critics are less hot on them. With songs like these, you can see a version, again, of what they could've been. To me, Albert and Allen and Buck could've been a different band. Like if they went all-in and had Jim Carroll write their lyrics, what a cool little band that could've been (laughs).

Martin: Or Albert, Joe and Allen.

Matt: Well, we actually get to hear what that sounds like, because of Brain Surgeons, and a little bit of X-Brothers, right? Albert and Joe collaborate. Later there's Blue Coupe. You don't get the Allen Lanier piece. But the main point is you lose what Buck would've added, because he can solo over those more sophisticated progressions.

Martin: And he's jazzy; he's got the Randy Bachman/Lenny Breau thing.

Matt: That's right. And to me, the only place they really do that is on "Don't Turn Your Back." We get that specific cool chord progression and Buck solos over it. And Albert is more of a writer on that one.

Henry: "Tenderloin" is also a little dirty (laughs) and there's something a little '60s pop about it, with that, "Treat her gently, treat her kind/ Tenderloin will last all night." Great little guitar part there that really propels it along. It's catchy, quiet, sexy, slightly dirty, romantic: "Nighttime flowers, evening roses, bless this garden that never closes." It's almost like Steely Dan or something. It feels like an earlier pop tune, but it also feels like a slightly jammier band and it's still very BÖC, but a jazzier version of BÖC. Probably unfairly overlooked when people talk about this record, but I think it really holds its own.

Rich: Funny you mention The Stranglers, plus I hear The Doors. And of course, The Stranglers were always saddled with the Doors comparisons. The song doesn't quite settle, given the way the chord progressions work in this, with that off-kilter phrasing. It doesn't quite build and resolve like a traditional rock chorus would. It doesn't quite get to where you think it might go, but it still works.

Jim: The solo section in "Tenderloin," that up-tempo section at the two-and-a-half-minute mark sounds like Steve Howe. There's a weird progressive element to that, and then earlier even, that may as well be Rick Wakeman soloing. But they also have a little bit of a new wavy thing going on too, although new wave isn't a thing yet. Are they heavy? Are they sort of punk? They were all over the map. I mean, I used to see them back in the day and they played pretty exclusively with all the heavy bands. It's an odd juxtaposition.

Martin: I love that! Steve Howe—I can't unhear that now. But this one is also a little Doors-y, but in a new way versus the earlier albums. What do you make of that connection?

Jim: Well, the black-and-white period was only like two or three years after The Doors ceased to exist. So I would say that's normal. This is the music that they grew up with, were influenced by and were using in terms of influences. They also drew from Steppenwolf and MC5, completely different sounds from The Doors, right?

I always find it kind of odd that old punks, like guys that are our age and older, loved Blue Öyster Cult. I'm just like, really? All the old punk rocker guys I know that are between our age and 65, they all love Blue Öyster Cult, those old records, the black-and-white records. And I could never get the connection. I'm like, Blue Öyster Cult was kind of psychedelic at that time, kind of post-psych Steppenwolf biker rock with some acid things mixed in. I suppose they had a rawness. I don't know if they were going for that rawness or they just didn't have a lot of money to do production. They were on CBS but I don't know what kind of budgets they got. But again, it's what makes Blue Öyster Cult unclassifiable, really. Because none of those worlds really meet, you know, psych, hard rock, art rock, punk and whatever The Doors are. It didn't really cross over, but they managed to pull a little bit from all of it.

Martin: Yes, true, very sensible. Okay, now we're at the end of this strange and varied album, and they throw us for a loop again with "Debbie Denise," the poppiest thing they'd done to date.

Rich: Yeah, not a favourite. I tend to think of "Debbie Denise" as a twin sister song to "Beth" by Kiss. I can imagine Peter Criss singing it, and ironically it's the drummer singing it here. But yeah, it's a song about being out with his band, taking attention away from the relationship. I'm not a fan of ballads, but I can understand why you'd close an album with that. It's a little soft for me, whereas "True Confessions" isn't. I think that one fits the overall feel of the album better, and provides some nice light and shade. But this one's a bit too sweet.

Jim: Yeah, I noticed the "Beth" thing too—he's singing to his wife who's at home and it's like, I'm not coming home. Musically it's almost a Meat Loaf-type thing, kind of dramatic, with this grand-sounding piano, really poppy. The vocals are swimming in reverb. And with Albert singing, it's weird for me, because my first real experiences seeing them, Eric Bloom was pretty prominently the front man. But then you go back and realize like, no (laughs), these three other guys sang lead vocals in the band—and for this one album, all four of the other guys! And Eric isn't even singing half the songs. And there's only one Donald on the entire album. Only "(Don't Fear) The Reaper," which is interesting. He became the voice of their hits, though, or at least the two biggest hits.

Matt: "Debbie Denise" is a maligned song among Blue Öyster Cult fans but I'm contrarian on this one. I think as a melodic pop song it's brilliant. The introduction, where it has the acoustic with that kind of keyboard, organ, almost Mellotron-type sound, is very majestic-sounding. I get the same feeling that I get from the first chord of "Free Bird," believe it or not, which is a weird thing to say. It's coming in big but very catchy.

In my unsophisticated view, when I first heard the song as a kid, I also thought this was their "Beth," right? It's talking about being on the road. I love "Beth" too. I'm a sucker for that whole mystique. This is a great thing for a teenage fan who wants to be in a rock band, to think about what the life of a rocker is going to be. You have to leave your best girl behind, right? It's so hard being on the road, leaving your girl behind.

But I think it's very well-written, melodically. You have those "la la la" parts at the end. I think it's very intentional, from a musicologist band who know their '50s and '60s music. That's on purpose.

But that's not the point I wanted to make. It's a Patti Smith lyric, right? And I now appreciate the lyrics of it, knowing what her intent was. This is a lesbian love song. But BÖC twist it around. They change the gender on it, change some of the lyrics. So now I can appreciate it in a more subversive way, knowing that it has this other meaning. But the point is that there is a prudishness about Blue Öyster Cult that they choose to follow because of commercialism. What would have been a cooler move, if they were really as urban, New York and sophisticated as they really are—like they actually are, legitimately; Allen Lanier is legitimately this New York poet guy—is if they would have kept the lyric or had Patti sing the lyric. And have this, you know, homosexual love song on there. That would've made it more sophisticated.

But no, we have to turn it into "Beth." That's a prudish, commercial decision. They then go and do the exact same thing on *Spectres*. You've got "Searching for Celine," a sophisticated Allen lyric about the French novelist. And instead you're kind of fearful or cautious commercially, like, we can't do searching for *his* company. No, we can't do that, right? So they change it to "her." And then there's "Black Blade," where they buried the F-bomb in the mix. There's always this little desire to be commercial that probably "Reaper" creates in them. They didn't do that before. I guess this is the record where they start. After this, I feel like they are chasing for the hits that comes with "Reaper." The success of that song introduces a conservatism that makes them be not quite as weird as they could have been. To their detriment. "Searching for Celine" could've been a cooler song if it stayed about a French novelist and the same thing applies here.

Henry: I've always loved "Debbie Denise," but with a tongue in cheek, with caveats. As mentioned, like "Beth" it spells out the travails of the long-suffering rock wife or the rock partner. Obviously "Beth" is the current granddaddy of the long-suffering rock partner songs. But then there's also a great one from the female perspective, from a band from Columbus, Ohio called Scrawl, called "Charles." It's sort of stay up and wait, you know, Charles, I might be out all night. Me and the girls are playing and we just can't get it right. It's a funny, interesting, little sub-segment of rock songs. Lyrically "Debbie Denise" is a little clunky although its heart is in the right place. Once again, it's kind of like, let's leave the record on an upbeat note. It's like "Redeemed," which is also a little dorky. But it's still a great song, an enjoyable song.

Also, Debbie Denise is like the weirdest name for anybody. Two names that you don't hear anymore, at least not in New York. It creates a weird stuck-in-time moment. I don't know, I grew up with a bunch of kids named Debbie and a bunch of kids named Denise, but never together. And why anybody would... if your name was Deborah Denise, why would you go by Debbie Denise? And you wonder, what was her last name? Was it Jones or Schlesselman? Debbie Denise Schlesselman. It raises a lot of questions.

But at the core, it's a good song, although kind of a comedy song to me. It's delivered with heart. Albert's voice is not as cool as Bloom's and he's not as sort of confident as Buck. But his performance has a straightforwardness. It's the kind of thing that would inspire people to do karaoke. They're like, they hear him sing and go, "Hey, I could do that." I don't mean to diss him. And it's nice that they break them up. You feel like the whole band is involved. Just like that whole gimmick where they would all play guitar together for a minute live. You perceive them as a family. Everybody can step up. It feels a bit like a cult because of that.

Martin: All right; anything to add before we move on?

Jim: Well, I'm just gonna go out on a limb here and say that *Agents of Fortune* and *Spectres* are basically BÖC's *Rubber Soul* and *Revolver*, right? What they started with *Agents*, I think they perfected on *Spectres*. I think overall *Spectres* is a better album, although neither have a lot of punch, again, because they're sort of heavy and sort of not. There's piano, synths, acoustic guitar and lots of folky harmonies. But it *is* 1976. The real heavy stuff hadn't really started other than Black Sabbath and Deep Purple. Even the Kiss records were kind of light. In '76 you had *Destroyer* and this is very much in that vein, where there's a lot of production but not a lot of bottom end or really, overall hi-fidelity. It's ornate but not punchy.

Martin: You bring up an interesting point. I tend to characterize the production on *Agents of Fortune* as bad, but I forget that besides the band, even the producers aren't thinking with a heavy metal hat on. Maybe that's why it sounds this way.

Jim: Right, it's pre- all of that stuff. In 1975 we got the big Fleetwood Mac record, a successful ELO record that year and a bigger one in '76. We've had those great Pink Floyd records, *Dark Side of the Moon* and *Wish You Were Here*. So there wasn't this, I guess, necessity to sound heavy if you were a hard rock band. It was more like, oh, let's make this interesting and put some piano in here; let's add some strings. That's why I like this period of music so much—'76, '77—because it wasn't, oh, we have to make it sound as heavy and as crunchy as possible. That hadn't really started yet. And that's what I like about these records—they have a lot of colour. Once you got to the '80s, all the songs sounded the same production-wise. You got the big guitars and they were phasing the keyboards out. So this is an interesting period to me for Blue Öyster Cult because they were getting experimental with lots of pianos and then synthesizers. I like that; I like the fact that it's not intentionally so balls-out the whole time.

Matt: Well, I'll just add that *Agents of Fortune* is a super-diverse record. You get lots of different styles. You really do feel like all five band members are contributing, despite Eric not writing a lot. Instead he's got some great vocal performances. So you hear everybody on the record, in all their diversity. Unfortunately, however, it sets the stage for some perhaps unreal commercial expectations going forward.

SPECTRES

Spectres
November 1, 1977
Columbia JC 35019
Produced by Murray Krugman, Sandy Pearlman, David Lucas and Blue Öyster Cult
Engineered by Shelly Yakus and John Jansen with Corky Stasiak and Thom Panunzio
Recorded at The Record Plant, New York, NY
Personnel: Eric Bloom – vocals, guitar; Donald "Buck Dharma" Roeser – lead and rhythm guitars, vocals; Joe Bouchard – bass; Allen Lanier – keyboards, guitar; Albert Bouchard – drums, vocals, harmonica
Guest performers: Newark Boys Chorus

Side 1
1. "Godzilla" (Roeser) 3:41
2. "Golden Age of Leather" (Bruce Abbott, Roeser) 5:52
3. "Death Valley Nights" (Meltzer, A. Bouchard) 4:07
4. "Searchin' for Celine" (Lanier) 3:35
5. "Fireworks" (A. Bouchard) 3:14

Side 2
1. "R. U. Ready 2 Rock" (Pearlman, A. Bouchard) 3:43
2. "Celestial the Queen" (Helen Wheels, J. Bouchard) 3:24
3. "Goin' Through the Motions" (Bloom, Ian Hunter) 3:12
4. "I Love the Night" (Roeser) 4:25
5. "Nosferatu" (Wheels, J. Bouchard) 5:22

Martin talks to John Alapick, Jim Bacchi, Rick LaBonte, Bill Schuster and Nick S. Squire about *Spectres*.

Martin Popoff: Jim, tell us your story about seeing Blue Öyster Cult for the first time. And stay with us, folks. This is indeed *Spectres*-related.

Jim Bacchi: Yes it is (laughs). So here's my story with *Spectres*. January 13th, 1978, I'm super-excited because I'm going to see my favourite band for the first time, who is not Blue Öyster Cult—it's Rush. Rush is opening for Blue Öyster Cult at the Nassau Coliseum. I'm 14. The weather forecast says we're going to have a storm. My mother's like, "I don't think you should go to that concert." I'm like, "Rush is my favourite band. There's no way you're not letting me go to that concert. I don't care. I don't care." So we go to the show. My dad takes me and my friends and we're gonna meet some other friends there. He's like, "I'm gonna stay at your uncle's house." He lives close by and then he's picking me afterwards. My mother's at home.

I go. There's snow, or at least flurries. It's a little cold. I come out of the show. Pouring rain, thunder. I'm running through puddles two feet deep to find my dad. You know, ro cellphones. "I'll be out by the entrance." That night the temperature dropped to freezing and everything froze— everything. Like all the trees on my street; all the branches were ice. And I live on a long street. I come home from the show and my mother, who was deathly afraid of thunderstorms, is sitting at the kitchen table with a candle. The power had gone out. And I just felt really awful. I'm like, oh my God.

But the show I saw was great and consequently I had just gotten my first guitar for Christmas two weeks earlier. The power went out for ten days in New York where I lived in Long Island. We had to go to my grandmother's house because they had power in Queens. And I brought my guitar and my *All the World's a Stage* and I was trying to learn all the guitar solos on a record player. It was the craziest winter storm ever.

But in that show I saw Rush for the first time and I saw Blue Öyster Cult for the first time, and Blue Öyster Cult were in their laser period. That was probably my second or third concert ever. You know, I was 14. I knew every Rush song intimately because I was so fanatical. It was *A Farewell to Kings* and they opened with "Bastille Day" and they closed with "Cinderella Man," which they've never played since. And that was the last time they were an opening act, that year, early '78.

But when Blue Öyster Cult came on, you know, I knew "Godzilla," I knew "(Don't Fear) The Reaper" and not much else because I wasn't really that familiar. My friend had an older brother who was a Blue Öyster Cult fanatic. But the laser show is what stuck with me most. Because the laser show at that time was so over-the-top. They had a sphere, a spinning mirror ball. Eric Bloom had mirrors on his wrists and they would shine the lasers on his wrist and he would move his wrist and the laser beams would go hit the mirror ball and send millions of laser beams all over. And I swear to God—I still remember this—I was ducking because I thought stuff was going to hit me. That's how intense the lasers were. My good friend who I went to all my concerts with was two years older than me. He was tripping on acid. So he's like, "Dude, that show completely freaked me out. I was on acid for that." I'm like, oh my God.

So I'm watching this incredible laser show and this band Blue Öyster Cult. I'm like, okay, I'm gonna go out and buy *Spectres*. And what's on the cover of *Spectres*? The lasers. If you get a minute, there's a little 20-minute documentary about Blue Öyster Cult and their lasers. And they actually show you these giant glass tube lasers. They spent thousands of dollars on them. Apparently, someone said to them, you know, OSHA is going to come down on you. These aren't safe. There were those stories where someone got blinded, but they're not true, but they decided to stop using them. So they had a very short period of *Agents of Fortune* and *Spectres* where they were using that crazy laser show and you can find a video about it on YouTube. It's wild. So that's my first really serious Blue Öyster Cult memory. That's why this album is so near and dear to me. I think it's my favourite.

And you know what's funny? At that concert, Eric Bloom was saying like, "We got our start out here" and I forget where it was in Long Island. But I never knew they were a Long Island band! Until he mentioned it at the show. Because I just thought they were from outer space. But he talked about the Jolly Rogers amusement park. "We used to play the Jolly Rogers amusement park!" And I'm like, wow, they're from here?! I had no idea because I was still a little kid when they came out.

Martin: Nice. Okay, so, guys, there's some context for you. What is the personality of this record?

Bill Schuster: I'd say they've moved more into embracing pop sounds but in a good way. I've always preferred this album over *Agents* for that reason. I think they wrote a bunch of great pop songs on here. No matter what the hard rock or metal trappings on a song or two might be, at the core these are good pop songs. They all have strong hooks—they're catchy.

Nick S. Squire: They're at cruising altitude. Personally, I think this is an album that builds on the strength of *Agents*. What I found with these older BÖC albums is that I like them maybe for different reasons now than I did in my teens or 20s. This might be controversial, but I think BÖC has more in common with somebody like The J. Geils Band than Deep Purple and Black Sabbath. They're never quite as heavy as you think they are. They have other elements in their music that I think are different than the traditional hard rock or heavy metal bands.

Especially on *Spectres* and *Mirrors*. The songs and the strength of the songs are often centred around piano. Allen Lanier's piano drives the thing. There's piano flourishes, there's grand piano, and he along with the rest of it works to create something that I think is different and unique. They rely on that; not rely, but it's there. But a lot of their music, especially on those two albums, it's almost '50s-centred. There are '50s-isms in there, whether it's vocal harmonies, the way they do a melody line, time signatures, or whether it's almost like a homage to girl groups. I find that to be a strength.

The other thing I like about *Spectres* is that despite them always having outside writers helping, it's a very BÖC-sounding album to me, however you define that classic BÖC sound, whether it's *Agents of Fortune* or later, maybe *Fire of Unknown Origin*. I think *Spectres* is right in there.

Rick LaBonte: They've kept that recipe of being accessible pop, reaching for the pop market a little bit. There are some moments here where they don't sell their soul for the pop scene, but they put more than enough pop in there. A lot of people among their peers were doing that about this time, because FM radio was king and it was starting to be a pop machine as well. It wasn't just underground albums anymore, or even just album-oriented rock. To get dominant radio, especially in the Midwest or Canada, you had to have a hit. So I think what they did is soften the blow. I mean, listen to "(Don't Fear) The Reaper;" it's a rocking tune but it's also surprisingly catchy. But what made that song so catchy in the first place was the pop vocal and the whole ear candy harmony stuff. And so even though it rocked, they put that pop hook to it.

So I think they thought like that when they came to this record: obviously people really liked that but they still want us to play. Because that guitar solo in "(Don't Fear) The Reaper" is nothing to sneeze at. But does it fit in this pop song? It's kind of wild. So I think they approached this album in that same way—a balance between accessibility and more musicality than most bands. It's a great rock record, but the more pop rock treatment made it accessible.

Lyrically, even though Sandy Pearlman and Richard Meltzer write a couple songs, we're getting away from the *Twilight Zone* and kind of *Night Gallery* song that they were coming up with, having all these weird theories. In the black-and-white album series, each album was almost like a book of short stories. Where here they're trying to write for the masses or for teenagers, even people who might roller-skate to it or bring it to the fire pit or play it on the jukebox at the pool hall. Yeah, they're thinking jukebox.

John Alapick: In my humble opinion, they tasted pop success with *Agents* and they wanted more of it on *Spectres*. And I think it helps and it hurts the album. There are songs on here where you could tell they were trying to do something that would get on the radio. Like I say, I think some of it works and some of it doesn't.

Martin: How would you characterize the production of the album?

John: As great as the quality of the songs were on a lot of these albums, the production, for the most part was subpar. *Spectres* certainly doesn't match what Martin Birch did, which was stunning. But a lot of their albums, outside of *Heaven Forbid*, which is actually way up there, yeah, there was something lacking. It felt restrained. And it feels restrained on here, even on a heavy song like "Godzilla." You listen to it and wonder what more it could have been, as great a song as it is and as memorable as it is. It never became a hit, but it might have been with more quality in the audio department.

But yeah, particularly when you saw what else was coming out around 1977, like *Rumours* which was produced very well, the biggest selling albums from that period all had stellar production. I mean, *Hotel California* came out around Christmas of '76 and that was all over radio and very well-produced.

Martin: Aerosmith *Rocks* sounds big and bold, certainly with both more high end and bottom end than either *Agents* or *Spectres*. And that's essentially a "New York" album.

John: Yes, and even Aerosmith *Draw the Line*. I mean, not quite up to *Rocks* standard. It was a little looser but still recorded pretty well. Them BÖC did the single live album but then *Mirrors*, which, I know you're a big fan of that album and I'm not. But I'll agree with you that it's gorgeously produced. But they were continuing even further in the pop direction than *Spectres* did, to try get more radio, more hits, more mass popularity.

Bill: I've never had a problem with the sound. It's pretty to my ears. It's clearly different from the black-and-white period, much clearer than it used to be. But I do find it interesting that there are so many producers credited.

I mean look; you've got Murray Krugman, Sandy Pearlman, David Lucas and the whole band all credited as producers. Doesn't that sound like too many cooks? Funny.

Nick: I described BÖC as having what I call a New York sound. And there's certain people that you see in this cabal of BÖC that also have a New York sound. For example, Ian Hunter, same town during this period, and he writes "Goin' Through the Motions." You see Ellen Foley—good luck finding an Ellen Foley album—but that same kind of stuff. Meat Loaf, Bruce Springsteen. I find the production not offensive but it's pedestrian. It's not the heaviest sound I think the production tends to play down the hard rock elements of the band. That's why, you know, the piano for me is more of a centring element. So it's a band that's sometimes considered a heavy metal/hard rock band, but I'm hearing piano, which to my ears, represents some kind of link to the question of production.

Rick: It's very much linked to the sound of the times. When I hear the "Golden Age of Leather" vocal, it sounds like Fleetwood Mac, with them bringing the girls on board in '75. This is just after *Hotel California* too. Sonically it's of its time and of what's happening with FM radio. They were really following current trends production-wise, with *Agents of Fortune* being the segue to get them to this place. But I do think that anybody who was a diehard BÖC fan might feel a bit slighted because they love that heaviness and rawness of the early albums. That's what we like about early Black Sabbath too.

But now they're somewhat polished. Is it a good thing? Absolutely, because you know what comes up eventually, *Fire of Unknown Origin*, which is an awesome, polished record but still has all the great things we love about BÖC. But here there's new territory covered and it doesn't sound like they're fully comfortable yet. Though vocally they sound awesome. For example "Death Valley Nights" has these beautiful ear candy harmonies. And it's wonderful because Albert, the drummer, is singing that one. But that's one that I say sounds a lot like Fleetwood Mac and Eagles when it comes to harmonies, the way they have that sweet high-end chorus happening. There's quality, dynamics, heavy/soft, high/low—it's fantastic. It's got what I like about Uriah Heep's "Circle of Hands" and even that, how to approach vocals, is a big part of production, even though people tend to focus on drum sound and how much bass and treble there is.

As for the drum sound though, I thought, well, where are the overhead mics? It seems like they just went direct. Or that's all they did was overhead mics and no separation on toms and stuff. Yeah, it wasn't as good as the album before and definitely not as good as when Martin Birch gets involved. To me that's their finest hour sonically. But here it's Murray Krugman plus a bunch of guys. There's a little bit of an identity crisis. There's a lot of hands in the cookie jar and that's gonna affect the overall outcome. That's why the album sounds different. The earlier ones were more like a cohesive package because all the songs are similar in vein, where on *Spectres*, each individual song is different.

Martin: Yeah, it sounds like they're checking off boxes, matching it up with *Agents*. Like we need one of these, one of these, one of these...

Rick: That's right; exactly. It's definitely a formula album versus the idea of this is what we had in the tank and this is what we're putting out there.

Martin: All right, well at least the album doesn't begin too terribly pop, with a "One of These Nights" or "You Make Loving Fun." "Godzilla" is pretty much this band's "Smoke on the Water," or at least it is if we're talking riffs.

Nick: Exactly. Even though I say they have more in common with J. Geils, of course the first track off the album is one of their heaviest (laughs). "Godzilla" is an undeniable classic. I can listen to it every day for the rest of my life and I won't get sick of it. Easy yet super-memorable riff, and the imagery conjured by the lyrics and the vocal too is so unique and different. I feel like I'm watching the movie. And when you're listening to the song, it's just heavy enough. You've got the great riff, you've got the imagery of Godzilla stomping around town, it's played well, you've got the vocal harmonies in there. They dialled that one in and they knew it. It's the first track, leading off the album, which means they knew that that song was going to be a good one.

One thing I'd like to point out is Albert's drumming; he's got a lot of tricks in there, little drum rolls, things that are subtle but drives that song besides the riff. And that's the one thing I came away with from re-listening to *Spectres* and *Mirrors* is that Albert is a really good drummer and Joe is a really good bass player. There's a cool bass line in that song, a descending bass line.

Jim: "Godzilla" is obviously played to death on rock radio and deservedly so. First off, it's certainly funny, very much tongue-in-cheek. You know, "There goes Tokyo, go go Godzilla." It was a funny song but with a great heavy riff. And that whole middle section with, "Godzilla, Godzilla, God, God" and all that, so cool.

One more quick story. So in 1998 my band Fuzzbubble is on the *Godzilla* soundtrack. A guy who's at this company called us kind of courting the band. He wanted to be involved with us because we were involved with Puffy. He threw us a party at the Plaza Hotel in New York. He rented the penthouse and he invited all these people down. Buck Dharma was there and I got to meet Buck. And I remember talking to Buck and Buck was really sour about not getting the "Godzilla" song on the *Godzilla* soundtrack. And I remember, like, yeah, you guys absolutely should be on there. That song should be on the movie soundtrack.

But I guess in 1998, Blue Öyster Cult were kind of not considered cool or whatever. But I was just like, I'm talking to Buck Dharma about a soundtrack that I'm on that he's not and he should be. It was a surreal moment. I also remember meeting Joe Lynn Turner and this is how he introduced himself: "Hi, Joe Lynn Turner!" I was just like, yeah, I know who you are, man. You're goddamn Joe Lynn Turner. You don't gotta tell me your last name. Just Joe would have been fine. So I'm in this room with these rock legends at a party for my band. But I remember meeting Buck and him kind of being sour about it.

Don't remember much more than that. Basically we got on the subject and I'm like, "Yeah, we're on the soundtrack." I kind of felt bad because I was on the soundtrack and he wasn't. I'm some nobody from nowhere. It was my first kind of real break. But he's like, "We're kind of bummed that they wouldn't ask us to be on that record." And I'm like, "You guys should have been, by all means."

Martin: Very cool, and then of course BÖC did a parody version of "Godzilla" all about not being included! So Bill, why do you think "Godzilla" was such a success?

Bill: I think "Godzilla" was a success because of its simplicity. And because of the cartoon, over-the-top nature of the lyrics I was talking about earlier. Plus it's easy pickings because Godzilla is just such an iconic part of pop culture. It has built-in fans because of all the Godzilla monster movie fans out there. There were always going to be people that would be drawn to the song because of that aspect of it. But yet Donald just came up with a good, simple but strong riff that plays well on the radio. It's not a favourite of mine on the album but I understand why it's one of their bigger songs.

Rick: In general during this era they're no longer trying to be the science fiction band but don't get me wrong, they know they can't alienate their base! Using the science fiction monster was a great idea for them, and "Godzilla" ended up being one of the most popular songs. People will be disappointed if they don't play that at a concert today. You want to hear people storming a place like Godzilla?—that's what would happen if they didn't play it. And then it obviously ends up being a great concert prop with the giant Godzilla breathing flames, at a time when stadium rock was doing that kind of stuff. What I love about this song most though is that it's got these dual vocal back-and-forth harmonies all the way through it, doing what they learned from "(Don't Fear) The Reaper" even. Buck and Eric are sharing the vocals. That's a great rockin' song, but it's one of those songs that many of us maybe don't need to hear as often because we've heard it a lot.

Martin: And back to the concert thing, man, I even remember seeing Albert's band, The Brain Surgeons in a tiny bar in Hamilton, Ontario, and he put on the Godzilla head thing. John, any wrap-up from you on this one?

John: Well, tongue-in-cheek, cool riff, cool chorus: "Oh no, they say he's got to go/Go go Godzilla." I mean, it's very memorable. You heard the song once or twice and it just stuck in your head. Interestingly, this was the second single off the album and it was somewhat of a radio hit for them. As far as their songs that have endured the most, you could put this number three right behind "(Don't Fear) The Reaper" and "Burnin' for You." It was a fun song to play live when I was in a band too. I used to play bass and this was always fun to do, given Joe's brief bass showcase in it.

Martin: Next is "Golden Age of Leather," which, weirdly, I always considered this the sister song to "Good Ale We Seek" from Starz's *Attention Shoppers!*. But putting that aside, what say you on this one?

John: I don't know, to me, the song doesn't really get off the ground. As strong as some of the playing is, it sounds like two songs put into one. A lot of times you hear that and it works, but here it sounds a little disjointed. They regularly do this one live because a lot of people like to sing that acapella opening of the song. I like this song. I don't love it.

Bill: Back to the biker themes again. I'd say it's a great story song, with this idea of a biker battle in the middle of the desert. I often wonder about that last old ranger who weathered the storm and what became of him. It's got that over-the-top Viking chant basically at the beginning, which is just an attention-grabber. "Raise your can of beer on high." Like John says, that's a great sing-along bit in concert.

Nick: I've always liked that song. I'm actually shocked at how it still turns up regularly in their set. There's a thing about mid-song which, I swear to God, I think they nicked that off of "Good Vibrations." You gotta go back and listen; he goes, "Ah" and then I'm waiting for them to start going to the Theramin and do "Good Vibrations." To me, it's almost note-for-note. And where it goes into that like Catholic monk hymnal thing, I think that's a really neat trick. So it tells me there's yet another element that this band can bring in. I found that sometimes BÖC maybe yearns to be less J. Geils and more even prog-sounding, so there are these prog elements that come in. And this goes throughout the album; there are time signature changes, tempo changes, shifting musical themes. And they like to do this at the ends of songs. So here they throw in this Catholic hymnal. Great way to end the song.

Rick: Opening with the acapella gives you that '50s vibe, that little golden era thing. I mean, it has nothing to do with The Fonz and *Happy Days* or *American Graffiti*, but it evoked that '50s trend that was going on then a little bit, and the fun of it. Then they start picking up the tempo and it become a little proggy, with great keyboard and guitar and behind them that cool driven rhythm. It's an awesome song. It takes you by surprise because you're listening to it and it's already rockin', but halfway through it, it speeds up and takes on a new life just like "(Don't Fear) The Reaper" does. You get delivered a left hook and it connects.

Martin: With Albert singing "Death Valley Nights," this feels like a follow-up to "The Revenge of Vera Gemini."

Bill: Sure, and it's one of my favourite Albert songs. Albert gives us a strong vocal here and creates such a cool vibe for the song. It's very eerie and it seems to be a forgotten song in the catalogue. In fact one of the strongest things about this album overall is that everyone brings something to the table songwriting-wise and vocally, with everybody except Allen. You get that multiple vocalist vibe that is so important for Blue Öyster Cult historically. Albert is such a contrast to Donald on the previous song, "Golden Age of Leather."

Nick: Nice song, but I find Albert to be slightly flat in places. He's like the

Ace Frehley in the band. But that vocal is an interesting counterpoint to the beautiful piano in that song. So I found that his sort of fragile vocal, coupled with the piano, makes the song for me. And the vocal harmonies in that song present another example of the idea that you've got to know what the hell you're doing in this band. If you're going to play in this band, you gotta know about vocals. I never picked up on this fully as a kid. But there's so much going on vocally with this band and the vocal harmonies, it's just top-shelf against any of their competitors doing this. Think about it. You have four vocalists—very rare to have that in a band. And they're non-traditional vocalists, but they all can basically hold their own.

John: This should have been the first single from the album. The first single was actually "Goin' Through the Motions," which we'll talk about later. But "Death Valley Nights" I think is wonderful. Excellent chorus, great harmonies, kind of classical music-sounding in the melody, and an almost spiritual feel to it during the verses.

Martin: Next is "Searchin' for Celine," sort of a follow-up to "Tenderloin."

John: Yes, both written by Allen Lanier, plus there's some great bass work from Joe. I like funk and they went funk here. A lot of people didn't like it. I enjoyed it. And Buck's solo in the outro is wonderful. More great harmonies during the verses. The piano plays a really prominent role in the song as well.

Bill: So here's Eric famously not wanting to sing about the poet. He didn't want to feel emasculated there, so he needed it to be about a girl called Celine and not the male poet. As for the R&B vibe, I think it works well. It's part of the variety of the album and I think the scope of the album is its greatest charm.

Rick: This one's got that cool bass line that touches on disco. That little bit of a disco thing was common at the time. I get a Gary Wright *Dream Weaver* vibe from this song. I think the guitars save it. Right up to the very fade, Eric and Buck are playing some fantastic guitar. This song doesn't quite feel like they're selling out, but anybody who's listening will notice that as a disco club bass line.

Nick: Yeah, "Searchin' for Celine" is one of those songs that sort of burrows into your brain. I happen to like the bass line and I know that Joe's actually playing it with a pick. But that chorus, "I've been searchin', searchin'/

Searchin' for Celine," that's an ear worm. And the more I think about it, here we are again with piano driving a song. I think BÖC are at their best when they're trying to keep things at least musically in-house, and this is a rare one from Allen. Allen Lanier is like the Swiss Army knife to me; he plays guitar, the piano, is a way better keyboard player and piano player than I ever gave him credit for, really solid. He's like the Paul Raymond of the band. He was this guy who could do everything, like Michael Lardie in Great White, one of those guys. I like that in the band, the flexibility of a keyboard guy who's competent as a guitar player.

Martin: And personality-wise, would you say that Allen is the most "downtown" guy in the band?

Nick: Sure, you know here he is with Patti Smith for a couple of years. Yeah, exactly. And there's his relationship with Jim Carroll. As an aside, when I was doing my first round of playing bass with Jim George, somebody in Philly knew Allen Lanier and he was living in Florida and not in the band anymore. But they said that he was not in good shape. This was from a girl who knew a girl who was shacked up with Allen. But, yeah, the description was of someone with a lot of bad habits and personal demons. And then of course we lost Allen not long after, in 2013. Anyway, great song from him here, and right in his wheelhouse and really, the band's wheelhouse too, given the range of the band during this era, definitely *Agents* and *Spectres*.

Martin: Closing side one of the original vinyl is "Fireworks," written entirely by the drummer in the band and then sung by him too—pretty rare in the industry.

Jim: Yeah, and great song. More of that ethereal thing. That's the Blue Öyster Cult that I liked the best, is when they're being kind of celestial like that.

Nick: I love that there's distinct sections of the song. I like the lyrics in it. In the chorus there's all this groove and those harmonies. I like that call-and-response in the harmony; they do that a lot. That's another '50s thing. It's almost like gospel, where they'll say a line and the line is then repeated. A lot of bands don't do that, it's like a lost art. It's really cool that they did that even then, but you never hear that now. And they did it without being like an overtly blues band, if you will, or gospel band. They're able to make that fit. And that has to come from either the production side or their influences. They also have a nice harmony twin lead guitar part in that too.

It's Wishbone Ash but good. I don't know why the Spotify algorithm said I should love Wishbone Ash, but every time I play BÖC it takes me there next. Everyone says I should love Wishbone Ash. I've tried to love Wishbone Ash. I cannot like Wishbone Ash. I don't know if it's the vocals or what but yeah, I found that twin lead like Wishbone Ash—but good.

John: I've been saying this for a long time, but to me "Fireworks" sounds like a Bob Welch song. I was never a fan of this song. To me it just doesn't fit. Bob Welch was big at this point. *French Kiss* from this same year went platinum. It sounds like something for the radio and I just don't think it works. But that chorus, I'm waiting for Bob Welch to jump in and go, "Your eyes got me dreamin'." I don't want my Blue Öyster Cult to sound like Bob Welch.

Rick: "Fireworks" is a great song, pop, beautiful harmonies, quite non-BÖC, sung by Albert, catchy phrasing vocally. That's one of the things I really like is this band's vocal phrasing, the layers, the separateness, the spaces in-between, pretty creative, actually. It's there on *Secret Treaties* too, with "dominance" and then "submission." The little things they do, it's just creative. There's a lot of thought put into it. I would love to have been a fly on a wall to watch them do the vocals on "Fireworks." Because I really appreciate vocal harmonies like that.

Martin: Over to side two, and it's another hard rocker, but one with a sweet, chewy centre.

Nick: Yes, and "R.U. Ready 2 Rock" is probably a top ten BÖC tune for me. I know it more from the live album *Some Enchanted Evening*, but they really haven't played it all that much live. It's been sort of forgotten following its use during this time period. Here's what makes it for me. I'm listening to the song and I'm like, what is it about this song? Piano's driving again, all these BÖC elements, but I'm like, Albert is copying Corky Laing on that drum beat. It's so sparse and heavy, it's like Corky, and Corky is a New York guy, right? Mountain had to have been an influence or friends or whatever. It's almost like a "Sunshine of Your Love" jungle groove. It really makes that song. And you've also got the driving piano, played frenetically, on top of that Mountain drumbeat.

More call-and-response in both the "Yes I am" and the "I only live to be born again" and then repeating it. The jam at the end is just ripping, with the bass and the drums. There's a time signature change at the end of that song, which again is another interesting element with this band. And that heavy, heavy jam just shows you these guys can really play, especially the Bouchard brothers.

Martin: You know, I love your theory about the piano and the '50s thing, because you notice both those elements—or that sort of combined element—in the two heaviest songs on here. "Godzilla" and "R.U. Ready 2 Rock" both have that Jerry Lee Lewis/Little Richard thing kind of shoved into these BTO or heavy Mountain songs.

Nick: Right, exactly. And you know what's good about that too, as I get older, I like that simple thing called dynamics, whether it's clichéd or not. It's being quiet and then building. It's going here and then moving there. It's being fast and slow. And those simple things in a song can sometimes make or break. It builds momentum. It's almost like telling a story. Maybe this shows my prejudice with music, but there's some subtypes of heavy metal where it's like you're just bludgeoning me to death with the same thing the whole time. And it's not just the same song, but it's every song and within the song.

So yeah, BÖC has this ability to kind of be quiet and loud, heavy and soft. And those simple things, really, it creates imagery, it creates a tension sometimes. Yeah, you can make or break. Just from my almost weekend warrior experiences playing live, you bring, bring, bring it down in the third verse, bring it down, don't let it all out. And then when they go and head for home you bring it up again. Stuff like that works in a live situation. The audience feeds off it. It's a tangible thing.

Bill: This song is built to be a concert anthem, although the title is a bit cheese with the short-form thing and the punctuation. But it sounds great here and works well in concert and is pretty central to the live album the next year, which went platinum for them—big seller.

Rick: "R.U. Ready 2 Rock" I think represents one of those boxes checked: "All right guys, we need some rock; let's stick this on there." But the guitars are loud and proud here, bigger than life. And I love that, "Are you ready to rock?" "Yes I am." It's a call-and-answer as Nick has noted. You can picture the crowd participation; it's designed to get people going, emphasized by the sort of gang chorus feel of it. Also I would say that the album as a whole has a good tracking order. Here they have an up-tempo, bombastic tune to kick off the side.

Jim: Sort of part two of "Cities on Flame with Rock and Roll." Not as crazy, but I love the "Who will rock with you?" because they're pulling from The Beatles, right? "Fixing a Hole." It perked my ears because I'm like, oh, they took that from the Beatles. Pretty sure it's intentional though; you can tell they did it. Super-poppy chorus but set against a sort of Led Zeppelin-ish riff.

Martin: Then we're into the first of two Joe Bouchard songs, with Helen Wheels writing on both of them, back for another taste after "Sinful Love" and "Tattoo Vampire."

Jim: Yes, "Celestial the Queen." I love the synthesizer on this. Again, big vocals. They use a lot of big reverb in the production again to get that spacey, spooky vibe.

Bill: I don't want to call it filler because I like the song. But it's another one that because certain songs on this album stand out more to me, I enjoy it more as part of the album experience rather than as an individual song. I've never quite figured out the song lyrically.

Nick: You've got this grand piano that is just regal and beautiful, but's it's driven by the drums. There are some quite modern synth flourishes that sit in there very nicely and are not over-the-top. It's not, "Hey, look, we got synthesizers we can we can play with." It's not overbearing where some artists at the time were like, "Hey, we're experimenting with synths now. We're just going to kill you with it." I thought he did a nice job. And then the piano is almost Rachmaninoff style, which, when I was a kid playing the piano, that was one thing about dynamics. My piano teacher said, "You hit the goddamn piano like it's Rachmaninoff. Everything's loud." I just wanted to sound like Jerry Lee Lewis—everything really heavy. But I like that song.

Rick: A very accessible song sung by Joe, the bass player, creative, and lyrically a fantasy sort of thing. It's a short and sweet song and not something they often play live.

John: It's got a majestic feel, which makes sense if you're calling a song "Celestial the Queen." It's melodic, and the keyboards are really high in the mix. It's a memorable song, but it sounds like they're trying to go for radio play. But this one works.

Martin: Next we have Eric Bloom, our heavy hitter, ironically singing what is probably the band's poppiest song to date.

Jim: "Goin' Through the Motions" is such an oddball track for them because it's so poppy but I love it. That middle section has a clear-cut Beach Boys moment in it. I love that synthesizer intro. The bridge is like one of the most perfect bridges ever written. It's funny, my singer in Hittman was never a big Blue Öyster Cult fan. I sent him that song and he's just like, "That's them?!" I go, "Yeah, dude." He goes, "That's an amazing bridge." That bridge is one of the most amazing bridges in a pop song I've ever heard. Pretty interesting that he wrote that with Ian Hunter. But yeah, it has a Mott the Hoople thing to it for sure.

But that bridge, oh my God, it's full-on Phil Spector. As soon as you hear that rhythm, it's Phil Spector. But just that chord progression, from the "To thee I dedicate this photograph," the way the key changes to "You'll sometimes look, you'll sometimes look"—pure genius. And that guitar solo, man. I wish they would play that live. I've seen them a couple times recently and they don't play it. That's another song that should have been a huge radio hit and just wasn't. It's so obvious, right down to the handclaps and everything. It's such a perfect pop radio single. It's amazing to me that it didn't do anything.

Bill: You see later in the career when Ian Hunter is back for "Let Go," and you wonder why did they keep bringing in Ian Hunter for these songs that are very un-BÖC, shall we say? "Goin' Through the Motions" is another fun song, but I think it's easily the weakest song on the album. I'd be curious if there's an interview out there with Ian Hunter where he discusses this at all, his involvement with these Blue Öyster Cult songs that are not considered among the band's classics, to be kind.

John: I love Ian Hunter with Mott the Hoople and I love Ian Hunter on his own. I don't think this quite works. I don't think this was the right choice for a single and I think this is what stopped their momentum. Maybe they weren't gonna get a result as big as "(Don't Fear) The Reaper" from this album. But I think there were better songs on here, most notably "Death Valley Nights," which may have gone top 40 had they released that as the lead single instead. It just doesn't grab you. No matter how many times I listen to it, it's just okay.

Nick: Okay, "Goin' Through the Motions" is maybe the most controversial song on the album. I didn't appreciate it at first, but later becoming an Ian Hunter fan, I now love this song. I always did without knowing who wrote it. I love "Goin' Through the Motions." Looking it up, I was shocked about how they barely played this song ever, possibly less than 20 times ever. Because it was the first single, right?

Anyway, here's why I like the song. I was trying to figure it out. It's distinctly an Ian Hunter tune, but what he does is he can take a very sad, emotionally-charged topic, like a breakup or strife with a significant other, and he makes it into a happy tune. That is genius. Some of the best songs ever written are like that. They take a tough, tough topic and they make it almost fun-sounding.

Okay, you're going through the motions. I mean, you're looking at the lyrics and it's not happy stuff. So it's the fact that he can do that and put the spin on it with the melody and the chorus and everything. One song that came to mind like this was Foghat's cover of "Somebody's Been Sleepin' in My Bed." I mean it's a tough song and they make it all happy, a happy song.

Also, I saw something recently on Rick Beato's channel where he said all the top hits on the charts, none of them have a key change—none of them. It doesn't exist anymore. And "Goin' Through the Motions" has a key change towards the end. And I'm like, that's another little subtle thing in songwriting where you go from one key, an A to a B or whatever, and it's sometimes magical in a song. And they do a key change in there and I think it works. By the way at the end, the "ya-ya" part is Bruce Springsteen to me. And finally, given this is Ian Hunter, this is like the sequel to "Irene Wild." He actually gets the girl and it sucks; it fell apart (laughs). He's pining away for Irene Wild. He gets Irene Wild. He's miserable.

Rick: Very poppy, and I agree with Jim that it should have been a hit. I'm back to thinking about Gary Wright and *Dream Weaver* with this one (laughs). Just that kind of vocal expression that's definitely appealing to the female population. They're not just writing songs for guys here. They're writing songs for actually men and women, to be accessible. It's not going for the hardcore BÖC fan exclusively.

Martin: Before we move on, what do you think of this album cover?

Rick: I think it's kind of cool because it's like, well, where's the Ouija board? It looks like they're gonna have a séance or something. Knowing the history, it's not a bad album cover to me, but does it support the music? Not really. Godzilla would have been cool on the cover if they could get the rights to it. It would have sold more albums, because, interesting enough, they put a dinosaur on the cover a couple of albums later. But I think this shows them as mysterious. It looks like a secret meeting. But like I said, does it suit the record? Not as much as the black-and-white period covers did. I would have thought the music would be a little darker than it is.

Martin: Into the home stretch we have Buck all on his own, hopefully doing what he did last time he was left to his devices. "I Love the Night" was subsequently issued as a single, but only in the UK.

Rick: This is another easy listening BÖC song again seeking out maybe a bit more of a female audience. Power ballads are starting to filter into rock 'n' roll at this time, or maybe not power ballads but just heavy bands doing serious ballads. Journey would get on board and there's Kansas obviously. Like I say, FM want to get to the pop masses and not just serve the underground, so the labels want to get both genders to buy the records. This was a formula thing and it wasn't just a normal BÖC song. This was written to say, you know what? We have to write for the general population. Because there was Kiss with "Beth" and even Styx with "Lady" a few years before. They're all throwing one of those tunes in there; it's a signature move. And we all know that it soon becomes the norm in hard rock and heavy metal.

Bill: Absolutely, and how this song was not released as a single here, I will never know. This should have been pushed by the record company and been all over the rock stations. It's just a gorgeous song, with a perfect Buck vocal. I have a version from the Dharma archives with an extra verse. But I would have liked for them to have done a more complete version with that extra verse. But even without it, this is just such a pretty song. As for that extra verse, if I remember correctly, it got more explicit about the vampire nature of the song. I always knew that there was more to it. My friends and I have always thought of it as a vampire song even though the lyric's not necessarily explicit about that.

Martin: Tell me a bit more about Buck as a guitarist.

Bill: Buck has a pretty consistent tone. It's a pretty sound. I think of Johnny Hodges in the Duke Ellington Orchestra. Johnny kind of walked the line between something that's legitimately beautiful and something that goes over into say, smooth jazz or muzak territory. I kind of see some of Buck's guitar sounds like that. Or some of his sounds are just so pretty, they could almost be in like Kenny G musical territory. But I think Buck knows how to walk that line tastefully and not ever cross over into muzak territory.

Martin: While we're at it, how about Albert as a drummer?

Bill: I've always enjoyed his drumming. He's never going to be talked about as a drummer on the level of any of the greats, but he's got a certain jazziness to his sound that I like. I found out later by watching Albert's blogs that apparently Albert is a big Duke Ellington fan. He did an episode where he was actually playing an Ellington song on piano that he had learned, which I thought was cool. So that explains some of that jazzy influence.

Martin: And Allen? What was his role in the band?

Bill: I've been trying to figure that out for decades and I still haven't come to a good conclusion. I'm not even sure if Allen knew what it was. It seemed like he was always doing something else and never completely in the band 100%. Whether it was playing around with Patti Smith or anyone else, Allen remains a mystery to me. Which, with a band like this, it's good to have mystery, of course. In the later years he almost disappeared completely. I mean, he had that famous "Let's throw him a bone" writing credit on *Heaven Forbid*, with the live version of "In Thee" being included. But really, as a creative artist, as a songwriter, he kind of disappeared. I don't know how much he might have had in the can still that he never let out, or if he just stopped writing altogether at some point. I mean, musically, obviously, he was great. He was a perfect utility man in concert, because he could play different instruments and fill whatever role they needed. But you look at his songwriting contribution, historically, it's been a wild subject, but if I remember right, I think there's something like seven Allen songwriting contributions throughout the catalogue.

Martin: Cool, Bill, thanks for that. Anybody else want to chime in on "I Love the Night?"

Nick: I'm surprised "I Love the Night' is played live. Matter of fact, they even played it in 2022. Of the songs on this album, I won't say I dislike it, but I found it to be almost a miss. It's sort of melancholic, but it just lays there. It's the same tempo and dynamic throughout the song. Maybe it's where it tracks on the album that bothers me. But I was surprised to see that it's still played live. I guess it resonates with fans, so good for them.

John: I love this track; it's slow and beautiful and sensual. This is probably the first time they did sensual and it really works. Wonderful track.

Jim: "I Love the Night," my friend Eddie Kurdziel from the band Redd Kross—he passed away in '99—when we became friends when I moved to LA, he was a big Blue Öyster Cult fan. And we were talking and we both said at the same time that "I Love the Night" is our favourite Blue Öyster Cult song. And it very well may be for me still. Such a beautiful song and the little guitar things Buck does, wow. It's weird, because bands that are really great at being heavy, usually my favourite songs are the lighter ones. With Led Zeppelin it's "The Rain Song" and "No Quarter." But "I Love the Night" is super reverb-y; I like the production. Again, the drums are not super-heavy or punchy on this record. But to me, they're in the right spot. The guitars really do the work on these records, or the guitars and the keyboards and the vocals. The rhythm section's kind of there, but it's in a '70s way like The Eagles, where the drums and bass aren't super-driving the band. They're just kind of supporting all of that great guitar work. And that's what I like about *Spectres*. It's pre-1980s metal where it all became about the big pounding drums and the super-hard rhythms.

Martin: Okay, and Bill, speaking of vampire songs, our last track, "Nosferatu," might be as overtly vampiric as the band ever got, even more than "Tattoo Vampire."

Bill: Yes (laughs). "I Love the Night" becomes the perfect intro, so to speak, to "Nosferatu," with the band creating like a mini concept album by putting these songs back-to-back. But with the lyric being very straightforward, it doesn't quite have the mystery that so many other songs do. But it's so well-recorded. It really sounds good. I love the keyboards on it and it's one of Joe's finest moments as a songwriter with the band. Those two songs together create such a strong finish to the album. They're meant to be paired like that.

Nick: Man, "Nosferatu," grand piano, the song is big, everything's big in it, the chorus is big. It reminds me of something that would fit on *Imaginos*. You know the band more than me, Martin, but I could see that song laying on that album both lyrically and just sound-wise. It makes for a great album-closer. They never play it live, really—I think they played it twice.

Rick: Beautiful piano, very epic, dark undertone, beautiful vocal—it's spooky and I like that.

Jim: That's their sound right there—spooky. But it's spooky and not necessarily heavy. Great piano part at the beginning. I mean, nobody really did that. I kind of wish they kept doing that. They did sort of but not like that. Super-cool. They do have a lot of stuff about vampires, huh? Like I said, my friend basically said like, yeah, they're vampires and space.

Martin: And bikers.

Jim: Right. Biker vampires in space (laughs).

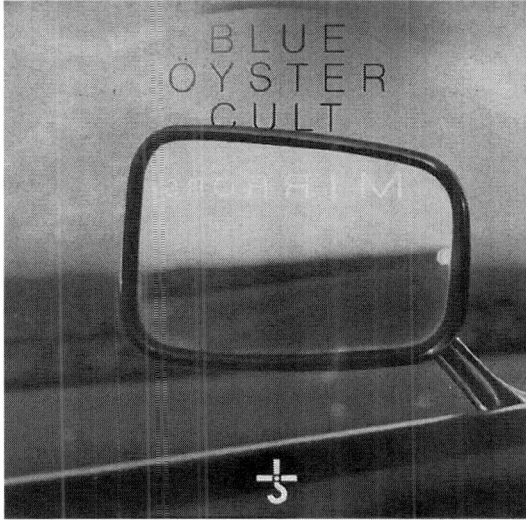

MIRRORS

Mirrors
June 19, 1979
Columbia JC 36009
Produced by Tom Werman
Recorded and mixed by Gary Ladinsky
Recorded at Kendun Recorders, Burbank, CA, CBS Recording Studios, New York, NY, The Record Plant, Los Angeles, CA
Personnel: Eric Bloom – vocals, rhythm guitar; Donald "Buck Dharma" Roeser – vocals, lead guitar; Joe Bouchard – bass, vocals; Allen Lanier – keyboards, guitar; Albert Bouchard – drums, vocals
Guest performers: Ellen Foley, Mickey Raphael, Genya Ravan, Wendy Webb

Side 1
1. "Dr. Music" (Meltzer, J. Bouchard, Roeser) 3:10
2. "The Great Sun Jester" (Michael Moorcock, John Trivers, Bloom) 4:48
3. "In Thee" (Lanier) 3:48
4. "Mirrors" (Roeser, Abbott) 3:44
5. "Moon Crazy" (J. Bouchard) 4:06

Side 2
1. "The Vigil" (Roeser, Sandy Roeser) 6:25
2. "I Am the Storm" (J. Bouchard, Ronald Binder) 3:42
3. "You're Not the One (I Was Looking for)" (A. Bouchard, Caryn Bouchard) 3:14
4. "Lonely Teardrops" (Lanier) 3:37

BLUE ÖYSTER CULT
MIRRORS
With one eye looking back and nine eyes on the road ahead, Blue Öyster Cult presents "Mirrors."
Blue Öyster Cult does it all with "Mirrors." On Columbia Records and Tapes.
Recorded and mixed by Gary Ladinsky. Produced by Tom Werman. Management: Sandy Pearlman & Murray Krugman.
"Columbia," are trademarks of CBS Inc. © 1979 CBS Inc.

Martin talks to Jamie Laszlo, Steven Reid, Nick S. Squire and Matt Thompson about *Mirrors*.

Martin Popoff: Okay, so now we gotta deal with *Mirrors*, which is pretty contentious, and frankly generally disliked. We did an episode of our *Contrarians* YouTube show where I called it my favourite of the catalogue, and although today I'd maybe put *Cultösaurus* or *Fire* higher, it's still at least top five for me. But I know I'm in the minority. What's the complexion of this record for you folks?

Steven Reid: What's the complexion of this record? Wow. I mean, we're not quite in the '80s yet, but it does feel like we are, doesn't it? We seem to be just a little half-step ahead. And at the same time, a half-step behind. It's an interesting idea. Blue Öyster Cult always felt to me like they evolved. There were changes made—that was then, this is now, this is what we're doing, but that's connected to here.

With hindsight, *Mirrors* fits into that perfectly. Admittedly, I was too young to buy this at the time. But at the time I can understand why people kind of went, "Whoa, whoa, whoa, excuse me? What is happening right now? Why have I got an AOR album?" That isn't what this is. I'm a big AOR fan. Yes, it's informed by that. The production is great by the way; the production is really good. It's crisp and it's clear. It's informative and helps everything on the album to come together. Separation is really good. Which is not something you can necessarily say about all of the albums in this catalogue. I think, actually, that the production itself is a triumph.

Whether that necessarily results in an album that's the same triumph in everyone's mind is another matter entirely. As I said, you bring yourself to an album. I like melodic rock. This is as melodic rock as BÖC ever really got, I think, but it does still feel like it's on their terms. But I can understand fans at that time going, "Just exactly what are we doing?"

Jamie Laszlo: I'd call *Mirrors* their most grounded album. I think it's the most song-oriented album. It's probably why it was my favourite growing up, because I was a song-oriented guy. That's why I was a Crosby, Stills & Nash fan at a young age. When a lot a lot of my peers were listening to other things, I was putting in *Déjà Vu* and stuff like that. Not that I didn't like metal as well. But I was also listening to the singer-songwriter stuff and I think this has a singer-songwriter mentality to it. It reminds me a little bit of if Crosby, Stills & Nash had a metallic edge to them. And I love the backup singers on three of the tracks. I don't think there's another album by BÖC that has female backup singers. Anyway, the album just goes down easy. There are other BÖC albums that are like a dark beer, or IPA. This is just your Dos Equis—it just goes down easy. I think the production helps with that smoothness. It's produced well, but as I get older, I think maybe it's produced a little too well.

Nick S. Squire: Just to let you know where I was at in life, I bought *Mirrors* around the same time I bought *Spectres* for $1. I can tell you that in my corner of the world in northeastern Pennsylvania, when I was a teenager and I'm discovering *Agents of Fortune* and *Fire of Unknown Origin*, you're going through the racks and you'd see the usual suspects. I'm here to tell you, I have never ever seen this album new in a store. And when I first saw it, I thought it was Buck Dharma's *Flat Out* album. I just thought it was like an alternate cover because of the similarity of the sky and all that. I'm like, what? And then I pick it up and I thought maybe it's a greatest hits. And then I'm looking at it like, wow, it's an actual album. I knew "Dr. Music" because *Extraterrestrial Live* was the first album by BÖC I got. But I was just amazed. As soon as I saw it, I bought it.

But I'm here to tell you just wherever I go, if I'm checking BÖC out, you just never see this in stores. It's sort of the forgotten album. And I know that you have a penchant for it. I like the album, but I can also tell you that the greatest thing about prepping for this exercise was discovering that this album is a lot better than its fate would suggest.

I know Tom Werman is criticised for his production. But I don't find that the production is all that different from *Spectres*. Why? Pianos are still front and centre; vocal harmonies are still front and centre. Both are still big in the arrangements and the overall dynamic, still part of the thing. There wasn't like a radical shift. Now we're gonna be a much heavier band or something. Those core elements are still there because the band is pretty much writing on their own. They have the usual lyrical help, but overall the album to me is not a marked departure from *Spectres*, except for being slicker and maybe in the kinds or songs that ended up on the album, if you will. There was no big song. You know, "Godzilla" is undeniable. When you hear the riff and it's a heavy song, there's nothing like "Godzilla" on this. So maybe that's the biggest criticism of the album is that you don't have a "Godzilla" or even an "R. U. Ready 2 Rock."

Matt Thompson: With *Mirrors*, I'd say that the repercussion of having such a big hit with "The Reaper" continue. The band experience a surprise hit with that song and with *Agents of Fortune*. They see the benefits of being commercially successful. They do try really hard with *Spectres* to have another hit—there's quality material on *Spectres*—but they don't catch lightning in the bottle the same way. They don't get anything near a "Reaper"-level hit. But I think there's a real strong desire for the band to create.

What's the next step we can do? Let's change the producer. I think they were really tired and fed up. They had sort of a three-headed production monster on *Spectres*, with Krugman, Lucas and Pearlman, right? And that's not a team made up of three people. Those are three independent people working individually on those songs. Now let's get someone in with some track record. Tom Werman has a track record with Cheap Trick and Ted Nugent and he makes records that sound good, and he'll have a more singular approach to this record. It'll have some cohesion. The band is still going with their *Agents of Fortune*-and-beyond songwriting approach of everyone bringing in demos. Let's run them through the gauntlet, we'll take some to preproduction. And they spent a lot of time on these songs. They did like three months of preproduction on this record. Tom Werman gets to pick the ones that make the cut. Turns out that there's a lot of sort of unrecorded or later-recorded nuggets that were done at this time, but by picking songs, his aesthetic is influencing not just the sound, but even the material.

Martin: I'll take umbrage that his Cheap Trick or Ted Nugent records sound any better than *Agents* or *Spectres*, but I gotta say it: a huge part of me rating *Mirrors* so high is because I think it's the best sounding album they ever did. It's actually got tops and bottoms on it, good warm bass and sizzling, hi-fidelity cymbals and high-hats.

Matt: Yeah, well, I love the vocals. It's the best vocal-sounding album probably that they've ever had. Excepting maybe the latest one, because that one shows good attention to detail. But all the singers sound really good on *Mirrors*. There's great sort of layering of vocals and it sounds really good. It has a nice cohesive production to it. I think the guitars are little bit wimpy sounding. I do think an advantage that the two Martin Birch ones that followed had is that they are harder-hitting with the guitars and a little bit harder-hitting with the drums. Werman's approach was much more perfectionist. I don't know if you can throw this into the production, but time is quite rigid on this album. In some cases that's good. If you're executing a pop song that you want to be sort of immediate, that works well. There's nothing really jarring in there. You do miss a little bit of Albert Bouchard's swing. It doesn't quite groove the way that previous albums have. It's a really interesting production. It stands out in the catalogue.

Martin: Steven, am I crazy? I don't think Matt is particularly agreeing with me here.

Steven: Well, I'm a bit of both. I'll agree that the BÖC records and the Cheap Tricks and Nugents, sure, they are all a little midrangey, but is the *Mirrors* production *too* good? Is that the problem? That suddenly we've got a really bold record where there's maybe too much being revealed all at once? Maybe that's the issue. For me, with Blue Öyster Cult, it was always about put it on, immerse yourself and get to know it. And I think with *Mirrors* it's still very clever but possibly too immediate. There's still a lot going on underneath, but we get caught up in big choruses, bolder keyboard sounds, much more obvious sounds, if that makes sense. But I get your point: it's to do with clarity. *Mirrors* is a very hi-fidelity album all around. It's high-gloss; there's a real sheen to it.

Martin: All right, I don't think I can win this one! Let's tear into the album, beginning with "Dr. Music." Thoughts? I mean, I always perceive this as quite the rocker, but the verse is kind of goofy.

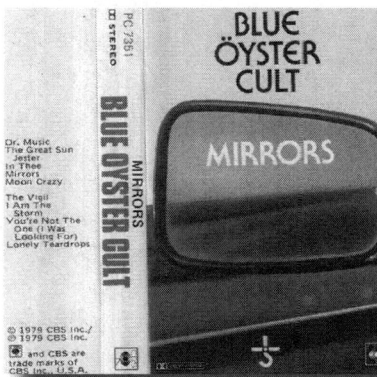

Jamie: My least favourite song on the album. I'm glad it's first so we get it out of the way because I know better things are coming. Yeah, it's heavy but it's got that primitive songwriting to the verse part, so I agree with you there. I think it's saved by the backup singers. Yeah, that verse is kind of corny-sounding and so is the whole "Call me Dr. Music" idea. I went to JCPenney when I was a teenager and they had scrubs for sale. But they were like cool scrubs, and it said "Dr. Music" on it. So I bought it because I knew the most music trivia of any of my peers. I wore it and became Dr. Music. So when I play this song, it reminds me of that goofy 16-year-old walking around with Dr. Music on his scrubs. And grown up now at 53, I'm thinking that was kind of cringe-worthy of me to do that. So I get a little cringey when I hear that song (laughs).

Steven: The start of a song says a lot. I don't know if it's Linn drums or some other kind of electronic drums, but that modern tom sound hitting you right at the very start, I remember going, "Something different." It's brave, a little cavalier, shall we say? But it's not all the way through, so you don't get those horrible things that lots of bands got seduced into trying. But it always makes me giggle when I hear that. Because a lot of Blue Öyster Cult, you listen to an album and can you place it in the year it came out without knowing it. Probably not all of it. As we've discussed, the earlier stuff sounds older than their years and then it moves around a bit for some of them. But there's very few moments on these albums where you'll listen to one thing and immediately go, yep, yep, early '80s—that's where we are, right at the cusp of electronic music going, "I can do something different." And I hear those toms and I go, "Why? They're not needed!" I mean, it sounds even earlier than 1979.

But to me the essence of this song are those glorious female backing vocals from Genya Ravan and Ellen Foley, the latter who worked with Meat Loaf on many a duet, by the way. They're just absolutely great on this. And that in itself takes you to somewhere else with this band. Yeah, it's a bit rock 'n' rollsy, with those vocals, and they've always alluded to tradition before in rhythms and beats and sort of guitar structures. But this is uncommonly happy and upbeat. Strangely, there were quite a lot of bands doing things along those lines at this point. There's some real kind of honky-tonk proficiency in here as well. It's definitely different from what we've heard before.

But you move past that slick—and I think interesting—production, there's still some bulging slices of guitars in here. They don't necessarily reveal themselves in quite the same way that we would have anticipated from what had come before And again, some of Joe's bass work, it bulges in all the right places. I will admit I'm someone that doesn't like harmonica— I'm not a fan. But give it to Mickey Raphael at the end of this song and it's dusty as hell. It just grates against you in all the right ways and it works a treat. And same again, it's those dynamics, it's those clever differences. There's a solo section at the end where it's just Buck wailing away over drums and suddenly we're in a completely different place from where the song started.

Matt: "Dr Music" is a riff-oriented BÖC song in the lineage of "Cities on Flame" and "E.T.I.," where you've got this ascending and descending riff to it, underneath a Richard Meltzer lyric. Eric's vocal is produced well, Buck's guitar sounds really alive and there's a lot going on. Mickey Raphael; that's Willie Nelson's harmonica player, so a real interesting collaboration. You've got some zesty percussion added to it. You get just this slight S&M reference in Richard's lyric. There are traces of this S&M thing in past BÖC songs, particularly in "Dominance and Submission," at least the title, and a little bit in "The Red & the Black," with "I got a whip in my hand" and "At leather's end." But it's very slight here because they are prudish and have a desire to be commercially successful (laughs). So it doesn't really show through on the song. In any event, "Dr. Music" becomes a good live favourite, right? It works as an opener.

Nick: They had four different singles for various territories and this wasn't one of them. But I love it. "Dr. Music" is timeless. Micky Raphael's harmonica, with that sort of old-style harmonica microphone, that gives it a Howlin' Wolf feel. He's been on everyone's recordings on the planet. BÖC and Willie Nelson were both on Columbia at the time. Mickey for decades has been the main man in Willie Nelson's touring band.

Quick story, stadium tour, Bob Dylan and Willie Nelson. Bob Dylan was terrible; one of the worst shows I've ever seen. Anyway, waiting outside to get into the venue at a minor league stadium, and we're all in line there, early enough, and walking down the street comes Mickey Raphael. I knew who he was because I'm kind of an idiot savant like that. He's getting closer and I just went, "Hey, Mickey, how ya doing?" He initially thought he knew me because of the way I was sort of gregarious. And he's like, "Hey, how are you?" Then he realized he didn't know me from Adam and he hightailed it out. But we shook hands, exchanged pleasantries, and everybody around is like, "You know Mickey?!" "Man, never met him."

The other thing is, you got Genya Ravan and Ellen Foley on "Dr. Music" and another song and those two are great. Genya Ravan produced the first Dead Boys album, *Young, Loud and Snotty.* "Dr. Music" is still in the setlist; they played it in 2022, and I believe "The Vigil" hasn't disappeared either. But yeah, I first got to know it through *ETL.* Anyway, great way to open the album, still holds up, and I don't want to beat it to death, but the girls singing in the background really adds something to the song. And you've got two of the best there with Ellen Foley, background singer for "Paradise by the Dashboard Light." I mean, fantastic.

Martin: I've raved about the production to no effect, but here's another reason I like this album so much: "The Great Sun Jester."

Jamie: They're all kind of similar, aren't they? With the acoustic guitars and big melodies going on. Again, it's the production and those acoustic guitars that make it go down so easy. And the songwriting is top-notch. I think writing songs like this is much more difficult than writing prog rock. Prog rock is just coming up with a bunch of different ideas that last about a minute, putting it all together and calling it a long piece. Coming up with a foundation for one four-minute song and making it memorable, giving you a hook like "Pretty girls can't look away," or "I'm the joker of the universe," that's not easy to do. That well goes dry. You don't even think of those hooks; those hooks come to you. You think of prog rock, you're putting the pieces together. This comes to you and it doesn't always come to you and when it stops coming to you, you need someone like Richie Castellano to come into the band and give you that spark again.

Steven: Many people accuse this of being the band's AOR album, and okay, with the keyboards here, I kind of get it. I mean, we're almost in Foreigner "Waiting for a Girl Like You" territory here. To me, this is the sound of a band trying to embrace maybe what's big at the moment. And that is not something that you would necessarily associate with BÖC.

Martin: You know what's big at the moment?—Styx. I mean, that's what this sounds like to me, BÖC participating in this short-lived pomp rock genre, which was mostly a handful of baby bands, but ruled in 1979 by Styx.

Steven: Well, yes, that's true. Good point. Which I'm a fan of too. Yeah, absolutely, it does. And yet the songwriting doesn't quite. When you listen to Styx, they were quite happy to kind of stop a song for 20 seconds and give you a huge bank of choral voices. That band is layered and layered and layered. Blue Öyster Cult are not going to do that because ultimately that's not their DNA. They're still a rock 'n' roll band. So there's these dualities fighting for supremacy on this album and it doesn't always work.

Yeah, I think it actually does, to be honest (laughs). This is one of my favourite Blue Öyster Cult albums. I mean, it doesn't necessarily sound like that, the way I'm talking about it, but I really like this album. There's always so much more to go back to here. Every time I put it on, I think, oh yeah, right. This is a dense album, but it's not a dense production.

And that's maybe part of its problem. In this song, I think musically and lyrically, we feel at odds here. Are they talking about the destruction of the sun? Possibly. I don't know. It's Michael Moorcock here. And then there's a response: Buck really bends that guitar solo into that kind of science fiction theme. He's always able to tell a story with what he's playing on the fretboard—really clever. And the way that it kind of swoops tastefully but excitingly as he goes for that kind of end section, also really clever and musical and fitted to the theme.

As a melodic rock lover like myself, there's so much here to enjoy. It's really well put together. The intricate piano runs that counterpoint those guitars... the ever-busy but never over-busy snare work—really good. It's crafted stuff. And to me it's as far from an AOR knockoff as it could possibly be. Modern criticism will tell you this is throwaway AOR. Whoa, it's absolutely not. It's absolutely not. It's really clever hard rock with a little bit of polish, is what it is.

Matt: The first of the Michael Moorcock collaborations. And Eric Bloom collaborating with John Trivers, who is a successful collaborator for him, going forward; this is basically the team for "Black Blade" and John Trivers helps him out with "Sole Survivor" and "After Dark." Some of it is based on the novel *The Fireclown*, by Michael Moorcock. It's more of a sci-fi than a fantasy lyric for him. It's got sort of bombastic acoustic guitars, combined with the electric, throughout.

All three of the Michael Moorcock collaborations are successful, but here's the sad part with respect to the recording of this album. Tom Werman does not like Eric Bloom's voice. He likes Buck Dharma, which makes sense with his pop sensibilities; he connects with that. Eric is left with not as much to do, and Tom doesn't really want Eric playing guitar on it either. And so this song is the one moment where Eric really gets to shine, although he also sings two others. It's Eric's lone writing credit and there are no inside BÖC collaborators with him on it. It's a very strong song for him, and it's going to kick off a successful trilogy.

Nick: "Moorcock also worked with Hawkwind, in various configurations. I like the experiment. I think that this song would have been a great album-ender, based on the lyrical content and just the mood of the song. I like the piano flourishes in it. There's a certain ethereal quality to the song. It builds in volume and in energy. Yeah, it feels misplaced after "Dr. Music," but I do like the song a lot and the acoustic guitar is fantastic. It's BÖC still trying to sound poppy but also a little proggy, and then they reverse course. *Mirrors* comes after three big albums in a row—*Agents*, *Spectres*, and then the *Some Enchanted Evening* live album did well. And then this one sort of just laid there. And then they reverse course a bit with *Cultösaurus Erectus* and try to be dark and heavy again, which, as it turned out, didn't stop the sales decline.

Martin: Next is "In Thee," and as much as I love this song, I could listen to it just to marvel at how good those acoustic guitars sound, and how Joe and Albert lock in as a rhythm section.

Steven: Agreed. There are a lot of nuances that get lost in this album. There's a gentle country inflection here, which is a theme that pops in and out of this album. I mean, it's maybe commercial '70s country, not really gritty with dead dogs and all this kind of stuff. But listen to the way that Buck twangs expertly against his own really excellent vocals. And it's bolstered by the kind of sway and sweetness of this song. Then you've got some strings courtesy of Jai Winding. It reinforces that feel but you're not being spoon-fed. It's smooth. But I can understand three songs in, people going, "What band is this that I'm listening to? What is the record on the turntable?" Lyrically it feels a little simple, but it's a beautifully constructed love song. It's not really the oeuvre that you would expect this band to be plowing. It doesn't really tick the boxes for me and you kind of expect a little bit more, but you know, I'm not gonna deny the band some love.

Nick: Whether intentional or not, given that Allen Lanier wrote it, boy, there's some tricks in there that are almost a lift from Harry Nilsson. I know that sounds off-the-wall but it's in the melody and the trick with the vocal and the way things stop. I know they're still playing it in 2022. I love the harmonies in the song which are again like classic '50s-type stuff. I wonder if that title, "In Thee," held this song back. It's odd. I don't know if American people could kind of wrap their head around those sort of Olde English words. Maybe you have to be a fan of BÖC to accept that. But on a superficial level, on radio, I don't know if that's going to connect with people. I was attracted because the song is great. I don't know why it didn't do more business, because it was put out there and it's got everything I like in a BÖC song. But yeah, Harry Nilsson. If you're gonna cop stuff from somebody, it's advisable to be him.

Martin: All right, onto the title track, which I think should have been a smash hit single.

Steven: Absolutely, for any of the naysayers that stuck it out 'til this point, oh, wow. It shimmers, this title track; it's of a world in itself. It's subtle, yet there's still these bristling guitars and a bass line that knocks you sideways. Simple but effective. Plus I'm a sucker for things like Vibraslap. Great vocal from Buck, but the backing vocals from Ravan and Foley steal the show; they become the focal point. And Buck decides to augment that with some really interesting, pleasing and short guitar bursts.

Martin: And you know, Steven, those completely charming backing vocals connect directly with the whole '60s girl group sub-narrative in BÖC, but so does that chorus, which I sometimes call "dependable 'Louie Louie' chords." And that all connects to New York rock, this sort of traditional '50s and '60s throwback feel of the New York sound you hear in BÖC.

Steven: Yeah, actually, you've put your finger on something that I couldn't quite articulate in my head when I was going through this album again. That is a girl group sound. Yes, absolutely. And it's so well-integrated in a couple of songs here. It should sound completely out of place because we're almost two decades down the line at this point, or a decade-and-a-half realistically, from that being a thing. Yeah. But it's natural here and it flows. And same again, it shows the band's dexterity, because it's them molding themselves into different situations without sounding forced and hackneyed.

And I like that there's both a strength and a fragility in those female vocals, that I think really lends itself to this song, which also really works well with the lyric. Are we talking about self-obsession? Are we looking in a mirror? Is that what it's all about? How do I look? How beautiful am I? Or are we looking into the mirror and saying, you know, who will I be today? Because what is reflected back is what everybody sees. It's not what is going on inside. That's a completely different thing. I've often wondered, is this song just about that vanity, or is it actually about the safety of people not really knowing more than what you see in the mirror? And the female vocals on this really convey that kind of difference in jeopardy really well. In the best possible way it leaves you hanging. You don't know if you should dislike the character that you're listening to here, or actually feel real empathy for her—or him.

Matt: It's interesting, first of all, that you get a title track! That's not something Blue Öyster Cult had done up to this point. Buck's wife Sandy sings on the demo version of the song, and so they keep that idea. It has a very prominent female vocal part to the song, in the chorus itself. It's not quite as hooky or as venturesome as the other Buck Dharma hit songs, so it does not become a hit. I mean, it's substantially hooky but it doesn't have a lyric quite as full-on, grab-your-attention, of a successful pop song. Throughout, you've got three songs with female vocals. It's an interesting thing they're trying to do. Again, kind of smoothing out the edges for pop success.

Nick: Absolutely, those backup vocals burrow into your brain. You gotta like that "Pretty girls can't look away." I felt the song was hit material, and it was issued as a single, but only in the UK. And I agree that it's a New York sound with those girls singing. This could be Ian Hunter. It could be BÖC. It could be Southside Johnny. But it's not Deep Purple and it's not Black Sabbath. "Mirrors" elevates this album. There's a subtle complexity. Even though it has the dependable "Louie Louie" chords, as you call them, it's everything working together. It's not "Godzilla," I guess, in terms of heaviness, but I just think the song is great.

Jamie: What I get from "Mirrors" is kind of like "The Machine" from *The Symbol Remains*, which talks about how we love our phones so much. "Mirrors" is about vanity, how we love ourselves looking at the mirror so much. So they're similar in a way. But I like how he describes what a mirror is in the beginning. I just like the texture of it, because he's talking about something simple, but he makes it sound complex at the same time. Maybe there's a hidden meaning behind it that I'm not getting.

The backup singers add a nice dimension to it. Man, this came out in June of '79. How was "Mirrors" not the summer hit of the year? It should have been the first single and it should be better known than "Godzilla." It's one of the best songs they ever wrote. It's infectious, so catchy, and the backup singers doing the "Pretty girls can't look away," that should have been on every beach radio as you walk down the beach in 1979. You should have heard that on everyone's little transistor radio as you walk by as the big hit of the year. And I don't know why it wasn't.

Martin: Side one ends with "Moon Crazy," which to my mind, lines up with the likes of "Tenderloin" and "Searchin' for Celine," these songs that are really only going to please the most dedicated BÖC fan and certainly nobody from the outside looking in.

Steven: Sure (laughs) and I have to say that it literally lets the side down. This is the only thing on this whole album for me that feels a bit old hat and a bit clichéd. But Buck seems to notice the peril, and steps in with a solo that twists things up. You know, it's straight rock 'n' roll themes but he's adding something a bit more mysterious. He saves the song from tumbling. But it's not the most memorable compared to what's come before. Again, you get a hint of country, with that intricate fingerpicking that Buck does at the end. It's fleeting, it's just a couple of seconds of it, it doesn't overstay its welcome. You get to the end and almost go, "Did I invent that? That didn't really happen just there, did it?" Because it doesn't need to be there.

It's just a beautiful little moment where you think, yeah, that's clever song construction. And I really do think that those little moments stop the song from being ho-hum in total.

Nick: I know you're gonna roll your eyes, but I could probably talk about this song for 20 minutes. First of all, they've never played it live. Second, it's got a '50s/'60s rock 'n' roll vibe, which validates the song being released as a single in Japan, with the rock 'n' roll revival thing that they do there. That piano-driven rock 'n' roll thing is all the rage in Japan at that time. Third, it's a shuffle, but I love how it goes from the shuffle into this Elton John/ Neil Sedaka chorus. It's not a time signature change but it may as well be, because it goes from shuffle to that straight time and then it goes back to the shuffle without an end. You know what I mean? It's just boom, boom, boom. Piano drives it. Bass drives it. There's walking bass lines, there's harmony vocals.

And then the end... I love the end. The ending of the song goes into like a Blues Brothers gospel revival with handclaps and piano, and I'm thinking about the Blues Brothers with them dancing in the aisles and doing backflips. And this is before the movie, which came out the following year. Yeah, I love love love this song. And I think it also tells you what that band can do. I know personally you don't like shuffles and have railed against them, but this is maybe a shuffle done right? It's a little quicker, plus you have the tempo changes and the gospel revival. So there's these dynamics back and forth, and it makes the chorus all that more catchy. But it's funny, the lyrics didn't resonate. I just cared about the music. If you asked me what moon crazy means, it's whatever; I just love the song.

Jamie: "Moon crazy, summer of changes, let the night shine on;" it's a little cheesy. Plus it's a start/stop song on an album that prides itself on being smooth-sounding. I guess that jarring juxtaposition adds weirdness. But it's not even a weird song. It comes across as a little bit of a joke to take you out of your smooth sailing conception of the record.

Martin: All right, over to side two, with "The Vigil," my favourite BÖC song ever and one we played live with our band Torque in the '80s. Bottom line, this does about half of the heavy lifting for me to vault *Mirrors* into my top five BÖC albums.

Steven: Playing it live—very cool. Yeah, if side one closes on a less interesting note, flip the record over and it welcomes you back. To me, agreed, it's better than everything that's come before on the album, and it's better than everything that's going to come. This is Blue Öyster Cult bold, threatening, unapologetic, getting the message across, melodic as hell, but still really dark. It seems like it's all of their specialities rolled up in one. It's classic Cult. I mean, that middle eight, the soaring harmony vocals played off those machine gun drums, it's taking you to different places, offering you different options at that point. You don't really even know where that song is gonna go. But the pinpoint guitar sprinkles... it takes you to the heavens that have been alluded to in the lyrics.

And the music is doing the same as the lyrics, so it's really coming together. It's really smart—and glorious, absolutely glorious. But then when the huge verse riff comes crashing back through the doors, it wipes all that away. It's doubled it down, hasn't it? You're left marvelling at just how mighty the whole journey has become. I'm not sure it gets much better than this, to be honest. Yeah, absolutely love it. I could listen to it all day.

Lyrically I like the subject matter too. I don't know; is it, "We're the aliens" or is it, "We can't be the only ones." Is it, "Why haven't they come to save us from ourselves yet?" Or is it, "Well, they already have and decided that we're beyond that and have left us to our own destructive devices." You're left with no conclusion. But you're left with all these possibilities and that is perfect for the song. It doesn't say, well, this is the defining factor. All of those elements just come together to make it much more than the parts would have been.

Matt: Really interesting song, right? It becomes a Blue Öyster Cult standard. Very well regarded in the canon and rightfully so. It's in the Buck masterpiece category, like "E.T.I.," where he writes the music originally to a different lyric. Or even something like "Lips in the Hills," where Buck comes up with some great musical ideas and is just matching it up with different lyrics.

Originally this was a Patti Smith lyric, "The Devil's Nail," and lyrically, I mean, that is out there. It's definitely too out there for a Blue Öyster Cult song. Their prudishness would not allow that; it would not fit their prudish commercial sensibilities at the time (laughs). So he writes, with his wife Sandy, a tremendous lyric, a UFO lyric, with references to Roswell. It pretty much fits in with the non-*Imaginos* aesthetic of the band lyrically, which is a lot of sci-fi, a lot of alien stuff like "Take Me Way" or "E.T.I."

Cool middle part, which is a Buck specialty. You got this middle part, instrumental break, that is a real changeup. You get it in "Reaper," you get it in "Harvest Moon" and now you get in "The Vigil." There's an interesting use of delay on the guitar and there's that really light melodic part. And I love his guitar tone on the lead part, which is not that much of a Buck Dharma tone to me. To me it reminds me of Brad Whitford on "Kings and Queen," the outro solo there. You've got a little bit more neck pickup tone and really just judicious use of delay and reverb, a really sweet guitar tone. Love that part.

Jamie: I thought it was a bit long, Martin, at six-and-a-half minutes. I think it out-textures itself a little bit, until we get to the middle where it becomes a bit like background music to me where I'm not paying attention as much as I should be. It becomes a wall of textured sound. Sorry to rip on your favourite BÖC song of all time.

Nick: We go from the swing of "Moon Crazy" to "The Vigil," with this precise, metronomic beat. It's a total contrast and I like that. You've got the vocal harmonies at centre stage and the end jam is really cool. They're still playing it live. I mean, this song gets more love… I didn't realize this song was played live more than "Dr. Music." That was a surprise to me. "The Vigil" is another song that could have been a hit, I guess. I don't know. I mean, if it was, it would be because of that super-memorable riff that they use during the verse, because otherwise it's a little involved.

Martin: Next is "I Am the Storm" which I always aligned with "Dr. Music." It's got that same bait-and-switch thing, with the heavy, complicated riff that gives way to something a little more straight-line at the verse. Same kind of tempo too, a little slower but close.

Nick: Yeah, and lots of that mid-paced groove, plus lots of piano. Bloom sings it but Joe wrote it, which is interesting. The imagery in the lyrics is really vivid, but man, that's a tough thing to read in 2023. It's basically about a guy being pissed-off at a woman and he's aggressive and he's talking about violence. I mean, the music is good, but unless I'm missing something in there, it's not the best narrative in 2023. Maybe you have to think about it in relation to somebody other than a significant other. But, again, on face value it's written about a woman and he's talking about basically obliterating the person off the face of the earth. So it's a tough listen in this day and age. I didn't pick up on that. Maybe that's my problem. It takes a while for me because I'm always listening for other things in a song. Not the best.

Steven: Shocking lyric notwithstanding, I'm gonna go out on a limb and say that following "The Vigil" with "I Am the Storm" might make this one of the best—if not the best—quick one-two punches in this band's catalogue. Eric

Bloom's vocals are at the peak of their powers here. Perfect match for the rolling guitars and the pounding rhythms. I used to play the drums many moons ago. I love how the beat switches from that almost straight four-on-the-floor, with the snare hauling the whole song along almost ahead of the beat, and then the ride cymbal takes it to the offbeat. Never underestimate the power of the offbeat. I mean, we are changing everything by changing very little. And I love how it comes and goes.

Before you really get to know the song, there are points where you think that offbeat is going to come back and it doesn't. That's good. I really like that because it's also a weapon that can be overused, but it really adds urgency. And that is to me is an element of something that's coursing through the whole band here. There's an urgency. The snare snap is constant, there are mini rolls on everything, the guitars are just searing. Everyone is responding to the call. Again, they're building a track ever higher and higher.

There's an anger, an innate seething-ness in this song. And lyrically, like Nick, I never really picked up on that aspect, which is disturbing. To me it was always more of a universal, "You've been warned. Don't cross me." And this song conveys that 100%. The whole song is saying don't mess with me. But to circle back, yeah, these two songs together create a sort of synergy.

Martin: Things lighten up considerable with "You're Not the One (I Was Looking for)" which, famously, Albert turned in as a bit of a joke on the popularity of The Cars.

Nick: I don't like the tracking decision here. The last two tracks were not the best ones to end the album. Like I say, I felt that "Sun Jester" could have been put back there and these songs buried somewhere else. "You're Not the One (I Was Looking for)" is an Albert vocal and it didn't grab me the way maybe it should have. After he does the lyric about the fancy ladies who can talk and talk, you hear the scrambled sped-up words. I love that. I'm going, "Where did that come from?!" I thought that was a neat little trick. There's this really cool chorus, and I like his off-kilter, slightly off vocal delivery. All told though, a bit of a ho-hum track for me.

Steven: I struggle with this song. Any song that has you singing the lyrics to something else over it as you'll listen to it, that's trouble. I had heard The Cars long before I'd heard this, so I'm singing "Just What I Needed" over the top of that song when I hear it. I know it was brought in as a parody. I know it wasn't necessarily even brought in as a serious option for the album. And other people kind of went, "Yeah, hey, but it's too good to put to the side."

It is. But in context, it's not—because it's been done. I mean, it really has been done. This is a rewrite. And it's a blatant rewrite. It doesn't pretend to be anything other than that.

Even the song title is almost a call-and-response to "Just What I Needed." You got just what I needed. You're not the one I was looking for. Are they kind of saying that anyone can do this? Yeah, the Cars song was a huge hit. Everyone loves it. Everyone's singing it. This is how easy it is to put that together. Well, it clearly is. Because you listen to them back-to-back, and while they're not the same song, it's the same song. And yet, if I put it on, am I going to bop along to it? Yeah, probably am. I mean, that's some good, fine, fluid guitar work here, so it's not a clunker completely. Had it not been on the album, would I miss it? Not really.

Martin: Okay, and to close out, we've got "Lonely Teardrops," a funky clavinet-driven song written by Allen and sung by Buck.

Matt: Yeah, so Allen is relatively engaged on this album, right? For him he's being prolific, he's bringing multiple songs—two—to the record. This was something that he wrote originally as "Wind in my Veins," or maybe it would have been vanes. It's moody, it's melancholy and I love the end part of the song. We get a bit of a drum break, not fancy at all, sparse, and then the Wendy Webb vocal kicks in with the "lonely teardrops" outro refrain—very haunting. It has that eerie urban-ness that the best Allen Lanier songs have, like "Tenderloin" on *Agents of Fortune*. It's different from what the rest of the band does. Strong song, under-appreciated; I guess it's a deep cut.

Nick: With the clavinet, you have what is almost a passé instrument driving the song, right? You're thinking Stevie Wonder with "Superstition" from years ago and early Stones and other bands. But in my sort of meat-and-potatoes rock world, the chord changes get to me. It's not exactly jazzy but there are some odd chord changes. I feel like I'm in the lounge of The Love Boat, listening to that song here at the end of the album. So those last two tracks for me are anti-climactic, compared to the first seven, which were fantastic.

Steven: The guitar tones and the keyboard sounds on this song have always reminded me of *In Through the Out Door* from Led Zeppelin. That's always where it's taken me. Again, it's got that slightly kind of countrified thing. There's a bit of a jaunt to it. And then you go back and look at it and go, hold on, this came out a couple months before *In Through the Out Door*. So it's complete coincidence.

One of the things that Blue Öyster Cult does is they like to close an album in an understated fashion. It's been a strange journey across side two. You've got an absolute behemoth of a song, you've got a fantastic follow-up, and then you've got a rock 'n' roll jingle/new wave thing that just kind of goes away. And then we're back for something else that's completely understated, with clever interplay between the Bouchard brothers, song by Allen, vocal by Buck. They're creative—aren't they absolutely great? Here we are at the end and they've opened up different layers and different textures. They allow so much more to happen in these songs because the guitars are never tied down. You know, we've built this—you go play. It's a really key aspect of this band. I think this song serves as a metaphor for the album as a whole.

Jamie: When that girl sings, it sounds like one lonely teardrop falling down your face.

Martin: Yes, nice! (laughs). Okay, so have we rehabilitated the reputation of this album or is it still deserving of its middling status?

Nick: Well, it's hard to tell. It seems like there are singles on it, right? You know, they had three bangers and the live album was a banger too—both live albums—and maybe people wanted son of "Godzilla." That's the only thing I could think of. That they're catering to more of a hard rock crowd and this did not give it to them. *Cultösaurus* didn't deliver any hits either. *Mirrors* is not them finding their way after a flop or something like *Creatures of the Night* was after *The Elder*. I mean, BÖC had platinum and gold right in a row so they're supposed to be building on that. And from my ears I don't see it as a great departure from *Spectres*. It has all those key elements in there including the piano and the vocal harmonies and everything. Is it because there's no "Godzilla" on it, something with a big, lumbering riff? Maybe all this subtlety worked against them. But you're right; there's too much going on here for it to be a record that I've only seen half a dozen times in 40 years in a store.

Steven: I hope we've convinced a few people. There are so many nuances that are both highlighted and hindered by the clean and crisp production. I feel like Tom Werman added a sheen and a gloss, but Blue Öyster Cult were still able to bring their own twist to it. Yeah, there's less mystery and that's maybe the issue that people had here. What you see, to some extent, is much more of what you get here. I think it makes for a strange journey, and maybe an uneven one, although I still love it.

That clever BÖC eclecticism is still present but it twinkles. It's not like that lighthouse turning that blinds you with moments where you go, whoa! Yeah, "The Vigil," I'll give you that—that's a "whoa" moment. The rest of the album is much more "oh" moments, an awful lot more moments that just make you think, "Oh, I like that. That's clever." It took me quite a long time before I thought that there were enough moments that twinkle on this album that now it's beginning to dazzle me. Because they have managed to evolve. And yet, there's nobody else this could be—they still sound like Blue Öyster Cult.

Jamie: I'll say it again: I can't believe that title track wasn't the summertime feel good hit of the year. It came out right on time, late June, right there—boom. It was my favourite album growing up. I played this a lot driving around in my '83 Escort. But my tastes change over time, Martin. I've gotten more adventurous as I've gotten older. And now that I revisit *Mirrors*, maybe I needed it to be a little bit more adventurous. You know, things I loved about it when I was a kid, I get a little... I'm not gonna say bored, but I want more. But I understand why I loved it and I still love it.

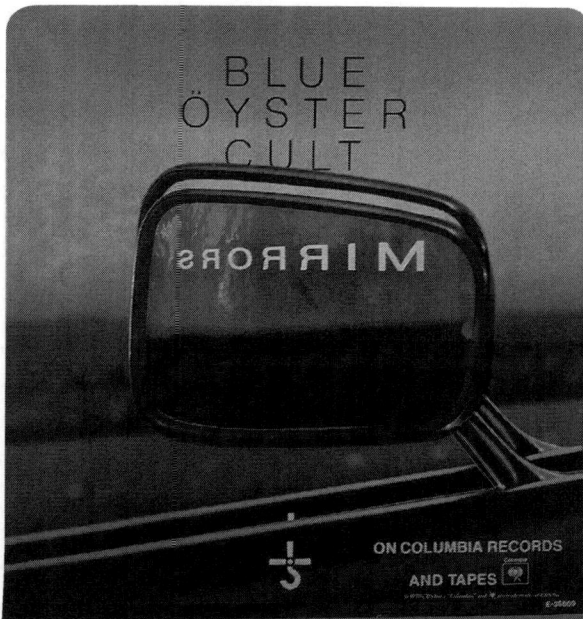

CULTÖSAURUS ERECTUS

Cultösaurus Erectus
June 14, 1980
Columbia JC 36550
Produced by Martin Birch
Engineered by Martin Birch, Second Engineer, Clay Hutchinson
Recorded at Kingdom Sound, Long Island, NY
Personnel: Eric Bloom – guitar, keyboards, vocals; Donald "Buck Dharma"
Roeser – guitars, bass, keyboards, vocals; Joe Bouchard – bass, vocals; Allen
Lanier – guitar, keyboards; Albert Bouchard – drums, vocals
Guest performers: Don Kirshner, Mark Rivera

Side 1
1. "Black Blade" (Bloom, Moorcock, Trivers) 6:30
2. "Monsters" (A. Bouchard, C. Bouchard) 5:14
3. "Divine Wind" (Roeser) 5:06
4. "Deadline" (Roeser) 4:28

Side 2
1. "The Marshall Plan" (Bloom, Roeser, J. Bouchard, Lanier, A. Bouchard) 5:24
2. "Hungry Boys" (A. Bouchard, C. Bouchard) 3:38
3. "Fallen Angel" (J. Bouchard, Robbins) 3:12
4. "Lips in the Hills" (Roeser, Bloom, Meltzer) 4:24
5. "Unknown Tongue" (A. Bouchard, David Roter) 3:58

A NEW MONSTER ALBUM
BLUE ÖYSTER CULT
CULTÖSAURUS ERECTUS
"LP"
STARRING
FEATURING
"THE MARSHALL PLAN"
"FALLEN ANGEL"
"MONSTERS"
"LIPS IN THE HILLS"
PRODUCER
MARTIN BIRCH
DIRECTOR
SANDY PEARLMAN
RECORDED ON LOCATION IN LONG ISLAND, N.Y.
GET THIS MONSTER BEFORE IT GETS YOU!
NOT FOR PERSONS OF NERVOUS DISPOSITION

Martin talks to John Gaffney, Steven Reid and Matt Thompson about *Cultösaurus Erectus.*

Martin Popoff: So new decade, what is the state of the band at this point?

John Gaffney: Well, *Mirrors* was mostly seen as a commercial and artistic failure for the band. All seemed to be in agreement that they needed to return to their heavier roots and get back to their more adventurous songwriting habits of years past. The first step turned out to be getting in Martin Birch, who had a long list of producing and engineering credits, most famed being Deep Purple with *In Rock* and *Machine Head*, as well as the Purple family-adjacent Rainbow *Rising*. He seemed to be the perfect man for the job and I would agree.

Around the same time period Birch would wind up at the desk for the rejuvenated Black Sabbath featuring Ronnie James Dio, with *Heaven and Hell* coming out three months before *Cultösaurus*. And Sandy's managing both bands during this time too, which resulted in the ill-fated co-headlining Black and Blue tour thing. A show from that actually came out sort of low-key on VHS, but never DVD, one would imagine due to a mountain of red tape. But I would recommend folks check it out, or at least see some of it on YouTube.

Matt Thompson: The changes here are very intentional, because of various types of dissatisfactions with *Mirrors*. First one would be commercial—they're on a downward trend. Next, Eric doesn't have a good experience with *Mirrors*, right? For whatever reason, Tom Werman doesn't like Eric's voice as much as he likes Buck's voice, so Eric doesn't get as much to do on *Mirrors*. So he's looking to come back and Albert is sort of the coach for Eric on this and he wants to get back to being heavy and sinister. So Albert is writing songs to be heavy, to be weird, and for Eric to sing. And of course you change producers. You've got Martin Birch versus Tom Werman, and that definitely makes it sound different as well. I think those are the reasons for the changes between the two records.

Steven Reid: Is it a reactionary album? Yeah, I think it probably is. I've often wondered, *Cultösaurus Erectus*, is this the band saying we've got to hit hard again, after what people's reactions were to *Mirrors*? Martin Birch's production is maybe perfect for that. It's not maybe a perfect production, but it's perfect for that. There was probably the impression that people weren't too sure about what the band was after with *Mirrors*. Let's be us again. *Who* will let us be us? Martin Birch will let us be us. And that's maybe what we want to do here.

Martin: Could you delve a little further into this production? What does Martin Birch do for them?

Steven: *Mirrors* has got a top end and a bottom end, absolutely. *Cultösaurus* doesn't really have a top end and a bottom end—it's got very much a middle. And in certain circumstances, that is perfect for what this band was trying to do here because it was necessary, to some extent, maybe thinking, "What can we do to feature the guitars better?"

Martin: Yet it's absolutely a better middle than what happened on the first five albums, right? Up to *Spectres*, they were kind of midrangey but flawed. This is like a purposeful crowding to the middle.

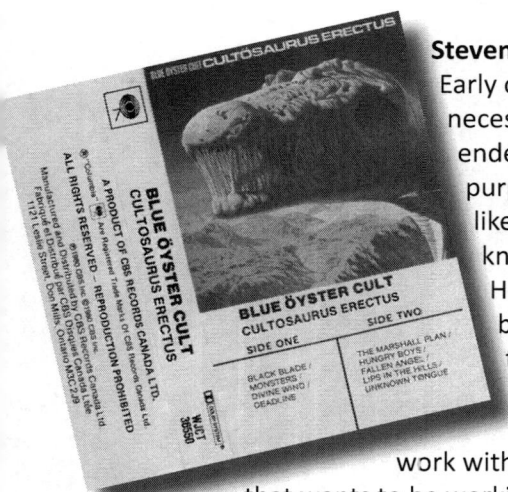

Steven: Yes, absolutely. This feels on purpose. Early on that kind of cardboard-y sound doesn't necessarily feel on purpose. That's what we ended up with. This to me feels very much on purpose. And we know that Martin kind of liked that dynamic as a theme. But we also know that he could do other things, too. He wasn't just bringing what Martin Birch brings. You listen to Martin Birch's albums; they don't all sound the same. And that, to me, is why we love him so much.

He was able to, in my opinion, really work with bands. *Cultösaurus* sounds like a band that wants to be working on this album. We're keen, we're hungry, we're getting to play. He's not going to knock about with us. I'm not saying that's what happened with *Mirrors*. I think the band were on board personally, although, frankly, I've heard both Eric and Albert complain about Tom. But I do think that right here, right now, they were going, "We want to be Blue Öyster Cult, the band that people know." But I don't think that's what really happens. I think we pour some of what happened before from *Mirrors* into here. This is much more melodic than what people frame it as, and I figure it's because of the journey that we've been on.

John: I've always loved the production on this album. I think it's one of their best from a clean all-frequencies-in-check but still punchy and dynamic perspective. For me, Martin Birch's style—which the guys talk about when they reference working with him—was more hands-off, letting the band be themselves but jumping in and giving them some advice and direction when they needed it. He really seems to tap into what makes BÖC special. For me they feel inspired instrumentally, vocally and most importantly, from coming off of the *Mirrors* album, which was a little predictable. They're exciting in the songwriting department here, where they're not afraid to take chances, something that I didn't really hear very much on *Mirrors*. I've always been a fan of what I call headphone mixes. This is when you can put headphones on and there's lots of layers and little nuggets to sonically to dig out of the recording and I think this album has a lot of that. It's got a lot of layers and details, with the keyboards especially adding some nice depth and texture to the sound, and the guitars all working together really nicely.

Martin: You say punchy, but it's also sort of tight and high-strung, kind of sober and all-business, right? I mean, the bass isn't super-deep on it.

John: I know what you mean, but for me, that way there aren't any frequencies to jump out as harsh. It's not too trebly, it's not too muddy, it seems to be right there in the middle, sure. Personally those are the kind of mixes that I like, where there isn't anything that's too overpowering. If we were to reference Martin Birch, *Heaven and Hell*, as much as I love that album, that album feels a little dry and boxy to me. *Cultösaurus* has more warmth and maybe that's where I feel the punch. I can really turn this record up and it just seems to sound better as I turn it up.

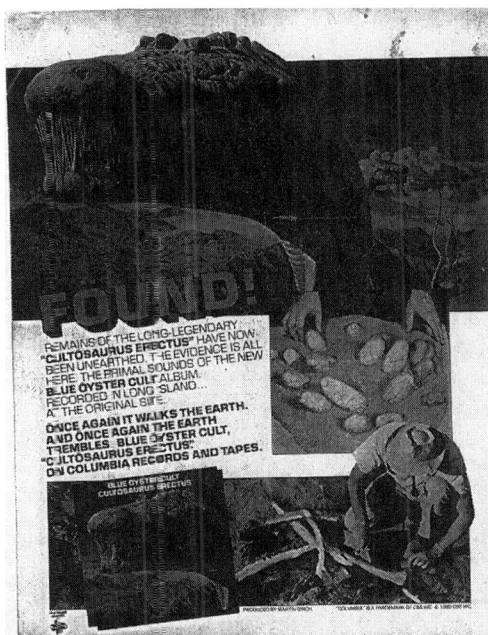

Martin: While we're at it then, how about a quick comparison between this production job and that of *Fire of Unknown Origin*?

John: They aren't too, too far off from each other. Maybe *Fire of Unknown Origin* is not quite as lush-sounding to me as *Cultösaurus Erectus*. I might align *Fire of Unknown Origin* more with what he did with Black Sabbath, although certainly not *Mob Rules*. But yeah, *Fire of Unknown Origin* and *Cultösaurus Erectus* are probably my two favourites from a sound standpoint.

Matt: Everyone liked working with Martin Birch. Part of the producer's job is the sonic picture but another producer role is getting the best out of the band. And by all accounts they were very relaxed in the studio, where, as I say, Eric didn't have a fun experience on *Mirrors*. Martin gets along great with all members of the band, so you're getting everyone's best efforts. And they're collaborating at a time when we know in our heads after the fact that Albert is going to leave the band not too much later—there's only one more record with Albert. So that adds a lot. Albert thinks that Martin was listening to their live records when he was dialling up the sounds for the record, and that it was more reflective of how they sounded live. I don't know what that means, right?

Martin: I don't really hear that.

Matt: Yeah, and I'm not an audiophile. I listened to these records throughout my life on poor equipment. But I agree that the album is very mid-ish, midrangey, but on cheap stereos and on the radio, it sounds great, right? It sounds really good. You hear everything. There's nothing getting buried. Everything sounds full again. Tom Werman does a great job on the vocals on *Mirrors*. The vocals sound better than on any other album. The guitars to me are a little thin; they're not that crunchy. So even on "The Vigil," where you've got a great riff, it's kind of thin-sounding. Whether it's because of Martin Birch or not, I don't know, but you definitely get more crunchiness to the guitars here than what you had on *Mirrors*.

Martin: Okay, so into the album, right away we get my second favourite BÖC song ever, "Black Blade," an epic, but not of epic length.

John: Yes, a personal favourite of mine too, and a great album opener. It starts with an explosion of sci-fi keyboard sounds and a triumphant-sounding chord which sets the mood perfectly. Written by Eric along with

Michael Moorcock and songwriter buddy John Trivers, who helped on "The Great Sun Jester." Moorcock would be back on the next album for "Veteran of the Psychic Wars." Cool lyrics, based around a character from Moorcock's book, *Elric of Melnebone*, who is controlled by his sword, the black blade or Stormbringer, with the sword needing to keep killing in order to survive. I think Eric's vocal delivery is great and you can really feel the character's pain and guilt through his vocals, especially when he sings that line, "And the whole world's dying and the burden's mine/And the black sword keeps on killing 'til the end of time." I love that line and I love the way Eric delivers it.

Great use of dynamics in this song, like in the verses where everything sort of drops down a little bit and gets slightly quieter. In my opinion, that's an underrated strength of Blue Öyster Cult. They're not constantly bludgeoning you with things. They know how to bring the dynamics down so that other sections and parts of the album jump out at you. I love the middle section with the descending and ascending fast chromatic line there. Birch got the guys to play really tight there. Then it sort of alternates between that and that triumphant chord that we heard at the opening of the song.

Then it modulates up a step and we get a rare studio bass solo from Joe. We heard him do a little mini solo in "Godzilla" but he does one here and it serves the song well. There's nothing overly flashy about it; it's just cool. He's doing these sort of big bends and the sound that he's using at that point adds to the spacey atmosphere of the song. Then there's this trippy keyboard melody before everything drops down again for another verse that finds Eric alone with just these kind of keyboard pads underneath him, again, adding more dynamic contrast. Then I totally dig that trippy, weird kind of computer going haywire and berserk sound that takes us into the end fade-out with the black blade speaking to us in its robotic voice explaining to us that we're all doomed. And if you listen very closely right before the song fades out, you can hear him say, "You poor effing humans." Love it—fantastic album opener.

Martin: Is it progressive rock, pomp rock?

John: Absolutely; in fact I'd say that both the first two songs are proggy. In "Black Blade" you get some pretty obtuse key changes, and then that nice modulation for Joe's bass solo.

Matt: It's the second of the Michael Moorcock collaborations. Eric, definitely being a true sci-fi and fantasy fan, reaches out to Moorcock and sends a fan letter and then they do this collaboration. It's not an in-the-room collaboration. It's Michael Moorcock sending lyrics in and then Eric working with a collaborator to come up with the music. It's one of the reasons why Blue Öyster Cult are sort of the patron saints of the *Dungeons & Dragons* roleplaying games. They have music that fits that, as much as Dio does, right? They are as well, because they have the bona fides of collaborating with Michael Moorcock, a giant of fantasy and sci-fi literature.

And I agree that it's a progressive-type song. It has lots of different parts. They do in two places on this album the sort of King Crimson fast unison thing that is rhythmically interesting—they do it again on "Monsters." It's probably as proggy as BÖC ever gets. Plus they've got really good keyboard synthesizer sounds on the two Martin Birch records and there's a cool little interlude part.

There's a great twist with the lyrics. Most of the song is written from the protagonist's point of view, which is Elric in this case. And then the last part, where they put the vocoder on Eric's voice, is written from the point of view of the sword, of Stormbringer, of the black blade. And it sort of shows that all of Elric's fears are appropriate, right? "It keeps calling me its master, but I feel like its slave." And then at the end, he goes, "My master is my slave" and laughs. So it's a fun little twist lyrically.

Martin: Speaking of synths, where's Allen on this record?

Matt: Well, that's a good point. He doesn't bring too much to this record. And if you want to criticize *Cultösaurus Erectus*, maybe it doesn't have as much Allen as we'd like. He's a little bit missing on this. I presume he's playing the keyboards throughout the record. At least he's coming up with some great sounds. Whether he's doing the piano boogie parts on some of them or if he's doing the more futuristic things, it sounds great. But he's not driving anything; he's in the backseat.

Steven: Who can resist a song that opens with a thunderbolt cracking across the speakers and hitting you right between the eyes? This is a mid-paced, atmospheric, thunderous song. It's really, really good. This is Moorcock giving us a song about a sword, the black blade, which can no longer stop killing, because that's what it needs. But the real message is that it's about abuse of power, how power breeds the desire for more power and really nothing else. And then you can no longer control it. That's conveyed in a beautiful way, both through the lyrics and in the music—it's a powerful song. It feels heady and almost like too much at certain points. Those warbling synths and those synthesized vocals at the end... you know that you've entered the world of Blue Öyster Cult. But those computer-y synths, when you analyze that part, it's uncomfortable. They make you think, whoa, I don't really like that. It's a tonal challenge but still it connects. This is one of those songs where you get to the end of it and you go, "Yeah, okay, I know exactly whose world I'm in, who's created this—and I'm on board."

Martin: It's interesting, but I just realized that both my favourite BÖC songs, "The Vigil" and "Black Blade" do that "My Sharona" thing, where there's this octave-jumping in the main riff.

Steve: That's true. I would never have picked that out. Now that you mention it, you see it. And that's another sort of tonal challenge.

Martin: As you say, John, "Monsters" is pretty proggy too.

John: Definitely, all sorts of gear shifts and chopsy things here. Makes me wonder if somebody was listening to a bunch of Zappa. So, "Monsters," written by Albert Bouchard with his wife, Caryn Bouchard, who helped him with the lyrics, and sung by Eric. It's another sci-fi tale, this time about a group of people escaping a dying Earth on a stolen ship. I love the line, "The four of us and Pasha dear, she to steer and we to fight." And the way Eric delivers that, there's a real intensity to his voice. Eventually love enters the picture and things go wrong with one of the characters, Joe, pulling a gun on the other side of the ship.

That tight opening to me, very progressive sounding, a pentatonic lick with the sax doubling it. Kind of throws me back to King Crimson. Then after that fast pentatonic sax-doubled lick, it drops down to the F sharp there, with these heavy, thick punctuated chords. Birch's production really adds weight to those chords. Then we get a sudden shift to a swing jazz thing, catching us totally out of the blue. Again, it's something you might expect from Frank Zappa, with some nifty sax work from Mark Rivera, who has worked with Billy Joel and a bunch of other top-shelf artists. Beneath it, Joe lays down this cool walking bass line. Whenever I hear this part, especially later when the crowd noises are added, I always think of that cantina scene from *Star Wars*. They're in a jazz club with a bunch of space aliens, you know, sitting around drinking funny-coloured liquids.

Then there's some tight syncopated blues scale lines doubled by the guitar and bass that take us to a sudden tempo drop and a half-step-up key change, which is totally out of left field. The intensity rises again and we get the sing-songy chorus of "Monsters monsters," like you might hear out of *The Addams Family* or something. Best part, there's a sort of false ending and then they return for the last verse. Love this song—fantastic. It's a one-two opening punch here that says BÖC are back. They're playing heavier and they've got their chops are all fired-up and ready to go.

Steven: Agreed, and man, that jazz part turns everything on its head, doesn't it? You've got a giant riff and then this deep saxophone work from Mark Rivera. Completely different feel, and you've got jazzy inflections later on too. I'm not so on board with those kind of crowd noises, the caterwauling, that comes in later on, but the riff is fantastic. And that "Monsters, monsters" chant; it's theatrical, it's almost showtime, isn't it? I can imagine that on a West End stage.

And then you've got that trademark solo from Buck Dharma. He does so many different things but he knows how to talk to the song; that's the key. You can't help but be impressed. It's not about that, though, is it? He was never the guy that you would say "guitar hero" in that sense of "Look what I can do." He's better than that.

And I also appreciate the false ending, because you think I'm in a safe world now and them you're right back in the maelstrom. Lyrically, you think, is this the end of us all? I mean four guys and one woman on the spacecraft. One gets jealous because everybody else is getting it on. That's the end of us. Maybe? Probably? What a way to go? I don't know (laughs).

Matt: Albert is trying to be heavy. So "Monsters" is a heavy song, and it's one he's writing for Eric to sing. It's a straightforward rocker, until you get to the jazz, which is hilarious, because it's pseudo-jazz, right? A jazz person is not gonna love this thing. But it shows a musical sense of humour, like they're throwing it in. And then they jump back into this heavy metal song. They're really having fun musically.

And there's even some Easter eggs, right? There's a little clip from a live recording where it's got someone going "Have another!" They're overdubbing these sort of cheering sounds, weird sounds, and they use the exact same sample on the other side on "The Marshall Plan." You can just tell they're having fun in the studio. I assume that was a George Geranios clip, their sound guy, that he had recorded somewhere on the road.

Martin: Nice, I didn't know that. Okay, next we have my least favourite song on the album, "Divine Wind," because who wants to hear Blue Öyster Cult actually doing a blues?

Matt: Well, yeah, to me this and "Deadline" are Buck's takes on the blues in a couple of very small ways. It does have a boring blues riff to it. And Buck isn't a very bluesy player at all, right? Like when he does vibrato, he often uses the whammy bar instead of just being bluesy like Eric Clapton. His contemporaries do it a different way. But sure, "Divine Wind" is not that interesting musically, not a lot going on with the rhythm section. But the lead Buck does is actually very cool. It's slow and atmospheric; to me it works.

But it's a Buck lyric that's not like his usual lyrics. He's usually crafting some sort of story and this is a political song about the Iranian hostage crisis and the Ayatollah Khomeini. But it's obtuse, spare. You wouldn't know that just listening to the song. On Buck's demo, his vocal delivery is very laid-back. And BÖC expert Bolle Gregmar has talked about the difference, right? Buck's almost indifferent in his vocal: "If he really thinks we're the devil, then let's send 'em to Hell." Whereas Eric does this really strong, angry, powerful thing, which fits his strengths. And he elevates it even better live. It's kind of weird, this album. You don't have an obvious single to it. But "Divine Wind" gets the Chu-Bops treatment, the little record covers with gum inside. It's "Divine Wind" that they put the lyrics to, yet it's not issued as a single. They're searching for a single and "Divine Wind" wouldn't have been a great one.

John: Dark and earthy 12/eight blues feel to this one, with lyrics inspired by the Iranian hostage crisis, which involved 52 US citizens. Great example of Buck's taste and sensitivity and sense of melody come solo time. He often returns to this little three-note guitar figure that sort of serves as a hook to the song. I hear shades of David Gilmour, with this blues-based, slightly clean playing, where he's always picking the right notes to play.

Buck is very versatile, able to switch between different styles. He can play that kind of shreddy '80s guitar style if he wants to, and you hear brief flashes on their various albums. But he normally defaults to just solid, tasty, melodic playing. I especially appreciate his tone, which is a lot cleaner. He goes for a cleaner tone than what a lot of guys were going for in the '80s. So you can always hear what he's playing. I just think he's a super-inventive player. He's sort of like Joe in the way that he's not a showboat. It's in service to the song.

Anyway, what he does here stops the song from feeling sluggish. That 12/eight blues rhythm might feel bogged down with too much heavy metal applied to it. Instead Buck gives it a nice lightness and brevity which is refreshing. He avoids the obvious of just doubling those low notes with some big thick Black Sabbath-style power chords.

Eric's vocals are nice and bluesy, laid-back when necessary and more aggressive when the lines call for it. Like at the end when he jumps up in his range and he sings, "If he really thinks we're the devil, then let's send 'em to Hell!" That's just great the way he sort of shouts that line out. Well-placed on the album after the two relatively fast and complicated numbers

Steven: Yeah, the pace of "Divine Wind" is divine indeed. There's a patient groove. It's almost languid, but you're left in no doubt as to the intent here. They've got a knack for making seemingly innocent songs threatening and menacing. You're never allowed to relax; it's always unsettling. The lyric represents a contrast against these beautiful layered backing vocals that feel like they've been ripped out of the AOR songbook. As for Eric's lead vocal, it's controlled, which makes the snarling, angry conclusion that much starker. Buck's playing is clean and sharp. It's incisive, never overdone, never overplayed.

And the lyric—what there is of it—raises a lot of questions. It's about Iran but we're turning our thoughts back on America too, I suppose. Should America be the world's leader? Should they be helping everybody? However, the words are constructed more like a Shakespearean potion being concocted and stirred in a giant cauldron. It gives it a completely different slant. Is it political? Hugely. Do you need us to shove that down your throat? Not really. You're left at the end with that killer line, "If he really thinks we're the devil, then let's send 'em to Hell." Who's to blame? It's open to interpretation. It's not telling you.

Martin: I like that! All right, next is "Deadline," as John says, lightly and politely bluesy but also I think a bit new wavy.

Matt: Yeah, and to me the bluesiness is in that call-and-response, right? In a blues song you sing a line and then you talk back with the guitar. And Buck does that throughout "Deadline." After a few words, he's got these nice little guitar lines in his characteristic style, still with whammy bar on it. He's much more Jeff Beck-like than Clapton- or Page-like. It's a kind of unusual phrasing influenced by jazz. But he's got a heavy metal sound too; he's playing with the whammy bar.

It's a very melodic song, but the bass line, which is played by Buck, is really interesting, because it's got a bend in it. It actually makes it hard for Joe to play live, because that bend goes basically throughout the whole song. Lyrically it's like a "Then Came the Last Days of May." So it's

another kind of early days crime-type story, apparently lightly inspired by Phil King and his murder. But it's written in a really smart way, right? Buck's not getting super-literal with telling the story, which he kind of does in "Last Days." I think it's more sophisticated lyrically than "Last Days of May" which is just you're driving out west and then you get killed. It's very literal. Here it's, "How long do you think that I could sharpen my knife?" Instead of saying, "I patiently waited." He's getting more sophisticated in how he's telling the story.

It's a catchy song on the record but even though it's put out as a single in the UK, it's not a hit. They have no hits from the record. And as for being new wavy, yeah, that's a good observation I hadn't thought of, but I totally see that. It's funny, it's Martin Birch who's this older heavy metal producer, but these two records are the most new wavy they'd ever get, more again on *Fire of Unknown Origin*.

John: "Deadline" turns out to be the only song sung by Buck on the whole album. A bit odd, but Eric's vocals are so great all over this record that I'm not complaining. So after the opening ringing guitar chords, we get that oddball bass line, done by Buck. Bass bends are not something you hear a whole ton of. It's something that hearkens back to Jack Bruce. But it drives the song along with some nice acoustic strumming going on in the background. The chorus is uplifting, with some nice little descending keyboard notes that sort of trickle down and fall in the background.

For me this song shows off Buck and his songwriting. Buck has a good melodic pop sensibility to his writing. His vocal delivery is always laid-back and also very melodic. And you're right, it does have sort of a new wavy, trippy, ethereal feel to it. There's quite a contrast between the music and the rather serious lyrics about an old friend who used to book the band who got caught up in owing the mob some money and he missed his deadline. Makes for a creepy storytelling vibe.

And you know, as for Allen, the keyboard playing in Blue Öyster Cult for me is not like a Deep Purple situation where the keyboard is dominant in the mix. It's more for texture. Like in the chorus there's that sprinkle of electric piano that contributes to the mood.

Steven: Again, I'm really revealing my melodic rock tendencies, but I love this song. It's the only song on the album that's written by one individual and then sung by them as well. And Buck does not waste a second of the opportunity. He's moody, sublime, melodic, quite beguiling. And he works off his own guitar lines during both the verses and the choruses. Wow, absolutely to-die-for; it's perfection, so in sync. And then there's another hugely scintillating and tasteful guitar solo proper. Plus it's got the grooviest of grooving bass grooves, and he played that too.

149

Martin: Any thoughts on the album cover art?

John: Love it. That's an illustration by Richard Clifton-Dey. I thought *Mirrors* was dull and boring and maybe too obvious. But this cover draws you in. It takes you to another world. I love the contrast. You've got this prehistoric fossil of the *Cultösaurus Erectus*, so are we back in time? And yet there's this spaceship flying around. Is it a futuristic world or are people from the future going back in time? It gets your imagination working.

The back cover's got two pictures and an artist's rendering. There's a lot of fun little nods to BÖC's past here. We've got the unfertilized egg from the female cultösaurus erectus found in the Stalk-Forrest, Stalk-Forrest Group being the original name of the band. It's near Oyster Bay, Long Island, New York, the boys being from the Long Island area. Photo courtesy of the Museum of Diz-Bustology, which is of course a reference to "7 Screaming Diz-Busters" from *Tyranny and Mutation*.

Figure B is a cultösaurus erectus discovered by Professor Victor Von Pearlman, of course, Sandy Pearlman, near Stony Brook, New York—the boys went to Stony Brook University. And the photo is courtesy of The Underbelly Institute, the Soft White Underbelly being another early name plus a name that the band would sometimes use for secret one-off shows. Then it says that the artist's rendering of cultösaurus erectus is "thought to be a distant relative of the Horn-Swooped Bungo Pony," which is taken from a line in "The Red & the Black" on *Tyranny and Mutation*.

Martin: Okay, over to side two and we get this sort of weak-tea rocker, not particularly funny, boring chords, not much of anything—not a fan of "The Marshall Plan" over here, if you couldn't tell.

John: And I understand that; this is where things take a dip for some people. Not so much for me though. But yes, "The Marshall Plan" is one that many people don't care for. It's a bit over-the-top in its silliness, like when that lo-fi guitar comes in quoting "Smoke on the Water." But for me, BÖC has always had a sense of humour, and I like Eric's theatrical delivery of the lyric.

And bonus points for the play on words with the political Marshall Plan and Marshall amps. Written by all the guys, and the only one that Allen Lanier gets a writing credit on.

It tells the story of Johnny, a rock 'n' roll fan who loses his girl when he takes her to a rock show only for her to leave with the band. To win her back he learns guitar to become a rock star himself. But alas, even this doesn't work at getting his Susie back. I love Buck's solo after the "It's gonna sound like" part and also after the Don Kirshner spoken word part, Kirshner being famous for his TV show, *Don Kirshner's Rock Concert*. And then Buck tears it up. He's stepped slightly outside of his blues box here and plays this really cool modal-sounding solo. And it's kind of shreddy too, showing that Buck could hang with the young axe-slingers who are about to come onto the scene. Overall, it's a fun song for me, but I know that I'm in the minority on that one.

Steven: The world is littered with songs that are about the myth of the rock star, and how great that is. And there are also a few that knock them right back down again. "The Marshall Plan," the title alludes more to America helping or trying to help Europe rebuild itself after World War II, and not necessarily working out the way that it should have done. And that's exactly what happens to our protagonist. Johnny does exactly the same thing. He sees Susie—Susie, again, as in Susie, dear—whisked off by a band after a show that they've been to together. And that is the fire in his belly. He's going to be the rock star. This is never gonna happen to him ever again. And he gets there. He achieves that goal across the length of this song. He becomes the huge rock star. And yet somehow, Susie is still not to be seen at the end. Susie is still off somewhere else. Is that a comment on him? Is it a comment on Susie? Is it a comment on the rock 'n' roll myth? I don't know. But it's a great journey.

And I love the little cameos in this song. That little snatch of "Smoke on the Water," it's almost played ironically, as if it's tired. That too is a comment on the rock 'n' roll dream, I think. And as a young guy from Scotland, I had no idea who Don Kirshner was. He's got the least rock 'n' roll voice you could possibly imagine. However, his little interruption is perfect for this, isn't it? So spot-on. This song is overblown and it's grandiose and it's not something that BÖC really did in those terms. But it lives up to the billing of the concept perfectly. I just think it's really clever. Johnny tells you what he's *not* gonna play. You know, he's not gonna play surf music. He's gonna play some heavy music. He's gonna play it loud, play it bad! But at the very end, "It's gonna sound like... it's gonna sound like..." You can't explain the best guitar solo in the world so you just play it. And that's exactly what happens. It's so well put together.

Matt: Yeah, Martin, I know your feelings on this one. What's interesting here is that they're intentionally trying to get along—it's the democratic song on the record. Everyone gets a writing credit on it. It's written in the studio. So starting with *Agents of Fortune*, songs have to go through a gauntlet to get approved for the record. You've got to do a home demo and then it's gotta survive the sort of pre-production demo process and then you gotta cut it for real. And this one doesn't go through that. It's written more in the studio.

It's lyrically not serious, right? It's a non-serious take on what becomes a trope for lots of songs, the origin days of becoming a band. But this is not really their origin story. It's just about some Johnny, some kid. And they make a goofy, campy video for it, featuring a shaven Eric Bloom, which appears in the *Black and Blue* movie. It's funny, but BÖC has two different versions of when they're funny, right? Sometimes it's tongue-in-cheek, but they also have a silly side to them. This is the silly side. Albert sort rued that later we got "Jukebox Hero" and "Summer of '69" becoming hits, which were basically treading in the same area.

Martin: Joe's Garage.

Matt: Oh yeah! Wow, I never thought of that, and that had just come out. And there's an example of silly but sophisticated.

Martin: Well, the same thing happens too, where the girl runs off with the band.

Matt: Yeah, yeah, and Frank goes there all the time. A lot of his lyrics are about life on the road and all the weird things that he's seen. But I would say *Joe's Garage* is funnier. It succeeds better that way. The sincerity works better for Foreigner and Bryan Adams. They get hits out of it. So BÖC is in this middle ground where it's probably not funny enough to be a funny song. It's not tongue-in-cheek, really, at all. It's a different kind of humour.

Martin: Well, the guy's name is Johnny. The Don Kirshner lines are dumb. They pick "Smoke on the Water" and then it sounds terrible. The chords are dull and then the arrangement with the piano is anemic. I mean, it's barely dad joke-funny.

Matt: Yeah, well—and this just popped in my head—so he's playing it like a kid playing "Smoke on the Water," kind of like when Alex finds the guitar in "2112," right? So I think everything's intentional there. And there's some very good lead guitar on it, not on that part, but like then when they do the little break section—pretty incendiary stuff. When this record came out, I loved that song. But I was 12 years old. I didn't have the history at that point of their more sophisticated material. I think they're just being funny in the studio; I'll cede that it's a bit of a throwaway in that regard. It does stand out against everything on the rest of this album, which seems more worked at.

Martin: Okay, enough complaining from me; I love to death the whole rest of the album, beginning with "Hungry Boys," which I've always framed as a pretty heavy one—but not so much after talking to you guys!

Steven: Absolutely (laughs). I cannot work out why this wasn't a single—because I think it's new wavy enough to fit with the times. And you do wonder—fate is a strange thing—how it would have impacted things. To go from "The Marshall Plan" into this on an album, that's brave stuff. It's saying don't pigeonhole us. We're going to do what we're going to do and you have to keep up.

John: Now here's where things go a little sideways for me. "Hungry Boys," an Albert- and his wife Caryn-written song, Albert on vocals and the only vocal appearance from Albert here. I agree that this has a strange new wave-ish feel to it, but it's like Missing Persons, with the vocal delivered in this staccato, deadpan, almost cartoonish style. And those electronic tom sounds—ouch. But that chromatically dropping riff at the end of each chorus I think is very cool and Buck plays a pretty shredding guitar solo in this one. But I do kind of enjoy the song because it has a weird, demented Devo-like feel, although it stands at odds against the subject matter, which is drug addiction. And back to the Zappa, this reminds me of his band around the "Baby Snakes" era, sort of jumpy and quick-moving.

Matt: Not a big favourite among BÖC fans, but I think "Hungry Boys" is underrated. It's fast and I agree with what you're saying: it's got a punkish-ness to it. I think what people don't like is the vocals. You get this combination of Albert and Joe both, I believe, doing a sort of falsetto-type thing. I love it. To me it's a foot in the old/foot in the new type thing. Those are musicologist guys, right? These guys listen to lots of stuff. They're not ignorant of what's going on around them. And they have the history to know the importance of falsetto in R&B music and stuff like that. So I think it's intentional and I think it works. It makes it cut through what is a fast and dense backing track.

It's a pretty straightforward drug addiction-type lyric, not a standout lyric but it's fine. The soloing is amazing but somewhat buried, presented like a punk rock song as opposed to classic rock. It's slipped in throughout and it's really incendiary. Buck is really wailing. So to me, this one's quick— it's in and out.

Martin: Next is "Fallen Angel," which sounds like a pomp rock song as performed by The Who, but circa *It's Hard*.

Matt: Oh definitely. It's got the histrionic Roger Daltrey style-vocal from Joe. And the keyboards have some of the pomp part that The Who had, although I'm thinking *Quadrophenia* style. I don't mean pomp negatively at all, and I don't know if I'm using it correctly from a pomp rock standpoint. You get a Helen Robbins lyric, so it's a little interesting, more of an *Agents of Fortune*-sounding lyric than the rest of the album. So it's, "Fallen angel, gonna ride up from Hell." It's not science fiction or fantasy-ish at all. It's a New York poet-y type version of that. And super-melodic. It's catchy and it doesn't stay too long—no fat on it.

Steven: Keyboards are a huge factor here and right across this album, but in different ways from the preceding album, *Mirrors* and from what came before. The guitars are given room to breathe here while the keyboards do a lot of the melodic heavy lifting on this album. Before they were used as a colour, as a tone. They were used to maybe change tack or rhythmically, with Allen on old school piano playing. Here it's melodic heavy lifting. And there are sections where you think, oh, there's no guitars for a little while, which wasn't really the band's calling card. It never really was after this either, I don't think.

But it helps to build the grooves as well. I liked that aspect a lot. Because it's not overplayed. Rhythmically, this is a strong song and the keyboard and the rhythm section lock in tight. There's an aspect that is maybe not spoken about as much as it should be for me is just how percussively and rhythmically strong this band always were. At this era, there's a telepathic link that's going on. Yeah, okay, you can say that's to do with family connections. But the ground is moving and yet the bass is always solid. That's a scarce thing but an important thing to have in a band, and it really comes across in this song.

John: "Fallen Angel;" love the upbeat, uplifting feel of the song and its super-catchy chorus. It's poppy, theatrical and over-the-top, like Meat Loaf. I'm a sucker for big hooks and this is a big hook chorus. And then Joe's vocals, man, he's totally pushing himself to his upper limit. I had no idea that Joe could belt out these kinds of notes. He jumps all the way up to a high C sharp which is very impressive. And I agree, like a Roger Daltrey, he adds a bluesy, gritty sound to the song. Man, that "Gonna ride up from Hell! I'm the fallen angel," you know, just fantastic. Buck's solo is also tasty and melodic as we would expect. I just wish the song was a bit longer; it clocks in at only 3:14.

Martin: John, bass is your main instrument; tell me a bit more about Joe as a bassist.

John: I've always thought Joe was underrated. He adds interest, but he's certainly not a flashy bass player jumping out and playing all over the neck, that kind of thing. But he adds interesting lines that contribute to the song. He does subtle things that if you were to take the bass out of the song, it would affect it. He has a background as a piano player and he's a really well-rounded musician. In fact after he left the band, he taught music theory and stuff like that and he's the guitarist in Blue Coupe, with Albert on drums and Dennis Dunaway on bass.

Martin: Time for a great rocker with "Lips in the Hills," which, surely this one you guys won't be calling a new wave song?!

Matt: No (laughs), this is indeed a blistering rocker of a song. The music's 100% a Buck Dharma-written song and it's quite heavy. But on Buck's original demo it's "Hold Me Tight." Buck does the sort of straightforward love songs a lot of times. That's his early AM music listening influences. I wonder if he had brought that in one year earlier, if he brings that to *Mirrors*, I wonder if Tom Werman loves it and he loves Buck's voice and there's no desire to change the lyrics. The rest of the band wants to change the lyrics. Like, "Hold Me Tight," this is stupid. I think Tom Werman would have gone for that. It would have had the *Mirrors*-type production and it would not have been as heavy. Plus the vocals would be Buck.

Martin: Could you describe "Hold Me Tight" in a little more detail?

Matt: The riff is there but it's not produced as heavy. It's the same music; they don't really change it, believe it or not, but it's a pop song. It's so weird. Instead the band recognizes it as having this great heavy metal riff. They play around with different sets of lyrics before settling on Meltzer's. And it's a Meltzer one that fts into the sci-fi part of the band, which he doesn't usually deal with. Maybe it's a UFO thing, maybe Roswell-related;

there's enough references there. I have no idea what he's on about, but it's great because we get some of the Meltzer-isms combined with the sci-fi BÖC things. Eric sounds great on it and it's a really fast metal one that's great live. It becomes a bit of a staple.

John: Okay, "Lips in the Hills," I dig that single-note, kind of pulled-off fast, little guitar lick that Buck plays, which sort of returns throughout the song. The main riff is hard, fast and driving, lots of energy here, very heavy and aggressive. Some speculate the lyrics are about the Roswell incident but I don't know. I always dug when BÖC dealt in mysterious lyrics that you're not really 100% sure what they're talking about, but it lets your imagination run wild. Eric's vocals are fiery and urgent and the background gang vocals add some punch to the chorus. I love the line, "I am gripped by what I cannot tell/Have I slipped or have I merely fell?" I like at the end of the song the way there's those weird, sustained kind of groaning noises. Just a cool heavy one that hits hard.

Steven: Yeah, it actually feels like a side-opener to me, with the guitars right at the start of the song. And then it is, by the standards of what we've got here, relentlessly energetic, almost punky in its outlook, at least musically. And the full song lives up to that. It introduces you in there and then you're waiting for Blue Öyster Cult to take you somewhere else. And sometimes it's actually quite a worry when they don't, and this one doesn't, really. This is get in, get your message across get out again. That said, there's still loads of guitar histrionics and the guitar that closes the song out and leads us into "Unknown Tongue"... I love those masterful little moments where you think, well, this is what we've got, this is where we're going and off we go. There's no breath.

Martin: Yes, and onward we go, to what is probably my second fave on the album, after "Black Blade."

Steven: Yes, it's an intriguing one, with piano and different flavours, with rhythm lines that slide and slither while the mood takes you to darker, less friendly places. But that mid-song breakdown, with the eerie piano, all punctuated by these really threatening beats... they create a massively unsettling atmosphere. There's excellent vocal interplay going on. Eric Bloom is back in the driver's seat, but ably backed by the rest of the band. So many of these great lead vocals are all about what else is happening at the same time, allowing the vocal to do what it needs to do. My only regret about the song is that it fades out. I always want a definitive ending at the end of an album. Yeah, there's some creepy and almost demonic vocals in there, but I really would have liked the song to have hammered its foot down at the end and then be off.

John: Man, fantastic song, fantastic album-closer. When it comes to BÖC lyrics, my favourite topics are the sci-fi things and when they delve into the occult conspiracy-type stuff. So I'm totally on board for the lyrics here, written by Albert and friend and songwriter David Roter. The lyrics Albert claims are a true story about a girl that David knew who used to cut herself and enjoy tasting the blood, although in your book, Martin, David Roter told you a somewhat different sort of inspiration for it. Eric's vocals just ooze all kinds of personality on this song. The chorus is especially cool: "Speak to me in many voices/Make them all sound like one/Let me see your sacred mysteries/Reveal to me the unknown tongue." Love it. And the spooky keyboard solo in the middle of song feels straight out of an '80s horror movie. An absolutely fantastic, great ending to a great album.

Matt: So here we get the first of the two David Roter songs. Interesting that they both show up on the Martin Birch albums. Although he's from the New York cabal of writers, he's different than the others. His lyrics are not like Patti Smith's; they are not like Helen Robbins'. He's quirky, he's funny, purposely, he's satirical; he's a different style of writer. So you get to a very different lyric. But they Blue Öyster Cult-ify the song, right? So it's not like a David Roter song at all the way they end up doing it. Before I knew who David Roter was, before I kind of knew what his intention for the lyric was, I thought it was just a cool take on what a teenager goes through. It's like a David Lynch, *Blue Velvet* kind of thing, right? Where everything on the surface is all fine and good, but underneath there's the horrors of suburban life. There's this sinister, "She took her father's razor/And watched it cut into her palm/She put her hand up to her mouth/To taste the blood so holy and warm."

And then when it comes out of it, "She got up in the morning/Put on her dress and patent leather shoes/Ate her cereal and kissed her mother/And caught the bus and went to school." So I thought it was that there's a seedy underbelly that we don't see. I actually don't think in retrospect that was his intention but I think it works great that way and I think they play it that way. And in the fade-out you have "Reveal to me" repeated over and over and the laughing. It's creepy; it's a headphone moment, kind of a fright if you fell asleep and then woke back up at the end of the record.

But of course, he's more infatuated with the symbolism of Catholicism as a non-Catholic and fascinated with girls in adolescence and menstruation and all this other stuff, right? I don't know if it works on that regard. That's kind of not how I choose to interpret the song. You get to hear his version more so on his *Bambo* album. You get the David Roter versions of those songs which Albert has a hand in but they're not very Blue Öyster Cult-ish at all. It's kind of neat to hear the difference. It's how he intended it.

Martin: Great, and what did *Cultösaurus Erectus* ultimately do for the band, through the rest of the year and into 1981?

John: Well, there weren't really any hits off of the record, but it was viewed as a correction after the AOR/pop slight misstep of *Mirrors*, although I think there are some redeemable things about *Mirrors*. They did the smart thing. It seemed like a lot of bands, especially bands from the '70s, knew that they had to change for the new decade. I don't know if they just sensed it in the wind, but there was a New Wave of British Heavy Metal afoot, and you get all these bands dropping fantastic albums in 1980. We've got Black Sabbath, Scorpions in '79, Motörhead with *Ace of Spades*, Saxon, Judas Priest, AC/DC with *Back in Black*. There's a shift away from the '70s, where sort of experimentalism and jamming gets left behind for tighter, focused songwriting and better production.

And for me, BÖC is right there with them. I don't consider BÖC to be a heavy metal band. To me, they're an intelligent hard rock band and that shows on this record. They can be heavy if they want to, and they could throw power chords down like anybody's business. But for me they've always been smarter than that. They're able to do their own thing, which is what's special about them. They're able to do all these different things and sort of tie them all together. So yeah, to answer your question, I think it brings them into the '80s even though it didn't really give them any commercial success, so to speak.

Matt: Yeah, so let's look at the goals that we think or we presume they had going into it. They had a goal around righting the ship commercially. Well, it fails. It does not do that at all. It continues the downward slide. They wanted to get heavier and a little more sinister—it's a total success. They kind of get the credibility back with the fan base, the average fan. So it works well. It did very well in the UK relative to their other records. I think it probably prolongs the career.

And maybe that does buy them enough time in advance of *Fire of Unknown Origin* where they actually do achieve the first goal of having improved commercial sales. They get to make another record with Martin Birch. So it succeeded enough that he's willing to do it with them again. So that's good. They had enough money just to pay him. And maybe that's the true success of *Cultösaurus Erectus* right there, that they get to perfect this relationship with Martin Birch and build a follow-up album that is considered by many to be the greatest Blue Öyster Cult album of all time, or certain top tier for most, as well as a significant commercial return to form.

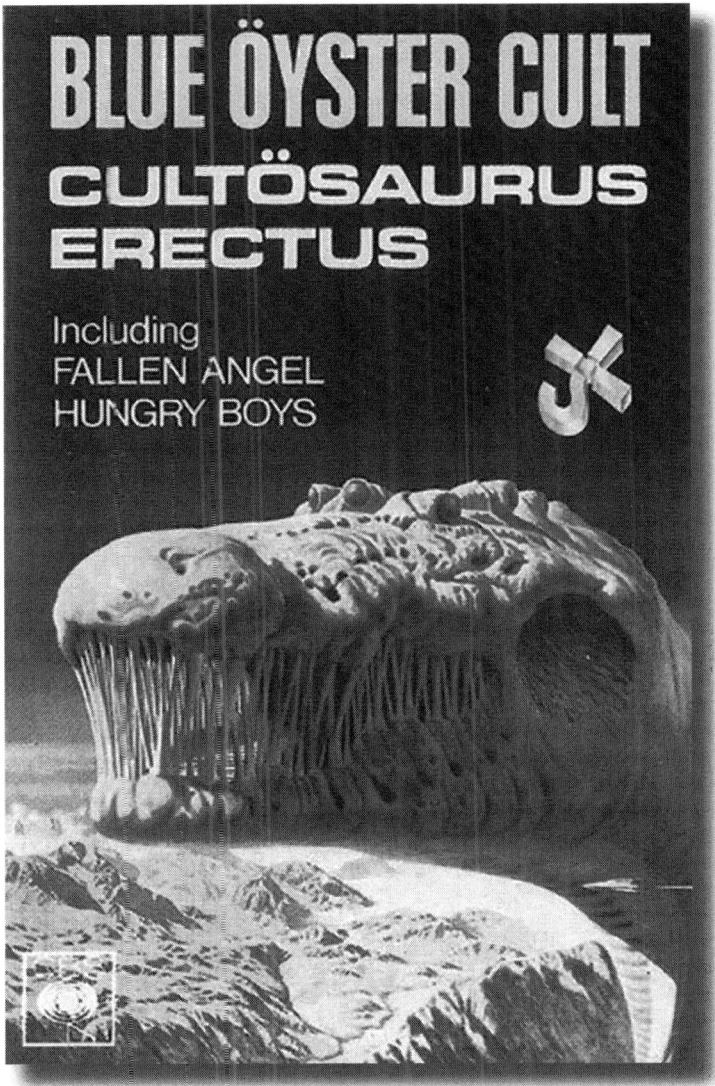

FIRE OF UNKNOWN ORIGIN

Blue Öyster Cult

9 CLASS A TRACKS

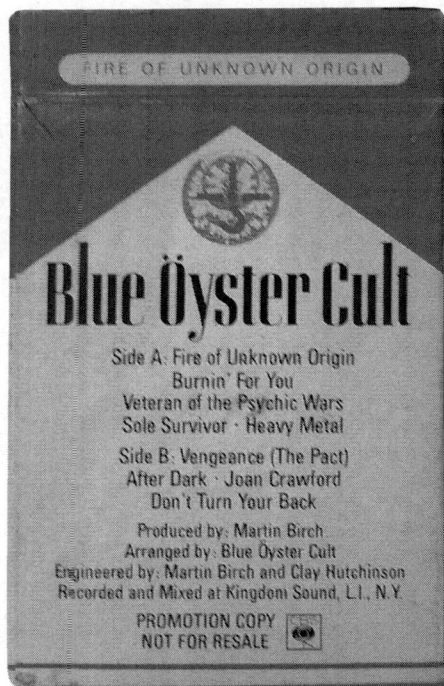

FIRE OF UNKNOWN ORIGIN

Blue Öyster Cult

Side A: Fire of Unknown Origin
Burnin' For You
Veteran of the Psychic Wars
Sole Survivor · Heavy Metal

Side B: Vengeance (The Pact)
After Dark · Joan Crawford
Don't Turn Your Back

Produced by: Martin Birch
Arranged by: Blue Öyster Cult
Engineered by: Martin Birch and Clay Hutchinson
Recorded and Mixed at Kingdom Sound, L.I., N.Y.

PROMOTION COPY
NOT FOR RESALE

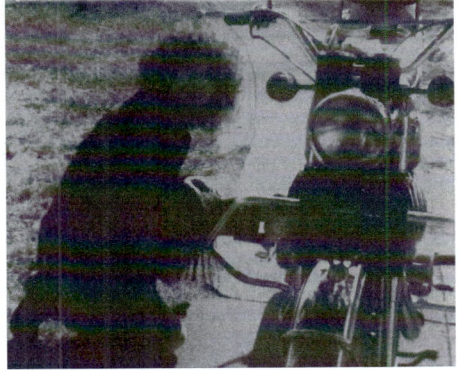

itage press shots and a couple of home casual shots. (Joe Bouchard Archive)

Oklahoma, 26th and 27th July 1975. (Rich Galbraith)

Cape Cod Coliseum, South Yarmouth, Massachusetts, 15th July 1978. Supporting was Cheap Trick. (Rudy Childs)

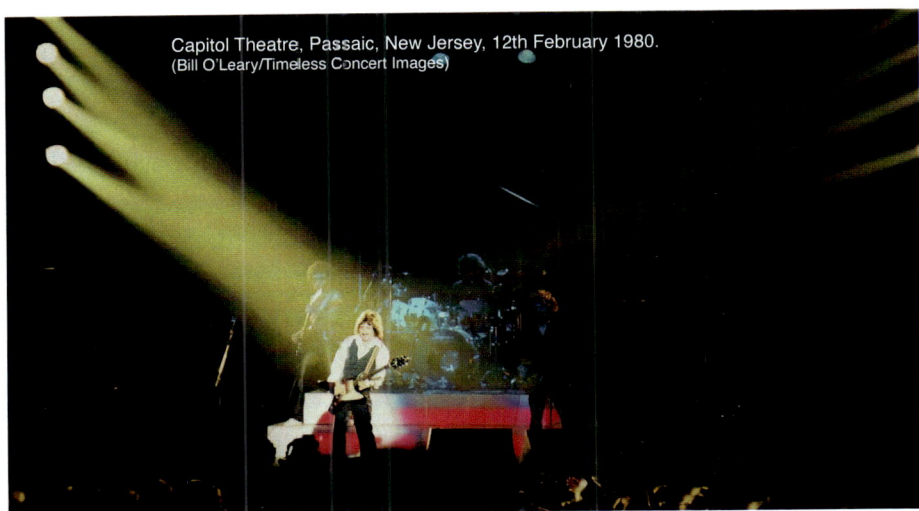

Capitol Theatre, Passaic, New Jersey, 12th February 1980. (Bill O'Leary/Timeless Concert Images)

Market Square Arena,
Indianapolis, Indiana,
8th October 1980. A Black and
Blue tour gig with
Shakin' Street and
Black Sabbath. (Rudy Childs)

apital Centre, Landover, Maryland, 26th September 1981.
hooting Star and Foghat were also on the bill. (Rudy Childs)

Ohio Center, Columbus, Ohio, 10th January 1984.
Supporting were Aldo Nova and Dokken. (Rod Dysinger)

...arly 2000s with Bobby Rondinelli and Danny Miranda. (David Lee Wilson)

With Jules Radino and Richie Castellano, Rotary Park, Last Fling Fest, Naperville, Illinois, 2nd September, 2012. (Greg Olma)

FIRE OF UNKNOWN ORIGIN

Fire of Unknown Origin
June 22, 1981
Columbia FC 37389
Produced by Martin Birch
Engineered by Martin Birch and Clay Hutchinson
Recorded at Kingdom Sound, Long Island, NY
Personnel: Eric Bloom – lead vocals, guitar, bass; Donald "Buck Dharma"
Roeser – lead guitar, vocals, bass; Joe Bouchard – bass, vocals; Allen Lanier –
keyboards; Albert Bouchard – drums, synthesizer, vocals
Guest artists: Tony Cedrone, Bill Civitella, Karla DeVito, Sandy Jean, Jesse Levy

Side 1
1. "Fire of Unknown Origin" (J. Bouchard, Smith, Bloom, A. Bouchard,
Roeser) 4:09
2. "Burnin' for You" (Roeser, Meltzer) 4:29
3. "Veteran of the Psychic Wars" (Bloom, Moorcock) 4:48
4. "Sole Survivor" (Bloom, Trivers, Liz Myers) 4:04
5. "Heavy Metal: The Black and Silver" (A. Bouchard, Bloom, Pearlman) 3:16

Side 2
1. "Vengeance (The Pact)" (A. Bouchard, J. Bouchard) 4:40
2. "After Dark" (Bloom, Trivers, Myers) 4:24
3. "Joan Crawford" (A. Bouchard, Roter, John Riggs) 4:54
4. "Don't Turn Your Back" (Lanier, Roeser, A. Bouchard) 4:07

Martin talks to Jim Bacchi, Rich Davenport, Rick LaBonte and Reed Little about *Fire of Unknown Origin*.

Martin Popoff: Well, the heroes of our tale make a bit of a rebound with *Fire of Unknown Origin*. What were your first impressions upon hearing this record?

Rich Davenport: For me? I mean, I like both. I tend to think of *Cultösaurus* as a heavier album, as a reaction against the softest albums that come before it. That's just my perception of it. And I think *Fire of Unknown Origin* is a more rounded album. I prefer it although I like both very much. Martin Birch slightly reframed the sound for the '80s without going too far. That came later. In terms of the creativity, there's a variety of different writing teams between the members and with the outside writers, which they've always chosen as opposed to the song doctors who were brought in later. It's got everything that you would expect from a Blue Öyster Cult album and it's a really good start for the decade. It's just a shame that things kind of came unstuck after this one, really.

Reed Little: Okay, so 1981 was a fantastic year in heavy rock. Previously I might have heard "The Reaper" or "Godzilla" on the radio, but I didn't really pay attention to those. I lived in a lot of cities and small towns that didn't have rock radio, so the first song that I heard that I went, "Oh, this is Blue Öyster Cult" was off of one of the most impactful albums of my entire life, 1981's soundtrack from *Heavy Metal*, the motion picture. That was actually where I first heard "Veteran of the Psychic Wars." I was 13 in 1981, and I won't go too much into the weeds, but "Veteran of the Psychic Wars" instantly became the anthem song for role-playing gamers all over America. This lyric is by Michael Moorcock, loosely based on the *Eternal Champion* saga. I knew gamers basically of my age who had never listened to Blue Öyster Cult in their life, but they loved that song. And it still has that kind of impact today. It was just so powerful.

Martin: What games specifically?

Reed: I'm talking like *Dungeons & Dragons*, but pretty much anything in that role-playing vein. Though in the '80s there weren't as many things available. *Gamma World* was out. There was *Tunnels & Trolls*, various things that were sort of riffs on the term *Dungeons & Dragons*. But really, if you were a gamer, *Dungeons & Dragons* is what you played. That was what was available.

And yeah, we were all too young to have heard Michael Moorcock's work in Hawkwind, right? So "Veteran of the Psychic Wars" was this huge thing. I was too young for my parents—rightly so—to let me go see the movie *Heavy Metal*, but I loved that soundtrack. It also got me hooked on Black Sabbath, because that was where I heard Ronnie Dio singing "The Mob Rules." Now that said, as much as I love that song, I actually didn't buy the album, because I grew up in a religious household and my parents were not about to let their kid get something from Blue Öyster Cult. So I didn't hear the full album until 1986 when a college roommate of mine owned that album. That album and Ted Nugent's *Double Live Gonzo!*, they were the only two we had and we listened to them all the time. So I know this album inside out.

Rick LaBonte: I heard this roller-skating in 1981. I was 11 and roller-skating to "Burnin' for You" and "Jukebox Hero," all the songs on the radio. So lo and behold, you wouldn't know it's the same band that did "Godzilla," even though that wasn't too far back. It definitely didn't sound like "Career of Evil." The musicianship had evolved; now they're well-polished for that FM age. Martin Birch did a good job. This is his second time so now he really had a good workflow. First album was good; it showed him what they could do, but I don't think the songs were there, even though it would be high in my ranking. But that's mainly became of the production and the way he helped bring the very best material out of them at that time. But I feel like they had a better workflow in the construction of this album. Not only do they know each other, but the guys in the band went in there knowing what was expected of them.

Jim Bacchi: Cool record—I mean, first of all the title and the cover alone again give you that thing that BÖC does so great. Amazing album art, amazing album title. In 1981, for me, I'm all about Judas Priest and Iron Maiden and the New Wave of British Heavy Metal, so this was a little light for me. But every time "Burnin' for You" came on the radio, I'm like this is a great song, I'm not skipping out on this. I saw it as "(Don't Fear) The Reaper" part two almost, very similar chord-wise, and of course Buck sang and wrote both of them.

Martin: How about a little more on the production? I feel like Martin brightened things up a bit this time, made it less puffy.

Reed: You're more production-focused than I am, but I went back and was comparing it with *Cultösaurus Erectus*, and I think *Cultösaurus* has more bottom end; it's a heavier sounding album. *Fire of Unknown Origin* is very trebly, which is unusual, because it has a ton of bass guitar. The bass guitar and keyboards are so prominent, much more so I think than in most Blue Öyster Cult music, but the bottom end is missing. So it's a trebly, or at least midrangey, bass guitar. Now, I don't know if that was intentional or what. I mean Martin Birch clearly knew what he was doing, so I have to guess that's what he wanted. But I always think that Blue Öyster Cult is a band whose material is written heavier than the way it comes out sonically, after it's produced and mixed.

Martin: Bass like that was pretty much the defining characteristic of a Martin Birch production, although not always, with *Mob Rules* being a notable exception. Jim? You're also a musician, what say you?

Jim: Best drum sound, I think, to date for them. The drum and bass thing, that's where it's starting to bring the punch and that's Martin Birch. It has that Martin Birch edge that you start to get on those Maiden records. Yeah, this record is definitely a big step up sonically from the previous one.

Martin: Rich, how would you describe the production on this versus *Cultösaurus Erectus, Heaven and Hell* and *Mob Rules*?

Rich: This is just my perception, but I think it's not quite as heavy. It captures the dynamics of the band but it's kind of radio-friendly, as proven by "Burnin' for You." But it's done that in a way that hasn't compromised or diluted anything. I would characterize the Sabbath albums as been heavier, with *Mob Rules* as the heavier, more aggressive album than all of them, with "Turn Up the Night" and all that. But there were quite a lot changes in terms of production in that shift from the '70s into the '80s. The aggression from the New Wave of British Heavy Metal… Sabbath and Blue Öyster Cult kind of got some capital with that. They didn't cash in on it, but they were in the right place at the right time.

BÖC had a big hit in the UK with "Burnin' for You." For them, it was a big, big chart entry and they wound up playing the Monsters of Rock Festival. Recently I did an interview with John Gallagher from Raven, and he was explaining that there really wasn't that much of a division between the old guard and the new bands. So for a band like Blue Öyster Cult, or Ozzy or Whitesnake, there's a wave of younger kids who were getting into rock in that time period who would think, "Right, another heavy band, great!" And they were enough of a force that Blue Öyster Cult could benefit.

Martin Birch was quite a hot producer at the time. He was a very skilled producer in that you didn't get the Martin Birch sound imposed on everything. He played to the strengths of a band, like Maiden for instance. And for Blue Öyster Cult, he seems to get a really clear and strong representation in terms of the engineering side of the band's sound. And because it was his second record, I think there's a cohesion this time where the different elements don't jump out in quite as pronounced a fashion as they would on say… and this isn't a criticism of *Agents of Fortune*, but there's so many different styles on that, and they kind of stick out and distract. Whereas *Fire of Unknown Origin* is more of a piece, more of a cohesive album.

Martin: Well, let's look at the songs, beginning with the title track, which has changed drastically from when Albert first started demoing it.

Rich: Yes, this features Patti Smith on lyrics and I really like this one. From what I picked up on in your *Agents of Fortune* biography, you made a comparison to The Stranglers on this one and I would agree with that. The bass line reminds me of "Riders on the Storm" a little bit as it builds up; it's quite hypnotic, almost like a loop. And of course The Stranglers are constantly getting those Doors comparisons.

Then the chorus is classic Blue Öyster Cult, very sweeping and epic but with a sinister edge. But they've got the harmonies and the tongue-in-cheek humour to balance that. So you get a contrast between the verse and the chorus. I like the middle section of the song, the breakdown, where you've got the synthesizers and the guitar harmonies. It's again quite epic but concise. And Buck's playing is lyrical and with a lot of feel but he can really rip as well. So yeah, it's an intriguing way to start, with a mix between expected BÖC and some new wave influence, topped with punchy sound.

Rick: Powerful song, strong lyrically, great rocker, love the keys on it. It shows the musicianship of the entire band—everybody's shining on it. They come right out of the gate as a serious rock band but with good sound that is hard-edged and shiny. We're seeing the success of Toto and Journey with "Wheel in the Sky" and stuff, and I feel like everybody is in the headspace of writing music that is accessible but not selling out. With the big hit but also with "Fire of Unknown Origin," BÖC found that healthy balance between pop and hard rock, where it's catchy but there's still space for great guitar playing.

Martin: Could you speak a little to this idea that they're moving away from acoustic and electric piano to more use of synthesizers?

Rick: Yes, well, on something like *Spectres*, there's a lot of piano playing. Now they're bringing in the synthesizers, which had been becoming popular through bands like Boston and Styx. Now the keyboard player has an even more dominant role in the overall tone of the record. Before, the piano was just fighting the frequencies. You can't hear a piano with all these heavy bombastic guitar. Now the guitars are mixed in to cater to the keyboard support, where the piano was in there struggling to find a spot in between the guitars—or even maybe a compelling reason to even be there.

Now everything is working together. The keyboard might be your whole atmospheric template, and the guitars are now a layer or a texture. It's a different approach. Even Albert gets a synthesizer credit. As for Allen, he probably had multiple keyboards around him, versus years ago maybe he had a handful. Now it's probably a whole circle, like you'd see in a prog band.

Martin: And the idea of equating synthesizers with futurism... that made sense for the tie-in to the *Heavy Metal* movie. Although in the end, they only got the one song on the all-important soundtrack album.

Rick: Yeah, "Veteran of the Psychic Wars" got on the album. But they had been very enthusiastic in writing a bunch of songs in hopes of being more involved, and that's where the album gets its heaviness. I think that's why this album becomes a favourite for a lot of people because as accessible as it is for radio play, it's definitely hard rock and even occasionally heavy metal all the way through it.

Martin: All right, and back to the first song on the album.

Reed: Yes, "Fire of Unknown Origin," which took his baby away—fantastic opener. Like you say, it's an older song that had been floating around since *Agents of Fortune* or there-abouts and somehow it never made it onto album. But it comes right in with exactly what the album is going to sound like: prominent bass line, prominent keyboards, with an Eric Bloom that is now at the top of his abilities as a vocalist.

I'm kind of surprised it's a Patti Smith lyric because there's really not much to it. There are some interesting couplets. You know, "Death comes sweeping through the hallway, like a lady's dress/Death comes driving down the highway in its Sunday best." I always loved that line. It makes you think about drunk driving right? Death on the highway. And yet that's not exactly unknown, as an origin, for something that took his baby away. I don't know. I sometimes think that looking too deep at BÖC lyrics for meaning is self-defeating. Maybe they're meant to be more evocative than they are mysterious and deep. I know people will argue about that endlessly.

As for the slathered-on synths, we're gonna get even more of that when we get to *The Revolution by Night*. But the '80s albums, as with so many artifacts of the '80s, they're dated in a way that you didn't get from the '70s. And that's because of the technology, right? It's not the songs; it's the fact that they're using different types of keyboards and those keyboards went out of date almost instantly because they had tiny amounts of memory and they were just replaced by better technology very instantly.

Jim: I totally agree with the Doors comparison with this song. I also hear "Riders on the Storm," but sped up. We're in 1981 and they're still flexing their '60s influences, you know, right there. I love that. At the same time they're writing heavy rock songs and finding interesting ways to retain their strong tradition of vocal harmonies from the '70s.

Martin: Next is "Burnin' for You," same speed, same length, same arrangement and level of heaviness, but all of a sudden, "Fire of Unknown Origin" seems nerdy and kind of off-putting in comparison.

Rich: Yes, true (laughs). Love it, absolutely killer single. Twin lead, which I'm always a sucker for—I'm a huge Lizzy fan. But there's a trace of a precedent as well, in a few songs, like "Tenderloin." They weren't suddenly like, let's throw some twin leads in for the sake of it. The construction of the song is so inviting, the way it starts with that wash of harmonies. It's almost like a 10CC choral effect. And the drum pattern is brilliant, great bass tone. There's a lot of energy and it really builds up well. And there's like an offbeat rhythm to the guitar line that brings what is almost a reggae feel. And then it really rocks on the pre-chorus section. In my notes I put more hooks than Ali versus Frazier!

Rick: Amazing song, specifically with respect to vocals, where after those lush opening harmonies that are so exciting and expansive, Buck delivers a laid-back vocal that is very soft. But everybody sounds inspired and that's what makes the song. There's lots of ear candy, but it's not the obvious kind, like you get in say "Black Blade" or "Monsters" or "Joan Crawford."

Reed: I love this song. Heck, I think everybody loves the song, which is the reason it was a hit. But that said, I don't think it's a particularly awesome song in terms of the BÖC catalogue. At this point in their career it was what they needed. It comes off very much as "The Reaper" part two to me. It's a love song, but it has some more interesting lyrics. We've got some couplets here like "I've seen suns that were freezing and lives that were through." That's not really standard love song material, right? But it's very pop-sounding and yet has these great heavy guitars. I say heavy just in that they're over-driven; they're not produced or mixed in heavily. It's not *Mob Rules* Black Sabbath. It's still very pop of construction.

Jim: Such a catchy song, man, beginning with those dual guitar harmonies at the beginning. I mean, my local radio station on Long Island, WBAB, that I grew up listening to, it's still there and they still play this song. It was on all the time and it got to a point where I got sick of it. But then I'm like, yeah, but it's such a good song, and so immediate.

And that reggae chord, it's modern, more like a new wavy stab with a delay on it. There are definitely parts of this record that skirt new wave, not punk or post-punk but American new wave. It's like they're going, oh, let's address this. We're still a rock band. But it's 1981. Like, what do we do?! We want to get on the radio. I don't know if they intentionally wrote these songs to get on the radio or because they wanted hits, because they had a bunch of hits already. Plus they just naturally and sincerely like accessible music. That's the great thing about them. But, yeah, that little delayed guitar stab thing was an interesting touch; it took it out of it just being a linear, smoothed-out hard rock song.

Martin: Next is "Veteran of the Psychic Wars," BÖC's version of "We Will Rock You," and to a lesser level of fame, Judas Priest's "Take on the World."

Rick: Yes, I love the marching rhythm, so dramatic and spooky. You can picture soldiers walking in uniform and thinking like something scary's gonna happen. There's something bad here. It's like you're under siege, and BÖC create the perfect music for that feeling. That's what I feel when I'm hearing this, that something is imminent. Like you see planes flying over the city and bombs are gonna start falling—that kind of scariness. The calm before the storm.

Jim: It's funny this made the soundtrack album but not "Heavy Metal: The Black and Silver" and they used two other songs called "Heavy Metal" instead. But this is arguably the best song on this record besides "Burnin' for

You," with that big pounding drum intro. Again, they're bringing in different keyboard sounds and not so much with the Hammond organ or clavinet or traditional piano. It's probably a Roland Juno synthesizer. That sound is all over this record. We're hearing BÖC as an '80s band.

Rich: Yeah, distinguished by that stomping military beat, regimented, clipped, topped with eerie keyboards. And I know you mentioned in your book that they were writing tracks for the *Heavy Metal* movie around that time, so like you say, the keyboards tie in with that. And then the song moves from the more regimented beat under the solo section, to being a bit more open rhythmically. It creates quite a nice flow to the track.

I love Eric Bloom as a vocalist. He's very expressive, quite high and clear with his range here and he's convincing with it. Don't get me wrong, I love metal—it's the genre I grew up with—but with some bands, it can be so cheesy with the lyrical themes. But BÖC can stickhandle their way through. There's that solid sense of the tongue-in-cheek, where they can sing a song like "Godzilla" because they've got enough humour in there. And on this one, it's not hokey, even though he's singing a science fiction-themed lyric.

Reed: This is the perfect example of what I mean when I say BÖC is not as heavy as people remember them. If you listen to this song, the individual components are not that heavy. The guitars are pretty distorted, but they're not deep, heavy guitars. The drums, I love that military snare drum. It sounds like a guy being marched to his execution, right? It has this synthesizer pad instead of these really complicated lines that are available elsewhere in the song. So they create an atmosphere. It's quite literally an atmospheric song.

And it's my favourite Eric Bloom vocal performance of all of them. But music is so spare and in the '80s now. Buck was a fantastic guitar player in the '70s. But to me, he kicks it up a notch every decade. He's just on fire on this album. But the solo on this song is not note-dense. It's very open and it's drenched in echo and reverb. Really, overall there's just so much space in this song. You feel like, okay, somebody could redo this and fill in those spaces and make it a much denser song but that would ruin it. And that's the magic of BÖC to me right there in one song.

Martin: Now we're into the deep tracks, with "Sole Survivor" lacking any sense of flash. They do however put a bit of an almost "Burnin' for You"-style chorus on it, but the verse is so staid, there was no way this was going to be a hit.

Rich: Yeah, unusual. Again, this is something that I like about Blue Öyster Cult in general, that kind of sinister, unusual, unsettling vibe that they have on some songs and then the payoff after that is a very melodic chorus. Or sometimes there's a dark undercurrent under a melodic chorus. That's a dark undercurrent as opposed to a soft white underbelly—I'm here all week, try the fish (laughs). So here we have an unusual, unsettling verse section with a clean guitar figure, very atmospheric with the synths, and then a big chorus, a big rhythmic payoff. They're all hitting the off-beat together on that. There are some nice backing vocals. Karla DeVito sings on this—she famously toured with Meat Loaf and she's in the videos from *Bat Out of Hell*, although it's Ellen Foley on the album. Very unusual solo from Buck. He's very good at playing those long, sustained notes; quite unsettling again, but it fits the vibe of the song.

Reed: "Sole Survivor" is a such a weird song. I love the opening bass line. And when I talk about bass and drums being prominent on this album, there are two songs that open with naked bass. And while I don't have an encyclopaedic memory for BÖC, I don't think that happens on any other album. Basically Joe Bouchard is substantially highlighted on *Fire of Unknown Origin*. Elsewhere it's got these atmospheric synth pads, over a really strange chord progression. It's not standard pop, it's not a one-four-five and it's not a bluesy chord progression—until you get to the chorus, and then the chorus has a much more standard rock chord progression.

The lyrics are very BÖC: last man on Earth, he's psychic for some reason and living alone so long that when rescue shows up, he doesn't even want to get rescued. It's territory that Iron Maiden would visit in another five years. But you think about 1981, I don't know of anybody else who could have done a song like this. One of the things about the '80s, weirdly, is that general rock audiences were starting to become less tolerant of strange lyrics. People that liked that sort of thing all gravitated to heavy metal but the rock audience was on their way over to hair metal, where it was songs about sex, drugs and rock 'n' roll and not the last of mankind who happens

to be psychic.

Rick: "Sole Survivor"—simple but memorable bass intro with the keys as great support. I like that song. Again, this is something they learn from the previous record, to have an accessible chorus despite whatever else they were doing, and I think they did that well.

Jim: Yeah, there's that Roland Juno synth sound again. Like I say, they got rid of the pianos now and they brought this in. Spooky song, catchy chorus.

Martin: Okay, it's funny, "Heavy Metal: The Black and Silver," with a title like that and how heavy it is, we're supposed to lap it up, but it's a bit underwhelming, isn't it?

Reed: Yes, and possibly because Albert Bouchard may be playing guitar on this instead of Buck—Joe said that in your book—and Eric is playing bass. And while it's rare to have a drummer that plays guitar as well as Albert does, he was no Buck Dharma. And I love the fact that the song starts and ends with squalling feedback, something that Martin Birch normally would have trimmed right out of any song. It just adds to that "We're just kind of goofing around" feel to it.

I appreciate this song because it's so different from everything else on the album. Clearly a song intended for the *Heavy Metal* movie. It feels a little rushed, a little unfinished. The lyric is about alchemy but there's not much to it. It's one of those that sounds great and then I go and read the lyrics, it doesn't really tell a story or have a point. It's just let's write a song that contains the phrase heavy metal and maybe they'll put it in the movie.

Rich: It reminds me a bit of "Godzilla," that kind of riff. And it's a more aggressive vocal from Eric. It's okay but like you said, it's not a complete knockout. It's not something I would skip, or in the old days, fast forward, when I had it on cassette, but it's not a complete knockout. I think what saves it is the general sense of eccentricity that Blue Öyster Cult have anyway, musically, which stops it being clichéd. It's not like typical Muppet metal. It plays to the band's strengths. It's a Sandy Pearlman lyric, with his spin on alchemy, as he mentioned in your book. That stops it being a typically clichéd metal song about metal. Maybe it shows through a little bit that they're writing to order for the film, where the title is a prescriptive element of the song. Yeah, not fantastic.

Jim: I love the feedback at the beginning and they give us a heavier riff, along with the heaviest arrangement and mix on the album. It's cool that we already got "The Red & the Black" and now we've got "The Black and Silver." I'm not completely in love with it but I like it. And like you say, as metalheads we're supposed to love it, but even though the bar is lower, you still gotta deliver.

Rick: I think the dissatisfaction comes from how it sounds like it's more from the black-and-white era. It's as much proto-metal as it is 1981 metal. It's got the thickness and darkness and doom of old school metal from the '70s but it's not the best riff, especially those chords under the verses.

Martin: Speaking of being obvious, or literal, what do you think of this album cover?

Reed: It's the ultimate BÖC album cover, right? When you think about Blue Öyster Cult, here's an album cover that's a Blue Öyster Cult. I mean, the kid on the front is actually holding a blue oyster. What do you want? It's perfect, it's creepy, it makes you think that maybe it's part of a story. It's wonderful. It's the type of thing that when you were flipping through the record bins, that would catch your eye.

Rick: Yeah, love it. You mentioned in the book that it gives you an indication of what a Blue Öyster Cult—or *the* Blue Öyster Cult—might actually look like. And it totally fits the music; it's an intriguing, atmospheric cover. Is it the fire of unknown origin that is making his face glow like that? Are they looking at this fire? Or are they waiting for the fire? There's obviously a story in the lyrics to the song but the imagery isn't too overtly stated. And it's a similar thing with the cover. You can try interpret it. There's a sharp, definitive image presented to you but you're not quite sure what it means.

Martin: Over to side two, we get "Vengeance (The Pact)," another heavy rocker, but with proggy tendencies as well. It's this record's "Black Blade" perhaps.

Rick: Yep, proggy, heavy guitars, good rocker, and then three minutes into it they pick up the tempo and it's almost speed metal, or galloping like Iron Maiden. Maybe the NWOBHM got into their collective headspace here or it's just something that happened, but they definitely flirt with the idea of speed metal here. And totally in their wheelhouse is this idea that they're almost writing little science fiction movies with some of these songs.

Jim: "Vengeance" just sounds like classic BÖC to me. It's interesting that they add that gallop part, that tempo change, seemingly out of nowhere. But that hypnotic mid-tempo plod makes a return. Yes, pretty heavy for this record, but still sounds like them.

Rich: I like the off-kilter element of this song, beginning with the fairground-type vibe to the keyboards at the beginning. Enter the booming drums and the big ominous riff. Joe's first and only vocal on the album, and interestingly, Albert sings none of the songs—it's all Eric or Buck. Quite a different vocal from Joe, more aggressive than what I associate him with, which is more of that lighter "Morning Final" approach. He comes in quite quickly, quite simple, but it sinks in the more you hear it. The solo section, they get looser underneath that as a band. Quite tuneful licks from Buck. And there's a key change when it gets faster. I can almost imagine Vincent Price doing some narration on it. But I agree: that's a sort of Maiden-style chug, you know, that kind of foot-on-the-monitor triplet thing towards the end. It's an unconventional arrangement, which is one of the band's strengths, I think.

Reed: This is another song intended for the soundtrack. Famously it's the entire storyline of the main kind of vignette from *Heavy Metal*, the motion picture, the story of Tarna, and it's also where "The Mob Rules" appears in the movie. One thing, I don't like the Bouchards as vocalists nearly as much as I like either Eric or Buck. Anyway, they follow the storyline so closely that it almost feels like a cheat. But at least following the script gives them a structure. Unlike "Heavy Metal: The Black and Silver," this is a song with a story. It has a beginning, a middle and an end.

Martin: Are you saying that where "The Mob Rules" happens, this would have been the song that would have absolutely lined up with that part of the movie?

Reed: Yes. And in fact, I don't know why the people who made the movie didn't include this as a closing credits song, right? So there's a scene where this evil orb comes down and transforms these people into monsters. And they come and they knock on the gates of this town. And then as somebody inside the town opens the gates, they hit the first chords of "The Mob

Rules." It's this really powerful marriage of music and picture, but man, I hate that movie. I don't want to sing the praises of this movie. But I love that one image of meshing Black Sabbath and the visual image. And that is where "Vengeance (The Pact)" would have gone. But of course, the vignette's, you know, 20 minutes and the song is seven minutes.

Martin: Interesting. Anything else you wanted to say about that one?

Reed: Only that a gallop structure like that wasn't common practice yet in heavy metal. Maiden just had two albums out, for example, so they hadn't beat it to death yet. But that galloping gives you the sense that the cavalry is coming, right? Which is what's happening at that part in the song.

Martin: Nice, okay, how about "After Dark?" Which I must say has become my favourite song on the album, over time. Plus it's the most magic Joe moment across the whole catalogue, as far as I'm concerned.

Rich: I thought the keyboards sounded a little dated on this one, which is not something the band generally suffer from. Nice licks from Buck, fast bass line, the synths are quite dominant initially. Then after the chorus, or sorry, in the pre-chorus, the guitars get quite rhythmic, almost punky. And then again, you're saying about Joe; there's a really nice walking bass line on the pre-chorus section, quite a complex riff on the chorus and a good hook line. But it's unconventional with a kind of... that thing that Rush did really well, of slotting in a twist on the time signature where it isn't in congress and it doesn't jive. You know, it flows quite well but it still grooves but it is quite a technical thing to do. And the guitar is more forthright on the second verse. Yeah, so again, I like the song, a lot of atmospherics going in there. And it's kind of a good example of the band's skillful arrangements again.

Rick: Yeah, great bass and drum intro, and I love when the guitars come in, with those two very distinct synth sounds. It definitely rocks and shows BÖC at its finest. It's short but just perfect. That's one of the things about BÖC in this era—especially from *Agents of Fortune* on—they don't overstay their welcome; they don't drag out songs. When this song ends, it sounds like there's still gas in the tank.

Reed: "After Dark" is such a weird song, and this is the second song on the album that opens with naked bass, with Albert laying down a great groove using snare and bass. And then there's that really high-pitched, almost like slide whistle-sounding synthesizer, which is kind of irritating, audibly, but I think that's what they wanted. It sets the mood. This is another lyric about a man being turned into a vampire. Seems pretty straightforward. But it's also another song where I think the intent of it, the overall desired effect, is actually heavier than the sonics allow. I can imagine Megadeth doing this song in '85 or '86 and the result would have been very different. It's still rock but it's not super-aggressive.

Jim: Pretty new wave, actually; sounds like heavy Cars. It's got that jerky, punky energy of their older records, but with the new wavy keyboards, layered actually with a bit of a '60s vibe, with that synth in there that sounds like Farfisa. And like Reed says, you hear the bass really great on this record. And that's the Martin Birch effect, because most of his records have that tight, high-slung bass in them. Yeah, "After Dark" is pretty out of character for them. But on an older Blue Öyster Cult record, the keyboards wouldn't be there. It would just sound like one of their up-tempo rock songs.

Martin: Of course who doesn't like "Joan Crawford?"

Rich: Oh, classic, classic song—amazing, and one of the highlights of the album. It plays into the fact that the *Mommie Dearest* book had come out not long before. Really ornate piano intro, almost a classical feel, very atmospheric and ominous and also quite dramatic. And then we get those aggressive eighth notes on the piano, with some really good punctuation from the bass and guitar and drums doing kind of rhythmic stabs as the song emerges. Same sort of piano situation as "Sinful Love." Great chords on the bridge.

You know, bombast and drama is usually not a substitute for good songwriting, but BÖC has got both. You've got the riffs but it's not like the vocal just follows the riff. You get riffs, but you also get good chord progressions with fresh melodies over them, if you see what I mean.

And what they'll also do, quite typically, they'll come up with a chord progression where you think you know where it's gonna go, and then it goes somewhere else. There's almost like a sour element to it. It's not quite like King's X, who do it more dramatically, where they'll throw in something really jarring and it's like, whoa, where did that come from? This is a more subtle version of that, sometimes with the harmonies, sometimes with the chord progressions or the chord inversions.

Another walking bass line comes in. Big chorus, and simple but with a twist. Accomplished arrangement with the sound effects. There's builds and there's breakdowns. There's that tense section with the bass drum pulsing like a heartbeat and some harmonics from Buck and then finally a pile of cinematic sound effects, which shows that humour creeping in again.

Rick: "Joan Crawford" gets heard a lot, but it's lasted because it's got a great chorus. What kind of band does a song about a Joan Crawford biography?! Pretty funny. The movie came after the book and this song, but now people who see the movie, they can listen to this song to get an even better picture of what she was like.

Jim: I remember hearing this on the radio; it was a minor hit where I lived. "Joan Crawford has risen from the grave." I mean, come on. Such a great song. And that great intro; Allen Lanier's a good piano player, man. That chorus sounds to me like something off of *Spectres*, melodically, in the harmonies. It has that classic kind of late '70s period Blue Öyster Cult sound, more in keeping with that than what is on this record. But the production overall is just so good on this record for 1981.

Reed: It's hard to believe this song got played on radio as much as it did, because it's so freakin' weird. The lyrics are completely surreal. Put your finger anywhere on the lyrics for this song and it's going to be weird. You know, "Policemen are hiding behind the skirts of little girls/Their eyes have turned the colour of frozen meat." What does that mean? And what it has to do with Joan Crawford, I don't know. But the chorus, when they come in with the gang chorus singing, "Joan Crawford has risen from the grave," that sounds awesome.

The lyrics are credited to David Roter, right? Apparently inspired by Al Bouchard's soon-to-be ex-wife screaming at him. And the movie *Mommie Dearest* came out just a few months after *Fire of Unknown Origin*, and the book it's based on came out in '78. So that may be why Joan Crawford was enough in this guy's consciousness that he could think up a frame for a song. Bear in mind there was also a sketch on *Saturday Night Live* about it in 1978 and everybody watched *Saturday Night Live* and those guys knew some of the cast. Otherwise it's the '80s—who's going to think of '30s '40s '50s movie star Joan Crawford? That's their point of reference, right? But it was in pop consciousness at that time, I guess, first because of the book.

Oh, and of course how can I forget the keyboard solo to announce the song? It starts with Allen Lanier and his best keyboard work, I think, on any Blue Öyster Cult song. And it's so out of place with the rest of the album. So we get this beautiful keyboard intro and then they start up this surrealistic, nightmarish story. I guess you could mostly see the song as Christina's nightmare waiting for mommy to come home. So yeah, it's a wonderful song, but it's so bizarre.

Martin: Okay, the album closes out on a wistful, melancholic note, with "Don't Turn Your Back." Are you buying what they're selling?

Rich: No, not a fan of this one. It doesn't fit the sequencing of the album, really, at least for my tastes. It's an example of that slight hint of sourness being brought to the forefront and perhaps not working. It's this unsettling feeling that sometimes works against the band, but that worked for them all the way through the a bum to this point. There's almost like a jazz fusion kind of chord progression to the song, quite jarring. Then there's a more melodic part with harmonies, but not much of a payoff to it in terms of chorus. This solo section saves it for me from being a complete washout. It's more melodic again, and the solo is inventive, quite original. But it's a bit of an anticlimactic ending to the album, really.

Rick: I don't know, I'd frame it as another sort of unappreciated gem like "After Dark." It's got the prettiness and catchy properties that we like about "Burnin' for You" and I'm surprised it wasn't a hit. To me it's a great pop tune with a timeless quality, and sung by Donald, who is supposedly the most saleable voice. I don't know, Quarterflash and bands like that are out by this time; there were all these melodic choruses all over radio. I'm surprised they don't play it live. It's not hard rock but it's just so catchy. When I turn off that album, that "Don't turn your back" warning over and over again in the verse is in my head until I put on the next album (laughs).

Reed: Surprisingly, it's one of the songs that was written for *Heavy Metal*, the motion picture, and it doesn't seem it would have fit at all. But if you watch there's a segment where they've got a film noir scene with this taxi driver, and this song is written about that segment. Honestly, I think it sounds like Blue Öyster Cult doing yacht rock. If you just think of the sonics of it, you can imagine Christopher Cross singing this song. Now the lyrics are a little weird for Christopher Cross but it's not completely out of the question. But it's not what I associate with the Blue Öyster Cult sound, although thematically for this album, there's that prominent bass line again. I know that as a band they could go to a lot of areas, but this is quite atypical. I'm not surprised that it was relegated to last track on the album.

Jim: Glad you mentioned the bass—love that groove. And those '80s keyboards, I mean, that's definitely different for them up to this point. Donald is singing over a chord progression that's a little weird. And then there's this suspended chord—strange.

Martin: It's a little like Rush in "Distant Early Warning," which comes much later, mind you.

Jim: Yes (laughs). Thank you! I'm trying to think, what is that sound?! And yeah, you're right, that's like three years later.

Martin: You might even compare Geddy's bass line in that song to what Joe is doing, somewhat.

Jim: Yes, yeah, wow, it really is a lot like it, isn't it? At least sonically.

Martin: And the keys!

Jim: Yes (laughs). The keyboard sound is probably an Oberheim, which is what Geddy was using, right? An OBX8 or whatever. I mean, that's exactly the "Distant Early Warning" keyboard sound.

Martin: Okay, let's not rush to any judgements (laughs). Now that we've come to the end of this album, what are your thoughts on what it would end up doing for the band?

Jim: Well, bottom line, *Fire of Unknown Origin* was probably too light for me at the time. It's 1981 and you're all into the newer, cooler bands. We're in the thick of the New Wave of British Heavy Metal, and I remember I was getting into UFO for the first time, although they're even older than these guys. But BÖC, man, they're that older band from the '70s that's still got beards and moustaches. And having a beard in '81, '82, '83 was about as uncool as it got if you're in a hard rock band. Soon it's like, you should be wearing spandex and looking like a girl or, you know, just looking more like a young rock guy.

Still, "Burnin' for You" put them back on the radar with the rock people because it was a huge rock radio song. I know the album almost got to platinum, but I can't believe it's not platinum by now. That song was on the radio every day. I may have a different perspective on things because they're a Long Island band and they probably got played a lot in our area. Growing up ever since "(Don't Fear) the Reaper" came out, you heard Blue Öyster Cult on the radio all the time here. You heard "Godzilla," you heard "(Don't Fear) The Reaper" and you heard this.

But it's weird. They didn't get two or three really big hits deep on any given album. It was always one song from an album, you know? And you're right. *Cultösaurus* and *Mirrors*, nothing off of those records became a hit. "Burnin' for You" was a comeback for them. But like I say, where I lived it was such a ubiquitous song. I can't believe they didn't sell more records. And they played arenas. I mean, when I saw them, they're playing Nassau Coliseum, Madison Square Garden, New Haven Coliseum, you know 15,000-seaters sold-out most of the time or close.

Reed: I wonder if the record only got so far because they included songs that they were intending to get put on this movie soundtrack, and therefore the songs are kind of all over the map. Plus they're trying to figure out how to join the '80s. A bunch of '70s bands struggled with joining the '80s, not just BÖC. So like you say, they're throwing in some new wave elements, and I don't know that the songs were necessarily new wave. And yet the instrumentation is somewhat new wave. And did that work? Well, I don't know. I mean, I think at the time you would say no. And nor would you say that their base was necessarily wanting them to be that way.

On the other hand, they've got, again, what I call functionally "The Reaper" part two in "Burnin' for You." So here's a song that gets radio play. Now, people hear that song. *Agents of Fortune* is by far BÖC's most successful album. So people hear "Burnin' for You" on the radio—this is a theory; I can't prove it—and they think that sounds pretty good. I sure liked that *Agents of Fortune* album. I'm going to pick up *Fire of Unknown Origin*.

So they get it to get "Burnin' for You" and it turns out to be one of the strangest rock albums to come out of the 1980s. I mean, I know a lot of people don't listen to lyrics, but pound for pound it's so in-your-face with songs like "After Dark" and "Joan Crawford" and "Veteran of the Psychic Wars," you cannot escape how strange this album is. And I have to imagine that anybody who was looking for a mainstream rock song, like "Burnin' for You," is going to listen to the rest of the album and go, oh, this isn't what I signed on for. And then that's reflected then in the sales of *The Revolution by Night*. It's an interesting theory, but yeah, perhaps in the strangeness of the rest of *Fire of Unknown Origin* after "Burnin' for You," therein lies the decline of the band that they've been experiencing ever since.

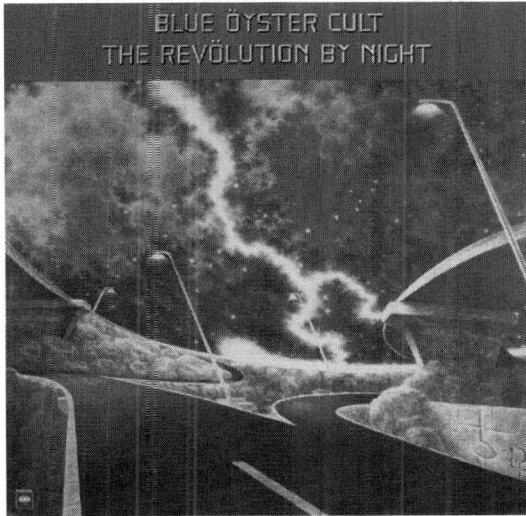

THE REVOLUTION BY NIGHT

The Revolution by Night
November 8, 1983
Columbia FC 38947
Produced by Bruce Fairbairn
Engineered by Dave Wittman; additional engineering by Ken Kessie
Recorded at Boogie Hotel, Port Jefferson, NY, Kingdom Sound, Long Island, NY, The Automatt – Studio C, San Francisco, CA
Personnel: Eric Bloom – guitar, vocals; Donald "Buck Dharma" Roeser – guitar, keyboard, vocals; Joe Bouchard – bass, electric and Spanish guitar, vocoder, vocals; Allen Lanier – piano, synthesizers; Rick Downey – drums
Guest performers: Mark Baum, Larry Fast, Randy Jackson, Aldo Nova, Gregg Winter

Side 1
1. "Take Me Away" (Bloom, Aldo Nova) 4:26
2. "Eyes on Fire" (Gregg Winter) 3:51
3. "Shooting Shark" (Roeser, Smith) 7:07
4. "Veins" (Roeser, Meltzer) 3:56

Side 2
1. "Shadow of California" (J. Bouchard, Neal Smith, Pearlman) 5:05
2. "Feel the Thunder" (Bloom) 5:47
3. "Let Go" (Bloom, Roeser, Hunter) 3:25
4. "Dragon Lady" (Roeser, Broadway Blotto) 4:04
5. "Light Years of Love" (J. Bouchard, Wheels) 4:08

Martin talks to Nick S. Squire, Reed Little, Bill Schuster and Matt Thompson about *The Revolution by Night*.

Martin Popoff: So here we are at *The Revolution by Night*. There's been another live album, a double, plus the band has experienced its first lineup change ever, with Albert Bouchard being replaced by Rick Downey. It's also been more than two years since the last studio album. What kind of record do we get out of these guys given all that?

Reed Little: *The Revolution by Night* was not as successful as *Fire of Unknown Origin*; it didn't even go gold. These were the first two videos I remember seeing from Blue Öyster Cult, being "Take Me Away" and "Shooting Shark." And "Shooting Shark," for a long time I remember seeing that video in the middle of the night and then not seeing it again for weeks, and then it just went to die. I'm going, "Did I imagine that song?" And I used to watch MTV obsessively. So I love those songs.

Sonically *The Revolution by Night* is much more in keeping with the general music of 1983 than *Fire of Unknown Origin* was with the music of 1981. But they have a problem with that. *The Revolution by Night* is an album of two sides and one of them doesn't sound like Blue Öyster Cult. To me, with the exception of "Take Me Away," the songs on side one could have been by any '80s band. It could have been Journey with Buck Dharma instead of Steve Perry. It could have been Toto. It could have been Manfred Mann's Earth Band, who had one song in the '80s, with "Runner," which was a cover of somebody, even. So they're another band from the '70s struggling to move into the '80s kind of unsuccessfully.

And even more than *Fire of Unknown Origin*, it's the '80s production that kills it. It's got the '80s drums, it's got the '80s synths, it's got the '80s reverbs. And it's so funny because it's Bruce Fairbairn producing and he was the '80s guy when you think of successful '80s albums. Bruce is one of the top producers but they didn't go to Vancouver to work with him. It was still recorded in New York.

Martin: But this is early for him. He'd had some Canadian success with Prism and wider success with Loverboy, but that's it at this point.

Reed: Right, but he's very much an AOR guy, and side one of *The Revolution by Night* is an AOR side.

Matt Thompson: Reed is onto something there. You did that *History in Five Songs with Martin Popoff* episode called "Go to Vancouver and Try Harder," about bands going there in the late-'80s and early '90s. And here they've got Bruce Fairbairn and so they're ahead of the playbook of what is going to be a successful recipe for bands. But it doesn't work in this case. This was not a successful record. It does worse than the previous records. Like Reed says, they don't go to Vancouver. They do it in Long Island, and for the mixing process, by all accounts from the band, Fairbairn is kind of absent. So they were kind of onto something that might've worked, but they didn't execute what became the best practice in terms of making that kind of record: go to Vancouver and work with Bruce—or Bob Rock—and then have him fully involved, and maybe they would've had a different outcome.

Martin: And how would you classify the outcome that they got? What do you think of the production?

Matt: Well, they'd had a bit of a break. They're not quite on their album-per-year cycle. There's some extra time, as they're kind of sorting through the impact of Albert leaving. Martin Birch had produced the two previous studio records and now you've got Fairbairn coming in a little bit before his biggest successes. They're kind of catching a producer certainly on the upswing, and it's a good catch for them at this point—at least going in.

They're going to introduce some new technology and sounds, notably the synth drum/electronic drum sounds for the first time. It's a mixed bag. Ultimately it sounds dated because of some of the drum sounds. So it's maybe not exactly "of its time," but it certainly sounds like an '80s record. It doesn't sound like an '80s hard rock record, but it definitely has some '80s sounds to it. If you go back to it, it'll sound dated, or in other words, it's not timeless.

It's a little bit bolder than the Martin Birch productions. The Martin Birch productions weren't necessarily bold, but they were very effective. The songs got across, they loved working for him and he was really impactful. But he wasn't making a bold statement. This one, they're going for it. They're making a bold statement. I think it works in some of the songs and not others.

Martin: What can you tell me about the change in drummers for this album?

Reed: Albert was apparently not well liked by the members of the band. He was somewhat domineering; they thought he was having too much influence. And maybe he opened his mouth one too many times and they got sick of him on tour and replaced him. Now that's always an interesting thing, when you replace a band member. Bands are a type of alchemy, right? A good band is not a group of individuals. So when you replace one member, you're always gonna get a different result. Cozy Powell and Bill Ward are both fabulous drummers, but they make different-sounding music, even playing with the rest of Black Sabbath. And Al Bouchard was a songwriter. He was a lyric writer. And even if he didn't directly write songs and lyrics, which he did, he's a voting member of the band saying, "I think we should do this, I think we should do that." And I shouldn't minimize that he absolutely was a vocalist. I just don't like his voice.

As for Rick Downey, new guy in a band... he's not going to have a say in whatever's going on. They're not going to be, "Hey, new guy, what do you think we should do?" He's in to do a job and he plays fine. The playing on this album is great. I think Buck steps it up. I think he takes a look at the '80s and goes, oh, I may not be up to standard here. And by the time we get to *The Revolution by Night*, he's playing easily on par with his peers.

Bill Schuster: The big thing here is the lack of Albert. Losing Albert was a huge loss for the band, especially his songwriting. And I think it's noticeable from the first track that Albert, the drummer, is not there. Rick Downey is clearly a fill-in guy. To me, it sounds like Rick just doesn't have the creativity that Albert had. This album is the sound of a band struggling with the loss of Albert and coming to grips with new technology. And obviously the songwriting credits are ridiculous. This is a band really reaching and bringing in outside songwriters, although they did find some good ones; they found some great collaborators. As for Bruce Fairbairn, he brings bright, clear production. We have entered the '80s completely. And for this album, I think it works. It's maybe a little over-the-top in places, but yeah, for 1983 the record sounds good.

Nick S. Squire: If I can compare, you know, BÖC is starting to have a stripped-down sound. The piano is not centre stage anymore; the vocal harmonies are not centre stage anymore. The '50s style and '60s style is not the focus anymore. They're starting to use more outside writers. I bought this album new so I've still got that muscle memory for it, but yeah, it still has all the core elements of BÖC, all the things you want in BÖC. But when you compare it to the previous records, it's more of an '80s production; you're getting synth drums in there now. You've got Randy Jackson guesting and doing slap bass. All told, track by track, this album is lesser to me than it was as a kid, compared with *Spectres* and *Mirrors*. It just doesn't have the complexity, if you will, and sort of the neat Easter eggs that *Mirrors* and *Spectres* had, whether it's dynamics, time signature changes, loud/soft, heavy/light that kind of thing.

Martin: The album cover is iconic Greg Scott. This is in the black-and-white style he drew in long after he was done with BÖC—sadly, we lost Greg January 10, 2021. Can you give me a bit of a critique of it?

Bill: That's a cool album cover; it's one of those that I used to hang on my wall in my teenage days. And I think the back cover might even be cooler, with all those Egyptian hieroglyphics. Back to the front, this is unfortunately one of the covers where the Chronos symbol is barely noticeable. Not quite as hidden as *Cultösaurus Erectus*, but it really blends in with the wall there on the side of the road.

Reed: I think it's completely lame. That picture does nothing, it tells no story—great, it's some lightning. It's a black-and-white picture. It's got a red banner across the top with the band name. It's the type of thing that if you're looking through the record bins, I just look at that and go they couldn't afford a good album cover. That's not a good sign.

Nick: Maybe not the best cover. You know, in the store, you certainly don't want to see 20 of these red banners when you're flipping through the bins. I remember picking it up and thinking, oh, damn, I'm the only one buying it.

Martin: The album opens with a chunky hard rocker, although I always felt there was too much going on in the intro music, which is also used for the chorus. But yeah, "Take Me Away" is the heaviest song on the album.

Reed: And it's by a wide margin my favourite song on the album (laughs). But it sounds exactly like what it is, and that's Aldo Nova. Aldo Nova's "Fantasy" was all over MTV, so when the verses of "Take Me Away" start, and then the pre-chorus, all you can think of is, oh, this sounds just like "Fantasy." It's just Eric Bloom singing instead of Aldo Nova and you get to the solo and even though it's Buck playing the solo, he plays it just like Aldo. Of course Aldo comes from that same school of east coast '70s rock players—well, he's from Montreal—so it's not really a surprise. You have a fantastic song, but to me it's not really tied to Blue Öyster Cult's identity as a band.

Martin: Yeah, Aldo had originally called it "Psycho Ward," and he actually plays the rest of the guitars as well as the keyboards. Bill, your thoughts on this one?

Bill: I don't know how complete Aldo Nova's version of "Take Me Away" was, but that's a stone-cold classic. And Eric's lyric is very much in the Blue Öyster Cult vein. As a teenager, I always related to those lyrics as the alienated kid waiting for the aliens to come and get me. That just seemed like such a cool thing. And of course, it goes back to the men in black from "E.T.I." on *Agents of Fortune*.

Nick: "Take Me Away," they were touring with Aldo Nova as opener and here he is now co-writing a song right after the fact. They were touring together in '82. I loved this song when it came out. It was on the radio for about three weeks and then disappeared. I loved the riff; thought it was a hit. I was like, oh my God, BÖC, great; you know, this is one of my bands. It was Kiss, Cheap Trick and then BÖC right in that order for me as a kid. So here I was getting the new BÖC album because I kind of missed *Fire of Unknown Origin* when it first came out, just given my age. But this came out and I just loved it. But "Take Me Away" was played on local rock radio and then disappeared.

There's synth in there but it's not overbearing and I love the riff. There's some synth drums in there and they're not over-the-top either. But the song just disappeared and I don't know why (laughs). It laid an egg. I felt right around that time... you probably can put your finger on it more than me, but in the rock world, sometimes bands tended to eat their own. You had a band like BÖC leading the charge, along with Ted Nugent and UFO, and then when heavy rock got more and more popular, those bands got pushed aside when they should have been still out there carrying the flag. That's the only thing I can attribute to this song failing: competition in the marketplace. This was the rise of Quiet Riot, Mötley Crüe, Ratt, Dokken and Twisted Sister, and instead of BÖC being the standard-bearer, it seems like they were pushed aside.

Matt: In a lot of ways, "Take Me Away" is a quintessential Eric Bloom song. It deals with subject matter for which he's very passionate. Eric loves science fiction. He loves the idea of there being life out there and he's talked about how, if given the choice, he would go, right? He would definitely want to find out more about what's out there in this universe and beyond. The Aldo Nova origin story is interesting and you've got Aldo Nova playing on it as well. He plays guitar and keyboards on the song. It works really well, right? It's a good, heavy rocker and a good way to start off an album. I like when they start with a powerful Eric Bloom song.

Martin: Okay, second track is "Eyes on Fire," a shock of pop after the squalling guitar noises across "Take Me Away."

Matt: It's a very sincere and competent pop song, an Eric Bloom vehicle, and a song very much in the tradition of "Goin' Through the Motions." Eric is working with a collaborator, Gregg Winter, consciously trying to make a pop song, although Winter gets sole credit. Like I say, it's competent. He sings well on it. But I'm not sure there was a market for sort of competent straightforward Blue Öyster Cult pop songs at that time. None of those here or from *Club Ninja* caught on.

Reed: Basically a Journey song. It could have been "Open Arms" or any number of other mellow Journey songs. It just happens to be Eric Bloom singing, but it doesn't feel like a Blue Öyster Cult song to me. It has a really short guitar solo and also for that reason it could have been anybody. Steve Lukather, Neal Schon... happens to be Buck. But didn't have to be.

Bill: "Eyes on Fire" is credited to Gregg Winter solely and completely. So it's not from a band member. One thing I noticed—I was commenting to my wife—I thought this was a strange lyric for Eric Bloom to be singing. Because at the heart of the lyric, this guy is kind of emasculated. And that's the type of thing that Eric, historically, doesn't wanna sing. He always strikes me as the macho, manly, biker guy that doesn't want to seem anything less than the big man and the guy singing this song clearly is not getting the girl. He's the "Oh, you're just like a brother to me" kind of guy. So I thought it was weird that Eric actually sang that lyric and didn't protest.

But even though it's not a BÖC-type song lyrically, it might have been smart for them to release this as a single. I don't know how successful it would have been, but in 1983 I think it would have stood a chance on the Top 40 chart. Probably lower rungs at best, but still "Take Me Away" might have been too heavy and "Shooting Shark" a little too long and esoteric with the lyric. "Shooting Shark" does not have a mainstream lyric to it. Let's just put it that way.

Nick: I like "Eyes on Fire," You've got some piano leading it off. It's an outside writer. So yeah, you've got the guys singing it and it's on a BÖC album but this is an example of how BÖC is kind of losing its BÖC-ness (laughs). Listening to it now, it sounds like music from a bad '80s cop drama.

So, where the song for me was always okay, now if I had this on CD, I'm skipping it.

Martin: "Shooting Shark" has a good reputation; it's somewhat this album's "Perfect Water" or "Harvest Moon."

Reed: Yes, all right, everybody loves this song. It's pretty, it's a Buck vocal—Buck sang all the pretty ones. It's got a great lyric based on a poem by Patti Smith. But again, to me, this song is generic. It's a Toto song. It's a Journey song. The opening reminds me of Tom Petty's "Don't Come Around Here No More," which of course was written by The Eurythmics' Dave Stewart. It's got that same techno rhythm and it could not be any more '80s. Now clearly, they released it as a single and it went pretty low, like No.83, so it did not do well. And I have to wonder if the guys were just scratching their heads and going wait, why wasn't this a hit? Maybe if Tom Petty or Journey had done it, they could have had a hit single but Blue Öyster Cult wasn't going to own that space.

And name one other BÖC song that has slap bass. But there you go. I actually had forgotten that Randy Jackson played bass on it. And it's very prevalent, not quite as prevalent as the bass is all over *Fire of Unknown Origin* as an album. But there's still a lot of bass and keyboard on this album. And also, man, every time I hear that song, it makes me think of Bruce Springsteen's "Hungry Heart," complete with sax solo, right? There's not many BÖC songs with a sax solo—there's True Confessions"—and "Shooting Shark" has two! So it's very Bruce Springsteen as well.

Nick: I loved "Shooting Shark" when it first came out and I love it today. I don't know why. It's a different sound for them. Randy Jackson on bass, didn't know that at the time. Of course, who was he? It was my foray into, oh, this is slap bass; this is kind of neat. It's atmospheric. It's a tad long, and I know they did a single edit that got it down to about four minutes, but still, I don't

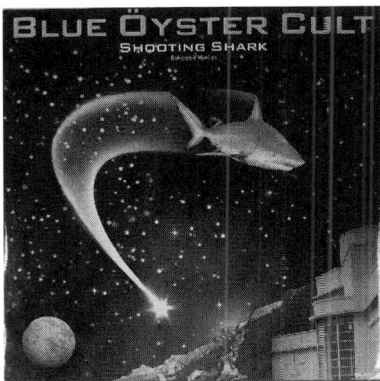

know how they expected this to be played anywhere on the planet. It's just too much.

It may be repetitive for some, but I do like Buck's melancholic vocal—that's what always made it for me. I don't know what it is about the song. It's an intangible for me, but I loved it immediately. That bass sound was foreign to me and I wouldn't have listened to some of those bands from the UK that were employing this kind of sound, but for me it was enough. That was me dipping my toe into that kind of sound. I heard them play it live and it was a little bit boring for the people I was with. But I was shocked that they played it live. And I didn't see BÖC until 2003. So here we are 20 years after the fact and they're still playing it. And they still play it from time to time.

Martin: I'm just thinking about this now, everything about that song seems really good to me, except the bass is distracting and the rhythm is clunky. It's almost like I want a whole new arrangement of it.

Nick: Well, you're right, and maybe it needs to be edited down. They have different bridges and things in there, but you're right. I always just felt it was the length of the song. But you're right. But what still makes it work for me is his understated vocal, counterpointed with the bass. That bass works for me, but I can see how after a while, it sounds like it's smacking you in the head just a little too much.

Bill: Despite the dated sounds, that's an all-time classic. I've always loved this song. I never understood the confusion about what a shooting shark is, because to me it was always very clear. "Shooting shark lighting up the sky." To me it's the subject of the song. She's flying away at night on an airplane after he sent her back for the last time. So I guess I never had any question about that. I was surprised to find out that was a sort of debated mystery, because to me that always seemed to be one of Patti's more straightforward lyrics.

Matt: "Shooting Shark" is one of these Buck compositions—there's a few of them—that are long but not epic. It's like a seven-minute-plus song. It's longer than "Astronomy" but it doesn't feel epic the way "Astronomy" does. It's much more atmospheric. And the production works really well. You've got some synthesizer sounds, blended well with the guitar, and you've got Randy Jackson doing the slap bass because Joe Bouchard doesn't really play that style. By all accounts Randy was a real pleasure to work with and spent time teaching Joe how to play that style.

One of Blue Öyster Cult strengths is collaborations, mainly lyrically, and one strong member in the bullpen with them is Patti Smith. She turns in a really good, mystical, love-oriented song, but in a very off way. And it's almost a hit. They get a video out of it, they get a little bit of airplay. Which is kind of weird. On the one hand Buck's voice suits radio well, but on the other, this is not really a radio-friendly arrangement.

Martin: And what did you think of Randy Jackson's bass part?

Bill: It sounds good but I still to this day wonder why when Joe was still in the band, why they would bring in an outside bass player. I'm not complaining about it. I love the way Randy played on it, but it still strikes me as a bit odd. By the way, in the demo collection, for "Shooting Shark," Buck said in his little notes here that he did the demo on the Roland 808. And the *Revolution by Night* recording was on the Drumulator. He thinks the tune is better suited to the 808.

Martin: Okay, last track on side one of the original vinyl is "Veins."

Bill: The '80s have definitely arrived here. The synth sounds on this and the electronic drums, oh my. But despite all that, I've always enjoyed the song. It's a cool mysterious lyric, with them going to the Meltzer well again, which never seems to run dry to this day. These guys are always reaching back, "Hey, look, here's another Meltzer lyric we have laying around." But yeah, wow, that is sonically one of the most dated songs in the catalogue, for better or for worse, depending on your personal tastes. Very locked in time.

Reed: "Veins" is an interesting song. Typically Buck doesn't get to sing the more aggressive, weirder lyric songs. And "Veins" is a somewhat fast, aggressive song about a guy waking up from blacking out, and maybe he killed somebody, right? That's the repeated refrain. He doesn't know if he killed somebody or not. And all of that would be well-trodden Eric territory. But the fact that you've got Buck with his sweeter, poppy-sounding voice on it gives it a very different dimension. Again, it's constructed... to me, it's much more of a pop song than it is hard rock or metal. So you've got that disconnect between a very aggressive, weird BÖC lyric and a pop song. And by '83 I don't think that's what the MTV-watching public wanted; they were listening to New Romantic music from England. They weren't into possible serial killers, right?

Nick: "Veins," I don't know what it is, but lyrically it wouldn't be something I gravitate to. But that song, I can tell you within the last week or two, I wake up in the middle of night to take a leak and that song is playing in my head (laughs). I don't know what it is about that song and the lyrics and the chorus, but it just gets in my head, "Veins in my eyeballs" and that whole state of mind. So maybe that's the sign of a good song. It gets in your head, burrows in your brain. Yeah, it does have the synth in there. Again, it's a different sound. But if it's burned in my brain, it must be a good song, right?

Martin: Sure, but like "Eyes on Fire," it's got that Rush *Power Windows* electro-clatter rhythm section thing going on, and I really wonder what it would sound like with a straight '70s arrangement. Anyway, flip the side and most of that kind of thinking is over with. Tell me about "Shadow of California."

Reed: Side two is what I think of as the more typical BÖC side, meaning it's the side that I enjoy more, with the exception of "Take Me Away" on the first side. "Shadow of California" is a fantastic song and quite weird. It name-checks several places in California and the shadow is this big, evil presence that's causing like earthquakes and these other events to happen. And all of that is exactly what I want from my Blue Öyster Cult songs. It's a hard rocker. It's got a great riff, muscular guitars. It's a fantastic opener for side two and I love the fact that it's got a writing credit from Alice Cooper band drummer, Neal Smith. I have no idea what Neal supplied to it, but I love the fact that Neal was part of the writing on that song because it's a great song.

Matt: Here you get a Pearlman *Imaginos* lyric, and it's kind of funny, because it gives you the *Revolution by Night* album title as well. So it seems like it's pointing to bigger things. But it doesn't advance the *Imaginos* plot. You don't actually learn more about the *Imaginos* story at a time when we're thirsty to learn more. We're going to have to wait five more years to get more information. It's pretty straightforward as a hard rocker and musically, it doesn't stand out as strong. You think about who is involved in the *Imaginos* lyrics up 'til now, creating music for them, and it's been Albert Bouchard. So of course his strengths as an arranger and sort of interpreter of Sandy's lyrics are missing here. So I'm not sure this one is as interesting as some of the previous *Imaginos* songs, or even the ones we get later.

Bill: This was a slow grower for me. I didn't used to appreciate it, but now it's right up there with "Take Me Away" and "Shooting Shark" which are my favourites on this album. I appreciate the way Albert has kind of included that in his updated list of *Imaginos* story songs. I don't think I was paying as much attention to that in the '80s. One of the cool little trivia bits about this song is that this particular lyric alone has given the titles to two separate Blue Öyster Cult albums, in both *The Revolution by Night* and *The Symbol Remains*. So yeah, that alone makes it a neat little song. But it's a classic Blue Öyster Cult song musically, upon reflection. It's something that would fit well on one of the previous albums.

Martin: Next is "Feel the Thunder," which, like the song before it, has one foot in pop and one foot in hard rock, never quite committing.

Nick: Yeah, well, this is the thing: "Feel the Thunder" is a bit like, we're BÖC, this is the reputation we've earned. Here's the song we have to write about motorcycles, right? (laughs).

Martin: The '50s is back though, right? It feels like one of those cautionary hot rod or motorcycle stories from a '50s or early '60s song. It's camp.

Nick: The '50s is back, at least thematically, and I guess for the music in the verses. The piano's not as much front and center, so it feels like a fairly heavy song. I would have loved to have heard that song live.

Reed: "Feel the Thunder" is well-trodden territory for Blue Öyster Cult. We're doing biker rock now. This one's about undead bikers dying on their way to a party or perhaps coming home from a party and it's kind of the same concept as "Ghost Riders in the Sky," right? Now they're eternally doomed to ride their bikes around and be literal hellraisers. This is not a complaint but it sounds like a complaint: it's stereotypical BÖC. If you think BÖC, these are the lyrics and this is the music that comes to mind, right? Certainly if I were to pick a song off of this particular album that is most BÖC-like, it's "Feel the Thunder."

Bill: I enjoy the song while it's playing, but I can't deny that it's pretty cartoony and over-the-top horror-type stuff. Not one of the deepest or most interesting lyrics. It's a good fun song. I've never loved it. It's definitely mid- to lower-tier Blue Öyster Cult.

Martin: Yet things go downhill further with "Let Go," which seems to expand upon or dwell upon all the things people don't like about "Feel the Thunder."

Reed: Yeah, okay, so I would not have picked Ian Hunter, necessarily, as a songwriting partner. But once you see his name, you're like, yeah, okay, I can absolutely hear the Ian Hunter influence. This song is too happy, too upbeat. I would even say it's peppy. There's kind of a tough lyric but then you get to the "BÖC, you can be whatever you want to be." Like it's The Electric Company singing it, right? And of course you've got a choir of people singing, "Let go!," which is way too close to the Ramones, "Hey ho, let's go!" I don't dislike this song but I think it's one of the lesser tracks on the album. One other thing about, "Let Go," ironically given that Neal Smith is on a previous track, I think that "Let Go" sounds like an Alice Cooper song. I could absolutely hear Alice Cooper doing that song.

Bill: I'm almost surprised Ian Hunter allowed his name to be credited on "Let Go." I wonder why they brought him in and what exactly he contributed here because lyrically there's not a lot going on, obviously. When you first assigned me this album, I said what have I done to myself? I put this so high on my list of candidates and now I'm the guy that has to defend "Let Go." And I've tried to come up with ways to defend it and I just can't do it. It's a fun song—that's about the best that can be said. It's very tongue-in-cheek. If they were to try to do this seriously at all, and really try to get the crowd going, like, whipping them up into a BÖC-loving frenzy, then that would be a jump-the-shark moment for the band. But if I just look at it as cheesy fun, okay then. It's fine while it's playing but I'm not sorry when it's over.

Nick: It's obviously a controversial song, but I hear the name Ian Hunter and I'm on board, or at least curious. I like Ian Hunter. Yeah, maybe the chorus is a goofy thing, but I like the song. I know they played it live a bunch of times. Maybe because of me as a teenager... I still haven't lost the excitement of that song. There's nothing wrong with an anthem for me. It's not very BÖC-sounding though. It's in the category of "Goin' Through the Motions." And you can relate it to the song on *Imaginos*, with the "We understand, we understand, Blue Öyster Cult" thing.

I mean, you have "Feel the Thunder," which is a heavy song, but you've got the mellower or middling recline of "Shooting Shark" and the slower "Shadow of California." "Let Go" is an up-tempo song, so maybe that's why I still feel a fondness for it. But I certainly appreciate why fans would be like, "What the hell is this?!" I'm a defender of Ian Hunter. Maybe the band changed the lyrics. I can't see Ian Hunter writing that. That might have been one of those in-the-studio things where it had a completely different lyrical bent and then they rewrote it for their own. I'd like to hear Ian Hunter under oath on that one.

Matt: It seems like they're just trying to write a song to do in concert. It's got the self-referential lyric, the "BÖC" chants. In concert, at the end when they go up on stage before the encore, you've got fans chanting, "BÖC! BÖC!" And it seems like it's designed to answer back on that call. The lyrics is pretty silly. It's a "Marshall Plan" kind of song. I guess it's self-aware. It's up to the listener to decide which end of stupid and tongue-in-cheek it falls on (laughs). I have to say that even though on the record it's pretty silly, it did work as a live song, during that time period, and even into the *Club Ninja* tour. I remember seeing it on the *Club Ninja* tour and it was the encore. The fans are chanting "BÖC!" and they come out, Buck kicks off that riff and it worked really well, as a live number. But sure, a little silly for the record. But it's short, right? Three minutes, in-and-out.

Martin: Moving forward, man, with "Dragon Lady," I'm feeling the same thing as everything on this side so far—and nothing else on the album, really—this idea that pop and hard rock are mixing a bit like oil and water.

Bill: I agree. I mean, once you get past "Shadow of California" I notice that everything's kind of mid- to lower-tier here. There are no real standout songs for me. "Dragon Lady" is fine. It's an okay, average Buck song musically. But I don't think the lyrics have a whole lot to offer, really. It's a song that I forget about when it's done playing. And again, that's kind of all of side two for me, other than "Shadow of California."

Martin: And you know, that one and "Feel the Thunder" both have a bit of that '60s girl group New York rock vibe, right? That little retro "Dead Man's Curve," Jan and Dean, Frankie Valli, Eddie Cochran thing, you know?

Bill: They should have brought in Ronnie Spector to do some background on that.

Martin: I'm also hearing Meat Loaf and actually The Tubes from this era, starting with *Remote Control*. It's all kind of camp, kind of Broadway. "Attack of the 50 Foot Woman" and all that.

Nick: That might explain why when I play this album on Spotify, the algorithm throws me over to The Tubes. But no, I like "Dragon Lady." You know, Buck is just an underrated, phenomenal guitar player. He doesn't get the credit he deserves. He's understated and maybe he likes it that way. He can play dirty, he can play ethereal. "Dragon Lady" is a great, great album track, you know, and not a single. I don't think it did much for them live, but it's one of the stronger tracks I think on the album. I kind of like what he does with the lyrics, with those stops and starts.

Reed: Another fast Buck song. So we get two fast rockers with Buck on vocals—if you think "Veins" is fast; it's certain busy—where he's normally the poppy ballad guy. And the lyric is about your mystical woman, which is much more what I would associate with Eric Bloom. But I think Buck really sells this one. It's my favourite Buck vocal performance on the album, even more so than "Shooting Shark." "Shooting Shark" is just so generically poppy to me. I mean, it's a good song, but I think he really makes "Dragon Lady" his. There's something about the way he enunciates that phrase "dragon lady" that is so uniquely Don Roeser, right? He owns that song and I appreciate that. Plus, it's got fantastic guitar hooks in it. It may be his best guitar performance on the album.

Martin: As a guitarist and actually a luthier and pedal expert yourself, what's your assessment of Buck as a guitarist?

Reed: Well, I would not say that Buck has a particular sound. He's very '70s. He came up in that same tradition as guys like another perennial favourite of mine, Dick Wagner, right? So you get these heavy guitarists from the '70s and they all sound similar. The difference is that Buck was very fast. Now there were other fast guitarists, but he was very busy. He wrote very busy lines, very busy solos. In the '70s, it was much more common to have fast phrases separated by longer, more languid passages. And Buck was much more straight-ahead, what in the '80s would be called a shredder, but nobody in the '70s used that term, right?

On *Hearin' Aid*, "Stars," Buck Dharma is one of the guitarists in the pool of guitarists on that song, a charity song put together by Wendy and Ronnie James Dio. You've got George Lynch, Vivian Campbell and Yngwie Malmsteen and all these other guys who are '80s hot shots—and he sounds completely out of place. Because, again, he's a '70s guitar player and he just doesn't fit into that world. But later on he's as good a shredder as anybody else playing that type of music in America. Buck just got better; he adapted. But in the early '80s he hadn't adapted yet—he was still a very '70s player.

Martin: What about tone and gear? Do you have any understanding of what he's sounding like or what he's using?

Reed: At this time he's using just cranked Marshalls and I think mostly an SG. He had a lot of custom guitars in the mid '80s. He would adopt

Steinberger, the headless guitars with graphite necks. Graphite necks had the benefit that they're not affected by temperature and moisture. So as you tour around the country, your guitars aren't constantly going out of tune. But headless guitars had a problem in that you had to have special strings for them at that time and they were not easy to get. I used to know a Steinberger endorser years ago and he said, "I got the endorsement so I could get strings—forget the guitars." Strings was the hard thing to come by. And he in fact still plays it. But Buck's got a very standard rock tone at this time, just cranked through a Marshall. Now the man has a very busy tone. He plays with like five different overdrive pedals. I watched a gear rundown of his and it's like five overdrive pedals. And he's like, "Yeah, I can turn any of these on in sequence when I'm in the mood for different levels of gain." And I thought that's too much work.

Martin: Nice, thanks for that. Okay, the album closes with "Light Years of Love," the only old school ballad I guess, given that "Eyes on Fire" and "Shooting Shark" are both made kind of dancey.

Reed: Yes, and I always hate finishing an album with a song I dislike but I really don't like "Light Years of Love." Multiple strikes against it. I don't like Joe Bouchard as a vocalist. I'm sorry, Joe. You're a fantastic bass player, you wrote some great stuff, not my favourite vocalist. And I can't believe Helen Wheels wrote the lyrics to this song because they are so subpar, so trite. And I'm not necessarily against Blue Öyster Cult singing love songs, especially if Buck is singing them, but this one is just so stereotypically a love song. It's pointless. It's filler. I would rather they have put something else on.

Bill: It's another one I like. I enjoy the sound on it. I think it's a good closer. Granted Helen's lyric is fairly basic, not one of her best. Not one of Joe's best musically, either. But it's a nice way to ease us out of the album.

Nick: I know it's another sort of ethereal and not heavy rocker that closes the thing out, but Joe Bouchard is on it and that was interesting. He's still in the band but his brother Albert is gone. I like his vocal on it too. As a kid I liked it and I like that one still today. That's one where if you're looking for a narrative through all the albums, I could see this being on *Mirrors* or *Spectres*. And Joe Bouchard, I have a lot of respect for. After this exercise as a player and as a musician, he became like an academic and music teacher. He's a serious guy. Even though bass players don't get credit, he's a serious, serious musician. I like it as an album-closer actually; I think it's pretty good.

Matt: "Light Years of Love," is a pretty effective song. It's a Helen Wheels lyric, with Joe Bouchard. So both Bouchards and Helen Wheels collaborated throughout the years. For her this is a little unusual. She's sort of wrapped up in this tough, bodybuilder, biker imagery and everything, and this is a really sincere love song. And Joe often goes for the lyrics that have a bit of a New York underbelly kind of thing, like a "Morning Final" or a "Hot Rails to Hell," or a vampire-type thing. And here he sings these sincere sentiments and it works really well, making for a good, ballad-y, big AOR-ish type song. Nice acoustic guitars, the production's good, nice vocal from Joe, the drums don't get in the way at all. But it's kind of a surprise given the writers.

Martin: Cool, well, from all that I gather that *The Revolution by Night* isn't exactly top-tier BÖC for any of you. Agreed? Any closing thoughts?

Bill: Well, I'll just say that I think it fits the vibe of 1983 perfectly—for better and for worse. I'm a big fan of 1983. That was kind of a musical coming-of-age year for me in a lot of ways. But I would rank this album nowhere near the best of '83 albums or Blue Öyster Cult albums even though I do love it and it has a couple of my favourite BÖC songs. As an album overall though, I think it's pretty weak and inconsistent. It goes back to what I said about the first album. Once again, it's a band that is questing. They're seeking an identity. Having booted Albert, they lost such a huge part of their very core, their identity. And you can tell they're floundering quite a bit here.

Nick: For me, unfortunately, *The Revolution by Night* is lesser today than it was back in the mid '80s. But it's so ingrained in me. I've listened to it so much. I know production-wise, Fairbairn gets slagged. It's a different sound for the band. There's less complexity to it. I think though that it suits the marketplace as it existed in 1983. The band had to change with the times. Allen's piano is gone and we're definitely into synth mode here.

But you know, with the synth drums at the time, I was going, "Oh, this is something new and exciting." Because in '83 and then into '84, I hadn't been bludgeoned yet, especially in the hard rock arena, with really crappy drum production. So this album was okay for me—it was like fresh. But then after you heard that Simmons sound too many times, it really got to be just so clichéd and hackneyed and cringey. And even more so when you listen back to it now. But I don't find that Fairbairn and Rick Downey were so obnoxious on this record that it became cringey. Maybe for another hardcore BÖC fan they were, but I thought it was well-positioned; they weren't over-the-top with it.

CLUB NINJA

Club Ninja
December 10, 1985 (album states 1986)
Columbia PC 39979
Produced by Sandy Pearlman
Engineered by Paul Mandl and Toby Scott
Recorded at Bearsville Studios, Bearsville, NY, Boogie Hotel, Port Jefferson, NY, Talysin Studios, Syosset, NY, Warehouse Studios, New York, NY
Personnel: Eric Bloom – vocals, guitar; Donald "Buck Dharma" Roeser – vocals, guitars, keyboards; Joe Bouchard – bass, vocals, guitar; Tommy Zvoncheck – synthesizers, piano, organ; Jimmy Wilcox – background vocals, percussion
Guest performers: Kenny Aaronson, Joe Caro, Phil Grande, Dave Immer, Joni Peltz, Thommy Price, Howard Stern

Side 1
1. "White Flags" (Leggat Bros.) 4:39
2. "Dancin' in the Ruins" (Larry Gottlieb, Jason Scanlon) 3:58
3. "Make Rock Not War" (Bob Halligan Jr.) 3:55
4. "Perfect Water" (Roeser, Jim Carroll) 5:28
5. "Spy in the House of the Night" (Roeser, Meltzer) 4:20

Side 2
1. "Beat 'em Up" (Halligan Jr.) 3:22
2. "When the War Comes" (J. Bouchard, Pearlman) 6:06
3. "Shadow Warrior" (Bloom, Roeser. Eric van Lustbader) 5:40
4. "Madness to the Method" (Roeser, Dick Trisman) 7:28

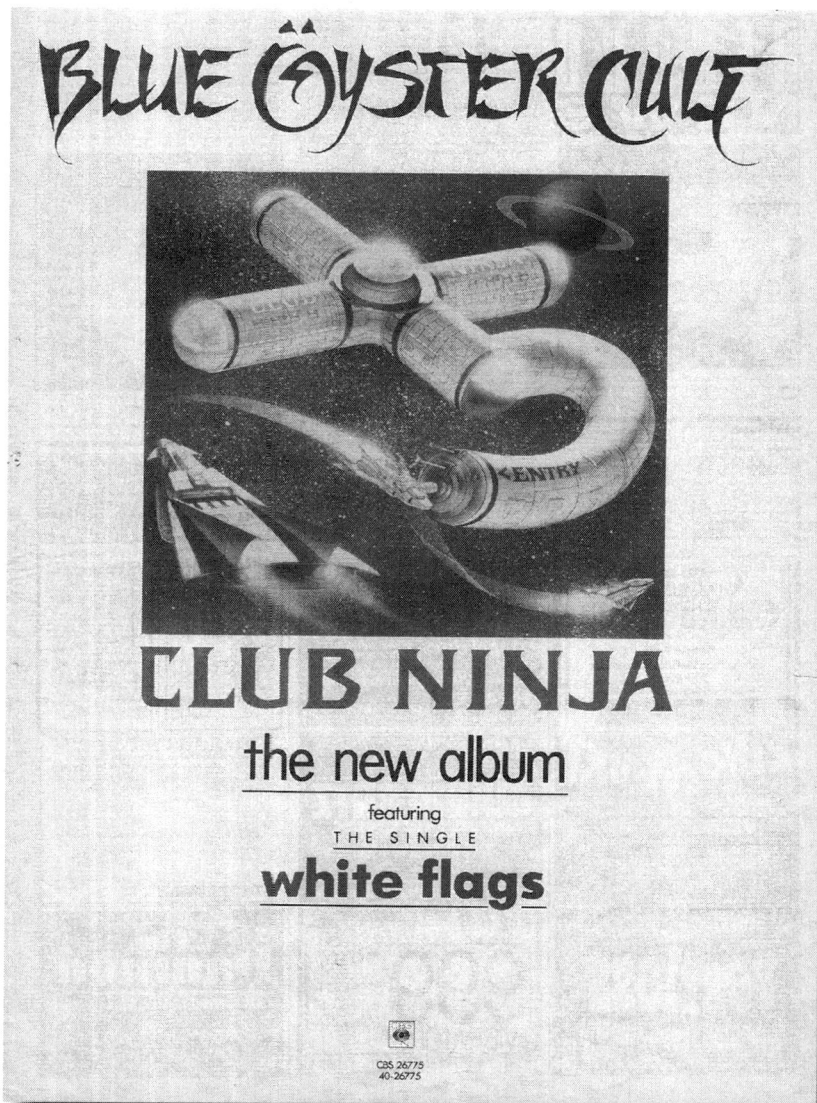

Martin talks to Rich Davenport, Jamie Laszlo, Bill Schuster, Nick S. Squire and Matt Thompson about *Club Ninja*.

Martin Popoff: Mirrors, Imaginos, Curse of the Hidden Mirror and Club Ninja... I guess these are the most contentious albums in the catalogue, right? And they're all complained about for different reasons. But on the chopping block right now is *Club Ninja*. What's your experience with this record?

Jamie Laszlo: It's the BÖC album that the fans love to hate. Is this their AOR album? Is it their soft rock album? Is it their hair metal album? I don't know. I do love the cover. Because the more something is thrown in your face, the less likely you're sometimes able to see it. And when I was 16 and got this album, I went a good year without seeing the symbol on the album cover, Martin (laughs). My buddy goes, "Dude, it's the spaceship" and I was like, oh, it couldn't have been bigger in front of my face and I looked right past it. I'm looking for the symbol *on* the spaceship.

Nick S. Squire: Yeah, the band is missing Albert Bouchard and Allen Lanier, the Swiss Army knife. The landscape is changing. I bought this album new, and when the album came out, "Dancin' in the Ruins" was everywhere on rock radio and I'm like, oh my God, they're using more outside writers, but then again they lost two writers, so I get that. I had no idea who those people were. They were definitely not in the fold, not historically used by the band. Perhaps that's why the sound of this album is even less BÖC than *The Revolution by Night* was. But yeah, "Dancin' in the Ruins" was, so how can you imitate yourself? But even though it's sort of son of "Burnin' for You," I love it. It's got a great chorus. But I heard it for like three weeks and then it disappeared.

Rich Davenport: I understand that it was quite a troubled and protracted birth for this one, quite expensive, drawn-out. And Sandy Pearlman said, quoting from your *Agents of Fortune* book, that it was the worst album he's been involved with. And I think it was Joe Bouchard in there that said they spent a huge amount of money on it. I have a soft spot for this one, because I think I'm right in saying that the first Blue Öyster Cult song I ever heard was "White Flags." I was like 13 in 1985 and I remember where it was. I was in the car with my dad, it was a Saturday morning, and we used to have this show on Radio One, which at that point was really bland and poppy. But we had the one rock show per week on a Friday night which was Tommy Vance with *The Friday Rock Show*.

But we're in the car, and there was a program on Radio One on Saturday mornings where they used to play… I think it was new singles that were coming out that week. And it was rare to hear, certainly in '85, any kind of hard rock song on Radio One, outside of Tommy Vance's show or any time in the daytime. That changed a little bit with bands like Bon Jovi and Europe a bit later on. But it jumped out and I loved the song and went, Blue Öyster Cult, oh, okay, that's what they sound like.

And then I bought the album, although not immediately. The next track I heard was "Godzilla" on a compilation, on *Axe Attack Vol II*, which was quite a big deal here. There was a series of compilations here in Britain. And I went, oh, that's completely different from "White Flags." And then the first album I bought was *Agents of Fortune* and then I got *Club Ninja* in a cut-out bin, but in '88 or '89. A British chain of record shops called Our Price that were part of Virgin sold discounted albums they wanted to get rid of. And I thought, well, it's got my "White Flags" on it, I'll buy that.

And I'd say *Club Ninja* is typical of what was going on in hard rock at the time for bands like Blue Öyster Cult and a lot of the southern rock bands. It's typical of the record industry at the time. We'd had the New Wave of British Heavy Metal and then there was a slightly glammier wave of metal that was coming in from America. And that had a detrimental effect certainly on anything more traditional. I mean, now we've got the classic rock radio format in. Back then that really didn't exist. I never heard the term classic rock. I know now that it's an American radio format.

But back then that was only starting to emerge and there was really nowhere comfortable to go for bands like Blue Öyster Cult. Record labels were forcing bands into a more commercial avenue unless they were having huge sales. And it killed off a lot of the southern rock bands, especially both Blackfoot and Molly Hatchet, who came off really badly. Both of those also had the outside songwriters being brought in. But by comparison to some of the absolute disasters that happened to some of BÖC's peers, who started out alongside them in the '70s, although this isn't a great album, it's a lot less of a blemish on the catalogue than some of those.

Matt Thompson: As Rich said, *Club Ninja* was a painful album to make. It was such a struggle for them. The touring success is starting to dwindle a bit after *Revolution by Night* and they're seeing dwindling sales. It's now starting to hit them in the size of the audience. You get a lineup change again in the drumming, and it becomes not a permanent change. So you're not getting continuity. Joe ends up leaving at the end of this. So the original version of the band is melting away, quite compromised. Buck talks about how it was really painful to record. My understanding is that he was flying to California back and forth to try and make this record work.

The interesting thing about *Club Ninja*, before it came out they were trying out some of the songs. And the one that worked the best in concert, in my opinion, and that people were really looking forward to, was "Wings of Mercury." Although it's a hard rock shuffle, Martin, and I know how you feel about shuffles (laughs). And that's written by one of the guys from The Dream Syndicate, Karl Preccda. You've got Sandy Pearlman doing some production work with The Dream Syndicate. It's a very biker kind of song, which you think would have been a really good fit. But instead they keep like "Beat 'em Up" and "Make Rock Not War," which don't really sound like BÖC. And they're contradictory, right? (laughs). They're contradictory messages.

Bill Schuster: My take? *Club Ninja* is Donald coming to the rescue. I think sonically this is a much more consistent album than *The Revolution by Night*. Some people really don't like the sound of the album. I'm a fan of it, personally, but I'm glad the whole catalogue doesn't sound like this. But for 1986 it sounds great. The songs all sound like they were recorded by the same band in the same studio during the same sessions. It's not an all-over-the-place mess, like *Imaginos*. So whether you like the songs or not, I feel like it works as a cohesive album. That's one of the things that I appreciate about it.

I've also noticed over the years that there's a theme of violence to this album. Most of the songs have lyrics about different forms of violence. There's a brief respite in "Perfect Water," but even that has hints of violence. And then "Spy in the House of the Night," you just think nice night, it's an escape, it's peaceful, but there's that spy there in the house of night waiting to do nasty things when you're not looking. But the rest is pretty direct. And if you can rationalize those two, there's never truly an escape from the violence on this album song by song. I like that thematic consistency to it.

Martin: How do the new guys do?

Bill: I actually like the keyboard sounds here a lot better than I do on *The Revolution by Night*. They're very mid '80s. Tommy Zvoncheck does a really nice job here. He's part of that consistency of sound throughout this album. I don't think Tommy gets enough credit. In fact it seems like he gets insulted more than anything and blamed for the direction of the album. But I think his playing and tones and textures are pretty important in setting that consistency of mood across the songs.

Martin: Okay, the record opens with "White Flags," which, man, even though they didn't write it, I feel like I'm instantly in a BÖC land of wonders.

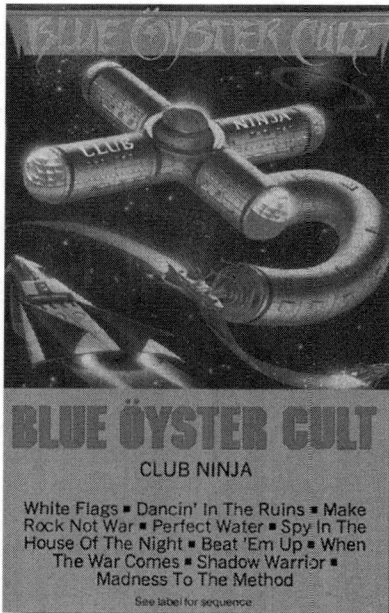

CLUB NINJA

White Flags ▪ Dancin' In The Ruins ▪ Make Rock Not War ▪ Perfect Water ▪ Spy In The House Of The Night ▪ Beat 'Em Up ▪ When The War Comes ▪ Shadow Warrior ▪ Madness To The Method

See label for sequence

Rich: Yeah, very true. I still love it. But I must admit, what disappointed me about this album is that in the past they always used outside collaborators by their own choice, whether it's Sandy Pearlman or Richard Meltzer or Helen Wheels or Patti Smith. While here, it's strangers. And overall, part of the appeal of metal and hard rock is that these guys write their own songs. And I was a little disappointed that the band hadn't written some of *Club Ninja*'s strongest songs.

Having said that, the opening two tracks, "White Flags" and "Dancin' in the Ruins," they're very much in Blue Öyster Cult's established style. If you didn't know they weren't written by the band, you would think they'd written them, if that makes sense. And again, something in their favour which killed off a lot of their peers, is that Sandy Pearlman was producing, so no superstar bigshot '80s producer. And even though he's been quite dismissive of the album, he still knew the band inside out. And although there are elements of that hideous '80s, drenched-in-reverb production that destroyed a lot of hard rock albums, it's not gone the whole hog. There's enough of the essence of Blue Öyster Cult here in terms of the production and the band's own playing and vocals and also in terms of the songs they've chosen from outside writers that it still fits the template.

So the album, when it works, it works well. The arrangement on "White Flags" is very much in keeping with what I'd expect from Blue Öyster Cult. Excellent vocal from Eric, very powerful and strident, upbeat and dynamic. It fits the song, which has a sort of smouldering, atmospheric tone. There's a malevolent, sinister kind of vibe to it. The absolute

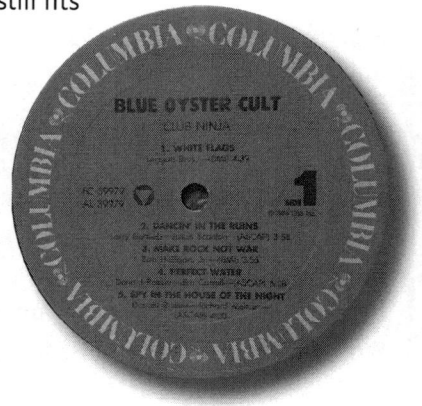

standout characteristic of the track is in fact the vocal, because he sings slightly lower and then shifts into his higher range quite dramatically. There's a bit where he goes for a high and really hits the note and it's like wow, this is really quite stunning.

Matt: They're using outside writers, but here it's basically a cover. Because the Leggat brothers, operating as Leggat, had this song on their *Illuminations* album and it's basically the same song. Generally on *Club Ninja* they're using outside writers mostly to not good success. These are writers outside the cabal, pop writers. But "White Flags" works great. What a great song, and lyrically it fits the ethos or mythos and it's got a really good Eric Bloom performance and great drums. It kind of simmers and burns. To me, that's a standout track.

Bill: I like "White Flags" quite a bit, but yeah, it's shocking to see that on those first three songs in a row, there are no Blue Öyster Cult band members in the credits. But I wouldn't have known any different, frankly. I would not have known this was a cover song. In fact I had this on cassette when it first came out and don't recall if there were songwriting credits on it, or if there were, I didn't notice. First three songs, no band credits—that's pretty bold to open the album like that.

Jamie: Believe it or not, I did not know "White Flags" was a cover until two weeks ago. When I did one of my "In the spotlight" episodes with a guy from Canada, he was showing some Canadian bands and he pulled out the album and says, "This has the original 'White Flags' that BÖC covered." So I'm thinking, oh my God, I gotta talk to Martin in less than two weeks and I just found out now after 40 years, it's a cover?! Right in time! (laughs). The original is a lot longer and has a proggy breakdown in the middle. I like their idea of cutting out the proggy interlude in the middle and making it more of a straight-ahead rocker. Kind of reminds me of Billy Idol when he redid "L.A. Woman" and he cut out the "Mr. Mojo risin'." Yeah, good idea, Billy. But what they did is they ended up making one of my favourite BÖC songs of all time.

I understand why the album is not a BÖC classic. But I don't understand why their cover of this song is not a BÖC classic, and why they don't do this in concert. They're out there doing a seven-minute "Shooting Shark" every single night. I say cut that out. Put in "White Flags," which is less than five minutes, and then you've got room for "Mirrors" which is another song that should have been a smash hit.

Martin: What do you like about "White Flags?"

Jamie: Oh, man, I don't want to go to war and I don't want to fight anyone, but if I had to do the charge… you know, I always think of the charges in *Braveheart*, where they're just running at one another. This is one of the songs I want on my playlist when I'm doing that. Plus it's infectious. The whole "Can't you feel my love," I mean, that just gets me going, man. I love it.

Martin: Next is "Dancin' in the Ruins," which, like you say, sounds like a Buck-penned hit but isn't either of those things.

Matt: Yes (laughs), it's in a series of '80s *not* hits. It's "Burnin' for You"-like, with the same level of heaviness and the smooth Buck vocal. But with respect to time and place, it's not going to catch on. The video got some good MTV video play because it had a skateboarder in it and kind of a good sci-fi theme, but it does not hit. It's written by someone outside of the usual cabal of lyric writers, but it works pretty well. Still, it's just another swing and a miss, ultimately, commercially.

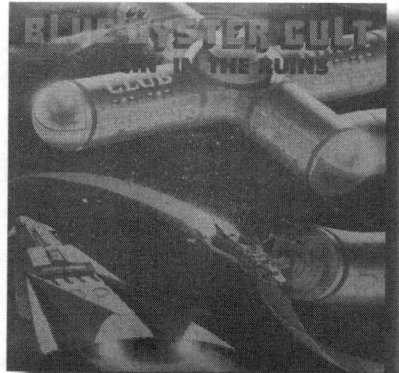

Martin: You know it's even got the rhythmic reggae punctuation chord from "Burnin' for You," as well as a matching intro drum hook and similar chords in the chorus.

Bill: Yes, it's pretty close, and it should have been a bigger hit than it was, really. Musically it's got all the traditional Buck pop hooks, even though he didn't write it. I don't really see it as a "Burnin' for You" sequel, because lyrically it's in a whole different headspace. People of my generation, the '80s generation, we were worried about nuclear Armageddon. We were worried about that mushroom cloud hovering over us. So "Dancin' in the Ruins" fit perfectly into that vibe. It seemed like something like that might have been picked up a little better by the general public, but unfortunately it wasn't to be.

Rich: It's in Buck's melodic style, it sounds like something he would sing and overall it's what we would expect from Buck—only this time it's *for* Buck, I guess. I wonder if the band were just really burned-out at this stage. Because I don't think it's as good a song as "Burnin' for You," which is one of Buck's own compositions. That was him and Richard Meltzer. So the band write better songs themselves, or certainly could. I don't think they've suddenly lost their talent. I wonder. But a lot of Blue Öyster Cult's peers were burning out around this time period. You had UFO, Thin Lizzy, Sabbath, Heep and to some extent Scorpions, and usually from that relentless treadmill of album/tour album/tour. I know they'd lost Albert, who had contributed a lot. But Buck wrote the biggest hit they'd ever had with "Reaper." It just seems strange that they would need outside writers.

Jamie: I love this song. It's got everything you want in a Buck Dharma song. I thought that video was great. A lot of '70s hard rock bands were struggling in 1986, and I'm not saying that "Dancin' in the Ruins" was a Top 40 hit or anything. But it got played on the radio and MTV was playing the video. And it was a well-produced video that made them seem hip because it had cool skateboarders doing cool tricks. So it brought these old guys kind of into the mainstream. Great hook, great melody, ear candy all around... it's the kind of rock song back in the day where your mom didn't mind listening to it when it came on the car radio when you guys were traveling somewhere. It goes down easy, but not too easy, so everybody in the car is happy.

Martin: What do you like about Buck as a guitarist?

Jamie: As I get older, I find that tone is becoming everything for me. I listen to new music quite a bit and I will fast-forward three minutes into the first song, capture the tone within a few seconds. If I don't like it, it's onto the next thing, Martin. I don't give albums any time. There's too much out there. I don't give anything more than a few seconds before I try and move onto the next thing. So I definitely love his tone.

Plus my favourite guitarists are not the Yngwie Malmsteens of the world. They're not shredders. They're the guys who add textures to the music and play well doing it. And Buck is one of those guys. He's not going to be out there going 20-notes-a-second, but he's going to wow you in other ways. I don't know, both the tone and the playing is clean. But you know, people like to say BÖC have had a career of evil, which is one of their songs, right? And there's something underlying in Buck's clean tone that comes off as a little evil at the same time.

Martin: All right, moving on, I don't think "Make Rock Not War" is technically four-on-the-floor but it may as well be given how loud the snare is. It's pretty thumpy—to the point of stodgy.
Bill: Yeah, and they also didn't write it. Still, I'm one of the few people that really loves this song. Outside of the cheesy title, which I can't defend, the rest of the lyrics though, if you get beyond that, it's really kind of a nice anti-war song. That goes back to that whole thing of all of us in the '80s worried about the mushroom cloud and waiting to go to war with the Soviet Union. So I was always very enamoured with the anti-war message of this song and I really found it to be a rather moving and meaningful anti-war anthem for my generation. I'm probably unusual in that. I don't think many people see beyond the cheesiness.

Jamie: "Make rock not war/What are we fighting for?" Awful title. And it has gang vocals for crying out loud. But I don't think it's as bad as it seems on paper. If I told you here's a song by BÖC with gang vocals from 1986 called "Make Rock Not War," you're going to think, oh my God, this is going to be the worst. I don't think it's that bad. It has the '80s production all over it, but I do find myself yelling along with the "rock not war" part. I'm not saying I would ever do that in public, but behind closed doors, Martin, yeah, I'm all about it: "Make rock not war!" I'm a little embarrassed to say that. It has a cool little guitar riff between the "Make rock not war" parts. But Martin, you have to be a little forgiving on this album to enjoy it. Not everyone is going to be forgiving. I get that because I'm not forgiving on a lot of albums by other bands. But it's a decent song on a decent album.

Rich: Now this Bob Halligan Jr., as an outside writer, he's less of a shock because he'd written for Priest. He wrote "Chains" on *Screaming for Vengeance* and "Some Heads are Gonna Roll" on *Defenders of the Faith*. And funnily enough, he got one of his first breaks writing with Rick Cua from The Outlaws quite early on, because Rick Cua, after he left The Outlaws moved into the contemporary Christian market. And Bob Halligan, I think, had come from a similar background and co-wrote with him quite extensively. But yeah, good writer. quite typical of the time stylistically, so this one is more consciously '80s or more noticeably '80s. I think Bob Halligan Jr. has written better songs than this but it's not a washout. A little bit generic at times, especially on the chorus. There's a nice solo, with quite quirky use of the tremolo from Buck. So yeah, I mean it's an okay track.

Martin: "Perfect Water" is pretty much the most well-regarded track on the album, and written using a time-honoured BÖC methodology.

Matt: "Perfect Water" is another Buck masterpiece. You get a Jim Carroll lyric and the lyrics are terrific. Jim Carroll had been orbiting around the Blue Öyster Cult echo-sphere during this time, right? He's friends with Allen Lanier. Allen references him n the "In Thee" lyric, "Jim says some destinies should not be delivered." And then that shows up on "Day and Night," that hasn't even been released yet. "Some destinies, they should not be delivered" comes out on "Day and Night" on *Catholic Boy*. So he's orbiting this sphere. Like most Buck collaborations, he doesn't collaborate in the room. He doesn't collaborate really ever. Buck goes off like a mad scientist and works by himself to create these things. But he's inspired by the really good imagery in the lyric and writes an absolute masterpiece.

Rich: Yeah, absolutely. And again, this is with an outside writer by choice, Jim Carroll, who wrote *The Basketball Diaries* and he released a couple of albums himself. Keith Richards helped him get his record deal with Atlantic so he's certainly in the Stones orbit too. The result is more typical Blue Öyster Cult. It's atmospheric and lighter with clean guitars at the beginning, and there's quite an interesting stutter effect with the way the bass and the drums lock in—quite unusual with the bass drum grace note thing. The chords on the verse are good and it builds well. It doesn't deliver a killer hook on the chorus initially, but it kind of waits until the sort of newer, secondary musical passage, where it almost becomes a different song. Then there's a section later on where there's lyrics and soloing going on at the same time and it gets a little busy. But it's definitely turning the song into the perfect definition of one that builds and builds. That strong hook might have had more impact earlier in the song. And with the solo going over it as well, it's a bit cluttered. Maybe that's their quirkiness working against them again.

Bill: Instant classic. I loved that one from the moment I heard it. There's a reason it has lived on in their setlist. But I disagree with Donald because I seem to remember that he has not necessarily been a fan of the original recording. But I think the original recording sounds perfect as it is. I don't feel like the live versions add anything that wasn't already there other than extended soloing maybe. Lyrically it goes back to the early days when you had those mysterious lyrics that you wondered what's going on here? There was the anticipation of some sort of terror just around the corner, just out of sight. It wasn't just Godzilla tearing down buildings. The idea of drowning is always terrifying to begin with. To me, that's a lot scarier than Godzilla tearing up Tokyo, or a cartoon skeleton coming to steal your soul.

Nick: Like Bill says, they're still playing "Perfect Water" live. They just played it in 2022. I think it's great. I love Buck's singing on that song as well as his guitar solo. That song could have been a hit at a different time, but timing was everything for them, unfortunately. Really chime-y guitar to this one, which is unusual for them, almost like they're listening to U2 or something. There's a call-and-response too, something that hearkens back to classic BÖC.

Jamie: It's this album's "Shooting Shark" but not as good. "Perfect Water" is not a perfect song. It's light, it's airy, it lacks a memorable hook. But the melody is nice. And Buck has a couple of solos that are nice. That's its biggest fault—this song is nice. And for a lot of hard rock fans out there, nice songs finish last. I know it's appreciated for Jim Carroll's lyrics, but I feel like that blinds people to the fact that the structure of the thing is just nice.

Martin: Closing side one of the original vinyl is one of the band's own, "Spy in the House of the Night." I'm hearing that J. Geils thing Nick brought up earlier.

Bill: Yes. This is Buck with Meltzer. I still don't know exactly what the lyric is about, but with Meltzer, do you really need to know what the lyric's about? Does he even know what his lyrics are about? I often question that. I think sometimes he just threw down a bunch of lines that he thought sounded cool. He had a John Lennon vibe to him, where it's, let's just see what they think of this nonsense here. I'll amuse myself as I watch everyone analyze this thing that doesn't necessarily mean anything at all. For what it's worth, Buck says in his notes for the demo collection that "Spy in the House of the Night" was recorded with the Drumulator drum machine. He said the demo has more odd time bars than the *Club Ninja* version.

Rich: Yet another Doors comparison, because they had "Spy in the House of Love" on *Morrison Hotel*. A nice energetic riff builds up well and provides an off-kilter feel. I like the harmonies, and the chorus is great; it has those clean guitar arpeggios on it which remind me of The Police. I get the impression that a lot of hard rock guys quite liked The Police. I know Rush obviously did and Sammy Hagar has that track on *VOA*, "Swept Away," which has a big Police vibe to it. I don't know if they were a conscious influence for Buck Dharma on this, but that's certainly what it reminds me of with those clean arpeggios. Solo is fantastic again, very complicated rhythmically. So yes, a strong end to the side.

Jamie: I like this song, but I feel like if it was beefed-up a bit, it could have been a bona fide BÖC classic. It suffers from the various production choices made on the album. However I like the groovy old school organ in this song. You may not even notice it when you first hear this song. The organ reminds me of the sprinkles on an ice cream sundae. You hardly notice them when you're eating them, but it's just cool that they're there.

Martin: Things aren't looking great as we flip over to side two. How bad does it get?

Rich: Well, Bob Halligan Jr. is capable of far better than this. I'd say "Beat 'em Up" is generic but not awful. But again, it doesn't fit for Blue Öyster Cult whereas earlier on "Dancin' in the Ruins" fit really well, as did "White Flags" and I think even "Make Rock Not War." This lyric stands out like a sore thumb. There's a line, "Jump to the music" and you're thinking, that does not sound right coming out of Eric Bloom.

Bill: This one's harder to defend than "Make Rock Not War," although I'm somewhat entertained by it musically. It's a good basic rocker if I'm in the mood to bang my head a little with music from that era. But yeah, lyrically this one doesn't have anything to offer. Possibly the weakest on the album.

Jamie: Again with the outside writers. Do you think it was the record company saying, look, we need to get you into the hair metal scene, more or less, and we're gonna help you out? There's a lot of things going against this album, and some people would say the songs are part of that. "Beat 'em Up," man, this one and three more on this side. Are you going to tell me, Laszlo, that you're going to try defend every single song on this album?! And my answer is yes! Yes, I'm going to. God, another awful song title. Would it be my first BÖC song I play for someone who's never heard them? No, especially with lyrics like, "You take a lickin'/Keep on kickin'" and, "We'll stop sockin'/When you start rockin'." Oh my God, it's cringe-worthy, isn't it? And there's more gang vocals with the "Beat 'em up" part.

But again, what it lacks in originality, it makes up for in a certain charm. And take charm however you want to take it. This is a "had to be there" album for sure. But then again, if you were a long-time BÖC fan in 1986 and buying this new you probably hated this crap. What I mean is, you had to be a 16-year-old still finding his way within the world of hard rock. You had to be a 16-year-old who thought Poison was too wimpy. But you couldn't listen to anything heavier than Maiden. You had to be a 16-year-old whose first BÖC album he ever bought was *Club Ninja*. Okay, so for me that's check,

check and check. So it might be less of a "you had to be there" album and more of a "you had to be me" album (laughs). And you know, there's only one me.

Martin: Nice, except this is wimpier than Poison (laughs). Okay, next we have a band composition, but man, "When the War Comes" is a hard one to love.

Rich: Yeah, I really don't like this one either. It's like you're waiting for it to go somewhere. And I'm surprised that this was Sandy Pearlman on lyrics. There's an old interview with Andy Scott from Sweet. He was talking about when they recorded "Block Buster!" and he remarked to one of the other band members that he thought it was more production than song, "Block Buster!," with the sirens and the vocal line. I mean, I like "Block Buster!" but I think this is very much a case of more production than song. It's more bluster than substance. And I find the stupid noises in the middle quite embarrassing, the "ooga chucka" bit. It's like, I remember playing that in the bedroom and thinking I want to turn that down in case anybody in my family think I'm enjoying this.

Jamie: About the spoken word intro by Howard Stern, I guess Stern's cousin was married to Eric Bloom at the time, and they got him to come in and do the spoken word. I remember hearing him on the radio saying he didn't want to do it, but he did it as a favour. And it comes off as a little silly, especially when you know it's Howard Stern and you hear his voice.

It's a moody song with prog instincts but it really struggles to find its identity. But here's the thing. I'm going to do another analogy. I know people might be sick of me doing analogies all the time, but this song, this album, it's the *Beastmaster* of Blue Öyster Cult albums for me. Okay, when I was a kid, I saw *Beastmaster* and I thought it was one of the best movies ever. Now I'm older and I see its faults—and there are many. *Club Ninja* and this song is like that. I see the faults as a 53-year-old in 2023 that I did not see as a 16-year-old in 1986.

But like *Beastmaster*, I still can't help but love it, even with silly songs like this and "Beat 'em Up." Come on, even you, Martin. I saw your quote on Wikipedia saying, "It's painfully constructed and baffling in its bad taste." Well, you know what, Martin? Some people can say that same exact sentence about *Beastmaster*. But I will say that the whole chanted "When the war comes" ending of the song is pretty badass, although why it's followed by more than a minute of tinkling, crashing sounds is anybody's guess.

Bill: "When the War Comes" represents the album's only Joe credit. As for the Howard Stern intro, it's a little over-the-top, but he does well with those words he's given to say. I just like the relentless plod of the song. It doesn't change a lot throughout. It's just constantly rolling and creepy and it works despite the "ooga chucka" (laughs). I'm able to ignore that "ooga chucka" somehow. It doesn't bother me because the rest of the song is so cool sonically. I understand how that can be a deal-breaker for people. It's a bit, well, why gentlemen? Why did you feel the need to put "ooga chucka" in there?

Nick: When I heard this, I didn't know who Howard Stern was. Stern is known to be a distant cousin of Eric Bloom. But at one point he was basically almost disavowing him as a relative, saying, "I'm supposedly related to him" blah blah blah. But at the time Stern still had this little bit of a speech impediment that he cleaned up years later. But yeah, I never noticed that he was on it until much later.

Martin: Moving on, I listen to "Shadow Warrior," and I'm thinking, this has got to be one of the worst travesties of a drum sound on any album. And I don't think the playing helps either. It's just fatiguing on every level.

Nick: Yeah, and in the construction, a fair to middling rocker at best, although the last minute is rippin'! If they had done that maybe earlier in the song, with the bass guitar and drums, it would have been much improved. And then it winds down slow again. It's that classic BÖC thing; they change the dynamics to let you know they can still tear it up. But even that part, you're right, you are complete distracted by the awful drums.

Jamie: I don't feel like I need to defend this one as much. I can see other BÖC fans thinking it's pretty decent. When I hear those lyrics, "No weapon, I carry no sword/Only my hands to protect me/No laws, I obey no laws/My spirit is righteous and free," it's like okay, I'm down, let's go kick some ass. It's a song that's able to break out of the chains that binds it. And what those chains are is the claustrophobic '80s production. It breaks free of that a little bit and dare I say becomes a little bit epic-sounding.

I'm not saying I'd join any clan called the Shadow Warriors if this was the recruiting song, but I can also say I couldn't blame someone else if they did. It has cool guitar solos that you can air guitar to and they come off as heavy—heavy for this album, I should say. That's the thing, it's got this doomy element that is wrestling with the synths and treated drums for dominance over the song. The band with this song almost wants to go heavier, but 1986 keeps pulling them back into 1986.

Matt: The interesting thing with "Shadow Warrior" is the Eric Van Lustbader lyrics. At that time he's becoming a popular writer. He has the ninja books at that time, and ninjas are hot in the '80s. They're hot with comic books and it's a popular thing. And then you get ninjas in the song lyric. He's an interesting guy, because he's got a music background professionally. He writes the liner notes for Cheap Trick's first record and he's done work behind the scenes, but then he's this fiction author.

That song was originally recorded with a different lyric; it was the "Rebel" song that was done for the *Teachers* soundtrack. They had this period where they wrote a few songs for the *Teachers* soundtrack: "Suma Cum Louder" and "Rebel," straightforward songs. But then they rework it to give it a more mystical lyric with this ninja-oriented thing. It works better than the original *Teachers* lyric, which is kind of stupid. But yes, "Shadow Warrior" is the updated version of "Rebel." Ultimately they don't get picked for the *Teachers* soundtrack. They were doing songs to be included on there, trying to get songs placed on it. It's a little bit like the *Heavy Metal* thing. Of course they get one on *Heavy Metal*, but they write more for it. Here they get zero, so it doesn't work out. But the lyrics are really direct, "I'm a rebel," really straightforward, and "Suma Cum Louder" is playing on the school type thing. That one shows up on *Electrocution of the Heart* by Deadringer, Joe's band.

Rich: A bit edgier than "When the War Comes" but still not a great riff. The production sounds very compressed and the chord changes are a bit jarring. There's a trace of a vocal hook that comes in partway through the song, and there's a fast section with a killer solo. In fact, there's two really good solos at the end which save it. It's not a complete dud, but it's not great.

Bill: Eric finally rears his head here in terms of songwriting. It's a decent song and it obviously fits the album title, *Club Ninja*. It works well within the context of the album for what it is. Clearly Eric is not the most important member of the band on this album. Eric and Joe have one credit each. Then there's the outside songs and then Donald took care of sort of three-and-a-half, but music only. That's why I was kind of speaking of Donald as the MVP of this particular album. He seemed to be the only one that was really trying to carry the ball artistically here, which is, considering how I've criticized him for his lack of songwriting at other times—even on *The Symbol Remains*—it's kind of funny that I'm actually defending him here. Plus he sings the two songs that have lasted the longest.

Martin: All right, well, among this trilogy of bloated, stodgy songs that take up most of side two, would you agree that "Madness to the Method" is the most creatively successful?

Bill: Yes, this has always been one of my favourites. I love the keyboard intro and it's got an artistic proggy vibe and I'm a prog fan. It's a sort of mini-epic with this lazy, languid feel, which is pretty odd in 1986. I like the little play on words there with "madness to the method" as opposed to "method to the madness." But there were a few odd lines in there, like "the wenches in the trenches" that I thought were cringey and throwaway but I guess worth a chuckle. For the most part though, I find the lyrics pretty solid on this one.

Rich: Yeah, I like this one. It's a good finish after a fairly... to be honest, I could live without the other three on this side. Well, certainly the first two tracks I would skip. "Shadow Warrior," if I was in the right mood I would listen to. As Bill mentioned, the title's got that nice bit of wordplay you expect from this band. It's got the atmospheric verse section with a lot of space, and then the heavier chugging section. And here's another example of them putting in a quirky time signature on the chorus, but subtly. It's not a cookie cutter chorus. The piano works really well on the chorus too, I thought. I'm glad it ends with this song rather than one of the weaker tracks.

Nick: "Madness to the Method" is a song as I could talk about for 20 minutes. I don't know why, I just love this song. I love the lyrics. I love the chorus. I don't mind the length, with piano setting the atmosphere like the classic BÖC songs—Tommy Zvoncheck, beautiful, beautiful piano in it, just gorgeous stuff. You know, as an older person, I think maybe I'm more radical now. I like the lyrical content. I know it starts sort of broad and then talks more on an interpersonal level, but I just like what they're saying. Buck lets it rip almost throughout the entire song, which is interesting. So it's great guitar and I love the build. It's got that quiet stuff and then it starts to build and then the chorus just explodes. To me, this is what BÖC is all about. It's funny, I listen to the song and at the end, I don't know what it is, but it's almost like I've had a workout.

Jamie: "It's "Dancin' in the Ruins" without the hooks. Basically, instead of hooks you get more gang vocals, "We want, we want/We need, we need." It's sloppily constructed, as far as I'm concerned. It could use some tightening up. But you know what, with a little editing, with less of an '80s production, with no gang vocals, maybe with a better identity, less meandering keyboards... you're right on this one. It's "painfully constructed and baffling in its bad taste," Martin. I'm finding it hard to defend this one (laughs).

Martin: Yikes, so how can we sum up the *Club Ninja* era for our readers?

Bill: Well, it's a record that is absolutely landlocked in 1986. If you're looking for this year in the encyclopaedia, this is one of the album covers that should show up. They were not shy about embracing the current technology and the current sounds. How much of that was the band's choice and how much of that was Sandy Pearlman's choice, who knows? But then again, I must say that it doesn't sound like any of Sandy's productions from the '70s. So I don't know how much of winding up with this sound palette has to do with Sandy himself, and how much is just due to the time it was created.

Martin: It's funny how they weren't really able to embrace hair metal, but instead they embraced a kind of earlier '80s pop metal sound.

Bill: Yeah, you absolutely would have expected them to go in a different direction. Maybe if they had released "Eyes on Fire" as a single and it had some success, that would have sent them more down the hair metal path.

Rich: Given how so many of their peers fared, I think as a mid '80s album from a band from an earlier generation, I still like it. In general, I do have quite a big soft spot for this album.

Martin: But again, a funny thing about this album, Rich, is that we're right in the middle of hair metal, yet they make an album that sounds like the pre-hair metal kind of poppy hard rock or even pomp rock of '78 through '82. It's almost as if this album was recorded before *The Revolution by Night* and then shelved and finally issued in 1986. They're not participating particularly in the hair metal market. It actually sounds about four years out of date at this point.

Rich: Good point. And maybe that's what these guys were being told was perceived to be commercial. Plus I can understand a band like Blue Öyster Cult shutting out the hair metal thing in general as like, what is this?! Maybe they're looking back at the *last* commercial trend that had substance in rock. Because quite a few of those guys from the more pomp rock bands came from a progressive background, didn't they? Like some of the guys from Foreigner and obviously Journey were quite progressive early on. So for a band like Blue Öyster Cult looking for something commercial to do, I can see this as a logical commercial sound to go for.

Martin: Interesting. So maybe *Club Ninja* could be viewed as a kind of neo-prog album like Asia or the tail end of Genesis, in a way. Rather than hair metal, which is the first thing you think of, because it's 1986. So yeah, it's almost like a '70s prog band going commercial, which takes you to Asia, Rush in the '80s, *90125*, *Big Generator* and GTR, rather than a '70s heavy metal band going commercial, which takes you to hair metal.

Rich: That's a great way to put it, yeah.

Nick: Yeah, that's a nice assessment. And you know, another band I'd throw in there is UFO, who also went sort of synth-y pop metal rather than what Kiss or Alice Cooper did, right? But along the lines of what Rich is saying, you think about BÖC, they've been around since '72, they're older guys. I could see them being presented with, "Oh, you've got to tart it up and wear spandex and do the hair." They're like, "What hair?" I could see them going, "We are not doing this crap." Whereas Kiss is like, all right, we can pull this off.

Martin: And they're all like five-foot-two, right?

Nick: Yeah, exactly. I can see BÖC laughing at it, screw that, we're going down with the ship, we're gonna find our mark and that's it. We're a mature band, we're a more sophisticated band, we're not going down that road. I can see them as particularly rejecting that whole thing, like Rush. We're not teasing out the hair. We're not doing any of that stuff. But it's a tough line for them to walk.

Martin: In essence, this is, you know, *Spectres*- and *Mirrors*-type material but just with every ill-advised '80s technology thrown at it.

Nick: Yeah, modern arrangement, more outside writers. It's almost like they're working the edges to try to fit in somehow. They're not going to be Bon Jovi. They're not going to be any of those metal bands. Like I say, I can see them being presented with this and going, "That's not us. We can't do this stuff." You know, again, my thesis is that they're closer to J. Geils than they are to Deep Purple and Black Sabbath. They're certainly not going to go the heavy, heavy route at this time. They're just not going to do it.

Martin: I like that J. Geils idea, but another one like that for me is The Tubes. You know, they go from that Zappa-esque prog thing pretty quickly into a sort of corporate hard-rocking pop direction.

Nick: It's funny you say that, because in the Spotify algorithm, over the last two weeks, I finish with these BÖC albums and it immediately goes into, well, first of all, it plays a lot of Moxy, because I'm listening to Canadian bands. And then it goes into The Tubes. So you're right. It's funny, it's almost seamless. Yeah, you're right about that. There's definitely a connection there. If you look at it from all angles as a band thinking about how they survive, they gotta put food on the table. But I can't see them saying, "Yeah, we're gonna be a metal band." I just don't see how they can do that. They're not going to recreate "Godzilla" necessarily, and that wouldn't have been heavy enough in the new marketplace anyway.

So yeah, in the end, I look at this album as less than the sum of its parts. Each song is good enough and some are great but as a whole, the nine tracks together lose something. My quick comparisons are Kiss *Unmasked* and April Wine's *Forever for Now*, which I think is a derided album in your homeland. Each song in isolation, you might rationalize as an interesting part of the catalogue, but as a collection, you're just confused and your confidence in the guys slips away.

Jamie: So if I hear you right, Martin, you're saying that it's a proto-hair metal album? Or is it BÖC trying to step into that hair metal space and botching it? Obviously it's too late to be doing proto-hair metal, but I guess that's your point!

Martin: Yeah, that's exactly what I mean—it sounds four or five years out of date.

Jamie: Yeah, maybe, but they're old, Martin. They're playing catch up. They were even old 40 years ago, you know, compared to everyone else doing it. So it's probably something they didn't want to do. Not that they knew how to do it anyway.

Martin: And I'm going to take the last word on this one. Because I disagree that they couldn't have gone full-on metal. Imagine if these guys looked at the New Wave of Heavy Metal and the success of Sandy's new shiny thing there briefly—Black Sabbath—and turned in a stormin' metal album at the end of 1982... Now they're competing with *Blackout* and *The Number of the Beast* and *Screaming for Vengeance*. Bring it on!

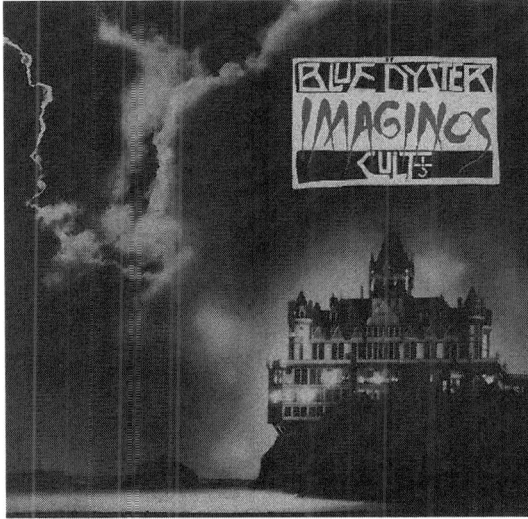

IMAGINOS

Imaginos
July 30, 1988
Columbia FC 40618
Produced by Sandy Pearlman; Associate Producer, Albert Bouchard
Engineered by Paul Mandl
Recorded at Kingdom Sound Studios, Long Island, NY, Boogie Hotel, Port
Jefferson, NY, Alpha & Omega Studios, San Francisco, CA
Personnel: Eric Bloom – vocals; Donald "Buck Dharma" Roeser – guitars,
vocals; Joe Bouchard – keyboard (sic), vocals; Allen Lanier – keyboards;
Albert Bouchard – guitar (sic), percussion, vocals
Guest performers: Kenny Aaronson, Marc Biedermann, Kevin Carlson, Joey
Cerisano, Tony Geranios, Phil Grande, Robby Krieger, Daniel Levitin, Tommy
Morrongiello, Aldo Nova, Thommy Price, Jack Rigg, Jon Rogers, Joe Satriani,
Shocking U, Tommy Zvoncheck

Side 1
1. "I Am the One You Warned Me of" (Pearlman, Roeser, A. Bouchard) 5:02
2. "Les Invisibles" (Pearlman, A. Bouchard) 5:31
3. "In the Presence of Another World" (Pearlman, J. Bouchard) 6:24
4. "Del Rio's Song" (Pearlman, A. Bouchard) 5:33
5. "The Siege and Investiture of Baron Von Frankenstein's Castle at
Weisseria" (Pearlman, A. Bouchard) 6:42

Side 2
1. "Astronomy" (Pearlman, J. Bouchard, A. Bouchard) 6:45
2. "Magna of Illusion" (Pearlman, Roeser, A. Bouchard) 5:51
3. "Blue Öyster Cult" (Pearlman, Bloom) 7:15
4. "Imaginos" (Pearlman, A. Bouchard) 5:44

Martin talks to John Gaffney, Sean Kelly, Jamie Laszlo, Reed Little, Bill Schuster, Nick S. Squire and Matt Thompson about *Imaginos*.

Martin Popoff: All right, we l, here's the "Be careful what you wish for" album from the Cultsters, right? Namely a concept album and with this band, *the* concept album of legend. A bit of a backstory to this one.

Matt Thompon: Definitely. And I think that part of the pleasure of *Imaginos* is how hard you have to work for the information that we, as Blue Öyster Cult fans, crave. So to set it up, I was an existing long-time fan before it came out. We had heard hints; we heard rumours, right? And the very first album, in the radio insert, Sandy mentions that *The Soft Doctrines of Immaginos*—two m's—is going to be the fourth Blue Öyster Cult album. It's mentioned in magazine articles, like the *NME* in 1975. The songs get demoed for other versions, and there are songs of course on the preceding Blue Öyster Cult albums that are *Imaginos*-themed songs.

So we're studying the green, lined printouts from when we sent away 50¢ for the lyrics. We're digging into it and trying to learn about this thing. But of course the album comes out in 1988 and it's pre-internet, so I had no idea it was coming out. The first I heard of it was "Astronomy" played on the radio with the Stephen King introduction, which was really kind of mind-blowing. We knew the connection with *The Stand* at that point from the book, not the TV series.

So I rushed out and I bought the record, and then you see on the back that the band is back together. I had recently seen them on the *Club Ninja* tour, and we know that they weren't together and now the band's back together, and they're doing the *Imaginos* concept. So I'm excited. I'm not gonna talk too much about how much I like or dislike about it—I'll leave that to the other panel members. This story is more about how the journey of being a fan affects how you might interact with the album.

So I see them on that tour and I do have a shirt that I got from 1988. It's kind of cool because it has the Stephen King part on the back with the "A bedtime story for the children of the damned" on there; so the merchandise is very, very cool. But they're only sort of touring the album, because immediately we find out that the band is not back together. Jon Rogers and Ron Riddle are in the band. They play three songs from the album. I saw them a few times on that tour, but I think they played "I Am the One You Warned Me of," they play "In the Presence of Another World" and they do the new version of "Astronomy." So you do get to hear sort of a single version of the band playing that song without all the layers but in the new format. So that's kind of neat to hear.

Now being a fan or trying to dig into this *Imaginos* thing, you have to be this esoteric, eldritch investigator going through all the resources that you can find. So I think after that album came out, there was kind of a cabal of researchers trying to really understand what was going on. There's John Swartz's FAQ, and even pre- that, the BÖC l (L) listserv. Martin, that was when we first interacted. Everyone's sharing the conspiracy theories about, you know, how this was going to make sense. That's a lot of where John got his information. John was a big leader on that group, trying to figure out what all this means.

Later we start getting the Brain Surgeons albums, so we start learning more about the story through these occasional old songs redone. I went to Bolle Gregmar's Museum O' Cult—best wishes for Bolle right now. And Martin, I know you had him extensively in your *Agents of Fortune* book, providing information and analyzing the songs, so it's great that we have that permanent record of Bolle and his scholarship on the band. He's right there in the first edition of your book from 2004, when it was called *Secrets Revealed!*. As the Blue Öyster Cult Fan Club, he put out *Morning Final* with Melne Murphy. So we were learning more all the time about this stuff. So yeah, I visited the Museum O' Cult, got to hear demo versions of these things.

Okay, so I think the question that then comes is that once you're in and your head is swimming with all this information, well, does it exist as an album? There's a recording of this thing, right? You can play these "What if?" questions. The album was supposed to come out as the fourth Blue Öyster Cult album, and then they demoed a bunch of the songs for *Spectres*. It could have been done at that time. But what would have happened had it been done as a sort of real Blue Öyster Cult album where they collaborated and it came out in the late '70s? What would that have done for their legacy? What would that have done for their popularity? I don't know.

But the question that I ask is, is it better if it didn't ever come out? You think about the things that influenced the H.P. Lovecraft writings. *The Necronomicon* was way more interesting and cool before someone actually tried to publish a version of *The Necronomicon*. *The King in Yellow*, the fictitious play by Robert Chambers, as you know, it's interesting, because it doesn't exist. The Beach Boys' *Smile* was probably more interesting before we got more actual versions of it. And then just to tie it to the BÖC thing, there's the book called *The Origins of a World War* by Rossignol, right? Like, that's way more interesting because it doesn't exist.

And so there's a part of me that thinks that *Imaginos* is better in our imaginations than it is in reality—because it was, of course, a huge compromise when it came out. That's it. I know I've talked a lot, but you guys know how I am about Blue Öyster Cult. So I'll leave it there.

Martin: Nice, Matt, that's excellent background. Nick, what was your experience with this record?

Nick S. Squire: Well, I wish that you had done the press and the marketing and the liner notes for this album, because your explanation of the story has always been clear and succinct, and I learned a ton. As opposed to reading the liner notes when I bought this on cassette when it came out in the summer of '88. Of course, there was a paucity of information about this album in magazines or on MTV or whatever. So, I didn't know much about it. And reading the liner notes, they're impenetrable. They're impossible to understand. As I've described it, it's a fever dream wrapped up in a word salad—it was really just brutal. But if you put the concept aside and just listen to the music, it's really good. And I'm a little embarrassed because I had it on cassette and never picked it up on CD. But I know all the songs and love the songs. Really, really good stuff.

But at the time when it came out in '88, *Imaginos* may have been a step behind what was going on. For example, Metallica had *...And Justice for All* and Living Colour's putting out *Vivid* and Jane's Addiction is out there. So there's new sounds out there. Still, this album is also better than a lot of the contemporaries that were still putting out albums during this time period. I mean, it blows away *Crazy Nights* and it blows away *Love Is for Suckers* and a lot of '70s bands were in fact not doing anything. Now Aerosmith had *Permanent Vacation*, but I think now 30-some years later, I'd rather have *Imaginos* than *Permanent Vacation*. But there's also Bad Company's *Dangerous Age*, Cheap Trick's *Lap of Luxury* and Joan Jett's *Up Your Alley*. So this stands up okay, or at least it didn't deserve the fate that it got. It was a marketing disaster and the band probably didn't do it any favours either. As Matt says, they only played a few songs live, and of course the guest vocalist didn't come out on the road with them.

Bill Schuster: Like you guys, I bought this when it came out in '88, also on cassette. I was 20 at the time and yeah, those liner notes were a mess. It was clear the record company was trying to make it look like the original band was back together, the way they had the credits. But it was kind of bizarre because Joe was playing keyboards and not bass—there was no bass credit at all! So things didn't look quite right.

But of course, we had no idea. And I remember an episode of Rockline at the time where Don and Eric had gone on and done an interview. I used to have the cassette of it. I wish I still had it, because it was hilarious. Eric was clearly under the influence of something at the time and he even alluded to that in the interview.

But they essentially seemed to make it as though this was just their current new BÖC album, and there was not this messy backstory behind it. They didn't really go into any detail, to my recollection, with regard to Albert's long involvement. And at that time none of us had any idea. So years later, circa 2000, I go online and I find a wonderful internet resource by a guy named John Swartz called the BÖC FAQ and that's where I first discovered the basic story.

And then four years later, I got your book, Martin, and it went into in greater detail, and as a side note, that book absolutely killed my Blue Öyster Cult mythology. Thank you, Martin. Every illusion that I had about these guys was brought down to earth. But it's such a great book. It taught me so much about them. And I still love it, even though I was kind of disgruntled that they're not quite the legends that I had thought in my younger days.

John Gaffney: Okay, well, *Imaginos*. I mean, if there was ever a band designed to make a great concept album, it was surely Blue Öyster Cult. Unfortunately for me the final product feels like a big letdown mired in all kinds of difficulties. As Matt alludes to, the album would take almost eight years to finish, right? CBS originally rejected it in 1984, feeling that Albert's vocals weren't strong enough to carry the full album. They insisted on the Blue Öyster Cult guys getting involved to help finish it. I forgot to mention that Albert's let go from the band and after he's let go from the band, this is when he decides to tackle this long-standing conceptual project. And anyway, the result is a messy, overcooked album, in my opinion, featuring the guys in the band plus an army of studio musicians.

Some names that jump off the guest list page are Robbie Krieger of The Doors, Joe Satriani and Aldo Nova, who had done with Eric "Take Me Away" from *The Revolution by Night*. I mean, the sheer amount of guests players only makes me question if this is even a true Blue Öyster Cult album, because it definitely lacks any of the chemistry and songwriting adventure of the classic albums. Plus as we'd learn, the main driving force for this record is Albert who is barely on it from a performing standpoint. He's there, you know, from a songwriting perspective, but oddly he doesn't really show up performing much on the album. Plus it would be their final record for CBS/Columbia and their last full-length for a decade.

I won't go into the whole thing, but the concept of *Imaginos* was started by Sandy way back in the '60s and worked on and expanded through the years with various parts showing up in BÖC songs. You told me on my YouTube channel that Sandy had a notebook that he used to leave laying around on top of amps or on top of a table that the boys could dig through if they were looking for some lyrical inspiration. All right and well, but what is the concept?

Well, to oversimplify it a l—at least the way I see it—a group of seven beings known as Les Invisibles, The Invisible Ones, begin to endow special powers to a modified child known as Imaginos. Imaginos is able to change his appearance and see the future. This allows him to manipulate events in history, one of the major ones being the onset of World War I.

For further study on the subject I encourage people to defer to greater minds than mine, like Martin's book, *Agents of Fortune*, or his fantastic *Flaming Telepaths: Imaginos Expanded and Specified*, which creates a detailed timeline of the *Imaginos* story, the protagonist's travels and impacts on important historical events, as well as the many other significant figures whose stories intersect with that of Imaginos. I know it's what they call speculative non-fiction and it goes way beyond what's reasonable (laughs), but all of the Imag nos stuff gets told as well.

Anyway, although the story is fun, and an exercise in imagination, I find it cumbersome and a bit much in the context of the *Imaginos* album, The plot is difficult to follow and lacks any kind of natural flow. Some of that may be to blame by the fact that the album was sequenced in a way that doesn't match the storyline, or the fact that this massive tale had to be reduced to a single album. Albert originally said that he had these great plans for this thing to be, I believe, like three double albums or something, or at least three albums, something extravagant like that. But here it gets chiseled down to one single album.

Either way, I find it difficult to embrace the story as there seems to be no natural flow. Unlike other concept albums, like say Pink Floyd's *The Wall* or Queensrÿche's *Operation: Mindcrime* which seems to deal with more identifiable characters, I get a bit lost here. Maybe perhaps if there were some spoken word sections between songs, or theme-type sound effects, it might have helped to glue things together and move things along, but who knows?

Jamie Laszlo: That's great, John (laughs) because I bought this album as a dumb 18-year-old when it first came out and now I'm a dumb 53-year-old and I still don't understand it. Plus I had no idea of the backstory or how it was recorded or how they were barely in the same room together. I didn't know the premise of the story. Fortunately there's an hour-and-40-minute video on YouTube and I watched it all and it's excellent. But still, I watched

225

the whole damn thing and I didn't understand one word. Not one word about the story of this album. You know why Martin is so damn smart? Not only did he understand the video, he wrote a damn book on it that's probably over my head that would confuse me even more. So if I never buy the book, Martin, it's because I'm just too dumb for it.

But the album itself, I've always sensed that even when I was a teenager, there's a mystique about *Imaginos*. I couldn't put my finger on it. Maybe it's the cover. Maybe it's the crazy names of the songs. Or because there's this chanting that kind of comes and goes on some of the songs—"seven, seven, seven." Whatever it is, it's got this weird vibe about it that I always loved it. To the point where I've always maintained that this album and *Mirrors* are my two favourite BÖC albums; it goes back and forth. But because of watching a confusing video about it and re-listening to it to prepare for this, it's now above *Mirrors*. Yeah, I love this album.

Reed Little: Well, there's no particular era of Blue Öyster Cult that in my mind is the correct era, right? There is no, oh, they should have sounded like this and the rest of it didn't sound like that so it doesn't sound right. On the other hand, it really throws into stark relief the plusses and minuses of things as you go along. I am a big nerd and have been a big nerd my whole life. I love occult stories. Although I guarantee you that no matter how many times you listen to *Imaginos*, you are going to know exactly nothing about the occult origins of World War I. I suppose it's in there, but you really have to read between some lines and look under some rocks.

I enjoyed Martin's book *Flaming Telepaths*. It's a lot of fun with great illustrations by Martin. But reading it, you still won't understand the occult origins of World War I. It's a very loose concept. It's like trying to find out the entire story of Ziggy Stardust from *The Rise and Fall of Ziggy Stardust and the Spiders from Mars*. It's just not there. But that doesn't mean that the songs aren't good. But after listening to the entire catalogue over again, my first thought listening to *Imaginos* was that this sounds like Toto. I've actually read reviews that said this was Blue Öyster Cult's most metal album and I went what?! In what freaking universe is this their most metal album? Maybe side one, I suppose.

Sean Kelly: Bottom line is that it's a bit of a mess of an album. It doesn't live up to the expectations of the fans with this whole story, this great billing of it being a concept album. And it's diving back into the origins of the band too. Some of the stuff appeared earlier. It definitely sounds like a dog's breakfast of record. You can hear it. You could tell. What's just fascinating was this adherence to concept though, where you compromise when you need to get something done. Because hey, we're going to do this triple concept album. It's going to be the whole story. Oh wait, we're going to lose our deal?! Okay, we'll call it Blue Öyster Cult and we'll slam it together. I don't care who sings on it. Let's get the thing done.

Martin: Exactly. Okay, how about a few words on the production of the record?

Bill: The production is big and it needs to be. I wouldn't want every Blue Öyster Cult album to be this overproduced and this big and bombastic, but for this project—which, again, is not really a Blue Öyster Cult album while simultaneously being the ultimate Blue Öyster Cult album due to its origins—the production is perfect. It had to be over-the-top.

John: Okay, so the credit goes to Sandy Pearlman with Albert Bouchard getting an Associate Producer credit. Albert had to go to court to secure getting his name put here on the production credits. Quite honestly, maybe I would have left my name off these production credits. I don't like the production on this album. For some people, this amount of reverb creates atmosphere. For me it just makes it sound kind of muddy and with everything too far back. I don't really like the drum sound, which is too boomy and bombastic. At times it makes me wonder if it's electronic drums or real drums. And the guitar sound isn't particularly pleasing to me either, especially when they're pounding out power chords. It varies, but it's often a typical kind of late-'80s processed guitar sound. To me BÖC is a '70s band—you know, "The Marshall Plan," Marshall amplifiers—and I'm just not hearing that. It's too processed for me. The mix distracts me and takes away from the album.

Martin: Let's move over to the songs. We open with "I Am the One You Warned Me of," which is a big slamming rocker.

Sean: It is but back to your question about production, this is what happens when you try to apply effects a few years after the fact to the tracks you have already recorded. You hear the application of these big reverb effects on the guitars and drums. I bet these chords and that riff sounded huge in the studio. I bet they're all sitting there going, "This sounds massive." But they kind of sound slappy in the final application, kind of floppy, right? I go back and listen to it and it sounds like somebody trying to make a 1988 record out of something they tracked in bits and pieces over a bunch of years. It's old Blue Öyster Cult music with a new coat of reverb paint on it (laughs).

John: For "I Am the One You Warned Me of," Imaginos, at this point known as Desdenova (sic), here he is after the shipwreck. But again I'm distracted. The song is an example of what I was talking about with the production. These big blocky power chords in the main riff, they just don't sound good to me. And they also sound very stock, like something you would hear from just some random '80s metal band. It's not that Buck doesn't do power chords, most famously maybe in "Godzilla." But even there he does some quirky little half-note slide-ups. And the way that chord progression is, it's kind of unique. This is just so stock to me—it's boring. But the vocal delivery from Eric is great. In general, Eric seems to put his heart and soul into the vocals. From what I've read, Eric understood that this was a lifelong dream of Sandy Pearlman's, so he kind of wanted to do it for him, if you will. So it does sound like Eric shows up. And the chorus of the song is pretty catchy, so I'll give it that.

Jamie: "I Am the One You Warned Me of" is the name of a song that you shouldn't remember, but somehow it rolls off the tongue and it rocks. But I still don't know what the hell they're talking about (laughs).

Martin: Things stay pretty brightly—if not mechanistically—heavy metal for our second track, "Les Invisibles."

Sean: Love this song actually. I like the background vocal thing and Buck's lead vocal. The song's got a dark vibe, but updated, with that cool angular riff. A lot of musical things happen in this record, I think, because of what Kenny Aaronson does on bass, where you hear Kenny moving the bass line underneath, which changes the nature of the chord. So you'll hear similar chords that are playing throughout the song, but because Kenny is changing the bass, near the end, that's how they were getting variation and dynamic. I like when that happens over static chords. Usually it's a static bass line and the chords move. But sometimes it's the opposite, which is the case here.

John: "Les Invisibles," Buck vocal… this one tells us about the origin of The

Invisible Ones. I mentioned that the songs aren't sequenced properly, which adds to the confusion of the whole story. This, I believe, should have been the first song, originally intended to be the first song, which would have made more sense because it sort of gives us the backstory, a little bit about The Invisible Ones. The repetitive bass line and riff create a hypnotizing vibe to pretty much the whole song. Those background vocals repeating, "Seven, seven, seven," seven times, over and over, sticks in your head for better or for worse. I unfortunately fall on the side of worse (laughs). When it just keeps going on, it's just kind of dry and deadpan the way it's mixed in there. I don't know; it starts to wear on me by the end of the song. On the positive end, there are some nice guitar melodies that serve as decent hooks here and there throughout.

Martin: "In the Presence of Another World" maintains the record's sense of majesty, right? To be sure, we're swimming in reverb, but it is panoramic and pretty darn epic.

John: Yes, I agree, and it's one of my favourites on the album, because of its various twists and turns. It's slightly prog-ish at times and it sets a nice, spooky mood. There's a Joe Bouchard and Sandy Pearlman writing credit on this one which is nice to see. The clean-picked guitars at the beginning set an ominous mood and you can hear some fretless bass. Now I mentioned earlier that there's just an absolute army of studio musicians listed on this record and I've heard Joe say that he's barely playing on this record. So I'm gonna guess that that isn't Joe but rather Kenny Aaronson, who is the only credited bass player. So yeah, I like the fretless bass playing, and Eric's delivery, which is especially mysterious at the beginning. Plus it's got a great heavy metal chorus with the "Your master, he's a monster" line. There's also an exciting '80s-style shred lead from Mark Biedermann. When I listen to this song, I do find myself sometimes staring at the album cover because that sort of dark stormy night and the house on the hill fits with the mood of this song particularly well.

Sean: Great Eric Bloom vocal, dark arpeggiated guitar on a beautiful chord progression. It kicks in, which is a classic thing. It's this nice beautiful chord thing that transitions into a classic BÖC riff. There's some shredding credited to Mark Biedermann, who also plays on the opener but that's it. He's really going for it and it's good, but you can kind of tell it was like they had an hour of studio time or something and said, "Okay man, just burn here. Don't worry about anything; we'll fix it in the mix!" This song sounds like something Queensrÿche might've done or was doing at the time.

Jamie: I love "In the Presence of Another World." It's got that "Your master" bit which is just another instance of this weird chanting going on throughout the album. It's infectious and catchy and gets stuck in your head.

Martin: "Del Rio's Song" is my favourite on here because it's got the most soul and the most melody. Yeah, I guess that's what bothers me about *Imaginos* in general—it's sounds like cold, anonymous stadium rock.

John: Maybe this should have been the single from the album. It's very straightforward in nature, it's got a very sing-able, easy-to-remember chorus and it probably would have connected with the audience. It's something you can picture people strumming on an acoustic guitar around a campfire, and everybody singing the song (laughs). The background vocals kind of drive the title of the song into your skull. It's a little too sing-songy and straight-ahead for me but hey, I'm not going to deny that you hear it once and the chorus sticks in your head.

Sean: It's a power pop kind of thing, with a guitar solo that sounds really off-the-cuff. It's just a fun song, a little weird. The chorus is a bit of a letdown, but the verses are strong and really melodic.

Jamie: "Del Rio's Song" could be annoying if someone else recorded it. I did hear the original by Albert Bouchard—BÖC does it a lot better. It's on the verge of being annoying, but it's not. Still it might be my least favourite song on the album.

Martin: Call it arena rock or Broadway rock, but whatever the case, "The Siege and Investiture of Baron von Frankenstein's Castle at Weisseria" is epic.

Nick: Man, "Siege and Investiture" is one of my top five BÖC songs ever. It's bombastic and the piano is like, "Holy, Jim Steinman!" The vocals are like Ronnie James Dio, but with more range. I thought that song could have been a successful single even though it's kind of an odd subject matter screaming about Frankenstein. But I just think the energy and intensity of that song is unequalled.

Sean: Love this. Definitely my favourite. I agree with Nick: the vocal sounds like Ronnie James Dio. This Joey Cerisano, yeah, man, what a vocalist! So much character and attitude. This is unmistakably Joe Satriani on guitar and he plays his ass off on it. It has old school vibes—classic heavy, gothic Blue Öyster Cult. I wish this was a Dio song to be honest with you. Imagine if this was a Dio song during this era; it would have elevated *Dream Evil* or *Lock Up the Wolves* for me. And very cinematic. At the end, the chord structure is one of the most beautiful pieces of music I've ever heard. I love that ending. And then like the piano—real piano playing—comes in. It's not just keyboards. Someone is actually playing beautiful kind of Franz Lizst-like lines. This is a really gorgeous piece of music, and to me it fits with that album cover I saw in the magazine ad as a kid. That's what I was kind of hoping *Imaginos* would be.

Reed: "The Siege and Investiture of Baron von Frankenstein" is their most metal song ever, possibly, with the exception of some stuff off of *Heaven Forbid*. But the rest of the album is not metal. They pull back the intensity at every turn. The vocals are not metal-intense, the music is not metal-intense. So I would not say that this is a metal album at all. Despite this one really heavy track and a couple other close ones.

I'm annoyed that they used vocals from two people who aren't in the band. Yeah, Joe Cerisano does a great job singing this song but he's not a member of that band. They should have taken his vocal off and put Eric Bloom on there. And yes, it would have been a very different song. Unquestionably, it would have been a different performance, but that doesn't mean it would have been a worse performance. But that way it would have felt much more like a band situation.

Now, let me go back to the Toto thing. Toto is a band of phenomenal musicians that are not known in the wider musical world for having a particular sound. Because they're so good, they can sound like anything, right? Toto just produces whatever performance is necessary. Which is why, you know, Michael Jackson's *Thriller* is basically a Toto album with Michael Jackson singing. And that's what I get from this album. It feels like really top-class studio musicians interpreting Blue Öyster Cult songs, rather than a Blue Öyster Cult album.

John: Despite its over-the-top and slightly pretentious song title, "The Siege and Investiture of Baron von Frankenstein's Castle at Weisseria" is my favourite song on the album. I absolutely love the gritty and dramatic vocal delivery from Joe Cerisano. It reminds me a bit of Australian singer Jimmy Barnes who sang with Bob Daisley and Lee Kerslake on the Living Loud project. It's kind of interesting that Joey appeared as a side guy on a whole bunch of different various projects. But man, his voice just jumps right out at me here. I absolutely love it. He's got a gritty, bluesy edge to his voice here, but way up in range, which really makes the song pop.

"Imagine he was me and I was called Frankenstein." It's just a great chorus, big and thunderous with big gang vocals on the word Frankenstein. Now, like Reed says, many people would say that this is BÖC's most metal album. I also disagree with that. I would probably give that honour, believe it or not, to their most recent one, *The Symbol Remains* and maybe *Cultösaurus Erectus*. But for me, this song can make that argument. It's got the big power chords and muscular groove and I just totally dig it. The long fade-out over the shifting chord progression is really cool too. The piano adds this classical gothic vibe to that particular section towards the end. Maybe if the whole album could have captured this level of energy and gothic overtones, I might view the whole thing differently. As it stands, this song really does it for me. I kind of wish that Cerisano might have sung some other songs on the album.

Jamie: I can never remember that title but my God it's so epic, especially at the end, and this guy who sings it, Joe Cerisano, he's actually made a living in the '80s. We've all heard him. He did jingles for Miller and Join the Navy and Sprite and Mountain Dew and Eveready, and he auditioned for Black Sabbath too. I watched a little thing on YouTube about him. I prepared for this, dammit. But he kills that song, man, kills it!

Martin: Before we flip over to side two, anybody want to say anything about the album cover?

John: The album cover is the Cliff House in San Francisco, which has long since burned down. It's a kind of a spooky, Frankenstein's house. When I first heard this album, I didn't know anything about the backstory. So looking at the cover, I guess it does fit the mood of it. I heard that Greg Scott—*Fire of Unknown Origin, Extraterrestrial Live, The Revolution by Night*—was originally contracted to do the cover and I've heard him describe what he had in mind, with all kinds of subtle symbols and the ship, the dogs and stuff like that. And the back cover was going to have some of the same symbols but sort of in different places like you see on an astrological sign and things like that. That gets my interest a bit more. I would have appreciated an album cover that had a bunch of details that you were trying to figure out what they mean to the story. This sort of stock photography is less appealing, given that we know what Greg Scott was capable of.

Martin: All right, side two offers us an old song dragged into the '80s, perked-up. I suppose it was inevitable that what is probably the band's most respected song after "Reaper" makes a return, especially given its centrality to the *Imaginos* saga.

John: Yes, good point, although I prefer the original "Astronomy" from *Secret Treaties*. Still, it is interesting hearing Buck sing the lead here. The slightly more up-tempo take and the repetitive 16th-note background rhythms make me wish, though, for the more open spaces of the original. This one flies close enough to the original that it makes me think of the original, again, which I prefer, which causes distraction. But when Buck moves higher up in his range and sings, "Call me Desdenova, eternal light" he really sells it for me. I could do without the "hey hey" refrain in the background—that's a bit much. I do like the ending with the sudden stop and then the crescendo and harmonized angelic-type voices. But again, I'll take the original or *Secret Treaties*, thank you very much.

Sean: Yeah, those very staccato guitars and the "hey hey" shouts make me think of "Run Like Hell" by Pink Floyd, right? I also like the one on *Secret Treaties* so much better. But yeah, one thing to look for, Buck is really good at going from lead to rhythm guitar playing on the same track. Also, as a trivia note, this was put out as a single in the UK.

Reed: The version of "Astronomy" on *Secret Treaties* is one of my all-time favourite tracks and I think it's superior in every way to the version on *Imaginos*. I think Eric Bloom's vocal fits the song much better than Buck Dharma's. But it's not just that. The version on *Imaginos* has got a hundred different guitar parts in it. It's just layer on layer on layer of guitar parts. It's got lead over lead over lead. There'll be like five or six lead lines going at the same time. And this is what people mean by overproduced.

I won't say the original is simplistic. It's not. It's still got layered guitars, but there's a lot less layers, right? And I do think the vocal fits it better. It's more intense plus that has my favourite moment in any BÖC song, which is when they pull back the dead little piano and then they ramp up the intensity again before they sing "Astronomy, a star" over and over and over again. You lose that entirely in the *Imaginos* version. It's all one intensity all the way through. And again that's a studio arrangement that's not the band because they clearly have a finished track that the band is coming over to sing on.

Jamie: So Eric Bloom sang it the first time and it's kind of garage-rocky. It's from the black-and-white period when they were a little bit proto-metal. I hear people say this album is over-produced. I think it needs it, for the layers and the textures and the "hey hey" chanting. It just works better when it's well-produced instead of garage-rocky. And I like Buck Dharma's vocals on it better, because he just adds that mystique.

Martin: Next is "Magna of Illusion," which seems to fall prey to the necessity of many concept album songs' tendency to have many parts, to tell a story in music as well as through lyric.

Sean: It's like Styx meets Andrew Lloyd Webber. It's got the big galloping guitars, very musical theatre, very Kansas-like. And this is one that Robby Krieger plays guitar on, along with "Blue Öyster Cult." But there's some weird choices. I know this was the end of the mix, but there's these weird low harmonies that kinda pop out. It's like, what the hell? They sound like some sort of Frank Zappa spoken word thing. Otherwise pretty cool, good tune.

Jamie: Those "Magna of Illusion" lyrics sound like he's singing a history lesson to me. Like I need to take notes. It was telling me, as an 18-year-old, something's going on here with this album and it's smarter than me. And that's why I like it.

John: "Magna of Illusion" is an Albert, Buck and Sandy co-write. Grand and epic sounding. Now this is a case where the mix works for me, because this song has a cinematic feel to it with the piano flourishes adding some nice kind of serious classical-feeling textures to the song. I like the hammer-on pull-off guitar line at the beginning too. The guitar playing in general on this song is great, with some really cool fill-in lines and flourishes that pop up here and there between vocal lines. Like I said earlier, maybe there should have been more stuff like this to help move the story along and help glue things together. This is my favourite vocal from Buck on the album.

Martin: I feel the same storytelling Broadway play vibe on the next song, "Blue Öyster Cult."

John: Yes, this is like a total concept album makeover of the Eric and Sandy song, "Subhuman." It really bears little resemblance to the original. Maybe that's why I like it, as opposed to "Astronomy," which flies a little too close to the original for me. This is really a completely different song, save for the lyrics. The melody line and background instrumentation are different. This song is much more ethereal and atmospheric. The "Ladies, fish and gentlemen" chorus really stands out for me; it kind of jumps out and works really well on this version.

The lyric is about Imaginos nearly drowning and washing up on shore to be approached by the Blue Öyster Cult. Albert sounds really good to my ears, this being his only lead vocal credit, which again is kind of... I don't want to say funny, maybe sad, because Albert was the guy that championed this thing and put all the blood, sweat and tears into this and he gets sort of yanked out. The record company thinks his vocals don't cut it. But on here he actually sounds good to me and this is his only lead vocal credit, even though in the song he does share his lead vocal with Buck.

The "We understand, we understand, Blue Öyster Cult" part towards the end of song is really catchy; it sticks in your head—very, very cool. Robby Krieger's solo that follows is great, bluesy and melodic but with some nice technical flashes. Honestly I didn't know Robby Krieger could play like that (laughs). So that's a nice surprise. When everything drops down at the end and the keyboard sound effects take over, it's very trippy and psychedelic. There should have been more mood-setting stuff like this on the album, in my opinion, like the end of this song with the weird keyboard sound effects. Like I said before, it might have helped sort of glue everything together.

Sean: Beautiful melody. It's not the strongest vocal on the album, that's for sure, Albert not being the natural singer that Buck and Eric both are. But this is his added fingerprints to a project that was his in the first place, or second place I suppose, given that it was him reviving something that had existed, but after he was out of the band. It's got character. It's kind of heavy but the guitars are buried in a very '60s way. It reminds me of when someone wants gravitas in a Disney musical, and they add a song like this. "We understand, we understand, Blue Öyster Cult." Or Toto or something; I don't know. But cool bass line development, and this has some very sophisticated jazzy guitar playing from Robby Krieger.

Bill: As cheesy as it is—and yes, it's very much right up there with "BÖC, you can be whatever you want to be"—I love it. It's ultimate cheese, but I like a little cheese in my Blue Öyster Cult. I like fact they have these different eras and that this is an odd little side-trip, really.

Martin: Speaking of side-trips, "Imaginos" takes us right down Broadway for a big repertoire wind-up number, seemingly designed to send patrons out of the theatre humming a happy tune.

Sean: Yeah, man, very musical theatre. I guess it's supposed to tie the whole thing together, right? But yeah, it's like *Rocky Horror Picture Show* (laughs). It sounds like a musical theatre production you would see, but by adults in a community theatre, where this is like the first song. Like *Waiting for Guffman* or something. I don't know. Or like you say at the end, to remember the name of what you just saw.

John: Vocals by Jon Rogers. For me they're okay but they don't really jump out at me, honestly. I would rather have heard Eric sing this one. "Imaginos" definitely suffers from not being sequenced properly on the album. It should have been earlier. On the original sequence, I believe it would have been number two because it tells sort of the early story of Imaginos. I guess his shape-shifting and him being in different places, Texas, Vermont, etc. It's fun to hear the bungo pony make a return. Last seen on the back cover of *Cultösaurus Erectus* and before that in "The Red & the Black" lyrics.

    There's some nice funky bass playing from Kenny Aaronson, I assume. It's a disappointing album-closer and title track for me. If they had to deal with this out-of-sequence thing, they should have ended the album with the song "Blue Öyster Cult." But there is some nice sax soloing at the very end. Makes me wonder why they didn't throw a bit more of that in there. It's kind of buried in the back.

Jamie: "Imaginos" is just an ear worm. "Ooh ooh, Imaginos." It shouldn't be. I know Columbia rearranged the songs and that should not have been the last one. It sounds like an introduction to the album, if you ask me, but I think it was originally like track two. They should have kept it at track two and it should have ended with the big epic "Blue Öyster Cult," which is seven minutes long.

Reed: Finishing the album with "Imaginos" is a bummer. It's like why put your worst song at the end?

Martin: I can't answer that! Any closing thoughts? Things you wanted to add?

John: Well, I'll just say that overall *Imaginos* is an album that I don't really return to very often. I did re-sequence the songs on a playlist and I did find that not only did it flow better lyrically but the music sounded better too. So for anybody out there, I would encourage you to go find the original track order of this album and maybe re-sequence it. It might help you enjoy it more. And also study the backstory in Martin's books. And if you really want to go down a rabbit hole, check out the YouTube video Jamie mentioned.

But yeah, when I'm ranking the BÖC albums, this is always towards the bottom for me because of the production and just because it took them so long to do it. It's overcooked. The cake has been in the oven for too long. If the whole band was there from the beginning and had been involved in all aspects of it, that might have helped too. As it stands it's kind of a chore to get through. I like "Frankenstein" and one or two others but overall it just feels like a chore in the listening as well as trying to decipher the story. Your sort of *Imaginos* extension book was a super-fun read as a story in itself. It would have been interesting if Sandy Pearlman maybe could have put this all together, got all his notes together and did it properly. But sadly Sandy is no longer with us, so that's impossible to happen. But as a single album from 1988, it just doesn't work. And honestly I can't see how three double albums would have helped the situation either.

Reed: Now, I will say I own Albert Bouchard's *ReImaginos*. God bless him for trying. I don't like Albert's voice. I can't listen to him. Albert sounds exactly like what he is, which is a guy who didn't have a fantastic voice to begin with and now he's 75 years old. And I mean, I give him all the props in the world for trying, but the result doesn't really do it for me.

But if you take his song order and reorder the tracks on *Imaginos*, it actually goes, "I Am the One You Warned Me of," "Del Rio's Song," "In the Presence of Another World," "The Siege and Investiture of Baron von Frankenstein," "Astronomy," "Imaginos," "Blue Öyster Cult," "Magna of Illusion" and it ends with "Les Invisibles." "Les Invisibles" is a fantastic song to end with. Like Jamie says with that chant, "seven, seven, seven," it's such a better way to end the album than with the weakest track. So as John says, go through and make yourself a playlist where you reorganize the songs according to the way Albert thinks that they should have been structured and see if that doesn't actually improve the flow of the album. I think it makes a big difference.

In the end, I think *Imaginos* feels exactly like what it is: it's a collaborative studio album with some vocal performances by Blue Öyster Cult. It's functionally identical to Metallica playing with a symphony. It doesn't really sound like Metallica. It sounds like a symphony with Metallica singing overtop of it, right? And that's how I feel about this album. It's good, but as a Blue Öyster Cult album, it lacks. I prefer the non-studio musician Blue Öyster Cult albums. If I had to rate it, I'd give it an appropriate 777/10.

Bill: I want to make sure to give Albert plenty of credit here because this has been his baby for literally decades. He's been a tireless champion for this and I'd like to definitely pimp his recent solo versions a little bit. These are the two re-workings that Albert's released so far. They are nothing like the *Imaginos* album that originally came out. As you've framed them, Martin, they're acoustically oriented. But they are really cool re-workings of the original songs, in addition to many other Blue Öyster Cult songs and some hidden gems that have only previously come out like on Brain Surgeons albums. We got the original version of "The Girl That Love Made Blind" on the Brain Surgeons *Malpractice* album. That was first time I ever heard that song, and then Albert redid it again for *ReImaginos*.

And there are many guest stars on *ReImaginos* and *Imaginos 2: Bombs Over Germany*. You have Buck Dharma, Eric Bloom, Joe Bouchard and Joey Cerisano, of course, who did "The Siege and Investiture" on the original *Imaginos* album. He does a version of "Quicklime Girl," of all things on the second volume. It's cool to have all these people coming back together to reimagine this concept. And it's nice to see that these guys are still able to be civil with each other, that all that water is under the bridge and that they're able to actually join in on each other's projects and take part in this. I like seeing that.

There's also, if you search YouTube, Albert has listed his original demos. But according to Albert himself, it's not the demos—it's the rough mix. So he has been very clear in stating that his vocals on that were not meant to be final. Whether that had anything to do with what the record company thought, I have no idea. I'm not sure if that's what they heard or if they heard the actual demos, but he did definitely state that don't judge it based on these.

But it's still really cool to go listen to that original version if you're a fan of this material, just to hear different aspects of it and what it was like before it was all tarted up with the production and the extra guest stars and Buck's and Eric's vocals. If I were to actually rate this album, I'm not gonna say it's my favourite Blue Öyster Cult album, but I do regard it very highly. But again, I kind of don't consider it a Blue Öyster Cult album. To me, listening to this record is near pure pleasure, but I acknowledge it's a chaotic mess and there are other minor irritations with it.

Nick: You know, when *Imaginos* came out, I knew it to be a project and I knew that there was extra personnel on it but I didn't realize that BÖC was in such disarray. Nonetheless I thought that the album deserved a better fate than the one it got. I think it holds up over time.

Matt: I'll just conclude with the assertion that the Albert Bouchard version is the most fully realized version of what the concept is and that we should approach it and experience it that way. I've been working on a zine that's coming out called *Critical Hit Parader,* and the first issue is a Blue Öyster Cult-themed issue. As I was writing it, I listened to Albert Bouchard's version for about two months straight every night as I was writing. And what happens if you absorb it that long, is that you get the taste of the other versions you've heard out of your mouth and you can kind of hear his two volumes of the story for what they really are. First, you know, 20 times listening to it, it's very hard to not hear the versions that you've heard before. And I actually think what he's done is a masterpiece. It's so good in terms of actually delivering on the concepts of *Imaginos* in a way that none of the other versions—basically his own demos and rough cuts, plus the *Imaginos* album—do. Bottom line: I'm excited for the third and final version of the trilogy from him to come out.

BLUE ÖYSTER CULT
HEAVEN FORBID
BLUE ÖYSTERCULT
The NEW Album IN STORES NOW!!!!
Featuring 10 NEW studio songs, plus one live treat!
Call your radio stations and request the singles "See You In Black" "Harvest Moon"
On CMC International Records

BLUE ÖYSTER CULT
LIVEFORME
From The NEW Album HEAVEN FORBID
CMC INTERNATIONAL
Manufactured and Distributed in the United States by BMG Distribution, a unit of BMG Entertainment, 1540 Broadway, New York, NY 10036. BMG is a trademark of BMG Music. Unauthorized copying is against federal law. Made in the USA
BMG DISTRIBUTION

HEAVEN FORBID

Heaven Forbid
March 24, 1998
CMC International 06076 86241-2
Produced by Buck Dharma; additional production by Buck Dharma, Eric Bloom and Steve Schenck
Engineered by Paul Orofino; additional engineering by Marc Senesac
Recorded at Millbrook Studios, Millbrook, NY, Minot, White Plains, NY and Alpha & Omega, San Francisco, CA
Personnel: Eric Bloom – guitar, keyboards, vocals; Donald "Buck Dharma" Roeser – guitars, keyboards, vocals; Danny Miranda – bass, vocals; Allen Lanier – guitar, keyboards; Chuck Burgi – drums, vocals
Guest performers: George Cintron, Danny Miranda, Tony Perrino, Jon Rogers, Bobby Rondinelli

1. "See You in Black" (Bloom, Roeser, John Shirley) 3:17
2. "Harvest Moon" (Roeser) 4:55
3. "Power Underneath Despair" (Bloom, Roeser, Shirley) 3:29
4. "X-Ray Eyes" (Roeser, Shirley) 3:48
5. "Hammer Back" (Bloom, Roeser, Shirley) 3:35
6. "Damaged" (Roeser, Shirley) 4:22
7. "Cold Gray Light of Dawn" (Bloom, Roeser, Shirley) 3:53

8. "Real World" (Roeser, Shirley) 5:11
9. "Live for Me" (Roeser, Shirley) 5:19
10. "Still Burnin'" (Roeser, Jon Rogers) 3:37
11. "In Thee" (live) (Lanier) 3:40

Martin talks to John Alapick, Sean Kelly, Reed Little and Matt Thompson about *Heaven Forbid*.

Martin Popoff: So here we are. It's been ages since we had a Blue Öyster Cult album, but with so many threats of one coming along the way.

Matt Thompson: Exactly, yeah. So the band's been away for ten years, and they've had some stops and starts throughout those ten years of thinking they might get to make another record. So they get dropped—they don't have a label. At various times they think they're going to get a deal. And so the songs are written over a long period of time, because they think they're gonna be doing something and then something falls apart. Eric at different times, at live shows, is sort of teasing that there's going to be a new record long before it actually ever happens. And they in fact, you know, in '92, play quite a few of the songs throughout that year live. "Still Burnin'" and "Harvest Moon," "Power Underneath Despair" and "Cold Grey Light of Dawn" all get played that year for a record that doesn't come. And then they take them out of the set. It's like this little tease.

My understanding is that because of this, *Heaven Forbid* is probably recorded at two main sessions, two different time periods. So you've got Danny Miranda on bass for something like eight of the songs, but then you've got Jon Rogers on bass for the three that were recorded earlier. So it's not quite a real band album. You've got Chuck Burgi on all but one song and Bobby Rondinelli is on "Live for Me," which is probably the last thing that gets done. So it's a little bit disjointed in terms of it being a single band that goes in at a single point in time and records an album. Given all that though, it actually has some pretty good continuity of sound throughout it. Surprisingly, they actually pull it off of not having it sound disjointed. So definitely kudos to them.

Reed Little: Probably like anybody, number one, I was kind of shocked that after ten years Blue Öyster Cult is putting out an album. And number two, that the album that they put out is frankly one of the best they've ever done. I love *Heaven Forbid.* It's an amazing album. Perhaps because of the benefit of technology, even though this is on CMC, not a big label, it sounds fantastic. And that is probably because with digital recording technology, it was now possible to get great sounds much more cheaply. They weren't eating up studio time and they weren't requiring roomfuls of equipment. They were just laying it down in ProTools and cutting it up. But I don't think BÖC ever sounded better.

This is their most heavy metal album. I know some people say *The*

Symbol Remains is heavier. I don't understand that. I think *Heaven Forbid* is a far more heavy metal album. The guitars sound amazing. It's a vocals and guitar album. Allen Lanier is still in the band, but they've replaced both the bass player and drummer. So they're in a little bit of that Spinal Tap rotating drummer situation that all rock bands eventually seem to hit.

But it's vocals and guitars that you get on this album and the vocals and the guitars all sound fantastic. The riffs sound great. Again, Buck has upped his game. He sounds amazing. He's just ripping off solos like the best of his peers. Right from the very first song, "See You in Black," it's a fantastic album. Now I will say that you notice the change very much in the lyrics department. It's John Shirley, horror writer. I need to track down some of his books. He is a much more, shall I say, blunt writer than Sandy Pearlman or Albert Bouchard or Patti Smith or Richard Meltzer. His stories are not allegorical. They're very much what they are. So when you read "Power Underneath Despair," it's a very straightforward story of revenge after this guy gets out of prison. You know, there's no mystery to it. So you're not really going to be hooking any conspiracy theories on it, hopefully. But the song construction to which it's attached is so wonderful and so aggressive.

John Alapick: As Matt says, we've had ten years between *Imaginos* and *Heaven Forbid* and *Heaven Forbid* was released on CMC International Records. For the longest time they were on Columbia. They were originally on Elektra before Bloom was in the band. And when their original singer left, they scrapped the album, and they got signed with Columbia; Sandy Pearlman helped to get them signed with Columbia and they were on that label right up through *Imaginos* and then they got dropped because the '90s arrive and the musical landscape changes. People are listening to grunge; they're not listening to '70s or '80s bands.

Blue Öyster Cult are not at the point where they're becoming a nostalgia band yet, but they weren't at that point where we were rediscovering them. These bands, they're not getting the hits they once did but they still have a lot to offer. They still have something to say. They still have some creative juices that they have to let out. CMC International gave the opportunity to these bands who were once popular and now the landscape's changed. They felt they should still have the avenue in order to record some good music. So you have bands like W.A.S.P., Lynyrd Skynyrd and Dokken amongst many others who were releasing some good music on CMC International.

And Blue Öyster Cult did that here with the *Heaven Forbid* album. By this point, Buck and Eric were doing most of the production. Also by this point, Albert and Joe Bouchard weren't in the band anymore. Allen Lanier was there but it was mostly the Eric and Buck show. I liked their production. I think the Buck songs sound really good and the Eric songs are heavy. They are heavy to the point that they don't sound like the same band. But they also had Chuck Burgi in here on drums, and his drum performance on this album, particularly on the Eric Bloom songs—the songs that Eric sings—is fantastic.

Martin: Excellent, and speaking of Chuck, wow, what he does at the beginning of "See You in Black" is basically this band's "Tom Sawyer" moment. And besides that, it might be the most heavy metal song the band has ever recorded.

Sean Kelly: Yeah, man, Metallica kind of vibes going on here. And a little bit of Dio during the *Dream Evil* era groove. He's got some double bass going on and then with the half-time part there's definitely a '90s Dio thing going on. There's a throaty Buck Dharma solo—man, when Buck plays heavy rock, he has a very throaty tone, very midrangey. When he wants to play grindy and bluesy, he does it better than anybody.

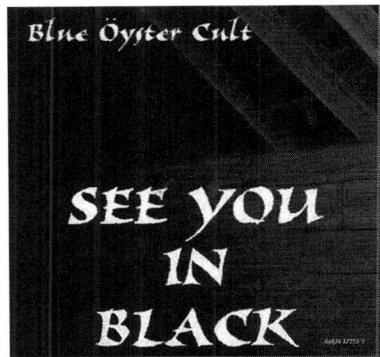

Matt: "See You in Black" got played in concert before the album came out, but not much before then—and it went over great right from the beginning. It's a great rocker. It's got the drumming and lead guitar intro, this really loose intro of maniacal drumming and guitar, and then it locks in with a very heavy metal, modern heavy metal—a little bit thrash if you want to be generous— riff to it.

And now we've got John Shirley on the lyrics, and this is one of his better ones. So again they're looking to collaborate lyrically with outside writers, but they've kind of used up the stuff that has been sitting around, like the Sandy Pearlman binder, and they're not really having much to do with him anymore. They don't have much to do with Patti Smith anymore also, right? So they're looking for a new collaborator and they go to a sci-fi author who doesn't have the popularity or necessarily the notoriety of Michael Moorcock in the biggest sense, but is well regarded in cyberpunk circles. He's known and is well thought of as an author. So it gives him some lyrical credibility throughout this and the next record and a little bit of *The Symbol Remains* as well. And it's a cool lyric, right? It's this morbid, clever, funny thing to say: "I want to see you in black." Why? Because it means your husband's dead. It's definitely a new take on this idea of stealing of your girlfriend.

Reed: Love it, fantastic opener. BÖC had a good track record of picking good songs to be their openers. And now kind of typically, as we'll see, I often say like Ronnie Dio after doing *Heaven and Hell*, every album he did was sequenced like *Heaven and Hell*, right? You have the fast opener and then you've got the long like epic track. And BÖC did that too except it was the aggressive opener and then hopefully this Donald song that will be a hit song, right? So you've got "See You in Black" which has got a very Blue Öyster Cult lyric about how he really he wants to see this woman in black because that means your husband's dead. And I love the production on it. It's not quite '70s timeless but it doesn't sound like the '70s and it doesn't sound like the '80s. It's just good hard rock. I think by the late '90s we're past the concept of timestamped production, unfortunately until we get to quantization and autotune, but that's a different story.

John: "See You in Black" is a case of I liked the song but it doesn't sound like BÖC. I mean, it's heavy but I never really thought of BÖC as a heavy band. Even though they did heavy songs, you listen to this and you're like, "Whoa!" This is heavier than anything they ever did, including songs like "Hot Rails to Hell" and "Dominance and Submission" which, I guess, granted, are heavy for their day but not beyond that. But "See You in Black" is a really cool opener and it grabs you just like many openers on legendary albums from the '70s do. On lyrics we've got John Shirley, who is a mystery and horror writer. He's writing a lot of lyrics here, taking the role that Sandy Pearlman and Richard Meltzer once had, although there's still a bit in the well with Richard.

Martin: Well, as Reed amusingly frames it, next is that golden Buck song. Basically, Blue Öyster Cult fans have deemed "Harvest Moon" a late-period classic.

Matt: Yes, that's right, and they've had this as a secret weapon for more than a decade. So Buck records it with The Red and the Black—it's a Red and the Black song, his band with Jon Rogers and Ron Riddle. And they have it. It's on all their demos but they don't get a deal, so it doesn't come out. Then they played it in concert throughout. So they know they've got a gem and they're just waiting for a record to put it on and they get to do it on this record.

Couple of things I'd like to say about this. So one, lyrically, it's very similar thematically to "Mistress of the Salmon Salt." There's this sinister thing in the small town going on where people are getting killed, and they're finding the bodies in the spring during harvesting and all that. So very similar. But what an interesting contrast to the way that Sandy Pearlman takes a very goth c approach to it, a very wordy approach to it, a very obtuse approach to it. For Sandy it's a Lovecraft style.

Buck takes a Peter Straub/Stephen King approach. Those are the books that he's reading, and it's more straightforward but still clever, right? So you don't find out 'til the end, that this is a horror story. It's the last verse where you learn it. The chorus lyrics are very wistful: "I love this time of year." It's wistful on the subject of autumn and things like that. And the lyrics don't tell you that there's a problem. This place has a history. It's very melancholy, and then you get the twist, where there's these killings going on, and they're gonna find those bodies in the spring. They find them all that way when the snow melts. So it's a really good modern horror story, and very melodic. It has all the strengths of a good Buck Dharma song, super-melodic, and they add a little twist to it, having the breakdown in the middle.

And if you'll indulge me one second, Martin. There's an alternate history here where things could have gone different in a couple of ways. So Buck is not prolific; he does not write many songs. But when he does, they're fully realized and they have a pop sensibility to them. They are of a melodic motif. He has delivered the most singles to this band. *Fire of Unknown Origin*, he demos "Burnin' for You." It's going to be for his solo album. They sort of force him to put it on *Fire of Unknown Origin*. And then he'll get the deal with Portrait to do a solo record. But he's got to give this to them.

So if you want to play the "What if?" game, what if he holds that and he releases "Burnin' for You" on a solo record? Maybe he has a minor hit with it. So then the next set of Buck Dharma songs that come along aren't Blue Öyster Cult songs—they're Buck Dharma songs. So you'd have "Shooting Shark," right? You'd have "Perfect Water." Those would be follow-ups. And he's building maybe this little career. I don't think he'd be super-successful, but to some extent he'd cover some ground and make a dent, and probably critically too. Those are sophisticated pop-type songs. You can see when he tries to write some other ones with The Red and the Black and it's kind of this new take on The Police.

So he's creating this little niche-y sophisticated pop career and then he writes and releases "Harvest Moon," which to me is a "Reaper"-level song.

I think it's better than "I Love the Night." Other fans love "I Love the Night." I think this new song is musically and lyrically superior to it. It's much more sophisticated. So anyways maybe he could have gotten that to be a hit, right? Instead it's released on CMC (laughs). They do try. I remember looking at the Friday Morning Quarterback magazine each week to see is this thing is gonna catch on at all. And you know, the world's changed and it's changing. It gets a little bit of teeny, tiny airplay but it doesn't become a hit.

Reed: I agree with everyone else that "Harvest Moon" is the classic Blue Öyster Cult song from the post-Columbia years. And while I generally prefer Eric to Donald, both as a vocalist and as a lyricist, I love this song. I love how creepy it is. Up on top you've got that nice plain story about a town in decline. But underneath it, you have this creepy, American, *Sleepy Hollow*-style horror story about people disappearing and how they find their bodies the next spring after the thaw. It's wonderful. It's everything that is missing from some of Donald's just straight-up love songs. You know, it's easy to forget what a great tradition of horror America has, and this is so New England-styled American horror. I love it. And it's got a great musical track, along with three guitar solos on it, all of which are slightly different. Not just the playing—I mean, the playing, he's obviously playing different notes—but I mean, the tonality of the three is different, meaning he probably recorded them at different times. Again, it's one of the BÖC songs that I put right at the top of the catalogue.

Sean: Buck plays these gorgeous, crystalline arpeggios—that's classic BÖC. And Buck, this reminds me, I know Albert didn't play on it, but it reminds me of classic laid-back Albert Bouchard-style drumming from the '70s, an AOR feel. I like when it goes to double time for the solo, and Buck keeps rolling, building and burning. And that's kind of his thing: I'm gonna roll a bit, it's going to get more intense and then there's bit of a lay-down. Just kind of a classic '70s guitar playing. And I love the way that Chuck Burgi responds to Buck.

John: This is a song they still play at every show. And people who are diehards love this song. If you're standing up front at a Blue Öyster Cult show, you're seeing a lot of people sing "Harvest Moon." This could have been a hit 15 years prior. This could have been the follow-up single to "Burnin' for You." The only difference is it gets really heavy during the solo. I mean, they pick up the tempo and it becomes more of a heavy metal song before it gets back into its main theme. Buck sings fantastic on this. It's a wonderful song.

Martin: Then we're back to another pumping, percolating stadium rocker in "Power Underneath Despair." Funny thing is, it sounds like the same character from "See You in Black," which is amusing.

Matt: It is—I like that (laughs). And I mean they are all John Shirley ones. And to me, it's sort of hit or miss, the John Shirley lyrics, right? Some of them are quite clever and some of them are really straightforward and to me they don't fit the BÖC aesthetic. But this one's really crunchy. It's a good heavy rocker, and then I guess that's something we could say across the board: this is a heavy album. This is actually a legitimate heavy metal album for a band that really doesn't do it that often. They had this one around from '92. It's kind of cool because it's got a little time signature twist to it on the chorus, which adds interest. Again, it's another John Shirley lyric, and it's also funny that it's sort of the same lyric idea as "Showtime" from the next album. So they kind of end up going to the well twice.

Reed: I'm torn on "Power Underneath Despair." I know you wouldn't think it to look at me, but I actually started my career in law enforcement as a correctional officer many years ago. And I hate songs and movies and shows about prisons (laughs). I just will never find that entertaining again. So I'm kind of conflicted because I think it's a great song and I love the chorus. One thing that they've really picked up and just pushed forward are those gang choruses, right? They rarely just have the one singer anymore. So they've got the whole chorus doing, "The power underneath, the power underneath." So I do like that one. Great song, very aggressive, very modern-sounding.

Sean: It's got a little bit of a Styx-style pomp rock chord progression, but also once again Dio. Long Island, upstate New York... Ronnie probably went to Long Island once in a while. It's got cool rhythmic displacement in the chorus which makes it very proggy. We've got these rhythms kind of flipping around, where there's accent on the snare where we're used to hearing it on the kick, which is very interesting.

John: Like "See You in Black" it's a very heavy song for them, and the chorus sounds like something out of doom metal. It's a cool song and as Matt says, pretty sure this and "Harvest Moon" and a couple other songs off this album they played as far back as '92, six years before they put out this album, *Heaven Forbid*. So these songs were already finished and they were ready to go and they already had worked them in front of a crowd for a while.

Martin: And even if they ever had songs written as heavy as some of these heavy songs, the production on this album is so heavy that they sound way bulkier than, say, "Godzilla" or "This Ain't the Summer of Love" or anything from the black-and-white period.

John: I would agree with that. Yes, no doubt about that. I mean they never sounded this loud and loud in a good way. This is not a loudness wars album. This is loud to the point where you really hear each instrument and it grabs you.

Martin: Then again, "X-Ray Eyes" reverses the jets, with Buck even massaging in an acoustic guitar track to go with his electrics. This is not structured like a metal song.

Sean: No, this has a '60s vibe, kind of note-y and jazzy, with a little bit of The Who in the verse. I call this "shlang guitars," as in "shlang," like hanging chords. And the jangly guitars, that's the Byrds thing and I know they loved The Byrds. You can hear it. Even when Buck sings, he's got that very "Mr. Tambourine Man" sound. It's very clean and enunciated and articulated.

John: This is another good melodic rocker from Buck that he sings really well. Nice harmonies on this one too, although I don't think it's a great song.

Reed: "X-Ray Eyes" is the first of what I think of as a '70s throwback on the album. It's not '70s-sounding in the sonics of it—the bass and treble, the frequencies you're hearing—but the guitar lines are very '70s. So this is Buck again, and Buck has hit an interesting point, I think in his compositional life, where he's starting to write a lot of retro-style songs. This is a very '70s-sounding song and the lyric references a 1963 science fiction movie starring Ray Milland, called *X: The Man with the X-Ray Eyes*. And he actually gets the date wrong in the song—he says it's from the '50s in the song, but it's from 1963. That's a weird point of reference for anybody, but how many kids looking for hard rock could possibly have cared about a cheap, old, science fiction movie from 1963? By the way, the movie is worth watching. But if anybody's fans were going to get that reference, it's Blue Öyster Cult's.

Matt: This one does fit lyrically because it's questioning a theme that permeates the Blue Öyster Cult lyrics which is, you know, the unseen, the starry wisdom and all this stuff. It's like, do you really want to see that? Do you really want to know what's going on? I think it's very clever the way it fits in with non-John Shirley lyrics, and the way that it's almost like an answer song to other Blue Öyster Cult songs. It's got the Ray Milland reference, which adds a '60s B-movie feel to it as well. And maybe that's the reason for the much-maligned album cover, which is more like a '50s horror campy cover. This is the only song that fits with the cover, perhaps.

Martin: It's like the cover of a pulp novel, like a noir detective story.

Matt: Oh yeah, yeah! That's a great way to say it; that's a better way. Absolutely. And this is kind of a pulpy song. And it's very well delivered. Buck's guitar playing has continued to grow. Although they haven't put out records, they've continued to play live, so his chops are totally up to speed on this album. And whether it's on the pop songs like this or on the rockers, you've got great leads throughout and so this is a little slice of sophisticated pop.

Martin: And it's jazzy pop too, right? He's often jazzy with his pop, and underscoring that with his solos, which are even more often jazzy.

Matt: Absolutely. That's in his DNA.

Martin: Then we're back to a groovy, grinding rocker in "Hammer Back," pretty accessible in the verses and then a pure headbang come chorus time.

Reed: Yes, so we have one song from the '70s and then we're right back to that modern heavy metal. And this is another song that I'm a little conflicted on the lyrics. It's a very straightforward song. The days of ambiguous BÖC are behind us—they left that behind in the '80s. So this is a song telling us that bad things happen, and you need to have your gun on you, and you need to be ready to use it. And I don't like that. Just going to state that. But it's impossible to tell whether this song is intended as a cautionary tale pro or against guns. So here's the ambiguity for you. Are they mocking America's tendency to think that you can solve problems with guns? Or do they really mean that you can solve problems with guns? I don't know. There's a little bit at the very tail end of the song. You've got a couple of sort of macho man sound effects which make it kind of not so serious, right? So maybe it is mocking. But you'd never get that from his vocal delivery.

John: Another heavy one, although like you say "Hammer Back" is quite melodic in the verses. It's when they go into the chorus that it gets really heavy, and it seems to get even heavier when they sing the chorus at the end of the song. It gets more and more menacing. That's how I would describe Eric's songs on here—menacing.

Sean: Cool guitar harmonies, sophisticated, weird, nice dark Phrygian mode. There's a million-dollar word for you. It's got that very dark thing where you're playing between the first two notes and there's just a half step (sings it). That kind of a *Jaws*-type thing. Yeah, they do these types of riffs and choruses really well. And the solo Buck does takes you right back to Uli Jon Roth and "The Sails of Charon."

Matt: For the Two Oyster Cult that they become, being Eric's and Buck's band, they're definitely ticking the boxes of what each does well throughout this album. This is an Eric rocker and so he has the appropriate menace in delivering the music. You get really good drumming throughout this record. Chuck Burgi is tremendous. I think he elevates this in a way that I would say doesn't get elevated on the next record. He's got some legitimate fusion chops as well, so he can kind of do both the rockin' to help the metal part but kind of indulge Buck's jazziness throughout. I think they play off each other really well. Lyrically this is in the straightforward John Shirley camp— it's fine. But musically it delivers the goods.

Martin: "Damaged" is one of the band' quirky songs that seems to make the point that they can be versatile and counted on for at least one completely new type of thing per album. Really much more that than, but at least one.

Matt: Yeah, this one is funky. The Hammond organ is sort of the highlight of the song and it's played by Tony Perrino. It adds a lot. This seems like something that could have been a good live one but I don't think they ever did play it live. I like the way Buck delivers the lyrics on it. It's interesting; it could have been an Eric song too lyrically. "Damaged, but I like it." That's more of an Eric thing to say. But instead it becomes more like a funk track. It would have been interesting to hear that in a rock style. The lyric fits.

Reed: We've had our modern rock and now we're back to Buck, and that means the 1970s. But this is now happening more frequently, where we get Buck on an aggressive song. Like Matt says, it seems more like an Eric thing. You've got Buck singing about being an unrepentant drug addict and violent drug addict who keeps telling his girlfriend that he's going to sober up and never does because he enjoys being damaged. So again, this is kind of like "Hammer Back." You end up going, "He doesn't mean that, right?" Is this meant as a cautionary tale? But you don't get that; there's no wink. It's not like "Flaming Telepaths" where the joke's on you, right? It's sung and it's presented in a very straightforward manner. But surely he can't mean it as a good thing. Also "Damaged" has prominent electric piano. Perhaps if you slowed this down and changed the tonality of the guitar and played it on acoustic instead of electric, it would sound like "Train True" off *The Symbol Remains*.

Sean: Buck utilizes a great in-your-face guitar sound. To me this one sounds like heavier Steppenwolf. When they bring the organ into play, it always reminds me of Steppenwolf, but the heavier evolution of where that type of vibe would've gone, where John Kay might've gone with the that type of vibe decades later. I'm also thinking, "Fabulous Thunderbirds go metal." I don't know why.

John: "Damaged" is really cool, especially when Buck is just singing over his guitar lines. And before the band kicks in and they go into that galloping rhythm, it's really cool too. I don't know if they ever played this live but it sounds like a song that would really go over live because it's got a catchy chorus that's very easy to remember.

Martin: Anybody want to comment on the album cover?

John: I don't have the one with Morgan Fairchild on it. I have the spookier one with the decaying face. You look at this album cover and you're thinking okay, this is gonna be a heavy album. And it is about 40% of the time. But yeah, you look at this and it screams death metal. I mean, even the way they write *Heaven Forbid* looks evil.

Reed: The album cover makes me think of Charles Band, the straight-to-video horror guy who did the *Puppet Master* movies. And who knows? I mean, he did *Bad Channels*, which was the movie they did the soundtrack for. So maybe that was intentional. I like the picture of Morgan Fairchild much better. But for a horror-themed album, the picture they went with was probably better. It was definitely an eye-catcher. But by this time you're deep into the CD age and I don't know that people were still making purchases based on the album cover alone.

Martin: All right, back to the contents and we have "Cold Grey Light of Dawn," another Eric-made rocker with a John Shirley lyric.

Matt: Yeah, very atmospheric too. This is the last record where Eric is sort of still at his peak, especially for ones that were probably recorded earlier in the recording cycle. I think he does a really good job of delivering the atmosphere on this. It's a slow groove, kind of a slow-burn song. Its merits are not obvious on first listen, because it's just less in-your-face than certainly "See You in Black" or something like that. But it's got a very good groove to it. Interesting harmonies on how they do the chorus too and all told it's a very successful song for the album. I think the sequencing works really well too, putting this between "Damaged" and "Real World." Sequencing on a CD is different than sequencing on an album, but I think this works.

Reed: Now it's time for Reed's controversial opinion of the day. I think that this is a grunge song. This song was apparently written in 1992. So what's big in 1992? Alice in Chains Nirvana, Soundgarden. I always say that grunge is the '70s in the '90s. And this song is very '70s. It's spacey, it's distorted. Actually, ironically, I think it sounds perfect for the soundtrack from *Heavy Metal*, the motion picture, but a few years too late. It's got a pretty typical lyric about not being able to run from the truth, right? Whether that's murder or old age or infidelity, themes that would have fit right in with the grunge movement. So in 1992 BÖC would have had to have been hearing what was popular and I wonder if this was them thinking maybe we can adapt to this music and put out something that fits into this. But then they ended up just holding onto it and not putting it on an album for another six years.

Martin: Like "Damaged," "Real World" finds the band funky and poppy, only this time missing the hard rock element.

Matt: Yeah, and it's a little out of place. This feels more like a Buck Dharma song—I think it's better suited as a Buck Dharma band song. It's mellow, right? Not distorted guitars at all. It sounds like a '90s alternative song, a little Dave Matthews-ish or something like that of its time. Lyrically it's another take on weirdness. It almost answers the question of "X-Ray Eyes;" you know, do you want to see what's really behind it? And here's one answer. It's like, no, I don't need to. The real world is bizarre enough for me. We don't need all this occult stuff. So that's kind of interesting. I think it gives the listener a break but it feels a little out of place. It doesn't really feel like a Blue Öyster Cult song.

Reed: "Real World" is straight-up country. Buck even adds an unnecessary twang to his voice in case you're not getting the point. To me it sounds like he's doubling the guitar with acoustic and electric so it's got a very different, very countrified tonality to it. Then he sings those lyrics that are about these strange occurrences, but then at the end he gets back to the moral of the story, which is, hey, the real world's plenty weird enough. You don't need to go off on all this strange stuff. It's a theme that shows up again on *The Symbol Remains*.

Sean: Nice acoustic guitar and yet it's funky. I like the acoustic/electric interplay. Buck has a great feel in his rhythm playing. He's very sensitive to what is happening rhythmically.

Martin: Then we're into "Live for Me," which always reminds me of "Your Loving Heart" from Buck's *Flat Out* solo album.

Matt: Yeah, except, I guess "Live for Me" is serious and "Your Loving Heart" is not, right? "Your Loving Heart" has the twist at the end where it's morbid. It's that '50s death song thing. It's like a "Tell Laura I Love Her" kind of '50s/ early '60s song lyrically, whereas this stays serious the whole time. And it really is a death song. You know, do all the things that I'm not going to be able to do.

So in some ways, now that I think about, it's an unsophisticated way to deal with death. It's much more straightforward. If you think about "(Don't Fear) the Reaper," that's a more poetic way to answer that. Instead of literally just doing the things that I won't get to do, which is what "Live for Me" is about, it's, no, we're going to transcend death and live together. It's a different take. But it fits into the Buck Dharma Blue Öyster Cult pop songs like "Burnin' for You" or "Dancin' in the Ruins." It works; it still feels like Blue Öyster Cult; it's got his poppiness. The underrated part to this song is the outro guitar, the little melodic things he does at that beautiful extended wind-down. He's playing these sort of more arpeggiated things where it's a little different for his style.

Reed: I have to jump a song for a second, because I've read multiple commentators say that "Still Burnin'" is a sequel to "Burnin' for You." Which I don't agree with but we'll get back to that in a minute. So I'm bringing that up because "Live for Me," the next song after "Real World"—and it's unusual to get three Buck songs in a row; they usually split them up a little bit more—but "Live for Me" does

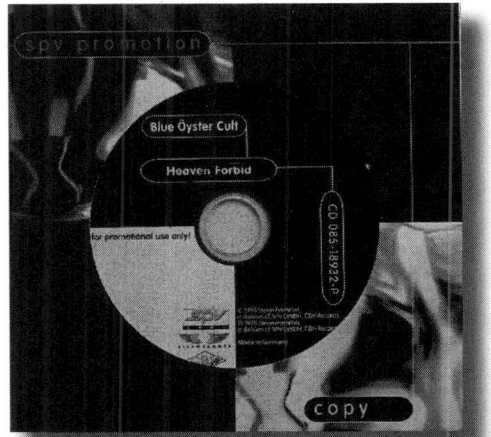

sound like a sequel to "Burnin' for You." I think it's even the same chords. I have not sat down with my guitar and tried to figure them out, but they sound very similar to me. It's just that instead of a lyric about lusting after this hot woman, it's about his brother being killed by a drunk driver. But the sonics of the song to me are very close. So again, this is Buck looking in his rear-view mirror as he's writing for this album.

Sean: "Live for Me" indeed sounds like "Burnin' for You" melodically, but it's a good update. To me it sounds like when Bryan Adams tried to write "Run to You" for Blue Öyster Cult. That actually happened. Vallance and Adams would get together and they would say, "Okay, ZZ Top? Who needs a song? Blue Öyster Cult? They're coming out with a new record. Let's write one that sounds like them." So it's all supposed to be aping Blue Öyster Cult "(Don't Fear) The Reaper," and they end up with "Run to You."

Martin: Were they literally writing "Run to You" for Blue Öyster Cult?

Sean: Absolutely, to give to them, yeah. Yeah, that's what they would do and that one was for them. I've got demos of Vallance and Adams doing that.

John: I agree: this is like "Burnin' for You" part two. Even though we're gonna talk about a song that was supposed to be "Burnin' for You" part two. "Live for Me" is great. That guitar line in the choruses, and then the harmonies behind Buck when he's singing the choruses sound superb. Love this track. This is another one of those songs where even more than "Harvest Moon" I think what could this have done if they'd released it in 1983 before MTV really took over and it became more about image?

Martin: I've never been a fan of "Still Burnin'." I just don't like those chords, or that vocal melody, especially when we get to the chorus.

Reed: Ironically, "Still Burnin'" is another '92 song, and it's another just rockin' metal song. It would fit right in with that kind of Alice in Chains heavy metal side of grunge. We can play "What if?" all day but if they had come out with a full album of that in 1992, I wonder how it would have done. I love "Still Burnin'," but again, musically it's a million miles from "Burnin' for You."

Matt: It's one that was around a long time. It's Jon Rogers; this is one where he plays bass. Conceptually, it's a good idea, right? I guess if you're coming back after ten years, you want to say that you're still burnin', which also includes the nod to "Burnin' for You." But unfortunately, I agreed with you. There's just not a lot to it. It doesn't really go anywhere. It doesn't really deliver the promise of the "still burnin'" idea that the rest of the album does, because the rest of the album does demonstrate that they are still burnin'. This one, not so much.

Martin: The album should be over at this point, but of course they gotta make it messy, just like having two different, both not-so-great album covers.

Matt: Right (laughs). Yeah, this is out of place. For me, it doesn't fit. "In Thee" is not the kind of song, even if they were to put a live song on it, that fits in with this record. It's a heavy record. And I'm not sure why you needed it in the first place. I mean, it's nice to have a live version of "In Thee" but it didn't need to be on this record.

Martin: There's pretty much no acoustic guitar anywhere else on this record.

Matt: No, that's right. That's a great point. So again, why is "In Thee" here? I guess the closest is "Real World." You get a little bit of acoustic there, but to your point, even there it's in the context of a traditional full band song.

Reed: I don't understand it either. They didn't need another track. It doesn't fit sonically with any of the other songs on the album. I don't get it.

John: Except I like this better than the studio version because I think it's just a pretty acoustic live version—they still play this song during the encores of their live shows. I think this works better without all the augmentation that they have on the original on *Mirrors*. This demonstrates how good the song really is. It stands out in a more stripped-down version. One other point, not only is it the only Allen Lanier credit on the album, it's the last Allen Lanier credit to date on a Blue Öyster Cult album. Obviously, given his passing in 2013, it's unlikely we'll see another one.

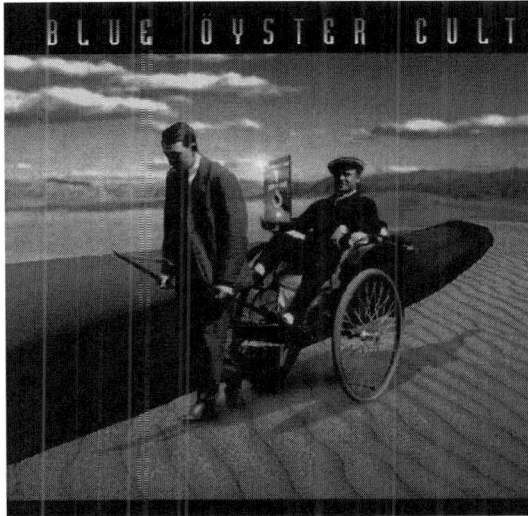

CURSE OF THE HIDDEN MIRROR

Curse of the Hidden Mirror
June 5, 2001
CMC/Sanctuary 06076 86304-2
Produced by Buck Dharma; Associate Producer, Eric Bloom
Engineered by Paul Orofinc
Recorded at Millbrook Stucios, Millbrook, NY
Personnel: Eric Bloom – vocals, guitar, keyboard; Donald "Buck Dharma" Roeser – vocals, guitars, keyboards; Danny Miranda – bass, vocals, keyboards; Allen Lanier – guitar, keyboards; Bobby Rondinelli – drums
Guest performers: George Cintron, Norman DelTufo

1. "Dance on Stilts" (Roeser, Shirley) 6:05
2. "Showtime" (Bloom, Trivers) 4:38
3. "The Old Gods Return" (Bloom, Roeser, Shirley) 4:36
4. "Pocket" (Roeser, Shirley) 4:15
5. "One Step Ahead of the Devil" (Bloom, Roeser, Danny Miranda, Bobby Rondinelli, Shirley) 4:16
6. "I Just Like to Be Bad" (Bloom, Barry Neumeister, Shirley) 3:54
7. "Here Comes That Feeling" (Roeser, Trismen) 3:21

8. "Out of the Darkness" (Miranda, Bloom, Roeser, Shirley) 5:06
9. "Stone of Love" (Roeser, Meltzer) 5:49
10. "Eye of the Hurricane" (Bloom, Neumeister, Roeser, Rondinelli, Shirley) 4:40
11. "Good to Feel Hungry" (Miranda, Bloom, Roeser, Shirley) 4:12

Martin talks to Rich Davenport, Sean Kelly and Matt Thompson about Curse of the *Hidden Mirror.*

Martin Popoff: It's three years since the band's last album but that actually felt relatively quick. Have the guys come up with the goods?

Sean Kelly: Sure, somewhat. I think generally what *Curse of the Hidden Mirror* is, it's a really good amalgamation of all the classic Blue Öyster Cult tropes, but with very dry production, very present production. It's a lot of really great melodic songs that serve as a vehicle for Buck Dharma's modal lead playing. And I love this rhythm section, Bobby Rondinelli and Danny Miranda. I love the way they react as players to this. These are the kinds of albums that excite me because I like bands that have had their heyday and are back in the market, and you can tell they were kind of fired up to bring something of quality to the table, right? And BÖC did. I think this was very successful. But you're fighting against all odds now. This came out in 2001 and it's tough out there, man. The market had been decimated in many ways. It's still there, people are still buying physical product and stuff, but they aren't necessarily lining up for the new Blue Öyster Cult album to come out.

Rich Davenport: Quite recently Frontiers have done this series of reissues where they added a few extras. They took care of this one and they reissued *Heaven Forbid*, and then there's the new album that followed. Plus they put out a couple of albums that had been kind of fan club-only releases, like live things. So I like all three of these most recent albums and I reviewed them.

What strikes me about this album—and I think I read this in your book—is that it was the first digital album they recorded, And what I like about it is that the dynamics are great and the production is a bit more in-your-face and upfront, perhaps, than *Heaven Forbid*. Not so much in terms of heaviness, more in terms of you can hear what's going on much more clearly. It's a more naked production in that you can hear the vocal tones and you can hear the guitar tones. And it's a modern guitar tone, a very clearly-recorded, overdriven guitar sound on a lot of it as opposed to a heavy metal full-blown distortion sound. It's a really good positioning of the band, kind of sonically, that should have, if it had gotten the attention it was due, set them on a good footing for the 21st century.

Unfortunately they were caught in that whole situation when first they were signed to a small, struggling US label called CMC. Then CMC was bought out by Sanctuary who were soon struggling themselves, and then bought out. So in 2007, CMC ceased to exist. But at the time, I think the band felt a bit lost at Sanctuary. It definitely turned out to be a curse. Because Sanctuary, never mind *Curse of the Hidden Mirror*, they just seemed to sign up so many bands and everything—or any one of them— just seemed to get lost rather than focussed on. You know, Sanctuary, you would imagine being known for managing Maiden and W.A.S.P. and bands like that, they would home in on that, but they just seemed to grab up everything. I mean, they even bought the reggae label, Trojan.

And unfortunately, a lot of albums have been out of print for so long. With metal and with reggae, you know, they just bought up everything and then got into pop. And when Sanctuary went into administration, or out of business—I'm not quite sure exactly what happened with the label but they definitely went under—the rights to a lot of this stuff went into limbo. So it put a lot of stuff out of commission and that happened to this album as well.

And here was Blue Öyster Cult yet again dealing with another shift in the rock landscape. As I was saying when we talked about *Club Ninja*, classic rock as a format didn't really exist then in any meaningful way. Whereas by this stage, 2001, it was much more established in America, and I would imagine, from what I've read in your articles and books, in Canada. Whereas in Britain, it really wasn't, although it was emerging, because *Classic Rock* magazine started in '98. But it was still fairly dismal over here for anything like that, and a lot of bands that reformed earlier or that had a big comeback in the '90s didn't really capitalize on that resurgence in classic rock, which seemed to come a lot later here, more like the early part of the 2000s.

Because I know myself, from being a musician playing in that era, the '90s was just a terrible time for rock in general, because the UK can be quite trendy in that sense. And even our rock mags jumped on the back of the grunge thing to the exclusion of traditional rock. It just seemed to be about throwing out the baby with the bathwater. I mean, I understand that it was completely oversaturated with hair metal, but even for a lot of the older classic bands like Deep Purple, Uriah Heep and Blue Öyster Cult, there just wasn't really much coverage outside of *Classic Rock* magazine, and not much of a touring circuit for it here either.

To give you an indication, I remember in 2005 when Judas Priest came back with Rob Halford, the Scorpions supported them here and they played the Hammersmith Apollo. But they had played arenas here before. So it was just starting to re-emerge. I think the big thing that tipped it over here was when Maiden came back. That put the whole classic metal/classic rock genre back on the map. And since then, the whole classic rock and classic metal genre—which, there's obviously a lot of overlap with the age group and the audience—it's much better now, you know, 23 years later. There's a far more established market for it. But when *Curse of the Hidden Mirror* came out there really wasn't.

Matt Thompson: Yeah, it wasn't really a friendly environment for a band like this, and from an American perspective, this would be the time of nu-metal. But *Curse of the Hidden Mirror*... it's remaking *Heaven Forbid*. But the difference is that they are a single band at this time. Danny Miranda has been in throughout the whole time and Bobby Rondinelli has been in the band for a while and they are a well-oiled live machine at this point. Plus you do get some contributions from those band members, with them showing up in the credits on four songs.

But for me, it doesn't quite work as well as *Heaven Forbid*; it's sort of a lower grade *Heaven Forbid*. And the reservations start with the sequencing. Opening the album with "Dance on Stilts" is just odd. They're starting with a six-minute song that's not an epic six minutes, right? It's like "Madness to the Method," which is a strangely long song. It's kind of weird that it's that long, so it comes off as strange as an opener. It feels like it's the live version of the song. But it's a very good pop song, right?

I love the "See me in a white suit" line and then the big punctuation, the stop. Because it's Buck singing it, so you think about the '70s Buck in the white suit. But in this instance it actually means a businessman. That's a cool but possibly unintentional throwback. But yeah, it's out of place sequentially; it's an end of side one of a vinyl record kind of song. They didn't start with an Eric Bloom rocker like they did on the album before it and after it, with "See You in Black" and "That Was Me" respectively. Let's go get 'em right away. This is a slow-burning pop song; it's relaxed with a relaxed arrangement. Kind of weird.

Martin: Rich, Sean, how do you feel about "Dance on Stilts" as an opener?

Rich: Much the same. I remember hearing this opening track and thinking, oh man, I hope this isn't gonna be a stinker of an album (laughs). Because it's not a great opener. It's unusually bluesy for them. It's stodgy and awkward and at an odd pace for an opening track. A little generic. The riff isn't overly welcoming. I always think if you're going to do a bluesy riff like

263

that, you've got to come up with something outstanding and original, or else it's just so easy to sound clichéd.

And that descending chord progression that the main vocal goes over... hmm (laughs). It's not particular catchy. His vocal is great and the solo is great, but as a song it doesn't really do much. And then there's an end section that saves it, where the harmonies sound like The Doobie Brothers, unusually, and where we get another pretty joyous and wailing solo from Buck. That's the best part of the song. There's this ascending riff that comes in that's better than what's in the main part of the song. But yeah, I remember hearing that and thinking, man, I hope the album isn't gonna stink.

Sean: Yeah, it's like AC/DC meets Bad Company, with a little bit of Cream's "Tales of Brave Ulysses" in there. I like the way Buck sounds like Paul Rodgers. He's a pretty good chameleon, this guy, as a singer. I don't know; I guess it still sounds like BÖC to me, or maybe BTO meets BÖC (laughs). It's a very '70s, mildly anthemic, AOR-driven rock thing. Great melodic Buck Dharma solo at the end and some classic kind of unison riffing where the bass and the guitar are mimicking each other. There are these thickening agents, I call them, in Blue Öyster Cult. But it's interesting. It's almost like, hey man, let's try for the single right at the first song, even though they blow it by making it so long.

Martin: Next we have "Showtime," which maintains the sort of sober, mid-volume vibe of "Dance on Stilts."

Sean: Yeah, but better tune. We have Buck experimenting a bit with some backward guitar—it's slippery. Actually, I couldn't figure out if it was backwards or if he was just manipulating the whammy bar, which is good thing; it just sounded cool. The song has an '80s vibe to me, with a sort of power pop pre-chorus, and there's interesting elements that periodically pop up in Blue Öyster Cult like the reggae and dub elements. You hear the delay on the vocal, the upstroke on the guitar, which you hear once in a while in the back catalogue.

And once again you can tell this is a band that came of age in the '60s where you're not afraid to take disparate influences and put them in your music. I also felt a bit of a Gilby Clarke vibe in the vocal. Yeah, kind of a straight-up rocker with a bit of power pop and a bit of Tom Petty. Cool tune. The lyric is about getting out of jail, but for all the talk about the quality of Blue Öyster Cult's lyrics, I gravitate right away to the music, because there's always a lot of substance there, although so much of it is subtle.

Rich: A much better song. Very striking opening with the backwards guitar. It's mid-tempo, but there's a lot of energy in it. The guitars have that kind of tremolo effect. Not tremolo as in whammy bar, but as in that effect that's on "Riders on the Storm." Robbie Krieger uses it and that is actual tremolo. Oddly enough, what most guitarists call tremolo is actually the vibrato bar. That's an odd bit of guitar trivia there for you.

Martin: Can you explain that a bit more there, Rich?

Rich: Okay, what most people call a tremolo arm on a guitar, it's actually more of a vibrato effect. And tremolo is an effect. I can understand people... I had this explained to me by someone who has much more technical knowledge than me. But if you listen to "Riders on the Storm" by The Doors, that's an effect there. And I had it. I bought a '70s amp when I first started playing guitar and it had this tremolo knob on it. I thought, "That's weird. Tremolo—that's the wang bar." And you put it on and it's the exact same effect as what's on "Riders on the Storm." It sounds like the guitar's going in and out, almost like a radio station you're trying to tune in. It's like a wave or an effect, but not a pitch waver. It's just the sound wavering.

So there's a nice sonic touch but in general you can hear the strength of the album's production in this song. It's very clear and in-your-face. You can hear the grit in the vocals. I also like the tempo switch where it doubles the pace and then backs down again. The melody and the harmonies remind me of something from *Agents of Fortune*, not to the extent where it's like copying, but there's a nice familiar echo of that.

There's an almost punky energy to the chorus and then a reggae section in the middle which I love.   love reggae anyway, and this fits. And there's a great melody and this muted backing vocal at this part. It made me think of other examples of hard rock bands maybe 20 years before this using a bit of reggae. You have the Scorpions on "Is There Anybody There?" and Krokus did it on "Tokyo Nights" and before that Tommy Bolin did it on "People, People" from *Teaser*. Plus Pat Travers covered "Is This Love?" and added some reggae on some of his own songs like "Crash and Burn." Even BÖC had an echo of reggae guitar right there on "Burnin' for You." So there's a precedent for it and I just think it fits in really well.

Matt: What's interesting is that they're repeating a lyrical theme, but not by the same guy. It's a jail lyric by Jon Trivers and on the last album we got a similar thing from John Shirley with "Power Underneath Despair." Kind of weird. "Showtime" had been demoed for *Cultösaurus Erectus*. It would have been interesting to see what it would have sounded like with Martin Birch and with where the band was at in 1980. But I'm glad it's here. Although I think Eric sounds a little better on *Heaven Forbid* than on this album, so it might have been better if it had been recorded earlier.

Martin: Next is "The Old Gods Return," which weirdly has both a heavier title and heavier songwriting than the way the song comes off in totality.

Matt: You know, "The Old Gods Return," you can see what they're trying to do, but I feel like they didn't get it polished enough for it to deliver. There's definitely good bits and the epic-ness is there but I don't think the parts connect as well as on some of their better epic songs. I think it required a little more craftsmanship, and frankly, maybe this is where a great arranger like an Albert Bouchard or a Richie Castellano could have smoothed some things out and elevated the song to a higher tier. Good song, but to me it's missing some of the sophistication that the best of their stuff has.

As for the lyric, it's interesting because you can think of it two ways. "Old Gods Return" is very Lovecraft-sounding, which is something they've dabbled in, certainly with Sandy Pearlman's lyrics. But you can also say it's the band trying to come back, like "Still Burnin'" from *Heaven Forbid*. But as a science fiction story, it's much more literal than a Pearlman lyric. And there's humour in it. I mean, Pearlman does do humour, but it's really dry and subtle. This is more straightforward. You wouldn't have a Pearlman lyric that says, "Now is the time that the apes take wing/And we recognize them from that Oz thing." But it works as a John Shirley lyric; that's more his sensibility. And if you're thinking of it as a nod to just the band itself, it's better executed than "Still Burnin'." That was not one of the stronger *Heaven Forbid* tracks.

Rich: Yeah, and it's got that sort of sinister, malevolent, dark, kind of eldritch vibe you associate with Blue Öyster Cult, plus a soundtrack feel from the keyboards. Again, the production really brings out those natural guitar tones. It's like classic rock overdrive, like I say, immediate without being full-on metal. This new era with respect to technology is benefitting BÖC in that sense. And the rhythm is great. Bobby Rondinelli is a real credit to the band and he fits in and locks in really well with Danny Miranda. And the vocals aren't conventional, with conventional hooks. This is what I was saying about some of the earlier albums, where there's a quirkiness with respect to the use of his vocal range, this singing from low to high thing that he does.

Sean: Once again you've got this classic Blue Öyster Cult trope with the dark arpeggios. That's a big part of their sound, where they have these clean, crystalline kind of arpeggios along with ominous kind of minor key riffs. For those who don't know, if you listen to the beginning of "(Don't Fear) The Reaper," that's an arpeggiated guitar figure. You're playing the notes of the chord one after another in succession and creating lines out of that. And Blue Öyster Cult does this to great effect quite often. So it's playing the chord's strings separately, playing the different voices, like in "Stairway to Heaven." Those are of arpeggios—it's the chord broken down.

Martin: I'm really starting to understand now what Rich is talking about with these guitar tones. "Pocket" is another one arranged all electric, with these hanging power chords, but it's not particularly heavy.

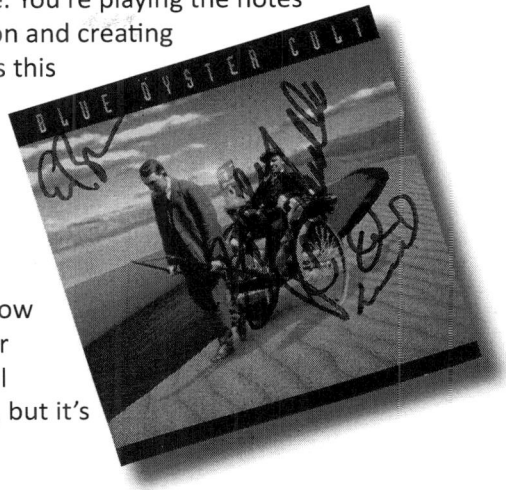

Sean: No. This is a very Who-sounding song to me, with Townshend-esque chords and Entwistle-esque bass and a conversation going on between them. Then there's a really melodic chorus, with nice overlapping '60s vocal harmonies, something that happens a lot with Blue Öyster Cult. It's a sort of support mechanism for the song, this chiming-in thing, almost like a bed underneath the lead vocal. So yes, this is a very thoughtful song to me. The verse reminds me of "Strutter" by Kiss, which is interesting; it has the same kind of chord movement. Great virtuosic solo, but kind of country metal (laughs). He's definitely got some fingerpicking country thing going on in his playing, which is nice and plucky and makes it very alive.

Which brings up another thing; especially throughout the '80s and '90s, things got compressed with guitar playing. As we refined distortion and saturation, everything got kind of compressed. So it was easier to play fluidly and play fast, but you lost character and identity. I find Buck Dharma never loses character and identity, tonal identity. He's always playing with a tone that's clear. And that's what comes back to what I said earlier, that when you're switching between lead guitar and rhythm guitar, you need skill to play those arpeggiated lines. I think he's got all that working very well. I recently saw some live footage of him playing on *The Morning Show*, and you see him switching and changing his hand positions and he always had that clarity and definition.

Rich: Like Sean, this reminds me of The Who, both in the note choices of the opening riff and then in the feel as it goes on. Obviously a lot of guys from this era are very influenced by The Who. It was quite striking that it was Bobby Rondinella because obviously I had known him from Rainbow and what he did with Black Sabbath. He's known for the more sort of rigid double bass drums and not really a looser Keith Moon feel. But he does that very well.

And it's an interesting lyrical idea, playing on that musician's term. I'm sure you know what being in the pocket means. It means playing really steady and being in the groove. So I suppose it's a nice interpretation of that lyrically, to be in the moment, you know, like a drummer would be. You're focused on the beat. You're focused on the moment, really locked in. There's a lot of chords in there, but again, this is that songwriting strength the band has—they make sure it's not a distraction.

Great solo again; you can hear that Buck has kept his chops up. He's really shredding there. It's kind of like classic shred. It's thick, he's not following any trends in guitar, but he's playing fast. And some guys from that era might just repeat the same licks over and over again. Whereas you can tell that both him and Eric Bloom have really kept the chops up, which is only to be expected from a band that tours like they do.

Matt: "Pocket" is a great Buck song. You want two of them on every Blue Öyster Cult album, right? You get more of them on this record because he's got the most left over and still high-quality material. This is a new one—he writes this one new—but then later they pull in "Here Comes That Feeling" and "Stone of Love," which are old, old Buck Dharma songs that were going to be for the second Buck Dharma solo album. So you get a lot of this style. Buck still sounds great, but it makes it feel less Blue Öyster Cult-ish. It's a little bit like what the band has become, right? He's taking a bigger role in the live performances, because his voice is more consistently there each night. And so now they've got to get more Buck songs on the record.

Martin: It feels suburban doesn't it?

Matt: Yeah, yeah, absolutely, and it just feels a little less BÖC. But "Pocket" is really good. I was going through some stuff and I found this "Pocket" bumper sticker. So they were trying to find a single and support it with some promotion.

Martin: Which begs the question, what do you consider to be Buck's personality as a soloist? What does he do more of or less of than other guitarists?

Matt: I think one thing he does is pay more attention to rhythm, the swing aspect of it. He grew up listening to big band and swing music. His father was a sax player and that really shows throughout all of his playing—his phrasing swings. And Albert can support that, right? So it works. Other drummers they've had sometimes don't support that style as well. So that's pretty unique. He's of that British blues revival generation, or whatever you want to call it. He's the generation after Clapton, Beck and Page, but he's not really that bluesy. He plays more chromatic stuff. He plays a little bit more... it's not really jazz, but there's a jazz sensibility to his phrasing, and he's very quick for his time. Later guitar goes to a whole 'nother level of speed, but he's very nimble as a player. For this time period, in sort of heavy music, he is quicker than his contemporaries who are trying to do this type of music.

Rich: I agree. He's got very unique phrasing. He still plays on the beat. He's not one of these guitarists that's like sloppy and messy, and it's unusual because of that. It's very much about his note choices. And for a guy from that era, making his mark in the '70s, he's got the chops and a sense of both melody and jazz in a way that really stands out. Then in measured doses he uses technique, speed, and flashier elements to make an impact rather than just beat that to death.

And he constructs the solos very well. It sounds like there's some thought gone into them. I remember reading that after the *Hearin' Aid* single "Stars" came out in '86, there was an interview with Ronnie James Dio in *Kerrang!* and they were asking him about putting that together and the production side of it. And Buck's solo was one of the ones that he picked out as being quite unusual and quite outstanding, you know, from all those guitarists. Which to me is one of his strengths. You've got that many guitarists on there, especially in the '80s where everyone was playing a million miles an hour, and they were hard to tell apart. And Ronnie flagged him as someone who was really standing out and really distinctive.

Sean: It's funny, like Rich, I was going to mention "Stars." It's famous for this big, long guitar solo, where like 20 guitar players all took a crack at this mammoth solo. And they're throwing in every lick they can—George Lynch, Yngwie Malmsteen, Craig Goldy, Vivian Campbell—and the two guys that sound different to me are Eddie Ojeda and Buck Dharma. And Buck Dharma takes a solo at the end, and it's funny, yes, Ronnie, who is producing and hearing everybody, appreciated what he did. He's coming from a generation before—'60s, '70s players, even '50s players—and Buck, he has tons of space in his playing. Very restrained.

But he can wail, he can play fast, but it's often this very kind of modal '60s thing. Almost kind of when The Byrds got influenced by East Indian music or something. So he's got these long kind of melodic lines and he's not afraid to use space. He's touched upon all the great '60s blues rock things from Clapton, Page and Beck—he had all those devices at hand—but more so he's made his own sound. And he's one of these guys who effortlessly can drop in and out. Like when he's playing a solo, he's often doing it on the same track as he's doing the rhythm guitar. When he's playing his rhythm guitar and the solo comes, he plays the solo. It means there's this fluid connection to the song. Plus I find he's a guy who consistently plays for the song.

Martin: What about his tone, and the fact that he plays very high notes quite often? I guess that's more related to note choice.

Sean: He does, but you know what? It's always with a warm and rounded tone. And his tone evolved nicely throughout his career too. As technology evolved, he wasn't afraid to embrace technology and different guitars, but he always sounds like him. His character is in his fingertips. He's got the sound that was developed from back in the day when he had a Les Paul or SG and a Marshall and that was how you generated your sound. It was generated through dynamics. The harder you play, the more sustain you got. And he got great dynamic control in his playing.

And I love his note choices too. I find it very interesting. He reacts. He's listening to the band and as the band builds, so does Buck. And this whole album embraces that theme. Like there's a lot of instances where Bobby Rondinelli starts picking up, and then Buck starts picking up and they're interacting and having a musical conversation, which is a very '60s and '70s concept. That kind of got eradicated in the '80s. The conversation was, "We need to have a hit record and I'll tell you what to do." But in the '60s and '70s the bands are still jamming and being improvisatory and adding those elements.

Martin: While we're at it, how about a comment on Allen Lanier?

Rich: He's very subtle compared to a lot of '70s keyboard players. I mean, he's not wearing a cape and doing a 50-minute solo. But especially on this one you get this rippling effect on the keyboard. He's a tasteful player and he can assert himself without being distracting, which is a difficult thing to do in any guitar band. He can assert himself and put in something noticeable. For example, going back to "The Revenge of Vera Gemini," his keyboards are so integral to it, they're like the whole backdrop to the song. But unless you listen closely, you'll almost miss him. So he can really put in something colourful and noticeable that's appropriate to the song, rather than one of these sections where it's like, "Right, let him have his 45-second solo to shut him up." So he strikes me as a real team player, and he's in keeping with the general Blue Öyster Cult feel of being a bit dark and unsettling.

Martin: Yeah, going back more so to the '70s band, the funny thing about it is you're not trying to wedge a piano player into a heavy metal band, because this band doesn't think like a heavy metal band. So there's always a place for him. It's like, oh, where's keyboards in the song? That's fine. It's not Black Sabbath, where it's a big deal if there's keyboards. Plus, as we've touched upon elsewhere, Allen to me is like the downtown New York guy. He's like the cool guy in the band in a way, right?

Rich: Yeah, and the Patti Smith connection; they were dating. And Jim Carroll. Again—and I know you mentioned this in your book—but Patti and he were quite cut off at one point, weren't they? Living as a couple and away from the rest of the band.

Martin: All right, next is "One Step Ahead of the Devil," a rocker with Eric really pushing air at the vocal end.

Sean: Yeah, this one reminds me of early Blue Öyster Cult riff-wise, although the chorus could have come from '80s Judas Priest. It's got that charging, chugging heavy metal eighth note thing, those fifth-y power chords. Cool tune. And yet, as we've discussed, there's a place for Allen Lanier, who adds a Jon Lord- or Don Airey-type thing to it.

Rich: Yeah, heavy one, but there's a Zeppelin influence in terms of that type of call-and-response riff between guitar and vocal. But it doesn't sound like they've copied Led Zeppelin in terms of the way the bluesy riff is written. And this is an example of a bluesy riff fitting much better than it does on the opening track, "Dance on Stilts." A much better example of integrating that blues feel into Blue Öyster Cult's own style. And again, it has to be said people associate that call-and-response with things like "Black Dog." But Zeppelin took that from the blues. It's more of a blues trope than a Zeppelin trope. But a lot of people will probably associate it with Zeppelin. Eric Bloom's very aggressive again, so that's good. They're not mellowing with age. And there's a lot of aggression in the fastest section of the song and a nice unexpected change for the chorus.

Matt: Well, "One Step Ahead of the Devil," you can like line up one-to-one many of these songs with their equivalents on *Heaven Forbid*, right? To me it's a cousin of "Hammer Back." It's a straightforward rocker and it's decent, but the lyrics are nothing. I prefer "Hammer Back," kind of, in the way that I prefer "Cold Grey Light of Dawn" over "Out of the Darkness," which is a moody rocker but just not quite as good or sophisticated as the previous one.

Martin: Do you find the production somehow less edgy or something, rounded-off, versus *Heaven Forbid*?

Matt: Yeah, I guess I find it lacking. The guitars sound more digital, more direct box kind of stuff. And they sound great on *The Symbol Remains*, by the way. They sound much more warm on *The Symbol Remains*. But sure, this is sonically not as pleasing to me as *Heaven Forbid*.

Martin: What do you think of the album cover?

Matt: Well, beginning with the title, it's a throwback in that it references a Stalk-Forrest Group-era song. The image is by Ioannis, known for Styx, Uriah Heep and The Allman Brothers. Fans thought that the *Heaven Forbid* cover was a misstep. But I think fan consensus—and I would agree with this—is that this is back into more appropriate themes for a Blue Öyster Cult album. It evokes *Imaginos*, right? You've got the two period-dressed people, so it looks of the time. That could be Imaginos getting a ride there. He's holding a mirror, and a mirror figures very strongly in the *Imaginos* story. But this is not the *Imaginos* mirror, right? It's not the Magna of Illusion.

Anyway, it's a cover that warrants some closer study. The shadows are not consistent. The image in the mirror does not really reflect properly. And there's no tracks, right? It's a desert landscape and there's no footprints or tracks to the wheels in that soft sand. So it leaves enough space, like some of their other albums, where we can kind of create our own story or interpretation.

Martin: Okay, back to the album with "I Just Like to Be Bad," and I'm not sure what to call this one. Hard pop?

Rich: Sure. I quite like it. It reminds me of "Sinful Love" in feel, again with a bit of a Who vibe, given this particular use of piano and some wilder fills from Bobby Rondinelli than you'd expect from him. And the way he punctuates the chorus reminds me of The Doors. That's a '60s psychedelic kind of drumbeat The Doors use on "Soul Kitchen" and "Five to One," that idea of punctuating every beat in the bar.

Matt: This to me is the least successful song on their least successful album (laughs). Speaking of the Bobby Rondinelli parts, it has a very heavy drum intro, and coming out of the breaks of the songs, the drums are still quite heavy. To my ears it doesn't fit with the overall tone of the rest of the song; it's kind of jarring. The lyrics are throwaway. It's a John Shirley lyric but it doesn't tell as cool a story as some of the other ones do. It doesn't have that evocative slice of life with a little bit of weirdness going on. Nor is it funny. But they do stupid, right? That's something that Blue Öyster Cult has done at times, but usually it would be with a humorous song. I don't find any humour in this song. I suppose what bothers me also is that the melody is kind of sing-songy, on both the verse and the chorus.

Sean: Weird song with a Meat Loaf or Springsteen kind of '50s vibe. It's a sunshiny hard rock thing, with a Byrds-y jangle on Buck's guitar. The chorus is weird. It's got that Blue Öyster Cult thing where you're getting that happy melody and then they throw in some kind of dissonant, tritone guitar chord that throws your ear off for a second. But then you're into it—once it's been established the first time and it's upset you, then you're fine that you're upset with it.

Martin: This brings up again the history of the New York sound, '60s girl groups, Vanilla Fudge, Young Rascals, Kiss.

Sean: Sure, The Vagrants, Mountain. The girl group thing is very interesting, and their influence on the New York Dolls. A lot of people don't talk about that, with the connection usually being made to the Ramones. But those girl group singles, they could also be very edgy. "He hit me and it felt like a kiss," The Crystals; that's a weird thing to sing about, you know what I mean? And the song is a sugary poppy thing.

In my hair metal book, Dee Snider talks about the Long Island thing, with Good Rats and Mountain. All these guys know each other so the cross-influence makes sense. All these guys are hanging out and playing the same clubs—Cinderella, Skid Row, White Lion—and they do have a sound. And to me, Rondinelli and Miranda, playing together is a very East Coast sound. When I played with Stet Howland he told me the same thing. He said they were all watching each other play.

Martin: Excellent, and honestly, I'm hearing a continuation of this idea with "Here Comes That Feeling," especially in the chorus.

Sean: Yeah, it's another plucky, melodic Buck Dharma riff, kind of classic '80s BÖC to me. The guy from Ghost really listened to a lot of Blue Öyster Cult. It sounds like this style of theirs was influential on Ghost. It also reminds me the band Asia, with that syncopated riff behind a very melodic chorus. There's this choppy, syncopated riff with a really nice linear vocal melody. And once again, another nice, modal, melodic solo by Buck. And when I say modal, it's like he's playing in the key, but he might alter one or two notes in the scale and emphasize those notes, which brings out a different melodic quality, often a mournful quality. There's something melancholic about his note choices. He's not going for the obvious kind of happy, major third resolution.

Rich: This one's what we expect from Buck, him being the poppier guy of the band. The introduction has a classic Blue Öyster Cult vibe, with great chords. Production-wise, again it's sort of naked, unvarnished guitar and crystal-clear vocal tones. As Sean says, the chorus is poppy but there's that subversive element of Blue Öyster Cult eccentricity that's keeping us off-kilter. It's not formulaic even though it's radio-friendly. They could've easily smothered that in harmonies and kept the beat simple. But they punctuate it and make it quirky. They subvert it from within, I think, is the phrase (laughs). When that's working for the band, it's a strength. As for the '60s influence and all of that kind of complicated New York pedigree thing, BÖC are one of those bands where you can bring those influences in and generally it doesn't overpower their own identity. They manage to distill all those things into one band.

Matt: This is one where the Buck Dharma demo is better. I think part of the problem is that Bobby Rondinelli is a great fit for them live at this time because he's such a heavy player. When they have to do the required drum solo, I'm not that into it but the crowd loves it! He's got good showmanship and really helps them in a live setting. However, I don't think it fits on the record, especially the Buck songs. It's kind of ham-fisted, the drumming, throughout these things. And so any of the parts where you might get some flaws in the songwriting, they're accentuated by the drumming. "I Just Like to Be Bad" is not a heavy song at all and yet the drumming is heavy and it's also out of place on "Here Comes That Feeling." So there's this incongruence between the performance and the songwriting.

Martin: "Out of the Darkness" pairs a John Shirley lyric with music that is attributed to Eric, Buck and Danny.

Rich: Yes, an odd credit for sure. This one starts like a typical power ballad, which rings alarm bells initially. But then it goes somewhere different, with a vocal and guitar figure that add a sinister vibe. Again it sounds like they're going to do something obvious and poppy and then they take it in that dark, vintage Blue Öyster Cult direction, which is great. The lyrics are quite unsettling again and it gets more aggressive as it goes along. Great writing, big chorus, there's warmth to the harmonies, but again it goes somewhere unusual with the hook line. There's a melodramatic, epic middle section, featuring another great riff under the vocal and some stately piano from Allen. I think it works really well, that one.

Sean: It starts out very much like Foreigner but the chords soon shift. It's tempered by Buck Dharma playing in this Chris Rea-type style; there's a sort of desert sadness happening with the guitar thing. It makes it feel darker. Eric provides a theatrical vocal, which, I don't know, I've always felt a sort of '60s hippie vibe from his voice.

Martin: Man, I love that. I've been thinking the same thing. Something about his actual voice, the twang in it or his phrasing, he sounds like he's smiling or suppressing a laugh, like he's just smoked a joint. Thanks for saying that. There's actually something Cheech & Chong about it, like a "Dave's not here" bit! Okay, not sure how that's going to go over, but let's move on: "Stone of Love."

Matt: Here we get a somewhat unexpected Richard Meltzer lyric. But this is one Buck had for a long time. The demo is great and this version is really good too; they do a good job on this one. "Stone of Love" could have fit on any Blue Öyster Cult album throughout the '80s, including the Martin Birch ones.

Martin: Very "Box in My Head," with the tumbling, sort of building block vocal phrasing.

Matt: Absolutely, and it's interesting because it's two different lyricists. That was exactly what I thought when I first heard that "Box in My Head" was gonna be the single. It was like, oh, that's interesting, we're kind of going to that well again.

Rich: Once more on the strength of the production, you can hear that the acoustic and electric guitars are layered together very simply, both playing this insistent, rhythmic riff. Sometimes when a songwriter says "Less is more," that can be a lazy excuse for not putting the effort in. But on this it's certainly not. It's simple but very effective—these notes have been chosen with some craftsmanship. Then there's an odd but effective transition from the clipped beat into these ringing power chords. This one also reminded me of "Sinful Love." There's a bit here with no vocals, isn't there? A very melodic empty section with no vocal. Which again is a bizarre choice for an arrangement. But we're talking about Blue Öyster Cult here, so it fits in. Yeah, again, an interesting gesture. Other bands might take a safer route with the song to make it more overtly commercial but BÖC take the road less travelled.

Sean: That choppiness, with the acoustic guitar doubling the riff, I thought was very cool—and very prominent in the speaker. You've got this acoustic guitar doing the same riff as the electric guitar and I love that effect. There's almost like a Stewart Copeland kind of thing going on with the high-hat when they take that pause in the chorus. Once again, very strong guitar and some neat drum and bass interplay at the end. And that's a concept that I feel is there throughout the whole album. It very much feels like, hey, we're getting together in the studio, you've got one or two days of preproduction, hear the songs, and I can just hear them knocking it off, probably in not a ton of time. It sounds vibrant.

Martin: From thoughtful pop to "Eye of the Hurricane," the heaviest song on the album, and, sensibly, it's Eric singing it.

Matt: Yeah, I saw this one performed live for the first time in January of 2000, so quite a bit before. So they're working it out live, and they did make improvements to the arrangement over time. This is one of the advantages of having a true band at this stage; it allows them to make some improvements and work the songs a bit longer. It starts with that descending Aldo Nova "Fantasy" riff to it, and then the keyboards kind of remind me of "Perfect Strangers" by Deep Purple. It's a different sound for them. And this is where Bobby Rondinelli fits great on the record. It's a heavy metal song, and heavy metal in a Deep Purple/Rainbow way, and of course he's an alumnus from Rainbow. There's a spot where he trades fills with Buck—it's a drum fill exchange with a guitar lead—and I think that works really well. Lyrically, it's John Shirley, who does all but three songs on the album. And this is in his style where it's not horror, it's not fantasy, but it's sort of a modern in-your-mind kind of lyric, which he does well, including on *The Symbol Remains*.

Sean: Good charged rocker, kind of dark, a convincing take on traditional heavy metal. These guys, when they want to, can deliver classic metal. And for contrast it has this cool, loping, blues change for the solo. I always think that songs like this, this is what my younger self as a kid wanted Blue Öyster Cult to be. Because Blue Öyster Cult was always this older band for me, right? I used to call them a small magazine ad band. When I would pick up *Hit Parader*, they were allocated a very small ad. Mötley Crüe had a full-page ad. Y&T gets a small ad and Blue Öyster Cult gets a small ad. So I'm going, okay, I'm not buying that one right away. I'll get to it eventually, but only because it's in the magazine (laughs).

Rich: Funny, yeah. Okay, the intro reminds me of the theme tune from *Psycho*. You know, Bernard Herrmann's classic theme from that. We get very heavy guitars and an ominous keyboard riff in creation of a sort of soundtrack vibe. Love the vocal melody and there's a hint of reggae again, just before the chorus. There's a subtle humour with that nice play on words, "There's an eye in my hurricane." And I like that fiery call-and-response between Buck and Bobby that Matt mentioned. They're obviously aware that Bobby Rondinelli is bringing a lot to the band and they're letting him off the leash here; they're using him to his full capacity. It's nice to hear him get the space to do that. They're letting him put his personality into it rather than making him only fit the template of the band and stay regimented.

Martin: All right, so the album closes on a bit of a goofy note, I think, with "Good to Feel Hungry."

Rich: Yes, an odd choice for a closer. The bass line is interesting. It's not conventionally melodic and there's a lot of energy. There's that call-and-response effect again with the vocals and the music. This one reminds me of "Ted the Mechanic" by Deep Purple for some reason, just the feel of it and the groove and the odd timing. There's a change to a minor key section with another odd time signature. It's quirky but it's grooving and not disjointed, even though there's a lot to it, a lot going on. Good chorus, not too sweet, slight disparity between the chorus chords and the harmonies. I mentioned King's X earlier on; those guys regularly utilize a more pronounced version of that idea. Again, Blue Öyster Cult are making a sweet chorus but not too sweet. They're putting that slightly... jarring is too strong a word, but something that makes it a little bit off, giving it that characteristic unsettling feel.

Matt: "Good to Feel Hungry" feels like a democratic song where they're just having a jam that celebrates the current band, who all sound good on it. This is where having the continuity of Danny and Bobby in the band for a while helps them cook up something groovy. So you've got a really good bass groove by Danny on a very bass-forward song, which is not what BÖC typically do, although there are a handful of signature Joe songs from the past like that. You've got kind of a long instrumental section with an organ solo and good guitar soloing where it really loosens up. John Shirley's lyric is sparse; there's not a lot to latch onto. I think it's more of a deliberate showcase for that version of the band to have a jam.

Sean: To me this is sort of an experiment in jazz. I like the floating, tremolo guitar in it, but this was the BÖC that I didn't care for in my youth. I'd think, that doesn't sound like the heavy metal thing that is in my magazine. But it does differentiate them and it's organic and kind of classic-sounding.

Martin: How about a few more words on Bobby, who is not going to be in the band for the next album.

Matt: No, he isn't. Like I say, Bobby brought a lot to the band's live show. At the time their whole business was the live shows. They get the small record deal and they're making a couple records, but certainly any income that is coming in is from concerts. And he's a really good fit for them live. He's heavy, so when they tend to do the songs heavier live, that's a really good thing.

But Danny will be there on *The Symbol Remains*. He slots in really well as a bassist. He gives them a bit of a different groove than they had with Joe Bouchard. He's not a copycat of Joe, but he's a competent bassist, which is proven when he is picked up by Queen when they work with Paul Rodgers. So on this record they sound like a band. There's stability in the lineup with respect to bass and drums, like they always had earlier. However, I think Rondinelli is a bit too heavy for them. Jules Radino shows more versatility and makes the next album, as a whole, work better.

Martin: All right, to wrap up then, how about ranking for me these three modern-era BÖC albums?

Matt: To me it's inferior. To me *Curse of the Hidden Mirror* is the worst of the three; it's the least successful. Although it has a singular sound—it sounds like a band, which you don't get on *Heaven Forbid*—the material on *Heaven Forbid* is stronger. You've got the better of the archive stuff, the things that were in the can, whether they were Buck demos or things like that. And you had sort of the first pick of the John Shirley lyrics. I think the John Shirley material is stronger on the first and third of that sets of records. Eric is not at his peak vocally during this time period. This is when he started to have some issues. *Heaven Forbid* was recorded before he was having those problems. Moving forward, I think Richie Castellano's ability to produce on *The Symbol Remains*, along with Eric's effort and his making some improvements to his voice, makes the new record stronger than *Curse of the Hidden Mirror*.

THE SYMBOL REMAINS

The Symbol Remains
October 9, 2020
Frontiers FR CD 1060
Produced by Eric Bloom, Buck Dharma, Richie Castellano; Executive
Producer, Steve Schenck
Engineered by Richie Castellano; overdub engineer, Buck Dharma, additional
engineering, Sam Stauff, assistant engineer, Steve La Cerra
Recorded at Mercy College Studio A, Dobbs Ferry, NY
Personnel: Eric Bloom – guitar, keyboards, vocals; Donald "Buck Dharma"
Roeser – guitars, keyboards, programming, vocals; Richie Castellano –
guitars, keyboards, programming, vocals; Danny Miranda – bass, backing
vocals; Jules Radino – drums, percussion, backing vocals
Guest performers: Andy Ascolese, Albert Bouchard, John Castellano, Phil
Castellano, Steve La Cerra, David Lucas, Jeff Nolan, Kasim Sulton, Kevin
Young

1. "That Was Me" (Bloom, Castellano, Shirley) 3:18
2. "Box in My Head" (Roeser, Shirley) 3:46
3. "Tainted Blood" (Bloom, Castellano) 4:17
4. "Nightmare Epiphany" (Shirley, Roeser) 5:30
5. "Edge of the World" (Castellano) 4:52
6. "The Machine" (Castellano) 4:14

7. "Train True (Lennie's Song)" (Roeser, Zeke Roeser) 3:57
8. "The Return of St. Cecilia" (Castellano, Meltzer) 4:12
9. "Stand and Fight" (Bloom, Castellano) 4:48
10. "Florida Man" (Roeser, Shirley) 4:08
11. "The Alchemist" (Castellano) 6:00
12. "Secret Road" (Roeser, Shirley) 5:24
13. "There's a Crime" (Jeff Denny, Jules Radino) 3:37
14. "Fight" (Roeser, Ira Rosoff, James Wold) 3:12

Martin talks to John Alapick, John Gaffney, Jamie Laszlo, Reed Little, Bill Schuster and Matt Thompson about *The Symbol Remains*.

Martin Popoff: All right, so here we are with a bit of a surprise at the end of our journey, a zesty, vibrant new Blue Öyster Cult album, from a band that feels re-engineered for survival—or something like that!

John Gaffney: Yes (laughs), after 19 years Blue Öyster Cult drop a new album. The band wasn't inactive during those years though, consistently playing live shows under their aptly titled Forever on Tour tour. I'd say that just like the crashing BÖC symbol on the cover dropping from the sky, this album packs a lot of punch and heft. It left a smile on many a BÖC fan's face, myself included. At this point, you've got Eric and Buck as the only original members and Danny Miranda on bass and Jules Radino on drums.

But the real secret weapon of the band and the person who really puts this album over the top for me is Richie Castellano, who on top of playing guitar and keyboards, he most importantly for me, adds another really strong voice. Plus he adds another really strong voice in the songwriting department of the band, getting a sole writing credit on three of the 14 songs and is involved in co-writes on another four songs. So a total of seven songs he's involved with on this record, and on top of all that, he also receives a production credit.

What makes BÖC special for me and what Richie brings back to the band and what I felt they were lacking on the two previous studio albums, *Heaven Forbid*, and *Curse of the Hidden Mirror*, is the early secret sauce of the band, which was the fact that there were multiple songwriters in the group, the dominant ones being Eric and Buck. But what people don't realize is how many songs were written by Albert, with everybody at one point or another basically getting in on writing a song. It's like Queen, where you have four guys that are really strong songwriters with their own personalities.

And much like Queen, the early BÖC had multiple singers, right? Eric and Buck take the majority of the lead vocals, but Albert has his fair share, Joe jumps in there and even Allen did "True Confessions." So to me, that's what was so special about the early BÖC. And on the last few studio records, the vocals were mostly all about Buck and Eric, and for me they missed that third voice. And here is that third voice for me: it's Richie Castellano. He adds just some great songwriting, some great vocals and this for me is what makes *The Symbol Remains* special and what really takes me back to classic BÖC.

Reed Little: So *The Symbol Remains* is the first album since 2001's *Curse of the Hidden Mirror*, and it did chart—sort of. It was 192 out of 200 on the Billboard Top 200. That's what they call tickling the bottom of the charts, right? But it did make No.10 on Billboard's Hard Rock Albums thing. And thinking back to 2020, I'm really having a hard time imagining what the other nine albums on that were.

It got generally positive reviews, and like a 77 out of 100 on Metacritic, four out of five stars on both Allmusic and Loudersound. And what I think is absolutely amazing about this album is that Eric Bloom turned 76 two months after this album was released. Buck Dharma was about to turn 73. I think Eric is 78 now.

Okay, so pretty remarkable for a late period album. But I am a true contrarian. When somebody tells me that something is good, I instantly look for reasons to dislike it. I don't like people telling me, "This is the greatest thing ever. You need to love this." And when *The Symbol Remains* came out, I remember, frankly, universal praise for it on the YouTube hard rock nerd community, in which I include myself. That's not an insult. It's just people that like hard rock a little bit too much, right? Everybody was talking about how awesome it was. So I was like, well screw that. I'm going to find reasons *not* to enjoy this album. And I did. There are reasons to not enjoy the album. Then I let it sit fallow for a while and damned if I didn't like it a whole lot more once I had gotten away from people telling me that I needed to love it.

But that doesn't mean I think it's flawless. I like the fact that it's kind of a tour of BÖC. It's not really a greatest hits, but it's a little bit of everything BÖC does. You have the poppy Buck Dharma songs like "Box in My Head." You have the numbers like "Secret Road" and "Edge of the World" and "Nightmare Epiphany" that are a bit more occult-oriented and they deal with conspiracy theories. Then you have some biker rock and you have some very nearly heavy metal. And that's like BÖC's career on an album. I think Buck Dharma has never played better. His lines are so fluid; it's just amazing. He may not have recorded an album since 2001, but he is a guitar playing fool on this album.

John Alapick: It's long. I think you could have taken maybe three songs off the album and it would have been better, perhaps "There's a Crime," "Train True" and maybe "Fight," the last song, which is still a good tune. That's another Buck song but he's got a lot of songs that are stronger than that. You know, I would probably have given it a 9/10 if you took them off because it's a little long. But that's me over time. I mean, at first in the '80s and '90s when albums were getting longer, I liked when albums were 60 minutes. When you start hitting 75 or 80, it's like, okay, I want quality over quantity. Now one thing about the music industry today is that bands are putting out albums on their own and saying, well, if we have eight or ten good songs, that's all we're gonna put out. So albums are getting down to 35 to 45 minutes again and I think it's better.

Martin: And what do you think about Richie's presence in the band? I mean, he offers a life extension, doesn't he? If Eric or Buck want to sing less or not at all, or, to be radical, if one or both retired, he's sort of like the bridge to another ten or fifteen years!

John A: Yes, interesting idea. He's definitely given them a new life. Richie Castellano is their musical director in the band. He's out there, he's playing guitar, he's playing keyboards on a lot of songs that Allen Lanier would once do and he's singing some songs too. He's singing "Tainted Blood." He's singing "Hot Rails to Hell" live. He's the secret weapon of that band. I think what these legacy bands have to have in order to have that extended life, you need a young musical guy who's got good ideas. Let's keep them true to themselves but let's add something to it. That's what Richie Castellano does. I think he's wonderful. I follow his YouTube channel. He's just a fan that got on with a great band. And he's making that great band better and I'm very happy for him.

Martin: You know, I've seen one sort of criticism of this album, and it's the idea that they're checking off a lot of boxes, right? Both musically and lyrically. And Richie is just as guilty of that as Eric or Buck or the band groupthink in general. Or Frontiers, the label or even Steve Schenck, the manager.

John A: Yes, that's true. But if the songs are strong, that's okay. My thing is, yeah, check off the boxes, but is the song still memorable? Is it something you want to hear again? That's why I think it works. I mean, I've seen videos where they've talked about that and I would agree with it. But as long as the songs are there, it's okay.

Bill Schuster: As much as I love Blue Öyster Cult, this was an extreme disappointment for me when it came out, although it's turning around pretty steadily and rapidly for me (laughs). But I was left underwhelmed after a 19-year wait since *Curse*. And I was so excited. You know, "That Was Me" came out and the video was fun. It was neat seeing Albert in there, claiming his cowbell in the video, back in the band for that little cameo.

"Box in My Head" I was less enthused about it. I just thought that was kind of an average poppy Buck song. As for Richie, I love Richie and his skills and what he brings to the band and he absolutely deserves to be there. He has earned his place in this band and on this album. It's great to have him and Jules finally on a recording. But I have to say that I have a hard time hearing Richie as a Blue Öyster Cult lead vocalist. As much as I like his voice, those vocals are jarring to me.

Matt Thompson: Bill, you mentioned that this album's growing on you. I think one reason why that might be is that there's a lot of attention to detail, a lot of sort of Easter eggs and ear candy, a lot going on with the vocal arrangements, the background vocals. So I do think it stands up really well to repeated listening. I find that I'm getting more out of it with each listen.

One of the things I really like about the album is that it's a collaboration with a lot of members of the cabal, as Martin has coined it. You've got a Richard Meltzer lyric, you've got John Shirley on there, but also David Lucas, doing a lot of background vocals right? And that's so cool, given the work that he did on *Agents of Fortune*, with the vocals on "(Don't Fear) the Reaper." So you can hear some real quality to the background vocals throughout this album and I really like that. You've got Kasim Sulton on it, so some of the newer members of the cabal get to participate. And then Andy Ascolese, who's part of the BÖC crew, plays keyboards. So he's really doing the Allen Lanier part of it and I think he does a great job throughout the album. So I really like the collaborative nature of the album although to me it sounds like a real band, and a band that has been together a long time. I mean, the rhythm section's phenomenal.

Jamie Laszlo: I agree. You know why I like this album so much? It's because they don't sound old and tired. And they're releasing an album in their 70s but they still sound like themselves. And I think Richie Castellano represents great new blood in this band and on this album. I know some people have trouble with him, and those people may call him tainted blood, wink wink nudge nudge. And I'll grant you that his songs don't sound like BÖC songs. They stick out on this album for me. But that's okay; they stick out in a good way.

Martin: How would you characterize the production? I mean, I'm still struggling with it. It sounds a little noisy or something.

John G: It's definitely lively. Richie's credited, along with Eric and Buck, so it's a self-produced album. I'd characterize it as tight, powerful and modern-sounding, but not so much that we forget that BÖC is a classic band that started in the '70s. You know, it doesn't sound too slick or anything but it also doesn't sound dated. It sounds modern, but still respectful to BÖC's heritage and past. The performances feel energetic and inspired and everyone shines at various points on this album.

Martin: Okay, into the album, the first salvo—as an advance track in the summer—was rumbling rocker "That Was Me," which showed promise, right? It was more electric and exciting and heavy than anything on the last record, that's for sure.

John G: Absolutely. The album opens with a bang, with heavy driving riffs and some really punctuated, quick, 16th-note things at the end of the main riff there. Eric, Richie and John Shirley get the writing credit on this one. Eric sings it with that mischievous attitude of his. He's telling us to look to him for most of the problems in the world. It's first-person; he's saying "That was me" but it's really a personification of evil or the Devil or something.

I especially love the line, "You see those bullet holes in highway signs" because that's one of those things when you're driving down the road, you go, "Who does that?!" (laughs). Well, apparently it's Eric Bloom from Blue Öyster Cult—that's who does it. So I really appreciate the kind of fun in these lyrics; there's a great energy. I love the chorus, "You'll feel me in the urban breeze/I'll be there when the moment's seized." I also dig the kind of halftime reggae-ish feel that they shift into there towards the middle of the song; it's a surprising twist. So yes, very strong opener—love it.

John A: "That Was Me" has a heavy riff but it's still really melodic. It's got a solid chorus and then that breakdown John mentions. Many of their cool songs have this great breakdown in them; they're not just the predictable verse/chorus/verse. So yeah, "That Was Me" grabbed me by the throat.

Jamie: Thunderous guitars, big riffs, this song sounds like the album cover. You know, we're back. Right away, you're picking up that the song has more of a hook than anything from *Curse of the Hidden Mirror*. *Hidden Mirror* came off as blah. I call that album creative constipation. Those songs sound as if they were forced out, that they worked too hard on them and that they wound up half as good as they wanted them to be. With this song it sounds natural, as if the song always existed and their muse is just kind of pointing them in the right direction to find it.

Martin: Also released at the same time was "Box in My Head." Fans had songs representing two expected pillars or legs of the stool, brutish Eric and thoughtful Buck.

John G: Yes, with "Box in My Head" the mood lightens, although it's still a pretty fast song with a lot of energy and a catchy melody. I like the way Buck keeps using and twisting the word box. There's a box in my head and inside is a box etc. It's quite creative. I like the mysterious kind of hanging chord at the end of the song too. Yeah, fun one.

Jamie: You know, Eric sounds like Eric on "That Was Me" and I'll be damned, Buck sounds like Buck on "Box in My Head." It's amazing how these guys found each other and all these years later they still sound like themselves. One didn't get weathered, while the other one stayed the same. No, they stayed right there. There's only a few bands that were... I don't want to age-discriminate, but a lot of bands, their lead singer has old man voice. You hear it and you're like, "That sounds like a 75-year-old singer." And it really throws me off.

ELO, 20 years ago, nobody gave a crap, and now they're filling arenas. How is this happening? Jeff Lynne still looks like Jeff Lynne. He may not look like him if you take off the sunglasses and shave his head, but with the sunglasses and that hair, he still looks like Jeff Lynne and I think that matters to people a lot more than they even realize. We want our rock stars to be like The Simpsons. The Simpsons have been on TV for 30 years. They look the same. They pretty much sound the same. That's how we want our rock stars to be. And by golly, that's what Buck and Eric are doing on this album. They're being The Simpsons. Especially Buck. You put this exact version of "Box in My Head" on *Mirrors* as the next song after "Mirrors" and you can't tell there's a 43-year difference.

John A: "Box in My Head" is fantastic. I had chills listening to that song the first time. Because I didn't hear the songs when they were putting them out on YouTube. I was like, I want to go in blind. I want to hear the songs when I buy the CD. And I bought it the day it came out and I remember hearing that and I'm like, oh my God, this is fantastic. It's a shame they don't play rock music on terrestrial radio anymore because this could be a hit.

Matt: One of the best Easter eggs ever, in my opinion, is in "Box in My Head." It's got the "Brandy" Easter egg. If you haven't caught that, go listen. On one of the choruses, they do a "You're a fine girl." They're musicologists, music geeks, and so there's lots to uncover in these songs.

Martin: Next is "Tainted Blood," and it's the first delivered shock. I think that's safe to say. I mean, we forget about hearing somebody other than Buck or Eric sing, and with such authority. And the lyrics... "(Don't Fear) The Reaper" for vampires?

Jamie: Yes, well, my favourite two songs on this album are written by Richie, although they sound like they're coming from a different band. On "Tainted Blood," I'm hearing Kansas, Journey and Meat Loaf with just dashes of BÖC. The hooks are strident and big—huge. Richie sounds like a bona fide rock star when he sings it. He doesn't sound like a guitar player singing. He sounds like a singer who might pick up the guitar every once in a while on stage, you know? He's just what the doctor ordered for this band. I think he gave Buck and Eric much needed energy and inspired them to write better songs.

John G: Man, I love this one. It's a love song for vampires. Maybe a love song between two vampires. I love when BÖC talks about sci-fi stuff, conspiracy theories and vampires. I'm all-in on this one. Fantastic melody, and a chorus that is absolutely huge. The build-up part to the chorus, that sort of two-tiered pre-chorus, I'm getting a shiver up my spine even talking about it: "No one to wipe my bloody tears/The life we had for 200 years."

And that chord progression, he does this weird little twist. It starts off in C sharp minor and he goes up a half step to a D and does this weird little twist-around to bring the chorus to F sharp minor, like a key change, and it's just so dramatic. It's so well done. Then there's a great melodic solo on the fade-out. You know, I gotta say that Richie seems to be really tapped into and understands what makes Blue Öyster Cult special. Because as we go through the songs here, you'll see he's involved in a lot of the heavier songs. And he knows the lyrical hot buttons to push to get the heart racing of any diehard BÖC fan. So yeah, this one totally works for me.

Martin: I'd describe "Nightmare Epiphany" as a sort of up-tempo jazzy shuffle. What are your thoughts on this one?

John G: Written by John Shirley and Buck, who does some nice lead playing on it. His clean lead guitar style, in my opinion, is one of his strengths, the way he can sort of almost like country finger-pick at times. And along those lines, there's this honky-tonk-type line that he plays before the chorus that is really fun, where he's doing these bends. There's almost like a pedal steel guitar vibe to it. I'm not exactly sure what the lyrics mean, but there's a lot of cool nightmare imagery in it. Maybe it's a girl dreaming about a man monster that she eventually meets in real life. It's mysterious, but I like when BÖC writes like that.

Matt: There's this trade-off lead guitar between Buck and Richie at the end of "Nightmare Epiphany" that I really like. So you get some Richie participation there within a fully realized Buck song. But like what they do live with "Last Days of May," where Buck has opened up his world to Richie to participate in, I think he did it on "Nightmare Epiphany" and it sounds really good. Richie's place in the band over the last 20 years, mostly, I guess, is really in the Allen Lanier role, right? So he's doing the keyboards live and he's also doing the second guitar live, although he joined the band on stage in more of a Joe Bouchard role—he started out on bass.

But I think on this album he's really playing the Albert Bouchard role, in that he's very prolific. He came in with the most songs. He talked about how when there's been rumours that the band was going to record an album, he'd go write some songs for a BÖC album. And so he was able to present a bunch of songs to the band for them to pick up. That's what Albert did. You look at all the things Albert would bring to the classic recordings. He always had the most material and he was very intentional, especially on *Cultösaurus Erectus*, where he was very purposeful in making Blue Öyster Cult sound like Blue Öyster Cult again. And he wrote songs intentionally for Eric's voice. That's what Richie did on *The Symbol Remains*—he was prolific and intentioned about both the band and about Eric and his singing.

Jamie: You know what my favourite thing about this song is? It's how it pissed off BÖC fans for half a second when they first listened to it. I also love how Buck, in the middle, for half a second, almost starts to rap. And I can sense every BÖC fan holding his breath thinking about "Roll the Bones" by Rush for a moment. But luckily Buck comes out of that sort of quasi-rap pretty quickly. Anyway, the band sounds very fresh and they're not afraid to extend the song, with this little jam at the end. It's them telling you, "We're putting in the extra effort on this, guys."

Martin: Okay, next is "Edge of the World," and man, I can't get past those yacht rock vocals on the chorus. Bill used the word jarring earlier—I'm fine with Richie on lead vocals, but I'm really not buying this particular line of reasoning.

John G: I don't know, I'm fine with it, and it's Eric on lead vocal, and he's the perfect choice for a song about conspiracy theories, another favourite BÖC topic for me. And alien abductions. So yes, again, Richie just knows exactly the buttons to push lyrically. When Eric sings the line, "The second time I was abducted, I tried to stay aware," it just puts a big smile on my face. It takes me back to one of my favourite Eric vocals, on the song "E.T.I." And I think those slightly whispered background vocals add to the ominous conspiratorial vibe of the song. When everything breaks down and it's just those background vocals, I think it sounds cool. I mentioned "E.T.I."—this album seems to throw an occasional wink and nod to the band's history, like the album title, for example, being a line from "Shadow of California" from *The Revolution by Night*.

Matt: Where Richie has something in mind, like with "Edge of the World," he's saying, you know, I'm thinking like a "This Ain't the Summer of Love" kind of vocal, right? So he's kind of coaching Eric. And, you know, Eric, sounds better than he's sounded in years on this record; he did a really good job. So the youth and energy that Richie brings... Albert didn't bring youth but he brought that high energy to the band and was kind of the catalyst to get things done. And I think that's important because Buck Dharma is not prolific.

Jamie: One of my favourites on the album. Right away when you hear the opening, it sounds a little different. You're thinking this one must have been written by Richie and it is. His songs seem to have a more modern vibe to them. And when I say modern vibe, I mean, they could be done by modern bands, but the bands that try to capture that old school sound. I'm not saying it sounds like Imagine Dragons or some crap like that. But those retro-minded new bands trying to capture the old sound often have a newer spin on things, and that's what his songs sound like on this album.

And those vocal harmonies, Martin, I disagree—unforgettable, pure earworm. This song, it's Saturday night party music! And if you don't think Eric is rejuvenated by Richie and his songs, listen to him during the chorus at the 2:32 mark of this song. He gives a spontaneous "Woo!" Like Rick Flair almost. And then a minute later he goes, "Edge of world! Oh!" and then another "Woo!" I mean, he sounds like he's a kid again. He's into it. He's improvising. He's just not singing the song. He's putting his heart into it.

Martin: Then we've got "The Machine," and as I said, I'm totally on board with Richie grabbing the mic with both hands and taking these leads.

John A: Yes, and it's a spectacular song. They're talking about something modern, how we're addicted to our cell phones. Yeah, that's a Richie Castellano joint top to bottom, writing to the lead vocal—although Buck is really prominent in the background vocals—and I wish they would do that one live. Amazing lyric, because everything's about how we're so connected to our phone. We're checking our phone every five minutes to see if we missed a message or something or some social media post.

John G: Every time I hear that ring tone thing at the beginning, I feel a slight Pavlovian body reaction, sort of proving the point of the song, that we are all prisoners to our screens. So I find it funny that the ringing there always catches my ear if I'm not paying attention walking around my house playing this album. I hear that and it makes my spider senses tingle a little. Fun song. I like the relevance to current times in the subject matter. Good upbeat driving feel to it also.

Jamie: I'm going to somewhat disagree with you guys. I think this is when they start to show their age a little bit, with these lyrics. It comes off as old men complaining about the new world they live in. He's singing about how we're all in love with our phones. Okay, I get it. But here's the thing. We've been addicted to our phones for 15 years. You're a little late to the party on singing about it. But I will forgive them because the last time they released an album, we all had flip phones. So I'll let them go. I'll let them get this out of their system now because they haven't had a chance for the last 20 years.

But I do like the hook that Buck sings when Richie and Buck are singing together. You can't tell who is the older of the two, which is what I need. That's how it should be in the band. I don't want one guy sounding like he's 40 and the other guy sounding like he's 75, unless you're doing some rock opera where you're playing different characters. I want it to sound unified. I hate seeing pictures of old bands like Foreigner and there's a young guy singing. It doesn't look proper. It doesn't gel right for me. With Richie, he may look younger in pictures but on here you can't tell the difference.

Martin: "Train True (Lennie's Song)" is written by Buck and his son Zeke. I saw an interview with Buck where he said Zeke's an attorney in Washington DC with three kids and is "almost middle-aged." I thought that was funny. But he's also a guitarist and a songwriter. I suspect I'm in the minority, but it's top-third track for me on the album.

Jamie: I see why a lot of people don't like this. It's a common style of songwriting, as is the cadence of the vocals. There's a forgotten '90s hit by Mary Chapin Carpenter, a country song called "I Feel Lucky." She's doing the same cadence that Buck is doing in this song. It's a storytelling cadence. "Well, I woke up this morning and this is my story/I went down to the corner" etc. It's pretty cliché, especially when the chorus comes in. It's called "Train True" and it starts to sound like a train moving through the chorus. And you got the harmonica, which I also find cliché. You know, the album was cruising along and with this song, I feel like we hit a train crossing. So I'm sitting in the car waiting, instead of feeling like I'm on the train. I feel like I'm at the crossing waiting for the train to go by so we can move on.

John G: Okay, "Train True" is probably my least favourite on the album. It's an upbeat country-flavoured blues number. I don't like the part where Buck starts singing really fast. It makes me think of those old-time auctioneers. Something different, I guess, but I don't really look forward to it in the sequence. Credit to the band though, for being able to tackle different rhythms and feels and make it work, which is another secret strength of the band.

Martin: "The Return of St. Cecilia" starts like "Highway Star" and it's even got Hammond organ sounds in it, plus piano.

Jamie: Yeah, I dig this one. Nice hard rock drive to it. It sounds like a lost Night Ranger song to me. And I mean that in the nicest way.

John G: For this one, Richie apparently beat the other guys to the punch by putting useable music to a Richard Meltzer lyric that had come in. The title is a reference all the way back to when the band was called the Stalk-Forrest Group—they had a song called "St. Cecilia." This one's a high energy, hard-driving '80s-style hard rocker. Richie's vocals have a lot of punch and energy to them. I especially like the way he sings the line, "Cecilia I never dug your trip."

Martin: "Stand and Fight" is probably the heaviest thing on the album, up there with the likes of "See You in Black" perhaps.

Jamie: Didn't you do a *History in Five Songs with Martin Popoff* podcast episode on when thrash slows down? Yeah, I think you did. This is that kind of song. It sounds like it came right off of Metallica's black album. I could see it being the next track after "Wherever I May Roam." I don't know if it suits BÖC. It does have some cool musical passages at the end, but the chorus sure leaves something to be desired. In general it's primitive-sounding, and maybe that's why I don't care for the black album that much. But it doesn't help having this song primitive-sounding surrounded by songs with so much melody and texture to them. I can see a lot of BÖC fans liking the song simply because it's heavy. Some people put heavy as one of their main priorities in music and that's lower on the list for me. But there could be a bunch of guys saying I don't know what I'm talking about.

John G: Wow, yeah, is this Blue Öyster Cult or is this Metallica? That descending half-step riff and low, open-string chugging makes me think of "The Thing That Should Not Be" from *Master of Puppets*. The big Accept-like tons of dudes hollering background vocals also add to the metal feel of this one. Eric is spitting some real venom here with his vocal delivery. There are also some nice leads filled with all kinds of crazy bends. The spot before the last chorus where the drums go double time makes me want to throw some horns in the air. Jules Radino's drums sound great on this record, man, really big and punchy, especially when he steps out and does some fills. Is this the heaviest song BÖC has ever recorded? Maybe. Plus I'd have to say that pound-for-pound, for me, this is probably the heaviest album BÖC has ever done.

Martin: By the way, what do you think of the album cover?

John G: Well, you've got the BÖC symbol crashing down upon some ancient ruins there, and it's pretty eye-catching. If you look closely, you can see some cryptic writing on the symbol, like various mysterious little images in the background. BÖC covers are always best for me when there's a sense of supernatural and mysterioso. And this one kind of has that although it's pretty direct and obvious. But I like album covers that make you look and go, what is that little thing over there? What does that mean? The back cover has the same thing going on. It's the symbol over what looks like a tablet with Egyptian hieroglyphics. I guess I would interpret this cover as implying that BÖC is back but also that they've been around forever (laughs).

Martin: All right, onto "Florida Man," which is my favourite on the album. Verse to chorus, top to bottom—I love it.

Jamie: Wow, top one, eh? It's a cute song, inspired by the newspaper articles and internet posts about, you know, Florida man does something crazy. But it's a little bit... I'm gonna use some of your language, Martin. It's a little too "ha ha" for me. It comes off as a parody song. But it's just so damn fun to have Buck back singing these smooth, melodic songs, taking the lyrics out of the equation.

Martin: In its defence, it reminds me of Jerry Seinfeld's parents. You know, Buck is a Long Island guy. How did I end up in Florida? It's a retirement song!

Jamie: Yes, I suppose it's got that personal angle. Nicko McBrain, Brian Johnson, Pat Travers... it's hard to think of them as Florida men, but I guess they are.

John G: John Shirley on lyrics, Buck on vocals. I live in Florida so I get the humour in this. Crazy things happen here all the time. The Florida man is real—it is not a myth. So this one puts a smile on my face. It provides some levity after the really big heaviness of "Stand and Fight." I do like the southern rock bends that Buck does in the intro.

Martin: Next is "The Alchemist," and yeah, unfortunately, I fall on the side of too rote, too expected with this one, right down to the plinking piano.

Bill: "The Alchemist" was the third song they released as a single, with the guys dropping a video for it on the day the album came out. While it's a good song, with a good Eric vocal and a nice Richie writing job, I agree, Martin—it felt like BÖC by numbers. It's like Richie was going out of his way to make a song that was classic BÖC for Eric to sing and that kind of bugged me. It wasn't natural. And I feel like there's a lot of that throughout this album.

Matt: I hear you, Bill. What you're saying right there, it feels like in some places he's kind of going out of his way to write a BÖC-styled song. Well, he is, right? Like, that is exactly what he's doing. He's played a bunch of the classic songs live over the last 20 years and has his thoughts on what he thinks the strength and nature of those songs are. And he absolutely was, whether you like it or don't like it. So I take your point.

Reed: But still, unquestionably the MVP of the album is Richie Castellano. And what's going to make or break the album for you is how you feel about that. So I do absolutely agree that Richie is trying to sound like BÖC. And he has to work at it, because he's not one of the original guys. Only the original guys organically sound like BÖC. Once you get past that, you have no choice but to try to recreate something. And even though I think he gets mighty close, it still makes it a bit artificial because he's not one of the original guys.

I like his songwriting a whole lot better than I like his lyrics. My main thing with this album is that it's constantly leaving me hoping for something better on the next song. I used to like their lyrics much better than what

I'm getting on this album. Even a song like "The Alchemist," which is a story-based song, it's a very obvious story. There's no subtlety to it. It's just a narration of events. I enjoy it. I enjoy the music, especially. I enjoy the singing. There are three songs where Richie's the sole credit. That's pretty amazing on a new BÖC album. So how you feel about Richie's participation in the album is, I think, how you're going to feel about the album as a whole.

Jamie: Ah, man, if you're missing that menacing song by BÖC—and I'm not gonna call "Stand and Fight" menacing; maybe caveman-like—"The Alchemist" is just menacing and evil-sounding. I could see this as one of the heavier songs on *Imaginos*, even if the lyrics don't fit the vibe, although they *do* fit the vibe of that album. It just doesn't fit the *Imaginos* story to a tee. I say who cares? Because no one understands that story anyways. And I realize I'm talking to a guy who literally wrote the book on that story. So I'll take that back and say most people don't understand the story to that album.

The song is epic, and on the last half of the song they really let loose. It makes me think, oh, my God, we don't deserve a BÖC album to be this good in 2020. Even with its few faults, it makes me want to call the guys and say thanks for putting this together. For us fans. You know, I could call Buck down in Florida and say, "Hey Florida man, I just want to say thanks, man."

John A: "The Alchemist" has more of that feel towards the '70s. It plays like an epic and I think Eric Bloom sings fantastic. I saw them do it live in 2020 and they did it as an encore. He came out dressed like the Grim Reaper and he's holding this big book as though he's reading a book, but he's singing the lyrics. And it worked so well even though a lot of people didn't know the song. A lot of them are there to hear the classics, but I'm like, oh my God, this sounds awesome live. They didn't keep it on their subsequent tours, but I thought it worked really well that night.

John G: I mentioned drums earlier; they sound great on this whole album and that fill right before the break for the first verse is just massive—totally love it. Eric is the perfect choice for the lead vocals on this one. He delivers all the medieval goods on this tale of vengeance for an alchemist whose father is wrongly accused of abducting the prince so his father, the king, has him killed. We even get some Iron Maiden-style leads right after the second chorus, some duelling guitars that I think would make Steve Harris proud. That ominous piano theme that returns at various points in the song I think is really cool. And the chorus is just totally epic and majestic. I love the lyrics here. "Because I'm the Alchemist, creator of your fears/I'm the Sorcerer, a curse throughout the years" makes me think of one of my favourite bands and songwriters, Leif Edling from Candlemass—it sounds like something he would have written. So yeah, cool song, super-heavy and I love the storyline and everything—great.

Martin: Then it's on to "Secret Road," which strikes me as one of those bluesy songs that might lurk on a BÖC album, serving as a segue between two flashier things.

Jamie: Yeah, good point. You know, we're deep into the album at this point and we're still getting those charming Buck Dharma pop rock songs with great hooks, this deep in. And it's at this point where I think the well isn't dry with these guys. They have more ideas and songs in them. And I hate the fact that they're well into their 70s. This album, to me, sounds like a new beginning. And this song sparks that idea in my head. It's an album that's bittersweet, because it reminds me that we all get older and eventually die. And against that, this sounds like a band that has another 50 years in them. And I ask myself, is this the best album ever by a 50-year-old-plus band? If it's not, what beats it? Uriah Heep? I'll leave that open-ended for anyone who wants to suggest something.

Matt: Great rhythm foundation to "Secret Road," which is missing from Buck's old demo version. His demo is great, but I do think the band elevate it. But yes, this is Buck bringing something forward from his archive, which he also does with "Fight."

See, Buck does not go and intentionally write songs for things. And he'll recycle older stuff—he's always done that. But when inspiration strikes, he goes off and writes a masterpiece, right? He doesn't just write lots of stuff and then picks out the best. It's like, when it really strikes him he goes and writes something. "Harvest Moon" was around for so long as a song with his band, The Red and the Black. But however he gets there, it's 12, 15 songs of greatness, whatever the number is. That's likely his lifetime output for songwriting. He expresses himself creatively I think during the live solos, right? That's sort of his ongoing, all-the-time creative juices. But yeah, he just gets these moments of inspiration. I gotta write this, this particular idea, not that I have to write a song, but I've got an idea. And he does. And that's why his demos are so fully realized.

John G: Buck's lead vocals are so good on mid-tempo and slightly laid-back songs like "Secret Road." Plus there's great lead chops, but as always with

Buck, he's very tasteful and melodic. He's so underrated, in my opinion. "If God had a heart that touched each and every one, we would reach for each other instead of a knife or a gun;" that's a really poetic line there. This is my favourite on the album—sublime, beautiful and well-crafted.

Martin: We're up to the penultimate song now, with "There's a Crime" being a sort of frantic MC5-like rocker.

John G: Yeah, a pretty cool one, written by Jeff Denny and Jules Radino, so there's no surprise that there's some nice drumming, especially those fast snare rolls. There's also a super-fast, crazy, finger-tapping Eddie Van Halen-style guitar thing that brings the lead solo in and I really wonder if that's Richie because it's so Eddie and so modern. Maybe not the most memorable song on the record for me but the energy is there.

John A: I used to love "There's a Crime" because it reminds me of heavier Thin Lizzy from the late '70s. But perhaps because it was so immediate, I liked it a lot but now when I listen to it, I'm like, you could have left it off.

Matt: I think this one supports what you were saying, Martin, about the heaviness of the material, or the heavier songs surprisingly not being the best songs. There's some uncomfortableness, maybe, around the heavy material. It's part of their legacy—that willingness or comfort in having some hard-rocking, heavy metal-type songs, where it's a very fine line between tongue-in-cheek and silly. They have them on either side. You've got "Let Go" and you've got "Beat 'em Up." It's a band that's comfortable having both "Beat 'em Up" and "Make Rock Not War" on the same album. Like, totally contradictory lyrical ideas, both kind of silly songs, perhaps compared to the usual highly crafted lyrics we usually get.

You know, Martin, I know your view on "The Marshall Plan" but I really like it. I think that one's on the tongue-in-cheek side and I think they declare that with the song title. "Beat 'em Up" is just silly. So to me, "Stand and Fight" and "There's a Crime," there's not a lot lyrically happening with either of them. They're rockers and there's some good lead guitar in them. Still, I would say they adhere to legacy but are middle of the pack, probably, at best.

Jamie: One small complaint I have about this album is that it's 14 songs long. I think a lot of people complain about that. And when you get to this song, you start feeling the duration. It's not that the song isn't good—it's fine. You get another Eric Bloom, "Woo!" I'll take that any day. But at the same time, yeah, I'm starting to feel its 60-minute length. This is one of the songs that could have got cut, especially hearing it now way up at the end. We're all getting a little antsy at this point, right? You hear this and you're like, no, we didn't need this.

But then again "Fight" is a great rebound from "There's a Crime." It sounds like classic mid '70s or early '80s BÖC. The guitar lick is—and I don't use this word often—tasty. There's an eeriness to the keyboards that are mixed in, and I love it when creative rock ideas are mixed in with Buck's velvety voice. Those evil sounds set against Buck's voice, you get a dark and light balance. But Buck's reassuring you: "Don't worry. I know all the ghosts and goblins here. If they show up, just tell them you're with me."

Martin: Anybody else on "Fight?" Or are you all worn out by this point?

John G: Yes, final song—finally (laughs). Buck on vocals and songwriting along with Ira Rosoff and James Wold. The slightly uplifting melodic slant of the song lies in contrast to what the lyrics are about: a fight not living up to its expectations. I love these lyrics. It's a clever look at an interesting but simple topic. There's this funny twist that there's a fight but nothing much happens. And Buck's slightly deadpan vocal delivery just adds to the humour of it. But there's a dark humour in lines like, "Nobody running to the glove box for the stolen gun" or "No one reached into his boot for a stiletto knife." I just love it. BÖC's sense of humour is something very underappreciated in my opinion. And the last line, "Last one, turn out the light"—great way to end the album.

Martin: Nice. How about some closing thoughts on what the guys have accomplished with this record in a general sense? After all, this could be the end. Or maybe not!

John G: Okay, well, overall, I love this record. It's a fantastic return after so many years. And I really love what Richie brings to the band, especially in the songwriting department. Long live the symbol, long live Blue Öyster Cult.

Martin: Like I was saying earlier, he's maybe the connective tissue to this band continuing on when perhaps we lose Buck or Eric.

John G: Yeah, possibly. Because he seems to be really in tune with what BÖC is all about. And he's 43, the perfect age, a whole lot younger than the other guys but not too young. Sometimes in situations like that, where you want to insert a different style, he could have been a square peg in a round hole. But he's been in the touring band and suddenly they're writing an album. That can be treacherous territory, because again, sometimes even though the guy may like playing with the band live, his songwriting and what he prefers may not align with the band. But it's very clear that Richie understands what makes Blue Öyster Cult special, what makes it work.

I would love to interview him and find out how much he had to do with inspiring the band to make this album, how much his youthful energy was a factor. Because 20-some years from the last studio album, you can read interviews with Eric where he basically says, like, "What's the point in even making a new record? You don't make any money." And he's right; in this modern age of streaming, it's hard to make any money from a new record. So through the years it seemed like the guys weren't super-motivated to put out a new record. They were content to be on these Forever on Tour tours.

Bill: I will say I've had to revise my view on this album overall. I find myself liking it more than I did initially. Some of these hooks are starting to get in. But there's a reason I wear this shirt I have on right now. This is the Buck Dharma Archive shirt. Back in 2000, Donald Roeser put out a bunch of his demos. And two of the demos made their way in new form on *Curse of the Hidden Mirror* the following year. And 19 years later, two more of those demos made it onto *The Symbol Remains*. "Nightmare Epiphany" and "Secret Road" were on volume three of the archive. And I listened to the archived versions earlier to compare and they're actually pretty similar here.

So that also was one of the things that bugged me. It seemed while it's great to reuse stuff, not let it go to waste, it also seemed like a bit lazy to me. Like really, Don? You've had almost 20 years to write some stuff and you're still recycling stuff from the '90s with these John Shirley lyrics? So I think they can do better. I mean, maybe I'm putting too high expectations on these guys. They're in their mid 70s. Maybe they just don't have as much spark as they used to, or motivation to write anymore—and that's fine.

I think maybe my expectations in general were too high for this album. And that's on me more than the band. Overall, though, as I said, I have softened to it, but I will say it is still my least favourite Blue Öyster Cult studio album. And there's no doubt of that. I'll take *Club Ninja* any day; I'll take *Revolution by Night, Curse* or *Heaven Forbid* any day, and certainly any of the classic original eight. But I'm gonna keep going at it. I'm encouraged by listening to it lately. There's definitely room to grow. I don't think anybody should ever feel locked into a first impression opinion. You take your circumstances into your music with you. As you change with time, it's only natural that your opinion of music should change with time.

Reed: Let's again remind ourselves: Eric and Buck are well into their 70s. It's just frankly phenomenal that they put out an album this good. Could it have been better? I don't think so. At this point in their lives, at this point in their careers, I really do not see how a better product would have been possible. But that doesn't mean that I don't think there was any room at all for a better product. The more I listen to it, the more I get into it, and unlike Martin, I actually liked the rockers better than I like the more mellow songs, the poppier songs.

I was shocked when they did "Train True" in concert. They did I think three songs off of *The Symbol Remains* in concert. I know they did "Train True" and they did "Tainted Blood." Maybe "Box in My Head" and/or "The Alchemist." I mainly remember that I was complaining before the show started that by the time they got to Dallas, they didn't have enough T-shirts to sell. And I thought, come on guys, first album in 20 years and you don't have enough T-shirts? It's pretty lame. Anyway, it's a fantastic comeback album just because of the amount of time that has passed. And yet based on the fact that everybody just heaps universal praise on the album, I have to call it overrated, from a semantic point of view. I even take issue with the word comeback, because they never went anywhere, right?

Matt: Look, *The Symbol Remains* is a very solid Blue Öyster Cult album. They wanted it to fit within the legacy and I think it does do that. To me, maybe it's not top tier but more middle tier. But I have a raging Blue Öyster Cult bias, right? In BÖC land, it's a seven out of ten, but out there in the world, it's a sold nine (laughs). It absolutely warrants continued listening.

Jamie: Let me just add this. I absolutely love the textures and the layers to the sound on this record, because it makes it feel big. Which is completely unlike another band about a decade ago that did a comeback album: Van Halen, with *A Different Kind of Truth*. Comparing that comeback album to *The Symbol Remains*, I want my comeback albums to sound big, just like the cover. Boom, baby—we're back! And that's what this sounds like. Van Halen's album sounds like we whipped this up for you over the weekend— hope you like it. And some people might like that. But I want my comeback albums to go big or go back home.

John A: Well, I'll tell you what. As far as ranking goes, you can't really go wrong with the first three. My favourites would be *Tyranny and Mutation*, then *Secret Treaties*, then the debut with *Cultösaurus Erectus* at No.4. My fifth favourite would be *The Symbol Remains*. I think this record is expertly produced and I love nearly everything on it, although it's a little long.

I'll agree that Richie Castellano is the secret weapon. I know some people aren't on board. I mean, they like him, but they don't think he fits in with Blue Öyster Cult. I disagree. I think that his songs on the album are very, very strong. As for Buck, we're always talking about how "Harvest Moon" and "Live for Me" should have been hits had they come out earlier. I could say the same thing about "Box in My Head."

And I'll agree with consensus that *The Symbol Remains* captures their whole career in one album. That's an accurate statement. Because you have a little bit of everything on there—the eerier stuff, the melodic songs, the heavier fare—and instead of "Buck's Boogie" you have "Train True" (laughs).

So yeah, in closing—wonderful album. And I remember buying it, right during the pandemic. I'm still going out buying music, going to the local record store wearing a mask and all that. And I remember that feeling when I put that album in my car—I still have a CD player in my car—and I was like, wow, this is fantastic. I felt like a kid again.

Martin: Excellent, and I love that as a way to wrap up. Yes, I agree that if this is the last album we ever see from the band, that the boys can definitely be proud of the way they closed up shop. Time to turn it back to the reader—hope you all have enjoyed this vast and amassed catalogue analysis and have found your interest in this band renewed just like I most definitely have.

CONTRIBUTOR BIOGRAPHIES

John Alapick

John "The Music Nut" Alapick is an avid music fan and concert attendee who discusses music on several channels on YouTube. He resides in Monroe Township, Pennsylvania.

Jim Bacchi

Jim's first band Hittman, a traditiona '80s metal outfit formed in 1985, released two records in 1988 and 1993 before moving on, only to reunite in 2018. In 2020, the band released a critically acclaimed third record called *Destroy All Humans*. Jim is also a recording engineer, having worked with Jon Brion, Charlotte Caffey of the Go-Go's, Sugar Ray, Rickie Lee Jones, Macy Gray and Rage Against the Machine to name a few. His latest recording projects are The Tikiyaki Orchestra and Fuzzbubble, an acclaimed power pop outfit whose 2022 album *Cult Stars from Mars* features performances from Mike Portnoy, Jeff Scott Soto, Chip Znuff, and Darian Sahanaja from the Brian Wilson band. Jim is also a regular commentator on Pete Pardo's *Sea of Tranquility* YouTube channel.

Rich Davenport

Rich Davenport is a writer, musician and stand-up comedian from Bolton in the North West of England. He's written features and reviews for *Classic Rock*, *Record Collector* and *Rock Candy*, and sleeve notes for classic albums by Rory Gallagher and The Ruts. Rich also hosted a long-running radio show on *Total Rock*. As a musician, he's played with Atomkraft, Radio Stars, Martin Gordon (ex-Sparks), has fronted metal bands See Red and Black Sheets of Rain, and is currently playing with punk band Vicious Bishop and former Radio Stars/John's Children vocalist Andy Ellison. See richdavenport.com for more.

John Gaffney

John Gaffney is a musician from Tampa, Florida. His past endeavours include the metal bands Sinister Realm and Majesty in Ruin. Currently he records dark electronic music with his project Chamber of Sorrows, who can be heard at chamberofsorrows.Bandcamp.com. John also has a YouTube channel called *Lair of the Alchemist* that discusses all things heavy metal and hard rock. Come see him over at YouTube.com/Lairofthealchemist.

Sean Kelly

Sean Kelly is a Canadian guitarist, educator, and author who has performed with Nelly Furtado, Lee Aaron, Coney Hatch, Alan Frew, Helix, Gilby Clarke, Honeymoon Suite, and Crash Kelly. He is the author of two books, *Metal on Ice: Tales from Canada's Hard Rock and Heavy Metal Heroes* (Dundurn Press) and *Don't Call It Hair Metal: Art in the Excess of '80s Rock* (ECW Press). In 2015 he performed in Twisted Sister frontman Dee Snider's *Rock N Roll Christmas Tale*, and is currently playing guitar in the Toronto production of the hit Broadway musical *Rock of Ages*. Sean is a Music Teacher with the Toronto Catholic District School Board.

Rick LaBonte

Rick is a singer/songwriter from Windsor, Ontario. He has been collecting music and studying rock history since the '80s. As a vocalist and multi-instrumentalist, he has been performing in the music scene since the '90s. He was inducted in Windsor's Musician's Hall of Fame in 2017. He has released albums that are available on Spotify, iTunes, and on his website, ricklabonte.com, namely *On a Mission* (2016), *The Blues Side* (2021) and a double album called *Living It Up* from 2022. He is a regular guest on the *Sea of Tranquility* YouTube channel discussing all things classic rock. He has appeared in *519* magazine and *Windsor Life* magazine several times. As part of his storied music career around the Windsor/Detroit area, he has performed on stage with Uriah Heep, The Tea Party, Jody Raffoul, God's Joe Konas, Powder Blues Band's Tom Lavin, Detroit's Queen of the Blues, Thornetta Davis, Larry McCray and Scott Holt, current vocalist for Foghat.

Jamie Laszlo

Jamie was raised in Pittsburgh, Pennsylvania and listened to the local radio station, WDVE, which helped teach him a lot about popular music. Even though the facts he learned at school faded from memory just days after each exam, the facts he learned about rock music seemed to stay embedded in his head. Jamie's best friend growing up introduced him to Blue Öyster Cult, leading to the purchase of *Club Ninja* and *Mirrors*. Both cassettes went into constant rotation, with *Mirrors* remaining a favourite from the band. These days, Jamie is a YouTube music commentator and moderator, regularly contributing to *The Contrarians* and *Sea of Tranquility* music review channels.

Reed Little

Reed began his love affair with music when he discovered Kiss in 1976. In the 1980s, MTV exposed him to new favourites such as David Bowie, The Cure and Iron Maiden. He took up playing guitar in the 1990s. Reed retired from a completely improbable career in law enforcement and is currently a part-time professor, a keen amateur luthier and the singer and guitar player in a cover band called Old Man Jam.

Steven Reid

Steven has been a staff writer with the *Sea of Tranquility* website for over a decade. His impenetrable Scottish twang can now be barely understood as a co-host on the site's *UK Connection* YouTube show and as a regular on *In the Prog Seat* and numerous other music discussion panels. Previously Steven spent over a decade as a writer for the *Fireworks* rock and metal UK print magazine and *Rocktopia* website, with the last four years of that tenure being as Assistant Editor. Steven has also contributed liner notes for albums by Robin George and numerous Eonian Records releases.

Bill Schuster

Also going by the name of Howler Monkey (founder of infamous music forums, *The Monkey House* and *CryNet*), Bill is a regular contributor to *The Contrarians* (co-commandeered by the author of this book), *Rock Daydream Nation*, *Grant's Rock Warehaus* and *Ryan's Vinyl Destination* among others. Bill is also a charter member of the Buck Dharma Archive and also a writer of lyrics and singer of songs. Bill is proud to say that he's been a fully indoctrinated follower of the Blue Öyster Cult and its many tentacles—Brain Surgeons, Blue Coupe, etc.—for four decades and counting.

Nick S. Squire

Nick is oftentimes a *Contrarians* YouTube channel contributor, a part-time musician, a one-time college radio Program Director, a sometimes counsellor to music artists and a long-time fan of rock 'n' roll. A student of bass and piano, Nick played bass in bands throughout high school and college during the 1980s. After a 20-year lay-off, Nick knocked the rust off his fingers to join Jim George in an original rock 'n' blues trio sharing stages with Gary Hoey, Starz, Humble Pie, Sonny Landreth, Joe Louis Walker and The Holmes Brothers among others. With Jim's passing, Nick looks forward to "one more ride" with a dynamic original artist.

Henry Tenney

A writer, television producer and musician based in Brooklyn, NY, Henry was the long-time head writer of *Pop-Up Video* for VH1. He's lead singer and songwriter in the bands Dondi's Bloody Sputum, The Cheese Beads and Highland Shatners, plays in a Jacobites tribute band and with demi-supergroup The Jackson Pinks. He also regularly contributes new works to the international songwriters' circle, Bushwick Book Club, and had his prog fate sealed courtesy of Robert Fripp at a record store Frippertronics demo in his native Cleveland. He also commandeers a podcast called *An Embarrassment of Prog* along with friends and fellow obsessives Charlie Nieland and Bill Tipper.

Matt Thompson

Matt Thompson is the creator of the zine *Critical Hit Parader: America's Only Rock 'n' Role Playing Magazine* (criticalhitparader.com). The zine provides tabletop roleplaying game (TTRPG) content in the spirit of vintage rock magazines like *Creem*, *Circus* and *Hit Parader*. His companion newsletter and podcast on the intersection of rock music and TTRPGs is available at criticalhitparader.substack.com. A guitarist and songwriter, some of his music can be found at mtpromise.com.

Special Thanks

A hearty appreciation goes out to Agustin Garcia de Paredes who applied his eagle eye to a copy edit of this book. Agustin is also the moderator of the *History in Five Songs with Martin Popoff* podcast and served as a panel member on the King Crimson book similar in concept to this one.

ABOUT THE AUTHOR

At approximately 7900 (with over 7000 appearing in his books), Martin has unofficially written more record reviews than anybody in the history of music writing across all genres. Additionally, Martin has penned approximately 115 books on hard rock, heavy metal, classic rock, prog, punk and record collecting. He was Editor-in-Chief of the now retired *Brave Words & Bloody Knuckles*, Canada's foremost heavy metal publication for 14 years, and has also contributed to *Revolver*, *Guitar World*, *Goldmine*, *Record Collector*, bravewords.com, lollipop.com and hardradio.com, with many record label band bios and liner notes to his credit as well.

Additionally, Martin has been a regular contractor to Banger Films, having worked for two years as researcher on the award-winning documentary *Rush: Beyond the Lighted Stage*, on the writing and research team for the 11-episode *Metal Evolution* and on the ten-episode *Rock Icons*, both for VH1 Classic. Additionally, Martin is the writer of the original metal genre chart used in *Metal: A Headbanger's Journey* and throughout the *Metal Evolution* episodes.

Then there's his audio podcast. *History in Five Songs with Martin Popoff* and the Youtube channel he runs with Marco D'Auria, *The Contrarians*. The community of guest analysts seen on *The Contrarians* has provided the pool of speakers used across the pages of this very book. Martin currently resides in Toronto and can be reached through martinp@inforamp.net or martinpopoff.com.

A COMPLETE MARTIN POPOFF BIBLIOGRAPHY

2023: Dominance and Submission: The Blue Öyster Cult Canon, Wild Mood Swings: Disintegrating The Cure Album by Album, AC/DC at 50

2022: Pink Floyd and The Dark Side of the Moon: 50 Years, Killing the Dragon: Dio in the '90s and 2000s, Feed My Frankenstein: Alice Cooper, the Solo Years, Easy Action: The Original Alice Cooper Band, Lively Arts: The Damned Deconstructed, Yes: A Visual Biography II: 1982 – 2022, Bowie @ 75, Dream Evil: Dio in the '80s, Judas Priest: A Visual Biography, UFO: A Visual Biography

2021: Hawkwind: A Visual Biography, Loud 'n' Proud: Fifty Years of Nazareth, Yes: A Visual Biography, Uriah Heep: A Visual Biography, Driven: Rush in the '90s and "In the End," Flaming Telepaths: Imaginos Expanded and Specified, Rebel Rouser: A Sweet User Manual

2020: The Fortune: On the Rocks with Angel, Van Halen: A Visual Biography, Limelight: Rush in the '80s, Thin Lizzy: A Visual Biography, Empire of the Clouds: Iron Maiden in the 2000s, Blue Öyster Cult: A Visual Biography, Anthem: Rush in the '70s, Denim and Leather: Saxon's First Ten Years, Black Funeral: Into the Coven with Mercyful Fate

2019: Satisfaction: 10 Albums That Changed My Life, Holy Smoke: Iron Maiden in the '90s, Sensitive to Light: The Rainbow Story, Where Eagles Dare: Iron Maiden in the '80s, Aces High: The Top 250 Heavy Metal Songs of the '80s, Judas Priest: Turbo 'til Now, Born Again! Black Sabbath in the Eighties and Nineties

2018: Riff Raff: The Top 250 Heavy Metal Songs of the '70s, Lettin' Go: UFO in the '80s and '90s, Queen: Album by Album, Unchained: A Van Halen User Manual, Iron Maiden: Album by Album, Sabotage! Black Sabbath in the Seventies, Welcome to My Nightmare: 50 Years of Alice Cooper, Judas Priest: Decade of Domination, Popoff Archive – 6: American Power Metal, Popoff Archive – 5: European Power Metal, The Clash: All the Albums, All the Songs

2017: Led Zeppelin: All the Albums, All the Songs, AC/DC: Album by Album, Lights Out: Surviving the '70s with UFO, Tornado of Souls: Thrash's Titanic Clash, Caught in a Mosh: The Golden Era of Thrash, Rush: Album by Album, Beer Drinkers and Hell Raisers: The Rise of Motörhead, Metal Collector: Gathered Tales from Headbangers, Hit the Lights: The Birth of Thrash, Popoff Archive – 4: Classic Rock, Popoff Archive – 3: Hair Metal

2016: Popoff Archive – 2: Progressive Rock, Popoff Archive – 1: Doom Metal, Rock the Nation: Montrose, Gamma and Ronnie Redefined, Punk Tees: The Punk Revolution in 125 T-Shirts, Metal Heart: Aiming High with Accept, Ramones at 40, Time and a Word: The Yes Story

2015: Kickstart My Heart: A Mötley Crüe Day-by-Day, This Means War: The Sunset Years of the NWOBHM, Wheels of Steel: The Explosive Early Years of the NWOBHM, Swords and Tequila: Riot's Classic First Decade, Who Invented Heavy Metal?, Sail Away: Whitesnake's Fantastic Voyage

2014: Live Magnetic Air: The Unlikely Saga of the Superlative Max Webster, Steal Away the Night: An Ozzy Osbourne Day-by-Day, The Big Book of Hair Metal, Sweating Bullets: The Deth and Rebirth of Megadeth, Smokin' Valves: A Headbanger's Guide to 900 NWOBHM Records

2013: The Art of Metal (co-edit with Malcolm Dome), 2 Minutes to Midnight: An Iron Maiden Day-by-Day, Metallica: The Complete Illustrated History, Rush: The Illustrated History, Ye Olde Metal: 1979, Scorpions: Top of the Bill - updated and reissued as Wind of Change: The Scorpions Story in 2016

2012: Epic Ted Nugent, Fade To Black: Hard Rock Cover Art of the Vinyl Age, It's Getting Dangerous: Thin Lizzy 81-12, We Will Be Strong: Thin Lizzy 76-81, Fighting My Way Back: Thin Lizzy 69-76, The Deep Purple Royal Family: Chain of Events '80 – '11, The Deep Purple Royal Family: Chain of Events Through '79 - reissued as The Deep Purple Family Year by Year books

2011: Black Sabbath FAQ, The Collector's Guide to Heavy Metal: Volume 4: The '00s (co-authored with David Perri)

2010: Goldmine Standard Catalog of American Records 1948 – 1991, 7th Edition

2009: Goldmine Record Album Price Guide, 6th Edition, Goldmine 45 RPM Price Guide, 7th Edition, A Castle Full of Rascals: Deep Purple '83 – '09, Worlds Away: Voivod and the Art of Michel Langevin, Ye Olde Metal: 1978

2008: Gettin' Tighter: Deep Purple '68 – '76, All Access: The Art of the Backstage Pass, Ye Olde Metal: 1977, Ye Olde Metal: 1976

2007: Judas Priest: Heavy Metal Painkillers, Ye Olde Metal: 1973 to 1975, The Collector's Guide to Heavy Metal: Volume 3: The Nineties, Ye Olde Metal: 1968 to 1972

2006: Run for Cover: The Art of Derek Riggs, Black Sabbath: Doom Let Loose, Dio: Light Beyond the Black

2005: The Collector's Guide to Heavy Metal: Volume 2: The Eighties, Rainbow: English Castle Magic, UFO: Shoot Out the Lights, The New Wave of British Heavy Metal Singles

2004: Blue Öyster Cult: Secrets Revealed! (updated and reissued in 2009 with the same title; updated and reissued as Agents of Fortune: The Blue Öyster Cult Story in 2016), Contents Under Pressure: 30 Years of Rush at Home & Away, The Top 500 Heavy Metal Albums of All Time

2003: The Collector's Guide to Heavy Metal: Volume 1: The Seventies, The Top 500 Heavy Metal Songs of All Time

2001: Southern Rock Review

2000: Heavy Metal: 20th Century Rock and Roll, The Goldmine Price Guide to Heavy Metal Records

1997: The Collector's Guide to Heavy Metal

1993: Riff Kills Man! 25 Years of Recorded Hard Rock & Heavy Metal

See martinpopoff.com for complete details and ordering information.